D1810084
eat
out
for around
£5

Contents and Key to Regions

N.W. Adam

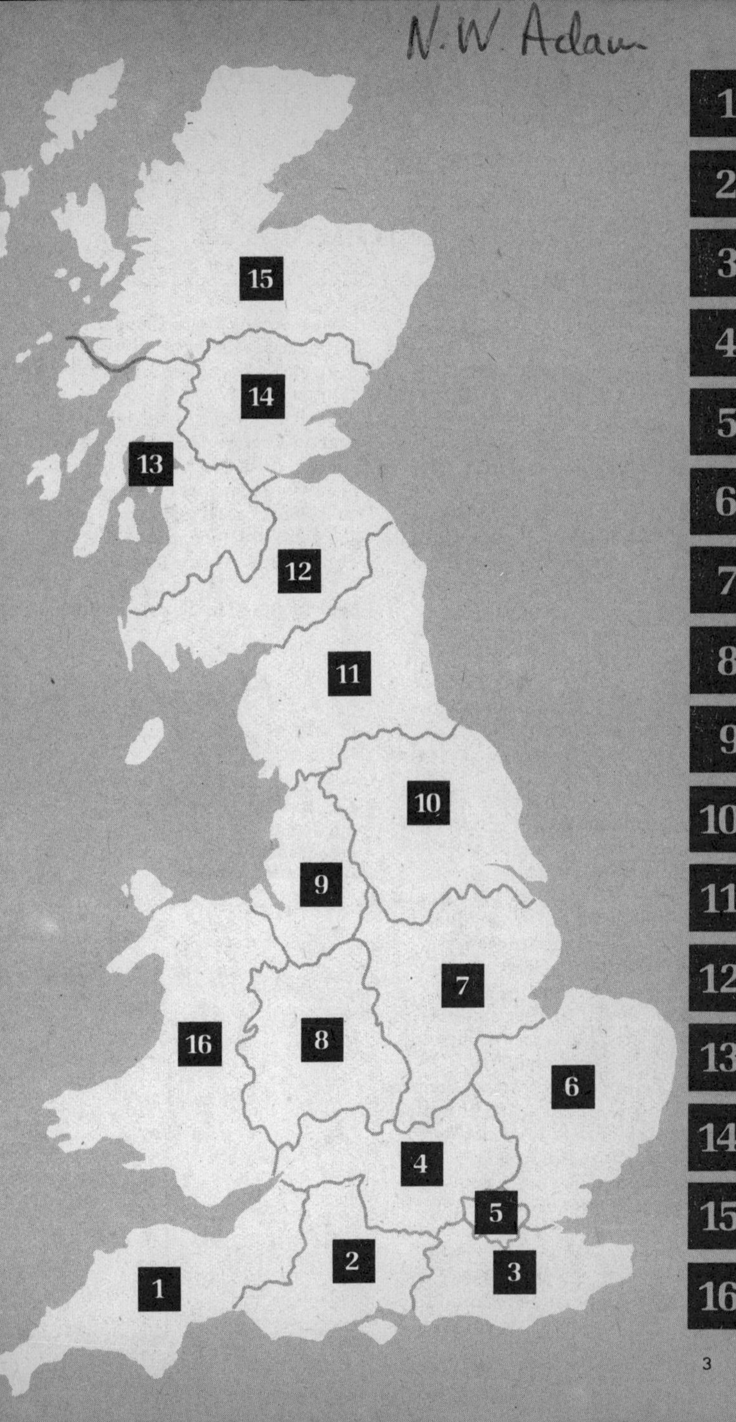

Counting the Costs

There is no doubt that a good three-course meal is one of the simplest yet most profound pleasures life can offer, but 'paying through the nose' for it at an uncaring restaurant can sometimes take the edge off that pleasure.

That's why the AA Hotel and Restaurant Inspectors have again taken to the road to bring you an even more comprehensive and far-reaching guide to low-price, yet high-standard eating places.

In these days of rising costs, when many people worry about high mortgages and growing families, it seems almost immoral to have to blow the week's wages – or the housekeeping budget – on a meal out for two people.

Fortunately, as this book demonstrates, there are over 1000 restaurants in Britain where excellence and economy are combined to provide opportunities for good eating out on a budget in congenial surroundings.

The AA Hotel and Restaurant Inspectors have visited and recommended all these places – a seal of approval from a group of established eaters-out!

My Inspectors are not peak-capped grading machines with slide rules, but thirty professional men and women with a profound appreciation of what is best and worst in hotels and restaurants.

The guide is divided into England, Scotland and Wales and sub-divided into sixteen touring regions. Each region is introduced by a map which indicates the location of the towns listed. In certain cases it may be advisable to use a road atlas where an inn is out of town.

All prices quoted are the latest available before going to press, but care has been taken to exclude places where prices for a three-course meal are likely substantially to exceed £5-£6 during 1982. As far as possible VAT and service charges have been included in the calculation.

I. M. Tyers

Ian Tyers
Manager Hotel and Information Services

My Kind of Place

****

Eating out with someone special or in a group of friends is high on almost everybody's list of social pleasures. And it's a proven fact that there are more business deals clinched, future plans formulated, proposals (and propositions!) made and accepted in the convivial atmosphere of a bar or restaurant than in any other one place–which is why most people nurture fond memories of a particular little bistro or restaurant. Maybe it was the scene of a momentous decision that changed their lives–maybe they just liked the food. Whatever their reasons *Eat Out For Around £5* readers feel strongly enough about their own favourite eateries to write and tell us about them, and we do our best to include them in our guide. But have you ever wondered where Britain's celebrities like to eat? We persuaded some of them to tell us of their secret hideaways . . . .

Actor **Derek Jacobi** is well known for his brilliant portrayal of classical roles such as the lead in television's *I, Claudius* and *Hamlet* and *Richard II* for the BBC's Shakespeare canon.

In reality quite a down-to-earth man and a Londoner born-and-bred, Derek names an Italian restaurant, La Barca Ristorante at 81 Lower Marsh Street, London SE1 as his kind of place. In fact, it's been a favourite haunt of his ever since it opened in the mid-sixties. In those days he was acting at the National Theatre, based at the Old

* * * * * * * * * * * * *

Vic in Waterloo Road, and recalls his and other company members' outrage when the old 'greasy spoon' café round the corner from the theatre suddenly became transformed into an up-market restaurant. But after a while actors from the Waterloo-area theatres began patronising La Barca and Derek became one of their best customers.

Nowadays he has no need to book; Luciano, the head waiter, has been known to rig up tables in his office for Derek and his friends on a particularly busy night.

Although the dynamism of his stage performance might suggest otherwise, Derek is the first to admit that he is not an adventurous eater. He tends to stick to a few favourite dishes, such as avocado with prawns or whitebait to start, followed by spaghetti bolognese. After an association of so many years it is hardly surprising that the staff at La Barca have got to know his preferences, and Derek recalls one occasion when he arrived at the restaurant absolutely determined to try something different, only to find a waiter serving him with 'the usual' without bothering to take his order!

Zany Scottish comedy duo **The Krankies** are in real life husband-and-wife team Ian and Jeanette Tough, an energetic couple who take their novel, music-hall style act all over the country. When on the road they like the clean, fast food served at the Little Chefs and also enthusiastically recommend the home-made dishes to be found at Motor Ross on the M62. When in summer season at Blackpool Ian and Jeanette head straight for a fish n' chip shop called The Cottage – a sort of unofficial meeting place for all the showbiz people playing Blackpool, and where for upwards of 50p per portion the couple can feast on what they describe as 'the best fish and chips ever'. For a local meal they recommend Oscar's at 43 Westborough in their home town Scarborough, where the cuisine is English, French and Greek.

Singer **Vince Hill** has very happy memories of the Brecon Hotel in Rotherham, South Yorkshire, where he and his wife would stay whenever he had cabaret bookings in the Sheffield area some years ago. He remembers the easy-going atmosphere of the place and the hospitality of the owner, Athol Carr, who never minded about the odd times Vince and his party liked to eat; sometimes returning ravenous after a show in the small hours of the morning.

The greatest tribute the Hills can pay to the good food and equally good vibes at the Brecon Hotel is to say that after many years of hoping for a child, their son Athol, now aged nine, was conceived there and named after the owner, who became a close friend. Vince says if they decide to have any more children they will certainly make a return visit!

Vince Hill – happy memories

Lenny Henry – embarrassing moment

✱ ✱ ✱ ✱ ✱ ✱ ✱ ✱ ✱ ✱ ✱ ✱ ✱

Lenny Henry, the talented impressionist and comedian who rose to fame from the chaos of ATV Birmingham's *Tiswas* and the BBC's *Three of a Kind* is 6ft 2in and broad-shouldered, and he admits to being very clumsy in restaurants. He recalls with embarrassment an occasion when he got up to pay the bill after finishing a slap-up meal without realising he had the tablecloth caught in his belt, and his companion ended up with a lap full of dirty crockery. It was an expensive night for Lenny – as well as paying for the meal he was literally taken to the cleaners. He names Jonathan's Restaurant at 16 Wolverhampton Street in his home town of Birmingham and Karachi Restaurant, 170 Old Christchurch Road, Bournemouth as his favourite eating places.

Actress and comedienne **Beryl Reid** votes for the Tarrazza at 45 Church Road Ashford, Middlesex. Above a row of shops the Tarrazza, run by two Italians, offers a three-course table d'hôte lunch for £4.75 and in the evening can provide an à la carte meal for around £15 a head. Miss Reid says that she has been to the restaurant at least three times in the last twelve months and is well content with the standard of cuisine and service. A typical set lunch has five starters including tagliatelli, melon, soup or eggs. The five main courses include chicken, pork, lemon sole or omelettes and eight different dishes are wheeled to the table on the dessert trolley. Miss Reid, a gourmet and keen home cook, particularly recommends the lobster as the main course, with crab cocktail and strawberries as a starter and pudding but agrees that this is the most expensive combination. Beryl Reid is now seen more in dramatic roles on stage, screen and television.

Kenneth Robinson, writer and broadcaster best known for his witty contributions to the *Start the Week* programmes with Richard Baker, takes his family on holiday to Oulton Broad in Suffolk and likes to go to The Moorings which is above a jetty and overlooks the waterfront on three sides. With his wife Mary and two daughters, he likes to eat plain but well-prepared dishes in pleasant surroundings. The menu The Moorings provides for around £5 includes prawn cocktail and soup, plaice, omelettes or hamburgers. Kenneth Robinson, who has recently published a collection of his writings with illustrations by his twenty-one year old daughter Lucy also holds one-man shows on one-night stands throughout the country.

Television personality **Barry Norman** personally recommends the Earl of Bradford's swinging place Porters at 17 Henrietta Street in London's West End. He featured the restaurant in *Barry Norman's London Season* in the summer of 1981. He says 'It's really a very simple place offering very simple food. English pies (steak and

Lena Zavaroni
– two choices

mushroom a favourite), with good side salads and vegetables and a fine range of house wines. It's principally a lunchtime place and two people can easily manage on £11 or £12 between them.'

Singer **Lena Zavaroni** originally hails from Rothesay, 'capital' of the Scottish Isle of Bute, but she now lives in North London with her family. Her favourite restaurants are Sale e Pepe at Pavilion Road, London SW1, where she loves the pasta dishes, and Grahame's Fish Shop in Soho's Poland Street, which is an upmarket fish restaurant with a thriving takeaway service. Now eighteen years old, Lena is no longer classified as a 'minor' in show business and is able to work longer hours. She enjoys the Country and Western style of singing and has starred in her own TV series.

Private Eye satirist **John Wells** likes to eat at Rugantino Italian Restaurant at 26 Romilly Street in London's Soho, a favourite of Private Eye staff for nearly twenty years. When he took to the stage in the witty Whitehall farce *'Anyone for Denis?'*, John Wells found the restaurant useful for late night parties with members of the cast. His favourite dishes are lasagne al forno or veal with lemon.

Why not write and tell us about your favourite hideaway using the reader's report form on page 283? If we print your recommendation in next year's edition of *Eat Out For Around £5* you will be entitled to a free copy of an AA book of your choice.

ENGLAND

The Punch + Judy, Petersfield

Lion Hotel, Shrewsbury

Tea House, Sandwich

The Red House Hotel, Exeter

The Ashburnian, Derby

'When I am living in the Midlands,
That are sodden and unkind,
I light my lamp in the evening;
My work is left behind;
And the great hills of the South Country
Come back into my mind.'

JOSEPH BELLOC

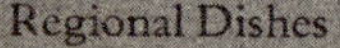

Regional Dishes

Cornish pilchards with cloves and allspice
Somerset jugged hare in cider vinegar
Devon ham in cider with damson sauce
Devilled Brixham crab
Somerset lamb braised in cider with currants
Dartmouth pie
Widecombe gingerbread
Somerset apple cakes
Lardy cakes
Saffron cakes
Cornish pasties

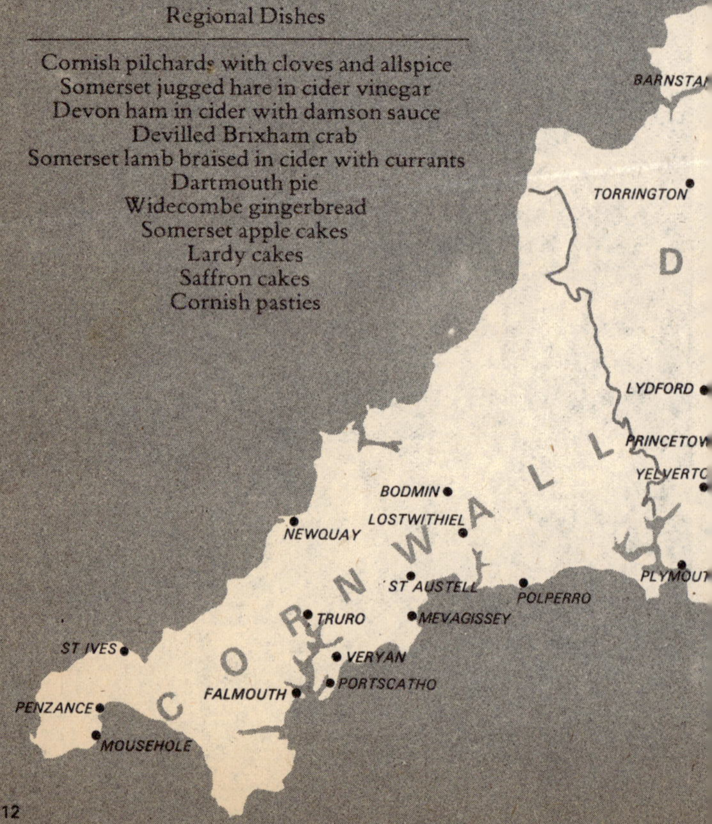

BARNSTA
TORRINGTON
D
LYDFORD
PRINCETOW
YELVERTO
BODMIN
LOSTWITHIEL
NEWQUAY
CORNWALL
ST AUSTELL
POLPERRO
PLYMOUT
TRURO
MEVAGISSEY
ST IVES
VERYAN
PORTSCATHO
FALMOUTH
PENZANCE
MOUSEHOLE

South West Peninsula

1

ALVESTON
PORTISHEAD
CHIPPING SODBURY
TORMARTON
BRISTOL
CLEVEDON
AVON
KEYNSHAM
BATH
WESTON-SUPER-MARE
WINSCOMBE
PORLOCK WEIR
LYNTON
MINEHEAD
BLEADNEY
WELLS
WATCHET
WASHFORD
SOMERSET
KEENTHORNE
CANNINGTON
STREET
WIVELISCOMBE
NORTH PETHERTON
LANGPORT
KNOWSTONE
TAUNTON
ILCHESTER
QUEEN CAMEL
OAKFORD
CHULMLEIGH
SOUTH PETHERTON
WELLINGTON
MARTOCK
YEOVIL
TIVERTON
SAMPFORD PEVERELL
CREWKERNE
VON
HONITON
THORVERTON
OKEHAMPTON
OTTERY ST MARY
EXETER
UTH
EAL
SIDMOUTH
KENNFORD
ORETONHAMPSTEAD
BUDLEIGH SALTERTON
BOVEY TRACEY
CHUDLEIGH
EXMOUTH
DARTMEET
NEWTON ABBOT
ASHBURTON
TORQUAY
CKFASTLEIGH
PAIGNTON
TOTNES
BRIXHAM
HALWELL
DARTMOUTH
KINGSBRIDGE

Alveston

THE SHIP, POST HOUSE HOTEL ☆☆☆
Thornbury Road (0454 412521)
Open: Mon-Sun 12noon-2pm

P

The Ship at the Post House Hotel offers a newly-devised wholefood menu which has a fine selection of dishes to suit the wholefood connoisseur, the weight-conscious and the hungry businessperson. Vegetarian pâté (90p), steak and mushroom pie with baked potatoes (£2) and various wholefood salads (from 55p) feature on the menu. To complete your meal a piece of honey pie is a must.

Ashburton

THE DARTMOOR MOTEL ★★
(Ashburton 52232)
Open: Mon-Sun 12noon-2pm, 7-9.30pm

C P

The three-course set lunch at this pleasant, modern hotel close to the A38 offers a good choice of main courses for around £3. The à la carte menu is extremely tempting, with an emphasis on fish and grills. Seafood special – scampi, prawns, mussels and cockles cooked in sherry and cream – is a delight, but you will have to choose a lower priced starter and sweet to keep within your budget when you sample it. Children are offered a half-portion lunch at around £2.

RISING SUN INN, Woodland
(Ashburton 52544)
1½m off southbound A38 Exeter-Plymouth
Open: Mon-Sun 11.30am-2pm, 7-10.30pm

C P

Once used by sheep drovers as an overnight stop on the road to Dartmoor, this rustic old inn houses an interesting collection of prints dating from the early 1920s. Many of the people depicted still form a faithful band of locals who meet and drink here. A sumptuous cold buffet, which includes home-cooked cold meats, fresh salmon, salads and pies, is very reasonably priced, and there are grills and basket meals for those who like it hot, all freshly prepared on the premises. Children can enjoy a meal on the covered verandah or in the pleasant garden to the rear. This is an ideal place from which to see the Devonshire countryside; Torbay and Plymouth are both nearby.

Barnstaple

BARNSTAPLE MOTEL ☆☆☆ Braunton Road (Barnstaple 76221)
Open: Mon-Sun 12.30-2pm, 7-10pm

[C] [♫] [P]

The restaurant and bar of this pleasant motel are ideal places to break a journey and enjoy good food. Hot and cold bar snacks include cottage pie, chips and peas. A three-course lunch in the restaurant is around £3.50. Choices include grapefruit and mandarin cocktail, roast lamb or gammon and pineapple and sweets from the trolley. A similar three-course dinner is £5, with a slightly larger selection of main courses, including beef chasseur.

ROBOROUGH HOUSE
Off A39 1m N of Barnstaple, down lane signed Hospital. (Barnstaple 72354)
Open: Mon-Sun 12noon-2pm, 7.30-9.30pm

[C] [S] [♣]

Set in fourteen acres of well-kept gardens and woodlands in a secluded position above Barnstaple, it's worth stopping here for more than a snack. The former private house was built in 1800 on a south-facing hillside overlooking the Taw estuary. Now a family hotel run by the Sneddon family, you can get breakfast, morning coffee, afternoon tea, bar snacks, and a table d'hôte lunch and dinner. Miss Fiona Sneddon runs the kitchen, specialising in home-made fare such as Devon-style chicken with apple, cider and cream sauce, or devilled lamb cutlets, tasty soups and pâtés, and her own fresh fruit cream ice. All these may be on the special tourist three-course menu for £4.95. Snacks range from Cornish pasty [50p] or egg mayonnaise salad [75p] to 8oz sirloin steak and chips at about £4. Dinner is nearer the £7 mark.

Bath

BARCELONA SPANISH RESTAURANT, 31 Barton Street (Bath 63924)
Open: Tue-Sun 12noon-2.15pm, 6.30-11.30pm

[C] [P] [S]

Suddenly it's Spain when you sample the intriguing cuisine at this bright and cheerful restaurant with its new, Spanish-style cocktail bar. Paella at around £4.50, kalamares marinera (squids with tomato and wine sauce) at about £3.50 or gambas parrilla (king prawns) for less than £4.50 are some choice examples. Tasty English dishes are also on offer, as are daily specialities shown on a board, including rape vizcanna (monkfish) and stuffed peppers. Choice of appetisers is wide, and an interesting sweet is pijama, a dish of assorted nuts and raisins served with a miniature flask of moscato.

THE CHICAGO PIZZA PIE FACTORY
1 St Andrews Terrace, Bartlett Street (Bath 333233)
Open: Tue-Sun 11.45am-11pm

[S]

Is your digestion system strong enough to cope with American-style overkill (as far as portions are concerned) and video shows of American football and baseball while you eat? You'll certainly need plenty of stamina to tackle the pizzas – the smallest available (from £3.45) is sufficient for two. But some good things have come from the US, you're offered a doggie bag in which to cart away the leftovers, and carrot cake (£1.05), an interesting variation on cheesecake, is presented with *two* forks. Salad – as much as you can fit in one bowl – is 95p. Kicking off with the stuffed mushroom starter is only advisable for expandable stomachs. Décor, thank goodness, is simple, spacious Chicago style, and there's a section for non-smokers.

CLARETS WINE AND SHERRY LOUNGE, 6-7 Kingsmead Square (Bath 66688)
Open: Mon-Fri 10am-2.30pm, 6.30-11pm (Sat 11.30pm), Sun 7-10.30pm

[C] [♫] [P] [S]

Clarets is a beautifully converted white-walled cellar, with pine-wood furniture. In fine summer weather, chairs and tables are set out under the large plane tree in the cobbled square outside. The owners, David and Lisa Tearle are thoroughly experienced restaurateurs and serve tasty dishes prepared from good fresh food. Choose from starters, casseroles (including a vegetarian vegetable and cheese version) with bread and butter and green salad (about £2.75-£4.50) and home-made sweets, with filter coffee to complete a very pleasant meal.

DANISH FOOD AND WINE BAR
Pierrepont Place (Bath 61603)
Open: Mon-Sat 11am-2.30pm

[♫] [P] [S]

The Fernley's Danish Food and Wine Bar [behind the hotel], although small and simple, is both stylish and comfortable, and well worth a visit for the variety of its delicious open sandwiches of meat, fish and cheese (around 75p). To these you can add salads (for a small extra charge), and finish with pastries and cream and good filter coffee. As an alternative try the cold table where, for from about £2, you can help yourself to as much cold meat and salad as you can heap on your plate.

THE EDWARDIAN, 36 Westgate Street (Bath 61642)
Open: Dining room: Mon-Sat 12noon-2.15pm, 6-11pm, Sun 12noon-2pm, 6-10.30pm, Cellar Bar: Mon-Sun 12noon-2.30pm, 6-9.30pm

[C] [♫] [S] [♧]

You'll have no trouble in finding and enjoying variety at this Edwardian hotel, close to the Abbey. The first floor Edwardian Dining Room is tastefully furnished in the period and a good grill section is available, with ice cream, fruit pie and cream or cheeseboard to follow. Starters are pricey, and without care, some will take you over the £5 limit. Sunday lunch can be had here for around £5, with half-price meals for children. In the cellar you can select hot roasts from the carvery in a sophisticated yet informal atmosphere, every day including Sundays.

THE LADEN TABLE, 7 Edgar Buildings (Bath 64356)
Open: Mon-Sat 12noon-3pm, Mon-Sun 6-11.30pm

[♫] [♧]

A fully-licensed wholefood restaurant seating about eighteen in a pleasant, relaxed atmosphere with soft background music. Proprietor Peter Slotter stays in the kitchen, concocting wholefood creations such as samosa (a crispy, deep-fried, filled Indian pastry at 35p) millet balls (millet mixed with fresh vegetables at 40p) or stuffed pitta bread at around £1. His partner, Valerie Tranter, waits at table, and she will draw your attention to the constantly-changing blackboard menu which lists dishes such as cauliflower cheese, chef's salad or curry, all under £2. Sweets include fresh fruit cheesecake and honey baked apple.

SPORTSMAN STEAK HOUSE, Rode Hill, Rode (Frome 830249)
11m south of Bath on B3109 Rode-Bradford-on-Avon road
Open: Mon-Fri 12noon-2.30pm, 6.30-11pm

[C] [P] [♧]

This converted stone barn has a copper-topped bar on the first floor, in an open-plan area where you can enjoy an aperitif while Philip, the resident chef, prepares your meal. Starters include fruit juices, prawn cocktail, and Strasbourg pâté with fingers of hot toast. Main dishes are unfussy but good, with two lamb chops, a pork chop or gammon steak at about £2.80, or a luscious, tender T-bone steak at twice the price. Not only do those prices include freshly-cooked chips, peas and mushrooms, but also ice cream or cheese to follow. Even with wine, you can keep around the £5 mark.

Bleadney

THE STRADLINGS, Bleadney (Wells 73576)
On B3139 near Wells
Open: Tue-Sat 11am-2.30pm, 6.30-10.30pm, Sun 12noon-2pm, 7-10pm

[P]

This sturdy, stone-built inn now boasts a rustic hop and wine bar where visitors to the country village of Bleadney can stop for lunch, dinner, or snacks. At lunchtime a businessperson's menu is available, with 'brunch', home-made steak and kidney pies and cottage pies in the range of £1.50-£2, or simple hot dishes – sausage and chips (£1.05), ploughmans (£1) or pâté (£1.20). The restaurant, a separate sixty-seater hall, is open in the evening, serving mainly grills and some house specialities, but this, at an average of £9-£10 with wine, is outside budget. A blackboard lists specialities which include mushrooms Valencia at £2, snails with garlic butter at £1.75, and many others.

Bodmin

CASTLE HILL HOUSE HOTEL ★★
(Bodmin 3009)
Open: Mon-Sat 7-8.30pm,
Sun 12.30-2pm

[P]

Ken and Sylvia Flint's Castle Hill House Hotel is an elegant Georgian mansion set in two acres of lawns and gardens. Delicious home-produced food such as soup, pâté and steak and kidney pie proves popular with guests and locals

alike, and it's as well to book in advance for dinner. The table d'hôte menu offers a three-course meal and coffee for about £4, and some items on the small à la carte menu are within our price range. A good selection of freshly-made sweets, including gâteaux and home-made fruit pies is served with clotted Cornish cream.

Bovey Tracey

RIVERSIDE INN, Fore Street
(Bovey Tracey 832293)
Open: Mon-Sat 11am-2.30pm, 6-11pm (winter 10.30pm) Sun 12noon-2pm, 7-10.30pm

[P]

This large inn by a stream enjoys a picturesque situation in the centre of Bovey Tracey, a popular touring area within a stone's throw of Hay Tor. On display is the sword, broken in two, which is said to have been used by the knight, De Tracey in the murder of Thomas à Becket. There are two eating places to choose from; the Cavalier Restaurant offers a substantial à la carte menu of grills, while the King Charles Buttery has a more budget-priced selection, such as basket meals, pizzas, sandwiches or salads. A choice from the à la carte of chef's own pâté, the Moorland grill (which includes kidney, egg, sausage, chop, gammon) with vegetables of the day and lemon sorbet, accompanied by wine and coffee would come just within our limit. On Sundays a set three-course lunch with coffee can be had for around £3 or thereabouts.

Bristol

ARNOLFINI, Narrow Quay
(Bristol 299191)
Open: Tue-Sat 11am-8pm

Presenting new developments in music, dance, theatre and cinema, the Arnolfini public arts complex boasts this airy and spacious bistro-style restaurant with its taped background music and blackboard menu, with salads, cold meats and cakes on display on long counters. There is always an exhibition of works of art on the walls. Once a docks warehouse, the restaurant overlooks St Augustine's Reach. Soups, pâtés and a hot dish of the day are all reasonably priced, and a three-course light meal can be enjoyed for around £2.50. Salads are particularly interesting, and a mixed salad of celery, apple, nuts, orange and mayonnaise costs about 45p.

LE CHÂTEAU WINE BAR
32 Park Street (Bristol 28654)
Open: Mon-Sat 9.30am-2.30pm, 5.30-9pm

[♫] [P] [S]

This informal, busy city centre wine bar brims over with business people at lunchtime – a tribute to good food and unpretentious but relaxing surroundings, with wooden furniture and lighting from candles in wax-encrusted bottles. Behind the Victorian bar a blackboard proclaims the range of hot lunchtime dishes – pork fillet kebabs in lemon garlic sauce, moussaka, chili con carne, kidneys Java at prices around £1.60-£2.20. Also at lunchtime and in the evening a selection of cold meats, pâté, cheeses, mackerel and attractively-prepared salads is on offer at about £1.75. Interesting desserts include peaches in brandy, and blueberry pie – both around 60p, as well as cheesecake, ices and sorbets.

THE CHEQUERS INN, Hanham Mills, Hamham (Bristol 674242)
Open: Mon-Sat 12noon-2.30pm, 6.30-11pm, Sun 12noon-2.30pm, 7-11pm

[C] [♫] [P] [⚘]

This riverside haven, close to the city, offers an 'economy lunch' which is likely to include a casserole or joint of the day for around £3.70. No wonder The Chequers is a popular haunt, attracting not only local business people but family parties, particularly for Sunday lunch, and even yachtsmen taking a spot of shore-leave. Apart from the restaurant offering a comprehensive choice of grills or 'Fisherman's Choices', the self-service bar has a carvery specialising in 'Roasters' – succulent rare beef or roast pork with vegetables for around £3 or cold ham off the bone for about £2.50. Lasagne, steak and kidney pie or turkey and ham in white sauce are also available for around £1.50 including vegetables. Snacks run from 50p and pastries and gâteaux are on offer at give-away prices.

CIRCLES RESTAURANT, Dingles, Queens Road, Clifton (Bristol 215301)
Open: Mon-Fri 9am-5.30pm, Sat 9am-6pm

[C] [♫] [S]

This comfortable, modern, self-service restaurant displays cold meats, salads, pâtés and a variety of sandwiches, all at very reasonable prices. Staff are on hand to help you to the various permutations of interesting salads which range in price from around £1-£2. Hot quiches and meat loaf are around 75p and soup costs about 30p. With cream gâteaux on offer at around 45p to complete the menu, this is a much sought-after filling station for shoppers.

DRAGONARA HOTEL ☆☆☆☆
Redcliffe Way (Bristol 20044)
Open: Captain's Cabin Bar: Mon-Fri 12.30-2pm, Garden Room: Mon-Fri 6.30-10pm, Sat-Sun 12.30-2pm, 6.30-10pm

[C] [♫] [P] [S] [⚘]

The Garden Room is a bright and pleasant restaurant within Ladbroke's Dragonara Hotel. A typical meal here might consist of pâté in the pot, followed by chicken breast provençale, with ice-cream to finish, at a cost of around £5. However, take care, as several of the main dishes will take you over the budget. At the recently introduced Cabin Bar though, you can choose from a variety of hot and cold dishes (eg, moussaka or salad of the day) after a bowl of soup, for as little as £1.50.

EDWARDS, 203 Whiteladies Road, Clifton (Bristol 311533)
Open: Mon-Sat 12noon-2.30pm, 7-11pm

[S]

The former Victorian shop has been recently modernised by owner/chef James Orchard. Lunch and supper menus offer an imaginative range of good food at sensible prices. Lunch can be chosen from an impressive selection of home-made soups, hot dishes of the day and a selection of grills. On summer days the cold buffet is popular. Sweets and vegetables are under £1. The dinner is more ambitious from both culinary and price aspects, but home-made beef, Guinness and oyster pie with accompaniments should be about £5.

GIOVANNI PIZZERIA, 15 Union Street (Bristol 22731)
Open: Mon-Thu 11.30am-12mdnt, Fri-Sat 11.30am-2am, Sun 5.30-12mdnt

[C] [♫] [S] [🍷]

Home-made pizzas are the speciality here. You can buy a simply-dressed tomato, oregano and garlic version, or go for a more elaborate one like pizza Giovanni – an extravagance of mozzarella cheese, tomato, oregano, salami and black olives, costing about £2.50. The skilful preparation of these and other dishes is on view to diners, providing interesting 'while-you-wait' entertainment. A more conventional form of entertainment is the nightly disco dancing and, occasionally, there is a live band at weekends.

THE GUILD RESTAURANT, Bristol Guild, 68-70 Park Street (Bristol 291874)
Open: Mon-Fri 9.30am-5pm, Sat 9.30am-1pm

[S]

The small Guild Restaurant, with its attractive extension on to a terrace, covered in winter, but opened in summer to allow patrons to eat in the sun, is a part of the smart Bristol Guild store in the city centre. Under the capable direction of Alison Moore, inexpensive lunchtime meals of good quality include a selection of home-made soup, quiches or pâtés chalked on a blackboard menu. Soup is around 65-80p, quiches are around 95p and pâtés with salad about £2.30. A hot main dish of the day could be spaghetti bolognese, moussaka, a roast or a casserole, all served with vegetables at around £2.50. Creamy desserts are delicious and modestly priced at around 85p.

LLANDOGER TROW, 5 King Street (Bristol 20783)
Open: Mon-Fri 12noon-2.30pm, 6-11pm (Sat 11.30), Sun 12noon-2pm, 7-10.30pm

[C] [♫] [P] [S] [🍷]

King Street boasts a number of impressive 17th- and 18th-century buildings, including the long-running Theatre Royal, first opened to the public in 1766. But none is more interesting, or has attracted more legends, than Llandoger Trow, built in 1664, one of the oldest inns in the city and now run by Berni. Duckling and T-bone steaks are specialities of the house here and the steak and duck restaurant does an extremely good local trade. In the smaller steak and sole restaurant, prices range from about £3 for fillets of place to just under £6 for fillet steak. Half a duckling costs around £5.

MARCO'S TRATTORIA, Queen Road (Bristol 28508)
Open: Mon-Sat 12noon-3pm, 6-10.30pm (Fri 11pm, Sat 11.30pm) Sun 6-10.30pm

[S]

Down a short flight of steps, below the

busy shopping street of Queens Road, you will find the quiet haven of Marco's Trattoria. This intimate little restaurant is simply-furnished with comfortable chairs and polished-wood tables in a cellar-type décor, complete with the original flagstone flooring. Your needs will be attended to by one of the charming waitresses dressed in an Italian-style costume which was cleverly-designed by manageress Tina Choules and made by the girls themselves. A satisfying meal can be based on the traditional English steak at around £3 or, for a little less, one of the Italian specialities such as bistecca al pizzaiola or scaloppine milanese for £2.80 or so. All meals are served with French fries (or spaghetti with the Italian dishes), garden peas, roll and butter, and include in their price ice cream for dessert or a selection of Italian cheeses with biscuits.

PARKS, 51 Park Street (Bristol 28016)
Open: Mon-Sat 11am-11pm,
Sun 12noon-11pm

Although the restaurant itself is only four years old Parks, situated in Bristol's busy Park Street and close to the city's lovely university and museum is housed in a Georgian listed building. It is fresh and bright, bedecked with attractive plants, grand mirrors and fans from the once-far flung Empire. Specialities here are savoury pancakes made with buckwheat and filled with such things as chicken in mushroom and white wine sauce, smoked haddock in cream sauce, or cheese with spinach and nutmeg, all at about £2.25, including salad and teas such as Earl Grey and jasmine served with milk or lemon, at around 30p per person. Main-course dishes, served with vegetables or salad, and jacket potato with butter or sour cream, include 8oz sirloin steak and chicken sauté with Madeira sauce at £3.45. In addition there is a Chef's Special. Desserts include gooseberry and elderflower ice cream at around £1. House wine is about 65p.

LA ROMANINA, 25 The Mall, Clifton (Bristol 34499)
Open: Mon-Sat 12noon-2.30pm, 7-11.30pm

The bright colours and cheerful atmosphere of La Romanina bring a touch of the Mediterranean to the heart of Clifton old town. Fresh flowers are on every table, and service is courteous and prompt. The pizza and pasta dishes are very good and cost about £2. Add on a further £2 to cover starter and sweet. The à la carte meat dishes, often accompanied by robust Italian sauces, are more expensive, but potatoes and fresh vegetables in season are included in the main price. Fresh salmon and lobster are also available in season.

TRATTORIA SORRENTO
239 Cheltenham Road (Bristol 45879)
Open: Mon-Thu, Sun 6pm-2am,
Fri-Sat 6pm-3am

P

This spacious, modern trattoria, bedecked with Chianti flasks, is noted for its home-made pastas and pizzas. Freshly made for each customer, the pizzas are rated by gourmets as 'the finest this side of Mount Vesuvius', and the Chef's Special is a particularly praiseworthy specimen – brimming over with Italian cheeses, tomatoes, bacon, salami, corn, peppers, mushrooms and anchovies! Pizza and pasta dishes cost around £2 but the steak and chicken dishes, English or Italian style, are from £3. So generous are the main courses that the luscious sweets, Italian cheeses and speciality coffees prove to be quite a challenge. Whatever your choice, dishes will be served to you in true Italian style by cheerful (and sometimes singing) Italian waiters who look as though they have just been plucked from the sunshine of Italy.

Brixham

THE ELIZABETHAN, 8 Middle Street (Brixham 3722)
Open: summer: Mon-Sun 12.15-2pm, Tue-Sat 7-9.30pm, winter: Mon-Sun 12.15-2pm

[C] [P] [S] [♧]

Small-paned windows, stuccoed walls, ceiling beams and dark, polished furniture lend an air of cosy antiquity to this small restaurant in the town centre. Fresh flowers are a complement to the fresh, home-made fare. The lunch menu offers a choice of main courses and desserts for around £2.40. Roast chicken, pork or fillet of plaice could be followed with apricot crumble or Devonshire junket with clotted cream. An appetiser such as home-made soup of the day, pâté or scampi, will set you back from 50p-£1.90. Dinners, served during the season, are 'Taste of England' dishes at their best. It would be easy to exceed the limit here, but soup, followed by duck in Armagnac and orange sauce and fresh cream chocolate puffs can be savoured without fear of overspending. The restaurant is conveniently situated opposite Brixham bus station and near to the multi-storey car park in the town centre.

Buckfastleigh

DART BRIDGE INN, Totnes Road (Buckfastleigh 2214)
Open: Mon-Sun 12noon-2pm, 7-10pm

[P]

Just across the road from the River Dart, this mock Tudor inn has pleasant gardens and a sun terrace. It is less than 100 yards away from the A38 Exeter-Plymouth road. The interior is furnished in pub lounge-bar style. Hot and cold meals are served, the former consisting mainly of grills with chips and peas from £1.90 to £4. A cold buffet with salads and meats costs £2.50.

Budleigh Salterton

THE LOBSTER POT, 16 High Street (Budleigh Salterton 2731)
Open: summer: Mon-Sun 10.30am-2pm, 7-10pm, winter: Mon-Sun 10.30am-2pm, evening by arrangement

[C] [♬] [S] [♧]

Near the sea front you will find this bright, white-painted restaurant with its small-paned windows and gay red canopy. Renowned for its fresh seafood specialities, you can enjoy an array of

other dishes too in the comfortable, Georgian-style interior. A three-course set lunch is available for around £2.75, and the à la carte menu gives a good choice for under £5. Particularly recommended are the pâté with salad garni and mixed seafood and salad. Dinner offers specialities such as scallops à la crème (scallops cooked in white wine sauce), and vegetables are included in the price of the main course. A three-course dinner rounded off with coffee can cost around £5.

Cannington

BLUE ANCHOR INN, Brook Street, Cannington (Combwich 652215)
Open: Mon-Sun 12noon-2pm, 7-10pm

[♫] [P]

This long, low, wisteria-clad inn was built in the 1600s. Rebuilt and greatly modernised in 1948, the Blue Anchor has enjoyed constant popularity for as long as anyone cares to remember. Proprietors David and Anne Rees provide an extensive range of bar snacks starting from soup, sandwiches and pâté and building up to steak and all the trimmings, and food is reasonably priced and well-prepared. There's a choice of two house wines.

Chipping Sodbury

THE LAWNS INN, Church Road, Yate (Chipping Sodbury 314367)
Open: Bar snacks: Mon-Sat 12noon-2.15pm, 7.30-10pm, Sun 12noon-2pm, 7.30-10pm; Restaurant: Mon-Sun 12.30-2pm, 7.30-11pm

[P]

Part of the Lawns is *genuine* Tudor – built in 1625. It is a popular eating place in lovely surroundings. The restaurant boasts authentic period plasterwork which complements the comfortable modern furniture. A bright little buttery offers a wide range of hot or cold snacks. The former, in the 70p-£1 price-range, include curry, cottage pie, lasagne and chili con carne. A three-course meal in the restaurant costs from £4-£8. Accent is on grills.

Chudleigh

THE WHEEL CRAFT CENTRE
Chudleigh Mill (Chudleigh 853255)
Open: Mon-Sun 10am-6pm

[P] [♿]

Created on the site of the original Town Mills which were used to grind corn, the

Wheel Craft Centre has a restored watermill complete with working wheel. Visitors can watch the group of craftsmen and women at work and browse around the wholefood and craft shops which form part of the centre. The 'Tea Shoppe' provides much more than cream teas. Home-made soup with a hot roll costs 45p, and you may follow this with one of the Special Hot Lunches – farmhouse stew at £1.25 and chicken in red wine at £1.65 are examples. Home-made desserts served with clotted cream cost from 65p. Lighter snacks include 'Things on toast' for 65p, omelettes with salad at 90p and vegetarian dishes from 95p. As yet The Wheel is unlicensed, though one has been applied for. A steaming cup of Rombout coffee at 30p is an excellent substitute!

Chulmleigh

FOX AND HOUNDS HOTEL ★★
Eggesford (Chulmleigh 345)
Open: Bar: Mon-Thu 11.30am-1.45pm, 6-9.30pm, Fri-Sat 11.30am-1.45pm, 6-10pm, Sun 7-9.30pm; Restaurant: Mar-Oct, 7.30-9pm

P

The Fox and Hounds Hotel, close to the River Taw, halfway between Exeter and Barnstaple, is a rambling country hotel, the mecca of fishermen from Victorian days. It has a large bar, the Eggesford Bar, which offers a wide range of snacks at a reasonable price. A salad bar in summer offers an impressive choice from £1.80. A Fox's lunch, consisting of French bread, ham and cheese, garnished with tomato and pickle, costs £1.20. In the tourist season, a four-course dinner may be had for around £5.50 in the hotel dining room. The menu is interesting and offers a good choice. You may even eat fish caught that very day as an entrée or a main course! A speciality is Chicken Fox and Hounds – chicken served in a white wine sauce with mushrooms and asparagus.

Clevedon

MON PLAISIR RESTAURANT
32-34 Hill Road (Clevedon 872307)
Open: Mon-Sat 12noon-2pm, 7-10pm

P

For Mr Luis Moran and his staff 'Mon Plaisir' is certainly the operative phrase, for here nothing is too much trouble and with their warm, friendly welcome they hope to make eating here 'your pleasure' too. You will dine in comfort at this Victorian house, set just off the sea front, where well-prepared food is served in generous portions. The three-course set lunch (with a choice of five main courses) is excellent value at around £2.15. In the evening a three-course dinner with a choice of sweets and starters, and a main course such as steak chasseur, gammon or sirloin steak and all the trimmings will cost around £5.

Crewkerne

THE OLD PARSONAGE ★★
Barn Street (Crewkerne 73516)
Open: Mon-Sat 12noon-2pm, 7-8.30pm, Sun 12noon-2pm

C P

On the corner of a quiet lane you will find this charming old rectory, personally run by Kenneth Mullins. Home cooking is the big attraction here. Interesting dishes such as cockles in cheese sauce and grilled rainbow trout with almonds and Pernod, are scattered liberally throughout the à la carte menu (most of which are unfortunately outside our price limit). The table d'hôte menus for lunch and dinner are reasonably priced at around £5. A traditional Sunday lunch of three courses plus coffee and cream costs approximately £3.50, with a special children's version at 50p less.

Dartmeet

BADGER'S HOLT (Poundsgate 213)
Open: Mon-Sat 9.30am-6pm, Sun 10.30am-6pm. Closed: Nov-Apr

C

The tumbling waters of the boulder-strewn river flow past this white-painted timber restaurant nestling in the shadow of Dartmoor. Rare birds such as the strange blue-eared pheasant from the Far East are on view in the garden. The food is not exotic, but is very good for all that. Table d'hôte lunch at £3.30 is outstandingly good value. A choice of starters includes home-made chicken and tomato soup served with fresh home-made bread, roll-mop herring or mackerel salad. Hot main course dishes such as roast turkey, loin of pork with pineapple or fried scallops with tartare sauce are served with ample portions of well-prepared vegetables. Home-cooked gammon or roast lamb with a mixed salad are two of the cold alternatives. Desserts include a delicious almond-flavoured trifle, apple pie or junket.

Dartmouth

THE STEAM PACKET, 3 Duke Street (Dartmouth 3886)
Open: Mon-Sun 12noon-2pm, 6.30-10.30pm (Sun 7-10.30pm)

S

Everything is shipshape in this neat little glass-fronted wine bar situated just 300yd from the river front, and as one might expect from such a nautical name, seafood is a speciality. As seating is limited to eighteen people you may have to wait for a place or book in advance – either way you'll be well justified in paying the Steam Packet a visit. Young owner David Hawke has a background of hotels and catering in this country where he did his training, and in the West Indies, Brazil and Switzerland where he worked. So you can be sure that when you taste his home-made quiche, pizzas or steak and kidney pie you're tasting some of the best around – and the price is right too!

Exeter

CLARE'S, 13 Princesshay (Exeter 55155)
Open: Mon-Sat 9.30am-5.30pm

P S

There are some classy shops in Princesshay, a pedestrian area just off the High Street and not far from the Cathedral, and Clare Dowell and Simon Shattock's brightly modern counter-service restaurant is just the place for a snack or lunch when you tire of looking in the gift shops and boutiques. It's justly popular with office workers, too, who have to find the quickest and cheapest good food around. 'Country style' hot dishes such as lasagne with rice and salad garnish, steak and kidney pie and gammon and courgettes in a cheese sauce cost around £1.85. A salad with quiche, pizza or meat costs about £1.85. Clare's is licensed to sell wines, beer and cider.

COOLINGS WINE BAR
11 Gandy Street (Exeter 34183)
Open: Mon-Sat 12noon-2.15pm, 5.30-11.30pm

P S

Tucked away in one of the older, interesting streets behind the main shopping area is this stylish, family-run wine and food bar where all the food is freshly-prepared on the premises. Beams and checked tablecloths create a welcoming interior and you can also dine in the converted cellars. An excellent range of meats, pies and salads is displayed on the long self-service bar, including such delights as chicken Waldorf and salad, tuna and rice salad and sugar-baked ham and salad, all around £1.55-£2. Hot dishes such as lasagne (about £1.55) and cottage pie are chalked up on the blackboard. There is a choice of about six sweets for around 50p-65p.

HOLE IN THE WALL, Little Castle Street (Exeter 73341)
Open: Restaurant: Mon-Thu 12noon-2.30pm, Fri-Sat 12noon-2.30pm, 7-11pm. Steak Bar: Mon-Thu 6-11pm, Fri-Sat 6-11.30pm

C S

One of the nationwide Berni Inn chain of restaurants, the Hole in the Wall is an old building of character. It provides a choice of two attractive, well-appointed restaurants, offering steak, fish and chicken dishes. Those familiar with Berni Inns will know that included in the price of each main dish are potatoes, vegetables, roll and butter, and to follow, ice cream or cheese and biscuits. The perfect finishing touch is the coffee, served in a glass with a generous topping of cream for about 30p.

NEW TAJ MAHAL, 50 Queen Street (Exeter 58129)
Open: Mon-Sun 12noon-2.30pm, 5.30-11.30pm

[S]

A compact Indian restaurant with somewhat grand interior décor equal to its name, the New Taj Mahal has walls of pleated multi-coloured silk and a silk-draped ceiling. A wide choice of Indian dishes is available but do take care when ordering curry – it can be very hot! The Tandoori Specials won't burn a hole in your pocket, though – they are well-priced at around £2.50-£4.75.

THE NOBODY INN ✕ Doddiscombleigh (Christow 52394)
South of Exeter, 2m east of Christow
Open: Restaurant: Tue-Sat 7.30-9.30pm. Bar snacks: normal licensing hours

[P]

At one time weary travellers would stop at this inn in vain. An unknown purchaser had refused hospitality by locking the door, causing them to continue on their journeys in the belief there was 'nobody in'. Now, in the heavily-beamed bar with its imposing stone fireplace, a varied range of bar meals awaits you, and more substantial fare in the charming 'character' restaurant. The menu here includes some comparative rarities – 'Nobody' soup, lamb sweetbreads and duck l'orange, but they will prepare your favourite dish on request.

POPPYS, 12 South Street (Exeter 73779)
Open: Mon-Sat 5.30-11.30pm, Sun 6.30-11pm

[C] [♫] [P] [S]

There are not many places in Exeter where you can get a not-too-expensive evening meal, and Poppys is understandably popular with theatre- and cinema-goers and students. Here they serve really beefy beefburgers with various toppings for £1.50-£2 inclusive of potato and salad: that's for the ¼lb size – the ½lb variety costs 35p more. There are slimburgers and vegetarian nutburgers too. Kebabs and quiches are in the same price range, and home-made cheesecake or chocolate gâteau costs about 85p.

THE RED HOUSE HOTEL ★ 2 Whipton Village Road, Whipton (Exeter 56104)
Open: Mon-Thu 12noon-2.30pm, 7-10pm, Fri-Sat 12noon-2.30pm, 7-10.30pm, Sun 12noon-1.30pm, 7-9.30pm

[C] [P] [🌳]

This imposing red brick building about a mile from the city centre has a warm comfortable décor with oak refectory tables and settles. There is an excellent bar menu from which one may select a snack or a satisfying three-course meal. A crock of delicious home-made soup served with French bread may be followed by a cold platter (a variety of cold meats, pâtés, pies and fish with self-service salad) from around £1.50-£2, or a bar grill such as minute steak, chicken or scampi for about the same price. There is always a good selection of sweets including gâteaux from around 60p-70p.

ROYAL OAK INN, Dunsford (Christow 52256)
6m south west of Exeter, just off the B3212 to Moretonhampstead
Open: Mon-Sat 11am-2.30pm, 6-10.30pm (11pm Fri & Sat), Sun 12noon-2.30pm

[♫] [P] [🌳]

A charming village inn in a rural setting, the Royal Oak offers sustenance either in the comfortable bar or in the dining room. An extensive menu includes home-made soup, prawn cocktail and chicken-liver pâté as 'beginners' from around 55p-95p. A selection of grills such as gammon and peaches or English steaks ranges in price from about £2.50-£4. Fish, chicken or steak and kidney pie are around £1.95 and a selection of salads about £1.50-£2.25 (prawn salad). Desserts include gâteaux with cream, or black cherries with meringue and cream and vary in price from around 65p-80p.

THE SHIP INN, Martin's Lane (Exeter 72040)
Open: Mon-Sat 12noon-2pm, 6.30-10.30pm

[C] [♫] [S] [🌳]

Sir Francis Drake wrote in a letter dated 1587 'Next to mine own shippe I do most love that old 'Shippe' in Exon'. Today, good wine and victuals are still there to be enjoyed, and at quite reasonable prices. The upstairs restaurant is perhaps a little dark and cramped, with deep red wallpaper and upholstery, high-backed settles, and windows within a few feet of the building across the lane, but the atmosphere is right and service is very quick and cheerful. All food is à la carte – the same menu for lunch and dinner. Starters include Scott's pâté at 80p and – a speciality of the house – whitebait, about 85p. Fresh Torbay sole is the most popular fish dish – around £3.20. Roasts and grills are equally reasonable, the most expensive being fillet steak garni which costs over £5. All dishes include peas or tossed salad, fried or croquette potatoes, roll and butter. Sweets include vanilla ice with cream and meringue Chantilly.

THE SWAN'S NEST, Exminster
(Kennford 832371)
4m south of Exeter on the A379 to Dawlish
Open: Mon-Sat 12noon-2pm, 6-10pm, Sun 12noon-1.30pm, 7-10pm

[P]

Mervyn and Joan Ash have run the Swan's Nest for fourteen years, and in that time they have managed to create a delightful and popular inn. Lots of rich, dark oak – and a fresh flower for every table – make for a warm welcome. The menu is simple but very good value – help yourself to crisp, green salads, cold meats, pâtés, sandwiches and fresh filled rolls; plus a superb selection of gâteaux, cheesecakes and fruit flans. Such a meal will cost you around £4.75 including coffee.

Exmouth

NUTWELL LODGE, Lympstone
(Topsham 3279)
3m north of Exmouth on the A376
Open: Mon-Sat 12noon-2pm, 6.15-10pm, Sun 12noon-1.30pm, 7-10pm

[P]

The vast lounge of this rambling Georgian hotel with its massive, dark wooden bar, glowing pink-shaded lamps, antiques, oil-paintings and intimate sunken area with soft upholstered settees serves a selection of snacks to tempt anyone's palate. Pork and red wine pâté with salad, chutney and toast is a meal in itself at about £1.50, and there is always a hot dish of the day, served in an earthenware pot and accompanied by a side-salad, chutney, hot roll and butter, for around £1.85. Platters of cold meats, crab, prawn, duck pie or game pie with salad are around £1.50-£3, complete with hot roll and butter. Sweets such as apfel strüdel with cream, gâteaux and cheesecake vary from about 70-80p.

PHANTASY, 19 The Strand
(Exmouth 5147)
Open: summer: Tue-Sun 12noon-2.30pm, 7-10pm; winter: Tue-Sun 12noon-2.30pm, Fri-Sat 7-10pm

[C] [S]

This town-centre 'emporium' sells gifts, groceries, confectionery – and good food. The candle-lit restaurant, above the shop, is ably run by Michael and Shirley Wilkes. Day-time eaters should secure a window-seat for the view over the flower-filled town gardens. Among the dishes they prepare is cuddled chicken (a charmingly-named concoction of chicken breast, ham and asparagus topped with a mushroom and cheese sauce – a favourite at about £3.75).

YE OLDE SADDLER'S ARMS
Lympstone (Exmouth 72798)
2m north of Exmouth on the A376
Open: Mon-Sat 12noon-2pm, 7-10pm, Sun 12noon-2pm

[C] [P]

Nestling in the picturesque village of Lympstone is this charming cream-painted inn, with tables and gay umbrellas in the pleasant garden when the sun shines. Bar meals are well worthwhile sampling, but so is lunch or dinner in the Manger Restaurant. An extensive à la carte menu offers some eight starters, including home-made soup at around 40p and mushrooms in batter at about 95p. Grilled fish, poultry and steaks feature as main courses, varying in price from around £3.65 for stuffed trout to £4.95 for 12oz rump steak. A selection of sweets at about 80p includes delicious meringue glacé and banana split.

Falmouth

COCKLESHELL RESTAURANT
Mawnan Smith (Falmouth 250714)
Open: summer: Mon-Sun 12noon-2.30pm, 7-10pm, winter: Tue-Sat 12noon-2.30pm, 7-10pm

[P] [♣]

Take the Maenporth road south west of Falmouth and you will come upon the small village of Mawnan Smith. Amongst the tiny cluster of shops, Mike and Sue's small restaurant offers a welcome in relaxed surroundings. Food is wholesome and fresh and lunches are good value for money. Typical dishes are lemon sole at around £3.65, mushroom provençale at £1.50 or chicken marengo at £3.55. An interesting range of home-made sweets is available for 50p. Traditional Sunday lunch – three courses – is a bargain at £2.80.

GREENBANK HOTEL ★★★
Harbourside (Falmouth 312440)
Open: Mon-Sun 12.30-2pm, 7-9pm

[C] [P]

Officers and passengers would leave their full-rigged packet ships and tea clippers at anchorage just off the pier of this attractive harbourside hotel before unwinding with a good meal. The names of ships and their captains and other nautical memorabilia adorn the walls of the Greenbank. Today this traditional hotel offers good honest food to a different clientele. The lunch is especially good value at about £3, offering a fair choice. And how could one better complement a main course of fresh grilled fillet of mackerel meunière than to sit before spectacular views of the mouth of the River Fal?

Halwell

THE OLD INN (Blackawton 329)
On A381 6m from Totnes
Open: Mon-Sat 12noon-1.35pm, 7-10pm, Sun 12noon-1.30pm, 7-9.45pm

[C] [P]

There's an emphasis on home-cooked meats, soups and sweets at this old country inn. Choose from a wide range of grills and salads (the cold meat platter is particularly good at about £2.40) and eat from a refectory table in the wood-panelled bar or, weather permitting, in the well-kept beer garden. A 1-lb T-bone steak with chips, peas etc, costs over £5, but you'll be well within the budget with the popular honey-roast gammon steak, fish, or basket meals. Sweets with clotted cream are all under £1.

Honiton

KNIGHTS, Black Lion Court, High Street (Honiton 3777)
Open: Mon-Sat 12noon-2.30pm, Wed-Sat 7.30-11pm
Closed: Mon during winter

C P S

Good, wholesome, home-made dishes are the order of the day at Knights. Try the cauliflower soup with cream and a slice or two of fresh granary bread for starters, followed by cider-baked ham, salad and foil-wrapped jacket potato with yoghurt and chive dressing – and, if you feel there's room under your belt for more, you can top the meal off with home-made sherry trifle or spicy rhubarb crumble with cream for a mouth-watering finale. Like the food, the décor here is natural and unfussy, with pine-clad ceiling covered with menus, wine labels and wine bottles, stone walls and pine refectory tables. Food is served on attractive Honiton pottery dishes.

MONKTON COURT INN, Monkton (Honiton 2309)
On A30 2m north of Honiton
Open: Mon-Fri 10.30am-2.15pm, 5.30-10.15pm, Sat 10.30am-2.15pm, 5.30-10.45pm, Sun 12noon-2pm, 7-10.30pm

C P

This imposing stone-built 17th-century inn with distinctive mullioned windows has a comfortable, welcoming interior – all dark polished wood and soft seating. Appetisers include pâté and toast for 80p and prawn cocktail for 95p. Hot main courses come from the charcoal grill – all served with coleslaw or fresh side salad and a choice of potatoes. Try German bratwurst (meaty pork sausage), American ranch steaks or ground steak hamburgers from the hot selection, or help yourself from the cold buffet (around £2.50). 'Afters' (you're in Devon now!) such as Dutch apple pie served with clotted cream are about 85p.

Ilchester

IVELCHESTER HOTEL, The Square (Ilchester 220)
Open: Mon-Sun 12noon-2pm, 7-9.15pm

P

Bang in the centre of this sleepy Somerset town, which is a through-route to the West Country, you'll find this unpretentious hotel-restaurant where orders are taken at the bar for the excellent table d'hôte meals both at lunchtime and in the evening. A three-course lunch can cost as little as £4. Appetisers include home-made soup or fruit juice and there is a choice of five main courses, including roast duckling and apple sauce. A home-made sweet or ice cream completes the meal. For around £5, a three-course dinner offers four choices of starter, including rollmop herring, five main courses and a wide selection of sweets.

Keenthorne

APPLE TREE COTTAGE HOTEL
Keenthorne, Nether Stowey (Spaxton 238)
Open: Mon-Sun 10.30am-2.30pm, 6.30-10pm

C P

This restaurant has a 1930s style dining room and a contrasting, olde-worlde beamed bar with a stone inglenook. Menus and meals are planned and produced by owner Manfred Krombas, who served his cooking apprenticeship both here and on the continent. Chili con carne, cottage pie, steak and kidney pie or speciality boeuf bourguignon are typical hot dishes, while meat salads, sandwiches and assorted ploughman's supplement the cold collation. A three-course table d'hôte lunch, with the choice of five starters and five main courses, a selection of fresh vegetables and a sweet from the trolley costs just £3.50 in the restaurant.

Kennford

HALDON THATCH, Bottom of Telegraph Hill, on A38 4m south of Exeter (Exeter 832273)
Open: Mon-Sun 10am-11pm

[C] [P] [🍷]

As you'd expect from the name, the restaurant is housed in an attractive thatched property, perched high above the road commanding fine views of the surrounding countryside. Décor is predominantly red with well-spaced tables and Ercol chairs. There are over a dozen starters ranging from 40p-£1.10. Of the main courses, you can sample a medium sirloin steak for £2.90 or deep-fried scampi at £2.20, and the Haldon mix grill (8oz hamburger, sausage, fried egg and bacon) is excellent value at £1.60. Desserts fall in the 35p-65p range, so you should see some change from £5. Traditional Devon teas are served during late afternoon and there is an à la carte evening menu, but choices under £5 are rather limited.

Keynsham

THE GRANGE HOTEL ★★
42 Bath Road (Keynsham 2130)
Open: Bar snacks: Mon-Sun 11.30am-2.30pm; Restaurant: Mon-Fri 6.30-9pm, Sat-Sun 7-10pm

[P]

Once the main farmhouse in the area, this Georgian building in the centre of Keynsham has a comfortable air. A collection of Cries of London prints and medallioned cartoon prints adorn the restaurant walls. Lunchtime bar snacks range from 45p-£1.35, and include pâté, chicken drumsticks and traditional pastries. Dinner in the restaurant may be selected from an à la carte menu, where you will have to restrict your choice, but at lunchtime a meal of tasty soup, fillet of plaice and all the trimmings, followed by wholesome apple pie and cream should leave change from a fiver.

Kingsbridge

GLOBE INN, Frogmore
(Frogmore 351)
Open: Mon-Sat 11am-2.30pm, 6-11pm, Sun 11am-2.30pm, 7-11pm

[C] [P]

Brian and Janet Edmond have given this 17th-century free house a complete face-lift since they took over in 1979. Emphasis is on local produce and home cooking, with starters, including a pâté of the day, ranging from 55p-£1. Devonshire lamb, baked in cider, tops the list of about ten main dishes, which are all under £2.50 (except rump steak – £3.80), and none of the delicious desserts is over 80p. Simple arithmetic will reveal that there's no need to forego coffee to stay under a fiver.

WOOSTERS, The Quay
(Kingsbridge 3434)
Open: Mon-Sun 12noon-2pm, 7-10.30pm (winter: open only Thu-Sat)

[C] [P] [S] [🍷]

Woosters – housed in a two-storey cottage – specialises in fish, which is not surprising since it is situated right on the quay. If you choose one of the superb dishes prepared from locally-caught fish you're likely not to be able to run to three courses within our £5 limit. Nevertheless, the blackboard menu lists inexpensive dishes such as pork and pineapple curry at £2.25 or steak and kidney pie at £2.55, which with a starter of seafood soup at 75p and a sweet such as chocolate fudge cake with Devonshire cream at around 85p will not break the bank.

Knowstone

THE MASON ARMS, Knowstone, near South Molton (Anstey Mills 231)
Open: summer: Mon-Sat 11am-2.30pm, 6-11pm, Sun 12noon-2pm, 7-10.30pm, winter: Mon-Thu, Sun 12noon-2pm, 7-10.30pm, Fri-Sat 12noon-2pm, 7-11pm

[S]

Beside the foothills of Exmoor a truly rural 13th-century picture-postcard inn is the delightful location of this warm and intimate restaurant. Here in the evenings an à la carte menu offers much fine fare at around the £5 mark, whilst at lunchtimes across in the bar there's a plethora of pies, prawn salad (£2.25) and ploughman's (£1) on offer, with soup and pâté as starters.

Langport

BROOKSIDE GUEST HOUSE AND RESTAURANT, Huish Episcopi
(Langport 250259)
Open: Mon-Sun 8.30-9.30am, 12noon-2pm, 7.30-10pm

[P] [wine]

If you like the personal touch, then this intimate guesthouse-restaurant is the place for you. Hungry early morning travellers can snatch a typical English breakfast for £1.50, whilst at lunchtime a variety of bar snacks and salads are available costing from £1.50-£2 (including a soup with roll). In the evening, after the residents have been fed, a quality three-course meal is on offer – but it's beyond our range.

Lostwithiel

ROYAL OAK INN ★★
(Lostwithiel 872552)
Open: Mon-Sat 11am-2.30pm, 6.30-10.30pm, Sun 12noon-2pm, 7-10.30pm

[P]

Charles I is said to have hidden in this 13th-century inn during the Civil War. Later it became the haunt of smugglers. Now, a less dramatic clientele is attracted by the wide choice of real ales and bar meals. The ubiquitous fried chicken/scampi/steak/salad choice is supplemented by the chef's home-made soup of the day, or complete meal-in-a-pot for around £1.70, such as chicken commoner or steak and kidney. Starters include escargots, and three filling courses can be well within the budget. Eat in a flagstoned or more formal lounge bar, or on the delightful sun terrace with views of the gentle valley.

THE TAWNY OWL RESTAURANT
19 North Street (Bodmin 872045)
Open: summer: Mon-Sun 9.30am-9pm, winter: Thu-Sat 9.30am-5.30pm
Sun 12noon-2pm

[P] [S] [wine]

This informal restaurant in the centre of historic Lostwithiel has softly coloured walls adorned with the work of local artists. Bench seating and pleasant, friendly service enhance the warm teashop image and there are several outside tables for summer use. Emphasis is on home cooking which predominates the whole range of delicious dishes, savouries, gâteaux and pastries. Home-made soups are about 60p and unusual open sandwiches include cottage cheese, walnuts, sultanas and apple as one combination costing around £1.30. Quiches, omelettes and salads are available and there are home-made Cornish pasties at lunchtime served with plain or savoury-filled jacket potatoes for around £2.50.

Lydford

THE CASTLE INN, Lydford
(Lydford 242)
Open: Mon-Sun 12noon-2pm, 7-8.30pm

[C] [P]

Close to the beautiful Lydford Gorge and next to the castle ruins is this superb example of a 16th-century English pub. The Foresters' Bar, where meals are served, has low lamp-lit beams and a great Norman fireplace ablaze with vast logs in winter or with a profusion of flowers in summer. At lunchtime, apart from a selection of soups, pâtés and basket meals, a sumptuous help-yourself buffet luncheon table is available which includes soups, roast chicken, duck, beef, home-cooked ham, crab, mackerel, smoked salmon, smoked trout, cold meat pies, salads, cheeses, sweets and coffee. The extensive à la carte evening menu could exceed our budget, but careful selection could give you a feast for around £5.

THE MANOR INN HOTEL ★
Lydford Gorge (Lydford 208)
Open: Mon-Sun 12noon-2pm, 7.30-9.30pm and normal licensing hours

[C] [P]

French-style cuisine is the hallmark of

this pleasant old inn, where Richard Squire prepares an enormous variety of fare. Satisfying bar snacks include curry or home-made steak and kidney pie for around £1.60 or Manor Hot Pot for 95p, but if you catch a whiff of the sumptuous aroma wafting from the restaurant you will find it difficult to resist. A four-course table d'hôte dinner could comprise ravioli Milanaise or Chef's chicken liver pâté, boeuf bourguignon or crepinette of seafood Mornay, a choice of sweets from the trolley, cheese and biscuits and coffee – all for £5.50. The à la carte menu includes eighteen starters and main course Manor Specialities such as Devonshire pork cooked with sliced apples and local cider, finished with cream and served in apple cases or boned chicken legs stuffed with creamed chicken and herbs, but main courses such as these could take you over the budget.

Lynton

THE BLUE BALL INN, Countisbury Hill, Countisbury (Brendon 263)
A mile east of Lynton on the A39
Open: Mon-Sun 11am-2.30pm, 6-11pm

[♫] [P] [⚘]

The Blue Ball Inn stands amid some of North Devon's most beautiful countryside, just over a mile from the picturesque villages of Lynton and Lynmouth. The inn still retains the charm and character of its 17th-century hostelry days with beams, real ale and a welcoming open log fire. In the evening familiar bar snacks such as ploughman's, ham sandwiches and salads are served, along with a selection of more substantial meals like rump steak, breaded plaice or rainbow trout, all at reasonable cost.

Martock

THE GEORGE INN (Martock 822574)
2m off the A303
Open: Mon-Sat 12noon-2pm, 7.15-10pm, Sun 7.15-10pm

[P] [S]

The George first appeared in church records way back in 1512 and there's a list of licensees dating from 1677 on display. However, most people will be more concerned with the food, of which there is a wide selection at reasonable prices. At the bar, try the 'George Special' of tender steak with onions and mushrooms in a buttered bap for about £1.60, or alternatively you might prefer a modest cheese and pickle sandwich or the venerable ploughman's. The small restaurant, adjacent to the bar, was once the local bakery. It has been converted into a cosy eating place where you can enjoy a three-course meal during the day and choose from the extensive à la carte menu available in the evening.

Mevagissey

MR BISTRO (Mevagissey 2432)
Open: Mon-Sun 12noon-2pm, 7-12mdnt

[C] [⚘]

This character, family-owned bistro is located at the harbour's edge in what used to be an old 'bark house' (where a preservative for coating fishing nets was made from crushed bark and resin). Hence, an old local expression for strong tea is 'like bark water'. Such tea would not be served at Mr Bistro, which caters for everyone's palate and pocket. Lunchtime fare starts with cook's own soup or freshly pressed orange juice for around 40p, followed by an interesting range of home-produced main dishes, with emphasis on seafood, all at about £1.75 with salad; examples are, seafood platter, fried squid, smoked salmon pâté and prawn quiche. A selection of desserts is available in the region of 70p and a children's menu for under £1 should satisfy any beefburger fan. The evening menu, whilst appealing to the most discerning diner, is unfortunately beyond the bounds of this book.

Minehead

THE DRAGON HOUSE, Bilbrook (Washford 215)
Open: Mon-Sun 12noon-2pm, 7-9.20pm

[C] [P]

This delightful, stone-built 17th-century house is surrounded by over two acres of beautiful garden. The passing motorist will do well to stop and sample the excellent three-course table d'hôte lunch which offers a choice of five starters, nine main courses and a selection of sweets from the trolley for around £5.50. Snacks in the bistro (a new venture) include home-made soup or ploughman's lunch for well under £1.25 and hot dish of the day at around £3. A wide choice of freshly prepared light lunches is always available.

THE GOOD FOOD INN, 34 The Avenue (Minehead 4660)
Open: summer: Mon-Sun 10am-10pm, winter: closed Mon

[C] [S] [♣]

Very few restaurants can boast of a service to equal the Good Food Inn: a staggeringly comprehensive menu of à la carte family fare offered for twelve hours a day and all extremely good value for money. Starters, ranging in price from 30p to over £1 include speciality gourmet soups. Steaks, seafood and poultry are offered in many guises, from around £2-£5 and all may be served in an appropriate wine sauce for another 50p. A numerous variety of pizzas, omelettes, burgers and salads is on offer. Sweets include a vast range of fancy pancakes, some served with liqueurs, priced around 80p-£1.30. Special two- and three-course simple grills are available for children at around £1.10, including a soft drink. As a special bonus, if you order and complete a three-course meal between 2.30-4pm, soup and sweet are offered free.

NORTHFIELD HOUSE HOTEL ★★★
Northfield Road (Minehead 5155)
Open: Mon-Sun 12.45-1.30pm, 7-8.30pm

[C] [P]

Built at the turn of the century as a tea planter's mansion, this splendid hotel has spectacular views of the sea and the Brendon Hills to the south. The magnificent three acres of garden were designed by Sir Edwin Lutyens and Miss Gertrude Jekyll – the ideal setting for a lunch to remember. At £5.20 the four-course lunch is exceptional value, with choices for each course. After a meal of cream of vegetable soup, roast chicken and salad, lemon layer pudding and fresh fruit or cheese, what better than a stroll around the tranquil gardens? A bonus to non-resident guests is the 9-hole clock putting green.

Moretonhampstead

RING OF BELLS, North Bovey
(Moretonhampstead 375)

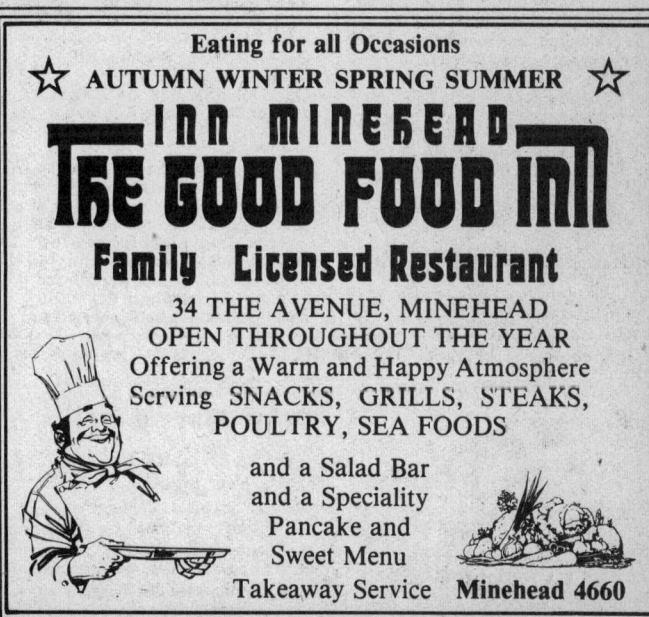

Open: Mon-Sat 11am-2.30pm, 6-11pm, Sun 12noon-2pm, 7-10.30pm

[P]

Just off the tree-studded village green in the pretty, moorland hamlet of North Bovey is this delightful 13th-century pub. A thatched roof, three-feet thick walls and low ceilings supported by time-blackened beams are features that attract moorland holidaymakers to the inn's door, but it's the quality of the food that has them returning year after year. A three-course dinner with coffee will cost around £5.75 in the restaurant, where corn on the cob, followed by pheasant with bread sauce and vegetables of the day, and a sweet from the trolley might be your choice. Bar meals for lunch or dinner include filled jacket potatoes, Stilton ploughman's, chicken quiche and fresh fruit and cream or gâteaux.

WHITE HART HOTEL, The Square (Moretonhampstead 406)
Open: Mon-Sun 12noon-2pm, (Sun 1.30pm), 7-8.30pm

[C] [P]

During the Napoleonic Wars, French officers on parole from Dartmoor Prison met at the White Hart. By then, this 300-year-old building was already established as a coaching inn. Its simple, elegant exterior is distinguished by the figure of a hind above the portico. The interior is unpretentious and comfortable. Lunchtime bar snacks are excellent and reasonably priced (chef's steak and kidney pie at £1.95). As part of the 'Taste of England' scheme, the restaurant menu offers some good basic English dishes (including Devon apple cake) and an excellent value, three-course tourist menu at £5. An effort is made to use fresh local produce wherever possible. Afternoon teas are served to non-residents in the hotel's charming lounge.

Mousehole

CAIRN DHU ★★ Raginnis Hill (Mousehole 233)
Open: Mon-Sun 12noon-2.30pm, 7.30-9.45pm. Closed: Oct-May

[C] [P]

A crow's nest view of Mount's Bay, from Penzance, past St Michael's Mount to the Lizard, can be enjoyed from Cairn Dhu. Donald and Angela Sibley's hotel and restaurant, perched about two hundred feet above the bustling village of Mousehole, exudes warmth and friendliness. Cuisine in this small character hotel is well-prepared and suitable for any occasion. Based on recipes from the 16th century to the present day, emphasis is on home-made British fare. Excellent value table d'hôte lunch or dinner offers three courses for £6. Typical dishes are crab pâté or potted tongue fillets, followed by skate with black butter, lamb Louise or home-made steak and kidney pie. Delicious desserts include strawberry shortcake, orange sorbet or peach and brandy ice cream. A wide range of international cheeses and a glass of French house wine round off an enjoyable meal. Bar food is available in the bar and on the sun terrace, where coffee and cream teas are served.

Newquay

THE BISTRO, 34 East Street
(Newquay 5444)
Open: summer: Mon-Tue 10am-10pm,
Wed 10am-7pm,
Thu-Sun 10am-12mdnt

[S]

A family operation which caters for families is a fair description of The Bistro. In the courtyard sun-trap behind the shop and on the forecourt, white-painted ironwork tables and chairs and flowers in pots and hanging baskets lend a gay informality. Inside, wooden tables have brown place mats, and red-flocked wallpaper and predominantly green carpet make this a cheerful environment in which to enjoy a meal. Miraculously, the family who run it can still serve a Sunday set lunch at around £2.25. A typical menu is soup, roast turkey with stuffing, three vegetables and ice cream. Apart from the à la carte menu, which includes such things as home-made steak and kidney pie with chips and peas at around £1.65, a good mixed grill and a 8oz steak with all the trimmings at under £5, there is a light supper menu at around £1.25-£1.70, which includes pizza and side salad. Snacks are available all day. Flans and gâteaux are made on the premises and Cornish cream teas are served.

CROSS MOUNT HOTEL ★★
Church Street, St Columb Minor
(Newquay 2669)
Open: Mon-Sun: normal licensing hours. Restaurant: 12.30-1.30pm, 6.30-9.30pm. Bar: 12noon-2pm

[C] [P] [S]

The Cross Mount Hotel is just on the outskirts of Newquay but enjoys a village environment. The building is basically 17th century and combines a small residential hotel with restaurant and bar. Burnt orange, toning with the mellow natural stone walls, is the basic colour in the dining room, giving a warm and cheerful setting for a nicely-presented meal. Table d'hôte lunch at around £3.50 and dinner (available 6.30-7.30pm) at about £4.50 are good value, as is the traditional Sunday roast at around £3.50. The 'tourist menu' all-in à la carte dinners for around £5 give a wider choice, and orders are taken until 8.30pm. Bar snacks include basket meals at about £1.70, garnished sandwiches priced at around 50p, omelettes 80p or so, and soup with roll and butter at about 55p. There are also salads at about £2.

THE LOWER DECK, 26 Fore Street
(Newquay 6520) Follow signs for Fore Street and Harbour
Open: summer: Mon-Sun10.30am-3pm, 5.30-10pm, winter: weekends only

[C]

A Pugwash character in a boat – the restaurant's distinctive logo – indicates your arrival at the Lower Deck. The seaside theme is continued inside the part pine-panelled, open-plan restaurant, slung with fishing nets and adorned with prints of old Newquay. The Lower Deck's a place for the family on holiday, with a children's menu and a good basic choice of food. Fresh fish and chips (£1.50), tuna fish flan and salad (£1.75) or a hot dish of the day such as moussaka, followed by one of the home-made sweets (around £1) will renew your holiday energy. And there's always the chance of a mid-morning home-made doughnut. The Upper Deck, open in the evenings, offers a more expensive à la carte menu.

Newton Abbot

THE DARTMOOR HALFWAY
Bickington (Bickington 270)
Open: Mon-Sat 11am-2.30pm, 6-10.30pm, Sun 12noon-2pm, 7-10.30pm

C P

A 'change' house in coaching days, this 17th-century cob and stone inn, three miles west of Newton Abbot, has a garden and patio where one may enjoy a meal on hot days. The large, open-area bar is furnished in oak, with wood panelling and hessian-covered walls. Here you may sample one of nine starters, a particular favourite being 'grotti nosh', a meal in itself for around 60p. Follow this with seafood risotto or steak and kidney pie at around £3, and complete the treat with fruit pie and cream washed down with fresh coffee and cream with a Turkish delight or mint chocolate.

North Petherton

WALNUT TREE INN
(North Petherton 662255)
Open: Mon-Sat 11am-2.30pm, 7-11pm (winter 10.30pm), Sun 12noon-2pm, 7-9pm

C P

A 19th-century coaching inn, this hotel has recently been renovated by its owners, Richard and Hilary Goulden, to make it a welcome overnight stop for the modern traveller. Prices are surprisingly low – from around £1.70 for an omelette to £4.20 for a steak. Snacks and light meals are available in the bar and there's a very accommodating children's menu, featuring all the old favourites.

Oakford

HIGHER WESTERN RESTAURANT
Oakford (Anstey Mills 210)
On the A361, 1½ miles west of Oakford
Open: Mon-Sun 12noon-2pm, 3-5.30pm, 7-10pm

P

This small, attractive restaurant is recommended mainly for its good lunchtime bar snacks, from a range of open sandwiches (such as chicken, prawns, salami from around 85p) to pâté and salad, lasagne, home-made steak and kidney pie or sirloin steak and chicken escalope. You can have a three-course meal, including soup and roll and a sweet, for anything from £3.50-£5 depending on your choice. There is a set Sunday lunch for around £3.75. Dinner is rather more expensive. Many a motorist will be relieved to find a good pull-in at such a remote spot.

Okehampton

THE COUNTRYMAN, Beacon Cross, Sampford Courtney (North Tawton 206)
5 miles north of Okehampton on the B3215
Open: Mon-Sat 11am-2.30pm, 7-10.30pm (11pm Fri-Sat), Sun 12noon-2pm, 7-10.30pm

P

This sophisticated, unusual inn in the heart of Devon is frequented as much for its excellent bar food as for its draught beers. Out of season, a business person's lunch can be had for around £2.25. A three-course meal from the à la carte menu will just about come within the £5 limit if carefully selected. A choice of ten starters, including pâté à la volaille (chicken pâté with Cognac) may be followed by one of six main fish courses, a grill, poultry, curry or home-made steak and kidney pie. Most of the home-made desserts, served with cream, will price the meal above £5, but an ice cream is an alternative. The cold buffet table includes a host of salads, ploughman's lunches and sandwiches.

Ottery St Mary

KING'S ARMS HOTEL ★ Gold Street
(Ottery St Mary 2486)
Open: Mon-Sun 12noon-2pm, 7-9.30pm

[C] [P] [S] [🚸]

Built in 1756, the King's Arms Hotel was originally an old coaching inn. Now the white-painted building commands a central position in this picturesque little town. The oak-decorated Tar Barrel Bar offers an excellent range of food – either snacks or a full three-course meal. Following soup of the day, steak pie, plaice fillets, chicken or beef curry, cider-baked Devon ham, and ham or beef salads are some of the choices for a main course, ranging in price from about £2-£3. Vegetables are included. A good choice of sweets is available for around 60p. The à la carte dining room menu is more pricey, but still good value and children are catered for.

Paignton

CHEZ MICHEL, 107 Winner Street
(Paignton 556100)
Open: Mon-Sun 12noon-2pm, 7-12mdnt (11.30pm Sun)

[C] [♫] [S]

The atmosphere is very continental at Chez Michel, when you dine by candlelight in the central courtyard at scrubbed pine tables bedecked with fresh flowers. The restaurant offers an impressive menu with a European flavour but for our budget-conscious readers the wine bar is the place. Charcoal-grilled chicken, steaks, rainbow trout or porc en brochette range from £1.50-£3.50 and this includes a jacket potato and self-serve salad. For a little over £1 extra you can have fruit salad or cheese and biscuits with coffee. Go along on Monday evenings if you enjoy live folk music.

LAI KIN, 33 Hyde Road
(Paignton 551005)
Open: Mon-Sun 12noon-2pm, 5.30-11.30pm

[♫] [P] [S]

The unusual marble-look frontage and smoked glass, 'porthole'-style door is an incongruous entrance to this Chinese restaurant in the main shopping area. Inside, the décor is more appropriate, with Chinese lanterns illuminating black chairs, white cloths and sparkling cutlery. Chicken with cashew nuts followed by apple, banana or pineapple fritters and syrup cost around £4.30 from the à la carte menu, and a business person's lunch is always available at just about £2.25 for three courses – terrific value. Chinese or Russian tea is served, as well as coffee.

LA TAVERNA, 53 Torbay Road
(Paignton 551190)
Open: summer: Mon-Sat 10.30am-2.30pm, 5.30-11pm, Sun 12noon-2pm, 7-10.30pm, winter: Mon-Thu 10.30am-2.30pm, 5.30-10.30pm, Fri-Sat 10.30am-2.30pm, 5.30-11pm, Sun 12noon-2pm, 7-10.30pm

[S]

A bit of the Mediterranean on the English Riviera where you can sample the delights of a fully-licensed, Continental bar as well as the excellent

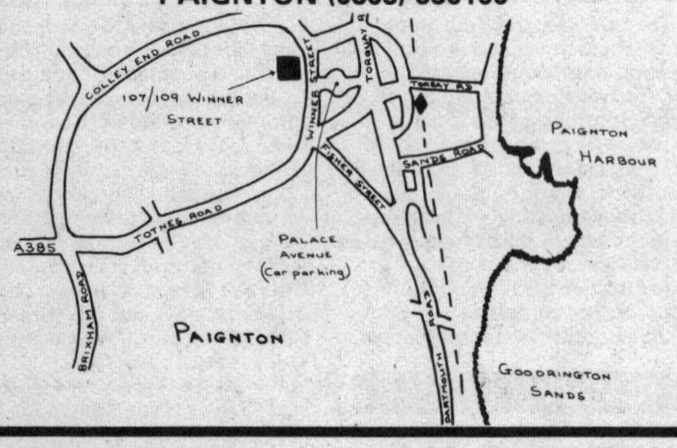

food. The arched and canopied front is set back from the road far enough to allow tables and sunshades to be placed outside in fine weather; wrought ironwork, white-rendered walls with painted murals and Italianate tiled floor in the dining area complete the illusion that the Italian sun shines outside. The family of the owner, Ernest Pelosi, has lived in Paignton since 1903, so it may be with a sense of nostalgia that the Mediterranean scene has been so carefully created. Small portions of pasta dishes are served as starters, or you can choose spaghetti bolognese at about £1.95 as your main course. Pizza specialities cost near enough the same. Other bar snacks (about £1.10-£1.35) include sausages, egg, beans and chips, and ploughman's lunch. There is a short list of other main dishes, including steaks, chicken, fish and salads.

Penzance

ADMIRAL BENBOW, Chapel Street (Penzance 3448)
Open: Mon-Sun 12noon-2pm, 6-10pm

C

In the early 18th-century, bands of smugglers known as the 'Benbow Brandy Men' made the Admiral Benbow Inn their headquarters. Here it was that the surplus tea, 'baccy, perfume, silk and brandy were hidden. Today, it boasts an equally desirable list of goodies to be chosen from the 'Vittals Chart', such as Cornish lobster, smoked mackerel pâté, roasts, grills and various

curries. Ice creams are the speciality – try the 'gooseberry lagoon' (coffee ice, gooseberries and iced fruit syrup) or the Southern Star (banana, paw-paw, peach and iced fruits), and wash it all down with a shot of finest rum. Buffet lunches are available in the bar upstairs at around £2.60. There is a set 'dish of the week' at around £3.

ROSIE'S RESTAURANT, 12-13 Chapel Street (Penzance 3540)

Open: Mon-Sat 12.30-2.30pm, 6.30-10pm

[S] [☙]

Rosie's Restaurant, situated within the heart of Penzance town centre, and under the personal supervision of attractive, auburn-haired Rosie, offers informality in cuisine, service and surroundings. A congenial bistro-style atmosphere is attained by the use of dark-stained wood walls and furniture, cheery red-checked tablecloths and half curtains, low-hanging white lamps and lush green potted plants and palms – the perfect surroundings in which to enjoy the well-prepared plat du jour. Typical dishes are home-made ratatouille, devilled kidneys, steak and kidney or fish pie, chili con carne, moussaka and cheese and potato pie as main courses. Good-choice mixed salads and interesting vegetarian dishes are also on offer. A limited but attractive range of sweets is available.

SMUGGLER'S HOTEL AND RESTAURANT, Newlyn Harbour (Penzance 4207)
Open: Mon-Sun 6.30pm-12mdnt

[C] [☙]

This 270-year-old character restaurant overlooks picturesque Newlyn Harbour, choc-a-bloc full of fishing boats, nets and weatherbeaten fishermen. Legend has it that there was once a secret tunnel direct from the restaurant's cellar bar to the harbour side, and the one-eyed smuggler whose sinister portrait acts as the restaurant's sign certainly looks as though he once drank his fair share of boot-legged whisky. Freshly caught mackerel makes a tempting starter at £1.15, followed by piping hot lamb barbecue, port Marsala or Mexican chicken, all under £3. Sweets are generously served from the trolley at around £1. David and Ann Reeve, resident proprietors, are always at hand to assure you of their best attention.

Plymouth

DARTMOOR UNION, Holbeton (Holbeton 288)
6m south east of Plymouth off the A379
Open: Mon-Sat 12noon-2.30pm, 6-11pm (10.30 in winter)
Sun 12noon-2pm, 7-10.30pm

[C] [P] [☙]

This old-established inn is in the Devon tradition – it's the centre of village life but caters for holidaymakers too. An old English cider press and barrels are housed here. Tasty vegetable soup served with hot crisp bread and butter at around 60p is just the thing to stay your hunger on a cold day. Basket meals cost from about £1.50, and there's a generous selection of main dishes including home-made steak and kidney pie and vegetables at around £2.50. Sweets are about 65p – and what could be nicer than a freshly-made fruit crumble with Devonshire cream? Dinner in the restaurant is likely to cost in the region of £6.

THE KHYBER RESTAURANT ✕✕
44 Mayflower Street
(Plymouth 266036)
Open: Mon-Sun 12noon-2.30pm, 6-11pm

[C] [P]

Pass the Khyber and you will miss the chance of enjoying a friendly, well-established Indian restaurant run with family pride since 1960. Décor and furnishings are very Indian, cuisine is authentic and of a high standard. Table d'hôte lunch includes a starter such as shami kebab (delicious round pats of finely chopped meat with spices and onions), a selection of curries and English dishes, and a sweet – try guavas and clotted cream – to follow. Several dinner menus are also around £5, and the reasonable prices also allow you the pick of the à la carte menus.

MERLIN'S RESTAURANT ★ 2 Windsor Villas, Lockyer Street (Plymouth 28133)
Open: Mon-Sat 12noon-2pm, 6.30-9.30pm

[C] [♫] [P] [S] [♣]

There's often something extra going on in this small hotel close to the city centre. Barbecues, Hallowe'en night parties, French or Greek evenings and beggar's banquets are Anne and Bill Proudman's specialities, but a no-nonsense lunch or dinner is always readily available. You'll be pleasantly surprised at the low prices of the well prepared dishes, served in an atmosphere of intimate friendliness. Table d'hôte menus offer, for example, delicious home-made soup, chicken chasseur with fresh and tender vegetables, and a sweet from the trolley for under £5; and much of the more exclusive à la carte menu is also within our budget – bar the lobster!

Polperro

CRUMP'S (Polperro 72312)
Open: Mon-Sun 10.30am-5.45pm, 7.30-10pm

[P] [♣]

Mike and Wendy Costello's tea room and bistro, in this most picturesque of Cornish fishing villages, is a low-beamed 250-year-old farmhouse, furnished in the late Victorian/Edwardian style and offering a range of cuisine to suit all tourist tastes. Daytime meals are pâtisserie-style; snacks and light lunches. Freshly prepared salads with fish or home-made pizza and quiche cost around £2.50, including soup, fruit juice or melon as appetisers. The bistro atmosphere is enhanced in the evening with white tablecloths and candles, when there is a choice of table d'hôte menus. In addition, the Family Wine Bar serves light dinners, similar in choice to the daytime menu.

Porlock Weir

THE PANTRY, Cottage Hotel and Restaurant (Porlock 862749)
Open: Mon-Sun 8am-11pm

[C] [P] [♣]

This attractive buttery, whose entrance is located by the Cottage Hotel garden, serves a good selection of meals and snacks throughout the day. A satisfying three-course meal can be had for a price well within our budget. For starters you could choose prawn cocktail or home-made chicken liver pâté served with French bread, both around £1 and a main course of home-made cottage pie with garden peas costs about £1.50. With a dessert of fruit salad with cream for around 65p and a coffee at 25p you have a full meal for well under £4.

Portishead

THE PEPPERMILL RESTAURANT, 3 The Precinct (Portishead 847407)
Open: Mon-Wed 9.30am-3pm, Thu-Sat 9.30am-10.30pm

[C] [P] [S] [♣]

Enterprising female proprietors occasionally give cookery demonstrations at this bright, clean restaurant in Portishead's town-centre precinct, and the results of their endeavours go on sale to the public for about £4.50 for a full supper. At mid-day, the business lunch costs around £2.65 with grills from £1.55 to £1.65, omelettes around £1.30 and home-made sweets at 55p. A lunch and dinner 'speciality' three course meal costs £5.95.

Portscatho

SMUGGLERS COTTAGE OF TOLVERNE, King Harry Ferry,

Roseland Peninsula (Portscatho 309)
Open: May-Oct: Mon-Sun
12noon-2pm, 3-5.30pm, 7.30-10pm

[P] [🍷]

Sailing and boating enthusiasts can drop anchor and pop in to sample the delicious home-made cuisine offered by Elizabeth and Peter Newman at this picturesque thatched cottage nestling close to King Harry's Ferry. Part of the cottage and the beach were used by the Americans in the preparation and planning of D-Day in the last war. At lunchtime there's an attractive cold buffet of home-produced quiches, fish mousses and meats, accompanied by original fresh salads. Alternatively, the Boathouse Bar-B-Q offers simple grills and hamburgers – ideal for the children. Informal suppers are superb value. Starters include stockpot soup at around 75p or smoked trout for about £1.75. For your main course there could be savoury pancakes or omelettes for around £3-£3.50. Gooseberry fool or strawberry Pavlova are a couple of the tempting desserts.

Princetown

FOX TOR, Two Bridges Road
(Princetown 238)
Open: Apr-Oct: Mon-Fri, Sun 9.30am-5.30pm, later times by arrangement

[P] [🍷]

Just a little more than a stone's throw from the famous Dartmoor prison, this licensed restaurant specialises in fresh, home-made fare ranging from scones and Devon cream to full three-course meals. Appetisers at 60p and under, include egg mayonnaise or soup of the day with home-made bread. For your main course you can enjoy sirloin steak with mushrooms, tomatoes, peas and buttered new potatoes for as little as £3.30. Sweets such as fruit tart or Devonshire junket are served with cream for 70p or less.

Queen Camel

MILDMAY ARMS
(Marston Magna 850456)
On the A359 Yeovil to Sparkford road
Open: Bar: Mon-Sat 12noon-2.30pm, 7-10.30pm, Sun 12noon-2pm, 7-10pm
Restaurant: Tue-Sat 7-10.30pm

[P] [🍷]

Mildmay Arms is a local stone-built 17th-century inn situated on the edge of this attractive village with a considerable history. Personally run by Maggie and Ken Evans, this is a friendly place to eat where home-made specialities such as poacher's game pie, or Somerset casserole of beef, cooked in cider are served complete with Maggie's secret additives. For a cheaper alternative to the restaurant the bar menu offers a comprehensive range of goodies from the Wiltshire ploughman's to the daily special and quiche Lorraine all at around £1. Cuts from the cold carvery range in price from £1-£2.50.

St Austell

HICKS WINE BAR, Church Street
(St Austell 4833)
Open: summer: Mon-Sat 11am-2.30pm, Tue-Sat 7-11pm (10.30pm in winter)

The Tudor frontage of Hicks gives way to a small, intimate wine bar of simple design with wooden tables and stools, and wine racks against the walls. Food is attractively displayed at one end of the bar and dishes can be chosen from a blackboard menu. Main meals are served with a selection of three salads such as curried rice or tomato, cucumber and onion, and an apple and celery mixture. These accompany various salamis, home-made quiche, gala pie or chef's home-made pâté – all around £1.20. There is a range of tasty hot dishes such as cottage pie, chicken casserole or sausage provençale for around £1.30. For dessert choose from Stilton, apple and biscuits, gâteau or cheesecake all at around 50p.

PIER HOUSE HOTEL ★★ Harbour Front, Charlestown (St Austell 5272)
Open: summer: Mon-Sun 12noon-2.30pm, 8-10pm

[P]

The Pier House Hotel, magnificently located right at the harbour's edge at the picturesque Georgian village of Charlestown, is well worth a visit though you must choose your dishes with care to keep within budget. The small harbour still exports china clay, and from the split-level restaurant of the charming, period hotel, adorned with masts, riggings and other nautical relics, one can view the complex manoeuvring of ships, laden with china clay, in the outer basin of the tiny docks. A la carte dinner offers good choices of French and English cuisine, such as Charlestown smoked mackerel pâté (about £1.15), followed by fresh local sole or râgout of seafood (both around £3.80), rounded off with lemon meringue or crème caramel (both about 90p), or a good choice of cheeses. Fresh seafood salads are also available.

St Ives

MASTER ROBERT'S HOTEL ★★★
Street-on-Pol (Penzance 796042)
Open: Mon-Sun 12noon-2.30pm, 7.30-10pm

[C] [♫]

Ideal for an informal 'quickie' lunch or the most well organised dinner party, this tastefully-decorated hotel with its character bar is located in the heart of the interesting and historic town of St Ives. An extensive buffet lunch or dinner of cold meats and fresh salad can be had to the accompaniment of live music and entertainment in season with hot meals also available.

Sampford Peverell

THE FARM HOUSE INN, Leonard's Moor (Tiverton 820824)
Open: Mon-Sat 7am-12mdnt, Sun 12noon-10.30pm

[C] [♫] [P] [♣]

This restaurant is a conversion of two cottages and set back off the road in its own grounds. Cooking is predominantly of the wholesome English variety and all meals from breakfast through morning coffee, lunch, afternoon tea, dinner and supper are served here. At lunchtime, as well as the à la carte choice, there is a special 'dish of the day' which costs from £1.50 to £2, and the three-course Sunday lunch, featuring traditional roast beef, carved in the restaurant, is around £4. If you prefer a lighter meal, a cold buffet is set out in the attractive bar.

Sidmouth

APPLEGARTH HOTEL ★ Sidford (Sidmouth 3174)
Open: Mon, Wed-Sun, 12.30-1.30pm, Mon-Sat 7-9.30pm

[C] [P] [S] [♣]

One-time tea planters Jimmy and Barbara Lyness have earned themselves an enviable reputation for first-class cuisine and excellent service since 1969, when they made their drastic change of career and took over the Applegarth Hotel. But it's not only the owners who can boast an interesting background, for Applegarth itself dates back to the 16th century when it was used as a staging post for monks who transported salt from the mines of Salcombe Regis to Exeter. The 'olde-worlde' character pervades the building to this day, not least in the restaurant with its beamed ceiling. The cuisine is always new and exciting – Barbara being a Cordon Bleu cook. For lunch, her array of dishes such as pâté Strasbourg, veau a la crème flambée and trout Applegarth will tempt the most discerning palate. More conventional dishes such as braised steak and chicken with honey and lemon sauce (both including starter, vegetables and sweet) cost around £3.50 but a two-course meal costs only £1.50 – one-course as little as 60p. Desserts are the responsibility of young chef Tracey, who produces tasty concoctions with the aid of fresh cream, sherry, brandy or liqueurs.

BOWD INN, Bowd Cross (Sidmouth 3328)
On A3052 2m from Sidmouth seafront
Open: Mon-Thu 11am-2.30pm, 6-10.30pm, Fri-Sat 11am-2.30pm, 6-11pm, Sun 12noon-2pm, 7-10.30pm

[P]

Strategically placed at Bowd Cross en route to Sidmouth is this attractive 12th-century inn, set in a welcoming shrub and flower garden. Low ceilinged, beamed bars are cosy and inviting and the choice of food is excellent. Starters such as whitebait at 80p, melon frappé at 60p or kidney turbigo at £1.10 are on offer. Main courses include home-made quiche Lorraine at £1.50, tongue, beef or crab platter at £1.90, beef braised in wine or sauté of chicken Parisienne at £2.70 and roast duckling with apple or orange sauce at £4. All dishes include potatoes or French fries and salad or vegetables of the day. Steak, fish, curries and Chef's dish of the day are also available. A selection of home-made sweets are from 50p.

SHERIDAN'S WINE BAR, Fore Street (Sidmouth 6724)
Open: Mon-Sat 10.30am-2.30pm, 7-10pm (10.30pm Fri and Sat)

[♫] [S]

Sheridan's is a smart double-fronted building near the seafront, serving inexpensive home-cooked 'rustic' fare. The well-presented range of savouries includes lasagne, cheese and onion flan with salad, rough pâté with French bread, smoked salmon with brown bread, and a variety of cheeses served with bread or biscuits. A large portion of fresh strawberry flan or chocolate gâteau with cream costs around 85p, and there's plenty of good, strong coffee. With good quality cutlery and china, and tables decorated with fresh flowers, this is a place for people who enjoy being pampered.

South Petherton

THE PUMP ROOM, Oaklands
Palmer Street (South Petherton 40272)
Open: Mon-Sun: 12noon-2pm, 7-10pm

C P

This attractive little food and wine bar lies at the back of Oaklands Restaurant (a good evening à la carte AA-appointed rosette and two knife and fork restaurant with menus a little above our limit). A variety of tempting dishes range from brandy and fish pâté, gammon steak with pineapple or home-made turkey and herb pancakes, and with a sweet and coffee the price should not exceed £5 at the Pump Room.

South Zeal

OXENHAM ARMS ★★
(Sticklepath 244)
Open: bar snacks: Mon-Sat 12noon-2pm, 7-9pm, Sun 12noon-1.30pm, 7-9pm, Restaurant: Mon-Sun 12noon-1.30pm, 7.30-9pm

C P

'The stateliest and most ancient abode in the hamlet' is how Eden Phillpotts described this beautiful, beamed inn, which was first licensed in 1477. The hamlet quoted is South Zeal, a cluster of houses found by taking a slight detour off the A30 east of Okehampton. Bar snacks offer an array of fish and seafood – from rainbow trout with potatoes and vegetables for around £2 to plaice and French fries for £1. Home-made fruit pie and cream is about 65p. On Sundays cold meals only are served in the bar – salads include roast beef or chicken for £1.65 and cheese for just over £1. Three-course meals served in the cottagey restaurant are excellent in both choice and value for money. Lunches are priced by the main course and vary from £3 for home-made steak, kidney and mushroom pie to £4.75 for rump steak.

Street

GREYLAKE, Greinton
(Ashcott 210383)
Open: Tue-Fri, Sun 9am-11pm, Sat 7am-11pm

C P ♧

Greylake is all things to all men, women

and children, but it is not one of your brash modern complexes, for the restaurant is housed in a 17th-century, whitewashed stone cottage, full of charm and character. There is a wide choice of food at painless prices. At midday, eleven different main courses are on offer (including deep-fried scampi and a mixed grill), and with starter, dessert and coffee, only the dearest steak dishes will take you over the £5 mark. A 'Sunday special', with roast pork as the main course, is around £3 (half-portions are available for children). Various salads and light meals can be had throughout the day.

KNIGHT'S TAVERN ☆☆☆
Wessex Hotel
(Street 43383)
Open: Mon-Sat 10.30am-2.30pm, 7.30-10pm, Sun 12noon-2pm, 7.30-10pm

[C] [♫] [P] [♤]

With direct access from the car park, there's no need to go through the hotel to reach the Knight's Tavern, so it is a good place to know about, especially for families with children. Pleasant cheerful service and comfortable modern surroundings make it a worthwhile stopping place. Rest awhile in the King Arthur Bar – aptly named in this Camelot Country, where at lunchtime you can choose from a wide variety of bar snacks, and there are joints from the carvery, charcoal grills, omelettes, pizzas or pasta dishes, curries, fish and many other favourites at budget-prices. You could choose a good dinner in the grill room/restaurant under the £5 limit too, though you could bust the budget if you ignored the menu prices. Fruit juice, followed by fillet of plaice and a sweet from the trolley would come within our limit, leaving plenty over for a glass of wine at 50p and a tip – and there are a number of other permutations under our price limit.

Taunton

HEATHERTON GRANGE HOTEL ★
Bradford-on-Tone
(Taunton 46777/8)
On A38 1m from M5, junction 26
Open: Mon-Sat 12noon-2pm, 7-10.30pm, Sun 12noon-2pm, 7-9pm

[C] [P]

This former coaching inn, dating from 1826 or earlier is easily accessible from Taunton or the M5. A wide variety of bar meals cost around the £1.50 mark and include Madras curry, steakburgers, home-made pies and salads (including fresh lobster and crab in season). Most of the à la carte menu presented in the small dining room is within our three-course budget. Basic favourites are supplemented by sweetbreads in sherry sauce, Swiss pork chop (stuffed with oregano, cheese, onions and mushrooms) or breast of chicken in a lovely lemon sauce.

Thorverton

DOLPHIN INN (Exeter 860205)
Open: during licensing hours. Meals: Mon-Sun 12noon-1.45pm, 7-10pm

[P] [&]

This two-storey inn enjoys a central position amid a picturesque village setting. Décor and furnishing in the Victoria Lounge bar would have pleased even the most discerning Victorian, and the deep-seated armchairs offer a place to relax with an after-dinner coffee. An archway leads through the bar to the attractive Gueridon Restaurant, romantically illuminated with oil lamps to produce a complementary atmosphere in which to enjoy some of the homely fare offered on the extensive menu. House specials include lemon sole with prawns and mushrooms, and home-made steak and kidney pie with Mackeson. Try the soup (also home-made) to start with, and for dessert there is a choice of cold sweets or ice cream – all reasonably-priced. Traditional bar snacks are available every day – the locally-produced pasty with gravy sounds like a tempting and cheap filler at about 40p. Lunch can also be taken in the wisteria-clad beer garden or in the separate real ale and wine bar.

Tiverton

POACHERS POCKET, Burlescombe (Greenham 672286)
10m west of Tiverton on the A373
Open: Restaurant: Mon-Sat 12noon-2.30pm, 6-10pm, Sun 12noon-2.30pm, Bar: Mon-Sat 11am-2.30pm, 6-10pm, Sun 12noon-2pm, 7-10pm

[P] [&]

This 17th-century inn gives you the choice of a pleasant bar or a peaceful restaurant. The bar offers a wide range of snacks, including seafood platter, scampi, chicken or sausage in the basket, gammon and pineapple, rump steak and turkey pie as well as ploughman's lunches and sandwiches. In the restaurant, the à la carte menu gives excellent value and you can feast on terrine provençale (a rough, spicy pâté), pheasant cooked in Madeira wine, and apfel strudel with Devon cream for around £5. All main courses include vegetables. Children are welcome and can eat food from the bar menu in the restaurant if their parents wish to eat à la carte.

Tormarton

THE VITTALES BAR, The Compass Inn, Tormarton (Badminton 242)
Off the A46 Stroud-Cheltenham road, and a few minutes from junction 18 of the M4.
Open: Mon-Sat 10am-2.30pm, Sun 12noon-2pm, Mon-Thu 6.30-10pm, Fri-Sat 7-10.30pm, Sun 7-10pm

[C] [P] [&]

This pleasant old country inn has four bars to choose from, but we suggest hungry travellers make straight for the Vittales Bar, where a tempting cold buffet is on display. Hot dishes are listed on a blackboard, and can often include rabbit pie, hot seafood casserole (both £2.35) or ham and asparagus in cheese sauce with salad at £2.25. Starters include prawns with mayonnaise or pâté at about £1.40. Various home-cooked meats with salad and sandwiches are also on offer, and sweets cost from 55p. Full meals can also be taken in the restaurant. Leading off the Vittales Bar is the Orangery, a pretty, glass-enclosed garden which draws families in the summer.

Torquay

THE COPPER KETTLE, Ilsham Road, Wellswood (Torquay 23025)
Open: summer: Mon-Sun 9.30am-10.30pm, winter: Tue-Sat 10am-5pm

[♫] [P] [S] [&]

This 'copper kettle' brews up not only for guests enjoying a refreshing cuppa after a meal but also for the picnicker on his way to the beach some yards away. Later in the day, day trippers about to make the long drive home are catered for. This is a special service offered by Leslie Bentham at his neat little Georgian restaurant in the heart of this holiday town. Many a thirsty tourist has had his flask filled to the brim with piping hot tea or freshly-percolated coffee by the enterprising Mr B. His wife, Elaine, specialises in high-standard home cooking – and the well-cooked roast lunch (with a starter) at around £1.75 and a Devonshire cream tea (with home-made scones) at about £1 is very popular. Salads are the house speciality; egg mayonnaise, chicken, fresh crab, salmon and many more – all from around £2 with special reduced prices for children.

THE EPICURE, 34 Torwood Road (Torquay 23340)
Open: summer: Mon-Sun 10am-9.30pm, winter: Mon-Tue, Thu-Sun 10am-5pm

[♫] [P] [S] [⚘]

With some thirty years' experience in hotels and catering behind him, proprietor Gary Dowland runs his attractive little restaurant with the emphasis on personal service and quality grill-style fare. Situated some 600yds from the harbour, in a row of shops, The Epicure is one of Torquay's oldest restaurants and instantly recognisable by its green stucco exterior with green woodwork and sun canopy. The deceptively small frontage leads into a long, brightly-decorated dining room. The cool exterior colouring is echoed inside with lush green plants. Best china and cutlery is used here and the walls bear framed prints of old sheet music. An extensive menu of fish dishes and grills is available, with home-made soups a starter speciality. Parents please note the special children's menu with main dishes less than half the standard price.

LIVERMEAD CLIFF AND LIVERMEAD HOUSE ★★★ Torbay Road (Torquay 22881)
Open: 1-2pm

[C] [P] [⚘]

The big attraction here is the marvellous view afforded by these sea-front hotel restaurants. Cream leatherette seats and velour drapes make for a very comfy inside setting and the uniformed staff are keen to ensure that everything is to your satisfaction. A set menu offers soup or fruit juice as a starter, with a choice of three hot main courses (battered fried whiting fillet, roast leg of lamb or chicken curry) plus a wide range of salads – the pressed ox tongue is delicious. Desserts include banana split and intriguing mincemeat turnovers. At £5.45 it is a little expensive, but there are special children's portions and those sea views really are lovely. On the seafront you will find Livermead House – a sister hotel run along almost identical lines.

THE PANTRY, Strand (Torquay 25123)
Open: Mon-Fri 10.15am-5pm, Sat 10.15am-12.15pm (5pm summer)

[C] [S] [⚘]

The Pantry is part of the Williams and Cox department store – a family business founded in 1837, which still upholds its reputation for quality and personal service. Overlooking the harbour, the restaurant has a modern décor with bentwood chairs and polished tables; service is provided by uniformed waitresses. Bill of fare is traditional, with quiche Lorraine and a chef's daily special (roast leg of lamb or beef casserole perhaps) on the hot table, and a selection of cold meats, salmon or cheese with salad on the cold table. You may, however, take a break from shopping any time as sandwiches, tea and pastries are served all day.

PIZZA-KING, 2 The Terrace, Fleet Street (Torquay 24365)
Open: summer: Mon-Sun 12noon-12mdnt, winter: Mon-Sat, 12noon-2pm, 6-11pm

[♫] [S] [⚘]

A cheerful, bright red canopy invites you into this rustic-style restaurant with wood-panelled walls and oak refectory tables. Red-painted chairs add warmth and colour to the simple yet attractive décor. There are twenty tantalising man-sized pizzas to choose from; and you can see them being prepared in the open cooking areas. You can make a feast out of the Pizza-King Special which is topped with cheese, tomato, salami, onion, mushroom, ham, pimentoes, to name but a phew! It costs about £2.40 and if your appetite can take it, 40p or so will add a baked potato and, at around 55p, a green salad. And for a mouth-watering finale, try cassata Seville – layers of chocolate and orange ice cream with raisins, walnuts and Grand Marnier – all for less than 80p. Between 12noon and 2pm, and after 7pm, there is a minimum charge of £1, though a special lunch for children costs around 80p. Wine is sold by the glass at about 65p.

Torrington

CASTLE HILL HOTEL ★★ South Street (Torrington 2339)
Open: bar: Mon-Sat 11am-2.15pm, 7-10.30pm, Sun 12noon-2pm, 7-10.30pm. Restaurant: Mon-Sun 12noon-2pm, 7.30-9pm

C ♫ P ♧

Magnificent views over the Torridge Valley and the hills beyond can be enjoyed from the garden of this delightful old hotel. A wide range of snacks is available in the bar, including a hot dish of the day such as curry, cottage pie or pork chops. The table d'hôte three-course lunch, served in the restaurant, is only around £2.75, with four or five choices of starter, three hot main courses – a roast and fish dish are always included – and a salad. There is also a generous selection of sweets from the trolley. Cheaper portions are available for children. The extensive evening à la carte menu features grills of all descriptions, and a three-course meal can be achieved for around £5.

Totnes

CASA DORO, 67 Fore Street (Totnes 863932)
Open: Mon-Sat 12noon-2.30pm, 7pm onwards

C S

Catch the distinct Spanish flavour of this small restaurant on the ground floor of a three-storey listed building. Heliodoro Lopez runs the place with the aid of his wife and mother-in-law, and together they produce a marvellous list of goodies. Tasty starters such as 'tropicanas' (layers of grilled ham, cheese and pineapple served on bread) or barquitas de apio (celery boats filled with tuna fish, peppers and olives) make interesting appetisers, with paella, chicken Espanol or a host of imaginative, cosmopolitan main courses to follow. Vegetables of the day are included in the price. Sweets, including delicious figs in brandy, are around £1.

THE COTT INN, Dartington (Totnes 863777)
Open: Mon-Sun normal licensing hours

C P ♧

A charming 14th-century building – long, low and warmly lit. The split-level, stone floor and timbered ceiling create a fine, olde-worlde atmosphere. Meals here nowadays are all home-made and presented buffet-style. Examples from the excellent daily spread are steak and kidney pie (£1.95) and gâteau (65p). So successful has the operation become, that owner Mr Shortman has recently added an extension to accommodate the growing number of diners.

CRANKS HEALTH FOOD RESTAURANT, Dartington Cider Press Centre, Shinners Bridge, Dartington (Totnes 862388)
Open: Mon-Sat 10am-5pm

P S

Cranks have made a name for themselves by serving appetising whole foods while at the same time encouraging crafts by displaying specially-commissioned articles and equipping their restaurants with craftsman-made furniture and pottery. This branch, in the interesting Cider Press Centre, which is dedicated to the encouragement and display of traditional crafts, is run on the usual Cranks lines with a buffet service counter serving soups, salads, and vegetable-based savouries, the accent being on compost-grown-vegetables and unchemicalised (their word!) ingredients. All food, including wholemeal bread, is baked on the premises. A substantial three-course meal with coffee is unlikely to cost more than £4.50 or so, and includes soup, a hot savoury such as spaghetti or carrot and parsnip soufflé, a sweet and coffee. There's outside seating for thirty.

THE SEA TROUT INN ★★ Staverton (Staverton 274)
Open: Mon-Sun 12noon-2pm, 7-10pm

[C] [♫] [P]

The à la carte menu is rather expensive and would surely take you beyond our £5 limit, but you need not deny yourself the pleasure of eating in this attractive old inn, for they also serve a comprehensive list of bar meals. A typical meal would be grapefruit cocktail, home-made quiche Lorraine with chips and veg, gâteau or cheesecake and coffee for around £4. The bar occupies the original part of the building, and with oak furniture, white-washed walls, beamed ceiling and stone fireplace it retains a certain 'olde worlde' look. Bar meals are limited on Sundays when a full lunch is provided in the restaurant, and in fine weather meals can be taken on the patio.

Truro

GORTON'S RESTAURANT, 10 Pydar Street (Truro 79140)
Open: Mon-Thu 10am-10pm, Fri-Sat 10am-11.30pm, Sun 12noon-2pm

[S]

Close to Truro Cathedral is this intimate new restaurant which is growing in popularity by the minute. An unbeatable-value three-course lunch menu brings together soup of the day or fruit juice, followed by home-made steak and kidney pie, a 'roast of the week' or a quarter roast chicken with fresh potatoes and vegetables, rounded off with home-made fruit pie or peaches and cream at only £2.25. A la carte eating is also possible, with the Chef's special chili con carne only £2.25.

Veryan

POLSUE MANOR HOTEL ★★
Ruanhighlanes (Veryan 270)
Open: Etr-Oct: Mon-Sun 7.30-8.30pm

[P]

Dinner at this spacious, elegant manor house, secluded beyond a tree-lined drive, is a peaceful and enjoyable experience. You'll find it midway between Tregony and St Mawes just off the A3078. Rex and Diana Dufty will make you very welcome in the gracious, country house-style restaurant. A typical table d'hôte three-course meal of home-produced, quality cuisine could include mushrooms with garlic mayonnaise, followed by roast duckling with orange and apple sauce, rounded off with meringues served with strawberries and Cornish cream at £5.

Washford

HOSPICE BAR ★★ **CHAPEL CLEEVE MANOR HOTEL,** Chapel Cleeve (Washford 202)
Open: Mon-Sat 10.30am-2.20pm, 7-10pm

[C] [♫] [P]

Furnished in keeping with its historic character, the Hospice is a charming eating place in which to enjoy the somewhat simple three-course meal at very reasonable cost. Soup with roll and butter is the only starter, followed by a good choice of main dishes, of which lasagne, steak, scampi, cottage pie, beef curry and rice, steak and kidney pie and ham salad are examples. Sherry trifle or chocolate mousse and a cup of coffee completes the meal which will cost upwards of £3.25. Near the sea, the hotel attracts holidaymakers at weekends, when live music is offered.

Watchet

RALEGH'S CROSS INN, Brendon Hills, Watchet (Washford 40343)
Open: summer: Mon-Sat 10.30am-11pm, Sun 11am-10.30pm

[C] [P] [ ]

Following recent full-scale alterations, this old Exmoor inn now has one large bar (which serves a variety of snacks and light meals), and a charming olde worlde restaurant for the discerning diner. Nearly everything is home-made, including soup served with a wheatmeal roll for around 90p, and liver pâté at about £1.90. Ham with egg and French fries costs around £2.70, while Brendon Hill Bobtails (rabbit casserole) and local pheasant casserole are about £3.50 apiece. Very nicely prepared desserts, all costing about 85p, include peach cheesecake, lemon soufflé and coffee gâteau. Somewhat beyond our budget is the Cordon Bleu Restaurant.

Wellington

BEAM BRIDGE HOTEL ★★ Sampford Arundel (Greenham 672223)
Open: Mon-Sat 11.30am-2.30pm, 6.30-11pm, Sun 12noon-2pm, 7-10.30pm

[C] [♫] [P] [🍷]

This small hotel on the A38 is an ideal stopping off place for the motorist. If you are in a hurry, the bar snacks are the thing – jacket potatoes with cheese, prawn or curry filling cost only 95p. Bill of fare in the peaceful restaurant offers a very wide choice, with a good range of starters. Deep fried breaded mushrooms with tartare sauce are delicious and cost less than £1. Chicken Kiev or lambs kidneys with herbs and wine sauce are interesting main courses. A host of sweets include crême caramel and black cherry and kirsch ice cream, which cost between 40p-70p.

MATILDA'S, 9 South Street (Wellington 4124)
Open: Mon-Fri 9am-5pm, Sat 9am-4.30pm, 8-10pm

[S] [🍷]

The traditional female touch is immediately apparent in this small, ground-floor, shop-fronted restaurant serving mainly breakfasts, lunches and teas. And no wonder, for the fresh, pretty atmosphere, with green print wallpaper and matching curtains offsetting pine furnishings is created by a mother-and-daughter partnership. The food selection is café, rather than restaurant fare (although Matilda's is licensed) – simple but definitely homespun, with vegetables, salads and fruit fresh from Mrs Stirling's garden. Full breakfast is £2; lunch may be Matilda's broth (75p), chicken with salad and potatoes (£1.95) or omelette (£1) and a chocolate or ginger sundae (75p). The quality reflects Mrs Stirling's experience in the catering world – until two years ago, she and her husband ran the red star hotel, Winter's Tale, in Burford. Matilda's is her retirement occupation!

Wells

RIVERSIDE RESTAURANT, Coxley (Wells 72411)
3m south of Wells on the A39
Open: summer: Mon-Sun 9am-11pm, winter: Mon-Sun 11am-2.30pm, 6-10.30pm

[♫] [P] [🍷]

This ten-year-old family-run restaurant was originally an 18th-century cottage which housed the local wheelwright in an adjoining barn. Nestling alongside the River Sheppey, it has retained its simple charm, not least because it is run very much as a family concern with Mrs Gorizia Reina looking after the kitchen, daughter Lucy the restaurant, and her father Angelo Reina supervising the business as a whole. Children are particularly welcome with a menu to suit their tastes; dishes like egg and chips or sausage and chips cost around £1. Main courses offer two house specialities: pollo al cacciatore (chicken with a sauce of wine, tomato, mushrooms and pimento) at about £3.50 and bistecca alla Siciliana (rump steak in a slightly hot red wine sauce) at around £4.25 – all include croquet, creamed or chipped potatoes plus vegetable of the day or mixed salad. Coffees include a rum, coffee and fresh cream concoction. Any dishes on the menu may be taken away at slightly less than the normal charge and you can place your order by telephone.

Weston-super-Mare

CHRIS'S RESTAURANT
8 Alexandra Parade
(Weston-super-Mare 23481)
Open: Mon-Sun 12noon-2pm, 6-11.30pm

[C] [♫] [P] [S]

Chris's Restaurant, formerly known as the Regent Steak House and under the same management, is a small, attractive, fully-licensed eating place with sixteen tables in polished dark wood, red/gold-patterned upholstered chairs with elegant green carpet and plush curtains, all of which add warmth to the room. Charcoal-grilled steaks are the house speciality, but, as these are priced at around £4 (including French fries and peas), care must be taken when choosing accompanying courses. Other grills, salads or omelettes are plain but less pricey. The 'chef's specialities' are more ambitious creations with tempting sauces, but these are likely to be outside our budget. For that grand finale there are six special coffees, including monk's coffee with Benedictine liqueur.

Winscombe

SIDCOT HOTEL ★★ Sidcot
(Winscombe 2271)
Open: Tue 7.30-9.30pm, Wed-Sat 12.30-2pm, 7.30-9.30pm, Sun 12.30-2pm

[P]

Set high in its own grounds and overlooking the beautiful Winscombe Valley, this imposing stone-built mansion has a pleasant dining room offering excellent-value three-course table d'hôte lunches and dinners to non-residents for about £4. Home cooking is the norm here, and house specialities include fresh cream Pavlovas. An extensive and reasonably-priced à la carte menu also operates.

Wiveliscombe

COUNTRY FARE, 4 High Street
(Wiveliscombe 23231)
Open: Mon-Wed and Fri 9am-5.30pm, Sat 9am-5pm, Sun 12noon-2pm

[P] [illegible]

Use Wiveliscombe's free parking and stroll down the High Street to Country Fare! This small family restaurant has an extensive range of good, fresh basic food, including home-made cakes and pastries. The Paskin family regard the comfort and satisfaction of their guests as of prime importance; home cooking is prepared and served to high professional standards. The daily 'bargain bite', consisting of dishes such as curried eggs and rice or two beefburgers and chips will set you back only £1, ham, egg and chips £1.30. A set lunch for under £3 might include soup, pork chops in cider (locally-brewed, naturally) or a roast, followed by fruit pie and cream.

Yeovil

THE PEN MILL HOTEL, Sherborne Road (Yeovil 23081)
Open: Restaurant: Fri-Sat 12noon-2pm, 7.30-10.30pm, Buttery: Mon-Sun 12noon-2pm, 7-10pm

[C] [♫] [P] [S] [illegible]

The weekday cold buffet consists of cold meats or pie with a selection of help-yourself salads from £1.95 or so. There is a hot daily special at about £1.95. Other bar meals include sausage, egg and chips at around £1 to a variety of steaks with all the trimmings from about £4.35. The restaurant serves a table d'hôte three-course meal for around £3.95 with a limited but good choice for all courses, and on Sundays this price buys a four-course meal featuring a traditional roast main course.

'This is the weather the cuckoo likes.
And so do I;
When showers betumble the chestnut spikes,
And nestlings fly:
And the little brown nightingale bills his best,
And they sit outside at The Travellers Rest,
And maids come forth sprig-muslin dressed,
And citizens dream of the south and west
And so do I. . .'

THOMAS HARDY

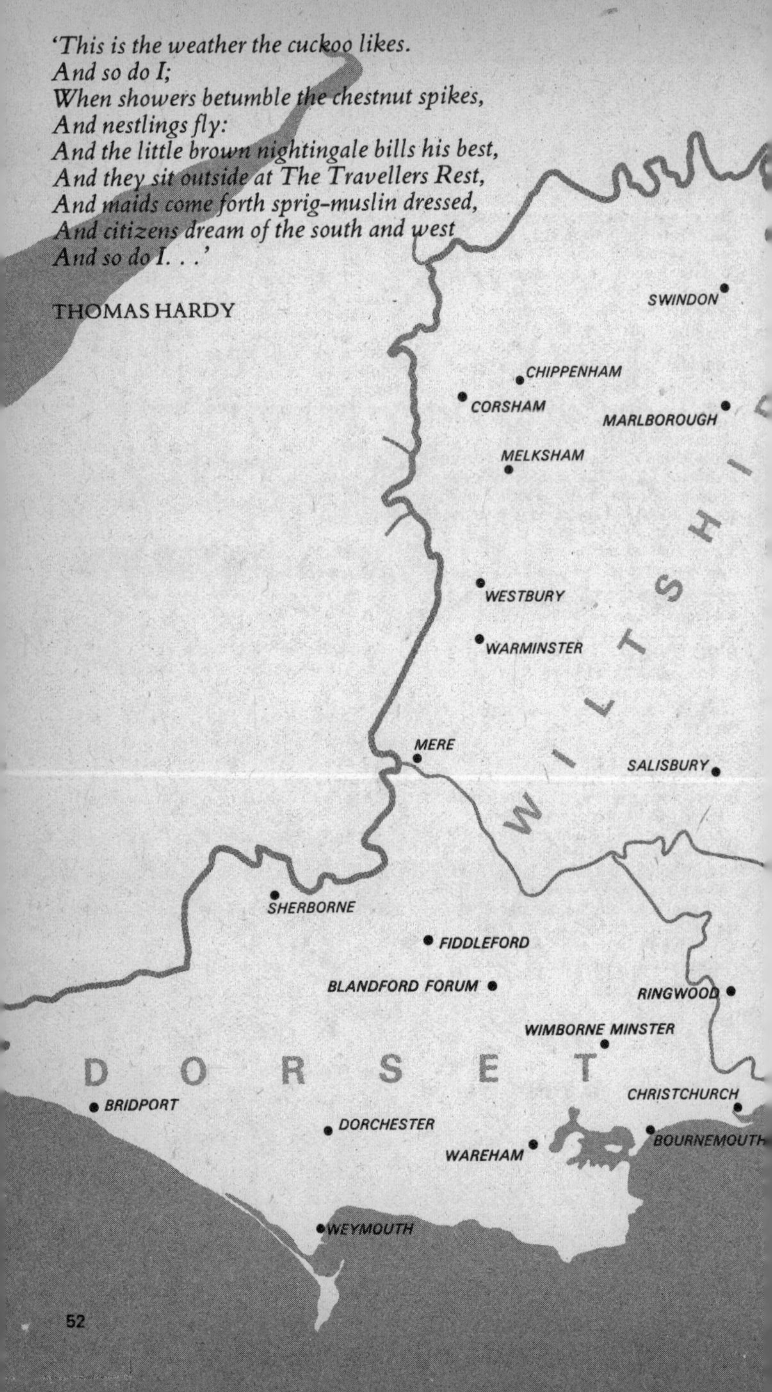

Wessex

2

Regional Dishes

Vectis pudding
New Forest venison in red wine sauce
Dorset chicken liver pâté
Poacher's pie
Jugged hare with redcurrant jelly

Aldershot

JOHNNIE GURKHA'S ✕
54 Station Road (Aldershot 277366)
Open: Mon-Sat 12.30-2pm,
5.30-11.30pm

Aldershot is better known as 'Home of the British Army' rather than a hunting ground for gourmets, but when engineer Hari Karki left the Gurkhas four years ago, where better to start his own restaurant than . . . Aldershot. He and his wife Meera have not only introduced the town to the rarities of genuine Nepalese food but have attracted much praise from Eat Out for Around £5 readers. Behind its unpretentious exterior in the 'downtown' area the restaurant is decorated with trinkets from Nepal, photographs of the Himalayas, Gurkha regimental memorabilia and a standard of service of which Kipling himself would have been proud. First-time visitors hardly need to move from the 'Nepali Special Thal' at £4.50 for three courses including a starter of mamocha – a soup with meat filled dumpling – well worth the twenty-five minutes it takes to prepare. Evening booking really is advisable.

Alresford

THE BODEGA, 32 Broad Street
(Alresford 2468)
Open: Mon-Sat 10.30am-2pm,
7-10.30pm (11pm Fri & Sat)

[♫] [P] [S]

The Bodega is a smart and sophisticated wine bar in picturesque Alresford – a small town which with its quaint shops, steam engine and watercress beds, attracts tourists from all parts of the globe. Interior décor is unobtrusive, with cream-painted panels and dark wood tables and chairs, but on summer evenings many patrons prefer to sit in the pretty covered courtyard, hung with the works of local artist Neville Paine. Start your meal with a home-made soup of the day and move on to a tasty Dutch speciality known as saté – a kebab of grilled pork in a piquant sauce, served on a wooden skewer at around £2. Sweets change daily, but could consist of chocolate mousse or ice cream with Grand Marnier. Specialities are chalked on a blackboard.

Basingstoke

THE BISTRO, 1 New Street
(Basingstoke 57758)
Open: Mon-Fri 12noon-2pm, 7-10pm,
Sat 7-10pm

[P] [S]

Doug and Suzy Palmer's homely little restaurant has deservedly acquired a very good local reputation in the few years since its conversion from a one-time doctor's surgery. Simple décor and furnishing create a typical bistro atmosphere. The lunchtime menu offers a choice of three or four main courses at competitive prices. For example, soup followed by roast lamb with orange and mint stuffing, plus peaches for dessert costs as little as £3.50. Alas, the majority of the evening menu (including daily specials chalked up on a blackboard) is beyond the budget, but this is one place where the excellent food and service warrants breaking the bank.

BURLINGTONS COFFEE SHOP AND WINE BAR, Seal House, Seal Road
(Basingstoke 66266)
Open: Mon-Sat 10am-4.30pm,
lunch 11.30am-2.30pm

[♫] [S] [♿]

Nothing but the best is available at Burlingtons departmental store and lunch is no exception. A trellis-work

ceiling with wicker-globed lighting and subtle exposed brickwork behind the serving counter complete a décor which is both relaxed and tasteful. A tempting array of food awaits you. Start with nourishing ham soup at around 40p, then choose from a wide selection of cold dishes, or a hot dish of the day such as chicken fricasée with peppers served on a bed of rice (this costs less than £2). Cold meat salads, including beef, chicken or ham are priced a little more, but the choice of salads is excellent – one example is rice with walnuts and sultanas. Delicious desserts such as feathery-light Black Forest gâteau or blackcurrant cheesecake are only around 50p.

CORKS FOOD AND WINE BAR
25 London Street (Basingstoke 52622)
Open: Mon-Sat 10am-2.30pm, 6-10.30pm, Sun 7-10.30pm

[♫] [S]

Corks goes continental in the summer when customers can 'take a pew' on the paved area outside the restaurant, beside a blackboard menu – strategically placed to tempt passers-by. Inside, behind a screen of brown half-curtains, is a dark and mellow eating place with soft music playing. Church pews make unexpectedly comfortable and intimate seating, and fine engravings decorate walls which are either white-washed or cork covered. Pots of leafy green plants and a large basket of beautifully-arranged flowers add a splash of colour, and the overall atmosphere is conducive to good eating. Starters such as burgundy pâté or smoked mackerel for under £1, plus hot casserole-type main courses with rice or jacket potato at £2.35 are always available. There are three or more scrumptious puds to choose from (all under £1) and an excellent array of cold meat salads (at less than £3). For £1.20 the special lunch of filled jacket potatoes or large brown baps with a glass of house wine is good value.

THE LIGHT OF SHAHZALAL
11 New Street, Joice's Yard (Basingstoke 3509)
Open: Mon-Sun 12noon-2.30pm, 6-12mdnt

[C] [S] [card]

Tucked away in an older part of the town, this Indian restaurant offers a wide range of food at surprisingly low prices. Service is the keynote here, with all staff genuinely anxious that you should enjoy your meal. A plethora of curries (marked hot, medium and mild on the menu to avoid burnt palates!) are available from £2-£4, whilst meat dhansak (hot sweet and sour) is around £2. Of the other specialities, chicken tikka with salad is heartily recommended at £2.80. For the less adventurous, English dishes, such as steak with mushrooms and chips at £2.50, are excellent value. Starters range from 70p-£1.30, with desserts (including jilaries, a delicious dough-based fritter) all priced at under £1.

TUNDOOR MAHAL RESTAURANT
4 Winchester Street (Basingstoke 3795)
Open: Mon-Sun 12noon-3pm, 6pm-12mdnt

[♫] [S]

Once the Midland Bank, this listed building retains its original stately exterior while the inside is transformed into a smart restaurant with warm red décor, wood-effect walls, Indian-style arches and nicely-positioned alcoves with hanging lights. Fresh flowers, candle-lit tables and soft background music complete the pleasant atmosphere. Cuisine is basically Bangladesh and Indian specialities with some Malayan, Persian and English dishes. A special three-course lunch costs around £1.75, with three choices for the main course including prawn, meat or chicken pillau. The à la carte menu includes a selection of original dishes – dhal soup with orange (around 50p) and beef Bangla curry served with fresh cream are worth sampling (at around £3). Sweets are fairly standard Indian dishes.

Blandford Forum

ANVIL HOTEL & RESTAURANT ★★
Pimperne (Blandford 53431)
Open: Mon-Sun 12noon-2.30pm, 6-10.30pm, (11pm Fri-Sat)

[♫] [P] [card]

Real wood fires are a feature of the Anvil, and the only restaurant between Blandford and Salisbury is housed in a beautiful, thatched 16th-century building, reputed to have originated as an Elizabethan farmhouse. Satisfying snacks may be taken in the newly extended and cleverly restored bar. Home-made fare such as cottage pie (£1.40), coquille St Jaques (made from fresh local scallops – £1.50) or beef curry with rice at £1.80 are the order of the day. Salads, soup, pâté and basket meals are also available. The beamed restaurant, with its brick floor has an à la carte menu which could easily break the budget. Soup, chicken à la crème (poached in a white wine and mushroom sauce) and a sweet is just within the limit.

Bournemouth

ANN'S PANTRY, 129 Belle Vue Road, Southbourne (Bournemouth 426178) Open: summer: Tue-Sat 10.30am-2pm, 6-10pm, Sun 10.30am-2pm, winter: Fri-Sun 10.30am-2pm

[S] [🍷]

This corner-sited restaurant, only 100 yards from the seafront, has an exterior reminiscent of a superior Victorian pub. At lunchtime there is an extremely reasonable à la carte menu with starters below 50p, and main courses, including pork chop and apple sauce and gammon with pineapple, range from £2-£3. Children's choices at around 60p include the well-loved bangers, beans and chips. A three-course set lunch is priced by the main dish – starting at about £1.50 for cottage pie or curry to around £1.95 for roast beef and Yorkshire pud. A three-course Sunday roast lunch costs around £2. Excellent table d'hôte three-course dinners are also served for around £3.50, and there is a slightly more expensive à la carte evening menu.

LA FONTAINE 141 Belle Vue Road, Southbourne (Bournemouth 420537) Open: Tue-Sat 12noon-2pm, 6.30-9.30pm, Mon & Sat 12noon-2pm

[S]

Tucked away in a residential suburb of Bournemouth, this cosy restaurant has attractive pine-panelled walls and ceiling. Ivor Jones and his wife Jane assure of a warm welcome. There is a regularly-changing chalked-up menu and an average three-course lunch costs just under £3. In the evenings prices rise only slightly to £3.50. Coffee is 25p extra.

FORTES, The Square (Bournemouth 24916) Open: Florentine Restaurant: summer: Mon-Sun 12noon-10.30pm, winter: closes 2.30pm. Coffee Shop: Mon-Sun 8am-6pm. Self Service Restaurant: Mon-Sun 10am-10.30pm

[C] [♫] [P] [S] [🍷]

This is a typical Trusthouse Forte operation, providing everything from takeaway snacks for the beach to three-course à la carte dinners in an elegant setting, at prices that represent very good value for money. The ground floor self-service restaurant serves an excellent lunch, high tea or supper at prices from little more than £1-£2, as well as cakes and pastries, sandwiches, bowls of mixed salad, ice creams and beverages. The Coffee Shop serves hot snacks and grills throughout the day, with soup, hotdogs, hamburgers and pizzas as just some of its attractions. The Florentine offers a choice of three-course lunches at prices from about £3.95 to just under £5, including various Italian dishes and a traditional weekend lunch at around £4.75. The à la carte menu is also reasonably priced.

THE OLD ENGLAND, 74 Poole Road, Westbourne (Bournemouth 766475)
Open: Tue-Sun 9.30am-3pm, 6-10.30pm

[C] [♫] [P] [S] [♣]

A warm welcome awaits you at this delightful olde worlde restaurant. Cuisine, though, is 20th century and well-cooked with fresh vegetables. A set three-course meal costs £4.25 (with big reductions for children), alternatively an extensive à la carte menu includes a range of starters from chilled tomato juice at 35p, to crab cocktail at around £1.65. Numerous main dishes are available, typical options being Dorset chicken (£3.80) and pan-fried gammon with pineapple (£3.95). Steak, unfortunately, should be avoided if you're to stay within the budget. Tempting home-made desserts such as crème caramel or fruit crumble cost around 75p. For light snacks or salads try the newly-opened Dickens Wine Cellar directly below the restaurant.

PLANTERS, 514 Christchurch Road, Boscombe (Bournemouth 302228)
Open: Sun-Thu 6.30-11pm

[♫] [P] [S]

This modern restaurant with its Hollywood movie theme and lively background music boasts a New Orleans-style cocktail bar with over fifty cocktails running from 75p for apricot sour to £2 for wild jaffa. The food is as expected, hamburger-based, with a few specials such as chargrilled steak and Oregon lamb. Spicy chili con carne with pitta bread and side salad costs around £2.40. For dessert there is an all-American line up of spiced apple pie, chocolate fudge cake, hot waffle with maple syrup and fresh cream and various sundaes for just over £1.

THE SALAD CENTRE, Post Office Road (Bournemouth 21720)
Open: Mon-Fri 10am-5pm, Sat 10am-2.30pm

[C] [P] [S] [♣]

This family-owned-and-run Salad Centre encourages and caters for sensible health-food, vegetarian-style, eating. Patrons are invited to refrain from smoking and family pets are definitely not admitted. The décor is clean and bright, if a little spartan, and the staff charming and most helpful. Everything is home cooked and made of the freshest, purest ingredients, with no artificial additives of any kind. There is a brave display daily of more than a dozen different salads, with quiches, nut roasts, savouries and – in the winter – various hot dishes. Fruit juices include apple, lemon, grapefruit and beetroot and there is a good range of beverages, though the Salad Centre is unlicensed.

TRATTORIA TOSCA, 12 Richmond Hill (Bournemouth 23034)
Open: Mon-Sun 12noon-2.30pm, 6-11.30pm

[C] [♫] [P] [S] [♣]

The cuisine at Edward Cobelli's charmingly informal Trattoria Tosca in The Square is, not surprisingly, Italian, but not expensively so. There is a good range of starters at prices from 45p-£1.85, spaghetti dishes at about £1.55-£2.10, and Italian specialities, including the romantically named filleto Casanova, at around £3-£5.50. Service is friendly, willing and speedy, but do book at the weekend if you want to be sure of a table.

Bridport

BISTRO LAUTREC ✕ 53 East Street (Bridport 56549)
Open: Mon-Fri 12noon-2pm, Mon-Sat 7-10pm

[♫] [P] [S] [♣]

Food and environment go together in this typical French-style bistro. Candles in bottles, check tablecloths, Lautrec posters and chalked-up menus make just the right setting in which to enjoy a lunch of terrine provençale at about £1, followed, perhaps, by stuffed green peppers with vegetables or salad for just over £1. Evening meals, in a more sophisticated yet still informal atmosphere, cost over or around £5.

BULL HOTEL ★ 34 East Street (Bridport 22878)
Open: Mon-Sat 12noon-2pm, 7.15-9.15pm, Sun 7.15-9.15pm

[P]

The Terleski family are in the process of restoring their 16th-century coaching inn. They are keen to offer good hospitality at a very reasonable price – and succeed. There's a wide range of bar meals, including a choice from the daily speciality menu costing between £2.25 and £3.25 for three courses, and hot or cold snacks from 50p-£4. It can all be washed down with a glass of real ale. The daily speciality choice offers unfussy dishes such as roast belly of pork and vegetables, and the usual range of grills is available. For dessert try crème caramel or apple strudel.

Burbage

THE SAVERNAKE FOREST HOTEL★★
Savernake (Burbage 810206)
Open: Mon-Thu, Sun 12noon-2pm, 7-9pm, Fri-Sat 12noon-2pm, 7-10pm

[C] [P] [♣]

On the fringe of the beautiful Savernake Forest, this charming old hotel specialises in home-prepared dishes. The Buttery Grill menu offers soup (65p) or home-made pâté (£1.20) as starters. Main dishes include quiche, chili con carne, pizza, shepherd's pie, smoked mackerel, fish pie, lasagne, interesting salads and an ever-changing hot dish of the day, all under £3. Traditional Sunday lunch costs around £5. An ambitious à la carte menu is available in the restaurant – unfortunately beyond the scope of this guide.

Chippenham

THE ROWDEN ARMS, Bath Road (Chippenham 3870)
Open: Mon-Thu 12noon-2pm, 7-10pm, Fri-Sat 12noon-2pm, 7-10.30pm, summer only: Sun 7-10pm

[C] [P] [♣]

On the main Bath Road out of Chippenham is this attractive, modern pub with a low rake, chalet-style roof and a colourful painted farmhouse wagon in the forecourt. You can sip cocktails in the comfortable lounge bar while surveying the very extensive menu offering freshly-prepared food. A selection of fourteen starters ranges from soup of the day for about 40p to more substantial hors-d'oeuvre at around £1.45. Fish dishes, grills, salads and specialities, such as loin of pork Marsala (at £3.30) and rump steak (around £4), are available for the main course and there is an impressive choice of sweets at a variety of prices. Among the more expensive (around £1) are banana split and rum baba.

WHITE HART INN, Ford (Castle Combe 782213)
Off A420 Bristol/Chippenham on slip road to Colerne
Open: Mon-Sun 12noon-2pm, 7.30-9.30pm

[P]

Idyllically situated beside a trout stream and overlooking the lush Weavern valley, this 16th-century stone-built pub is the epitome of Olde Englande. Low, beamed ceilings, log fires and suits of armour set the scene, while Ken Gardner, Fleet Street journalist and writer, personally attends to the food preparation. Home-cooked ham-on-the-bone or braised beef, served with vegetables cost around £2.50 in the bar, and for less than £3 you can savour locally-caught trout. Some dishes from the à la carte menu could be sampled within the budget, but venison in port wine or creamed pheasant cost around £5, so you would have to forego a starter or sweet course.

Christchurch

SOMERFORD HOTEL, Lyndhurst Road, Somerford (Christchurch 482610)
Open: Mon-Sun 12noon-2pm, 7-9.30pm

[C] [P]

Lunch in the attractive dining area and bar of this impressive Tudor-style hotel is superb value. The table d'hôte menu offers three courses, including chicken, traditional English roasts and locally caught fish dishes and a good selection of sweets for about £3.50 but with fresh Christchurch salmon the price goes over £5. There is an excellent cold buffet and a variety of bar snacks is available. Children are specially catered for in the summer with a pets' corner and their own play area and bar, and they are equally welcome in the dining area. The à la carte dinner menu includes an abundance of local fish and seafood as well as grills and roasts, but you could break the bank by selecting without care.

Corsham

METHUEN ARMS HOTEL ★★
(Corsham 714867)
Open: Mon-Thu, Sat 12noon-2pm, 6-10.30pm, Fri 12noon-2.30pm, 6-11pm, Sun 12noon-2pm, 7-10.30pm

[C] [P]

Situated midway between Chippenham and Bath on the A4, the hotel is in close proximity to Corsham Manor, the country seat of Lord Methuen, whose heraldic arms are displayed above the entrance portico. In fact, the building is steeped in history and Winter's Court, where lunch and dinner are served, retains the oak beams and Cotswold stone of a grandiose bygone age. A midday three-course businessperson's meal is a bargain at £4 (especially as minute steak is on the menu), but unfortunately the candlelit dinners are just beyond our range. However, there are further options in the Long Bar such as sandwiches, basket meals, and a cold table, all reasonably priced. Liquid refreshment includes a glass of house wine at about 60p.

Dorchester

JUDGE JEFFREY'S RESTAURANT
High West Street (Dorchester 4369)
Open: summer: Mon-Sat 10am-5.30pm, 7-9.45pm, Sun 12noon-2pm, winter: Fri-Sat only

[S]

Viewed as a building, Ann and Anthony Coletta's Judge Jeffrey's restaurant is of great historical and architectural interest. It was sympathetically restored and put to its present use in 1928, but had been first monastery property and then a private house for something like five centuries before. Judge Jeffreys lodged here in 1685 while making his mark in the town with orders for seventy-four executions. Today, the restaurant which bears his name is a friendly place, full of atmosphere, providing morning coffees, bar snacks, lunches, afternoon teas and dinners at prices which could hardly be accounted a trial to anyone. You can buy a substantial lunch for about £4 or eat à la carte for very little more. The evening à la carte menu is very English, listing scampi, veal, gammon steak and Dorset pork fillet all reasonably priced, with £6 the average price for a dinner. Children's half portions are available from the main menus at half price and there is a special children's menu with dishes costing around £1.50.

Fareham

GABBIES, 30-32 West Street (Fareham 284853)
Open: Mon-Sat 12noon-2.30pm, 7.30-11.30pm

[C] [♫] [P] [S]

This smart hamburger restaurant in the older pedestrian shopping area boasts far more than weighty burgers on its menu. You can enjoy a good three-course meal here, choosing from seven starters and a number of tasty main courses such as seafood platter or chicken Maryland. Sweets include gâteaux, cheesecakes, and ice cream sundaes. If you have a taste and appetite for burgers, Gabbies special is excellent – a ¼lb or ½lb lean beefburger topped with mushrooms, peppers, tomato and melted cheese served in a toasted roll with French fries or salad for around £2.55 or £3.45.

Fiddleford

FIDDLEFORD INN
(Sturminster Newton 72489)
Open: Mon-Sat 12noon-2pm, 7-10pm, Sun 12noon-1.30pm, 7-9.30pm

[P] [🍷]

This creeper-clad inn makes a welcome stopping-place on the beautiful, but remote A357 – the Sturminster Newton/Blandford road. Informality is the keynote and your hosts Geoffrey and Jill Fish ensure that there's a warm and cosy atmosphere. A lunchtime blackboard menu offers regularly changing speciality dishes, whilst an example of standard fare would be smoked mackerel pâté at around £1, chicken curry (around £2) or quiche and salad (£1.40). Sweets include coffee meringue and chocolate roulade at £1. In the evening, if you avoid steak the budget will not be exceeded.

Hambledon

THE BAT AND BALL INN
Broadhalfpenny Down, Hambledon Road, Clanfield (Hambledon 692)
Open: Mon-Sat 12noon-2.15pm, 7-10.30pm (10pm winter), Sun 12noon-1.45pm, 7.30-10pm

[C] [♫] [P]

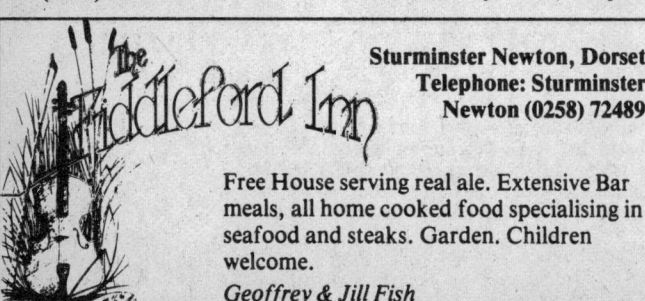

Even in the mid-18th century, when the cricket club at Hambledon became the strongest team in England and turned a rustic pastime into a national sport, the Bat and Ball was a hit with the locals. The inn overlooked the pitch on Broadhalfpenny Down and the players (wise chaps) would repair to it after, and sometimes even during, a match to indulge in 'high feasting'. Today the inn is even more popular despite being way out in the country, so it's always advisable to book a table. Hosts Frank and Katherine Rendle (Katherine does the cooking) have retained a cricketing atmosphere in the front bar; curved cricket bats, two-stump wickets and all, while the other bar is decorated in the more traditional beams-and-brass style. Order food at the bar and eat here if you like, or have your meal waitress-served in the cosy restaurant which overlooks an attractive garden. You really have to be something of a glutton to bust our £5 budget because prices are very reasonable. All five starters (from soup to a generous prawn cocktail) are under £1 and eight main courses range from about £1.10 for a Jumbo sausage, through mouth-watering meat pies (around £1.40) to grilled sirloin steak at about £3.80 – great value, considering that all the main dishes are served with chips, peas, mushrooms, onions and salad garni. Salads and ploughman's are also available. If you're not stumped when it comes to the sweet course, try an apple pie (40p) or gâteau (70p) or finish off with cheese and biscuits. No children or dogs allowed except on the front patio.

Hartley Wintney

WHYTE LYON (Hartley Wintney 2037)
Open: Mon-Sat 10.30am-2.30pm, 6-10.30pm, Sun 12noon-2pm, 7-10.30pm

[C] [P] [&]

East of the picturesque village of Hartley Wintney, nestling in a hollow beside the A30, is the rambling, historic one-time coaching inn now owned by Schooner Inns. Peter Cole, who assists the manager, claims that part of the building dates back to the 14th century. At present two grill bars, heavily beamed and partitioned in the usual Schooner manner, offer a range of old favourites at competitive prices. The Portcullis Restaurant has a salad counter from which you can serve-yourself to as much side salad as you want. Ice creams or cheeses are included in the price of the main course, which could be rump steak (around £5), half a roast chicken in barbecue sauce (around £4) or plaice and lemon (about £3.50). A starter will add about £1 to your bill. Apart from a bigger selection of starters, Dover sole and duckling, the Cromwell Bar boasts the ghost of a girl who hanged herself in that very room – the rope is still there to remind us! So popular is the Whyte Lyon with the locals that a third restaurant – the Hartford Grill has been opened upstairs.

Hook

WHITE HART, London Road (Hook 2462)
Open: Tue-Sat 12noon-2pm, 7-10pm (10.30pm Fri & Sat)

[♫] [P] [&]

On the old coach road from London to Exeter stands the White Hart, one of the oldest pubs in the country. Entrance from the car park is through an out-of-the-past courtyard, by a row of old cottages which were once the stable boys' quarters. The dining room, with its dark-wood fittings and a lattice work of beams, has one wall etched with the ghostly outline of a coachman and his horses. Fruit juice, pâté or soup followed by a mixed grill served with chips or new potatoes and the vegetable of the day will cost around £3. A sweet such as apple pie and cream or cheese and biscuits completes the meal. Bar snacks are of a high standard, and a three-course meal of cream of chicken soup, a veal or pork dish or sausage and mash and strawberry gâteau can cost as little as £2.50.

Lymington

THE SMUGGLER'S COVE, 6 Queens Street (Lymington 72603)
Open: Mon-Sat 11am-3pm, 7-11pm, Sun 11.30am-3pm

[P] [&]

Like all the best Smuggler's Coves, this tiny restaurant is not easy to find. Look out for the orange floral awnings when travelling on the one-way system at the point where the Bournemouth and Lyndhurst roads meet. Locally-caught fish from nearby Muddiford Beach features on the menu and mackerel is smoked on the premises. Proprietor Alan Stone also makes all the pastries – his steak and kidney and fruit pies are delicious. A meal of soup of the day, fish platter with French fries and side salad followed by a lighter-than-air pancake with lemon juice should cost no more than £4. Children are accommodated with reduced prices and they will be fascinated by the seashell wall collages in the restaurant.

Lyndhurst

THE BOW WINDOWS RESTAURANT
65 High Street (Lyndhurst 2463)
Open: summer: Mon-Sun 10am-10pm, winter: Mon-Wed 10am-6pm, Thu-Sun 10am-10pm

[P] [S] [♧]

The little town of Lyndhurst is on a major holiday route in the heart of the New Forest . . . and gets very busy in the tourist season. With this in mind, Bow Windows is particularly conveniently placed opposite a large free car park. Behind those bow windows is an interior decorated with mirror tiles and large murals of forest scenes. The menu is extensive and conventional. Good value table d'hôte choices at lunch and dinner will cost under £5 with coffee, and may include a roast, fish, or curry dish. Tread carefully as far as the à la carte is concerned; the cheapest dishes, such as steak and kidney pie or omelette will cost about £3.

Marlborough

ATTILIO'S WINE BAR, 13 New Road (Marlborough 52969)
Open: Mon-Wed, Fri-Sat 12noon-2pm, 6.30-10.30pm, Sun 6.30-10.30pm

[S]

A cheerful aura of Italy in a corner of rural Wiltshire, Attilio's interior is simple and attractive, with an emphasis on natural textures – rush, cane, brick and wood. The excellent pizzas – with fresh tomatoes and oozing with cheese – can form a filling base for a within-the-budget three-course meal. Lunchtime meals and snacks range in price from 60p-£3. Our inspector was impressed by the home-made crusty rolls, served with a large dish of creamy butter. You'll need a bit of mental juggling to keep the price of an à la carte selection down.

Melksham

THE WEST END, Semington Road (Melksham 703057)
Open: Mon-Sun 12noon-2pm, (Sun 1.30pm), 7-10pm

[C] [P]

This attractive mellow stone and tile hostelry has an interior with a farmhouse look – beamed ceiling, open-stone fireplace and scrubbed table tops. A limited menu offers simple but well-prepared dishes with emphasis on succulent steaks, all with interesting names. You may wrap your lips around the 'Farmer's Daughter' (a 8oz sirloin for around £3.25) or perhaps you'd prefer a Ploughboy's lunch or Hungry Horse? Three courses including a village pâté for a starter and Emmerdale apple pie with cream will cost between £5 and £6 with coffee. For a cheaper meal try the hot platter of the day or salad for under or around £2.

Mere

PESTLE AND MORTAR, The Square (Mere 860263)
Open: Mon-Fri 9am-5.30pm, Sat 9am-5.30pm, 7.30-10pm, Sun 12noon-5.30pm

[P] [S] [♧]

This restaurant bears a very apt name as the stone townhouse in which it is housed was originally the apothecary's, dating back to the 17th century. The comfortably-modernised and tastefully-decorated interior boasts an attractive restaurant with aperitif bar/coffee lounge plus a smaller separate area for morning coffee and afternoon snacks. Personal attention awaits all visitors by owners Wendy and Jerry Anderson. Wendy is to be seen 'out front' while husband Jerry prepares food in the kitchen. A newly introduced

Countryman range comprises various home-made pies and pastries, all below £2. An evening à la carte menu is also available at proportionately higher prices which are still within the limit if chosen with care. Try 'Taste of England' dishes here.

Petersfield

THE PUNCH AND JUDY RESTAURANT, High Street (Petersfield 2214)
Open: Mon-Sat 8.30am-5.15pm

C P S

This attractive olde-worlde building dating from 1613 has plenty of charm and combines a bakery, coffee shop and small restaurant. A set menu of good basic English fare includes starters such as sardine salad (around £1.15), smoked mackerel (about £1.25), salads in the £1.80-£3 range, fish dishes such as rainbow trout at around £4, grills from just over £2.50-£4.75 and a selection of desserts from 75p-£1.25. There is also a dish of the day on offer such as roast loin of pork served with a good selection of well-prepared vegetables for around £3.

Portsmouth

THE HUNGRY ONE, 15 Arundel Way, Arundel Street (Portsmouth 817114)
Open: Mon-Sat 9.30am-5pm

P S

For the very best kind of snack bar, in clean, comfortable, purpose-built surroundings, try Michael See's Hungry One. Fresh salads are a speciality of the house and range in price from Cheddar cheese at just over £1.50 to red salmon at around £2. There is a good selection of substantial snacks from about £1.50 for chicken or plaice and chips to nearly £2 for scampi and chips. There is a range of delicious desserts from around 50p. No alcohol, but finish with the locally-esteemed coffee with fresh cream.

Ringwood

ANROES, 35 Christchurch Road (Ringwood 3671)
Open: Mon, Wed-Sat 10.30am-2pm, 7-10pm, Sun 10.30am-2pm

S

Blackened beams and brass and copper ornaments recall the building's 300-year past. Whether James and Anna Robinson still use the old baker's oven in the kitchen for their delicious sweets is not known, but their attentive service and standard of cooking certainly suits the modern palate. The three-course lunch menu is particularly good value at £3.60, with four starters (including maybe, hot mussels in garlic butter) and main courses such as goujons of plaice or braised beef, and a sweet table to make your choice from. Dinner is more elaborately prepared and priced at £7.50 a head. Fresh vegetables and local fish are featured when available.

PEPPERCORNS RESTAURANT
9 Meeting House Lane
(Ringwood 78364/4361)
Open: Tue-Thu 10am-2.30pm, Fri-Sat 10am-2.30pm, 7.30-11.30pm, Sun 12.30-2.30pm

P S

Hanging flower baskets, bright against the whitewashed walls, pick out Peppercorns. Exposed beams and hunting prints create a relaxed atmosphere, enhanced by displays of fresh flowers. Appetisers range in price from soup of the day at 50p to prawn cocktail at £1.10. Main courses, served with vegetables of the day, include a variety of omelettes from £1.10-£1.75, lamb chops with redcurrant jelly at £1.85 and trout meuniere at £2.25. Cold buffet items cost from £1.45-£2 – home-cooked ham, roast beef and chicken included. Daily specials such as chicken curry (£1.35) or braised liver and onions (£1.40) change every day. Desserts, for example, Bakewell tart, fruit salad or Black Forest gâteau are in the 00p-05p range. Sunday lunch is a special feature, with a choice of four starters, two roasts or fish, two hot sweets or a selection of desserts from the trolley.

Romsey

THE WHITE HORSE, Ampfield (Braishfield 68356)
Open: lunchtime licensing hours

P

Nestling at the foot of a wide curve of the A31 is the welcoming sight of the picturesque, black-and-white-timbered White Horse pub. Inside, the large lounge bar is all beams and comfort, with a cavernous brick fireplace. Cindy and Ron Bagley offer astonishingly good bar lunches and you will find it difficult to spend as much as £5 for three courses, wine and coffee. Cindy does all the cooking and even the generous cottage pie, which comes in an individual dish, is full of surprises – with peppers and sweetcorn it only costs 65p! Beef curry, chicken supreme or sweet and sour pork are all under or around £1, and salads are available. Start with pâté and finish with delicious, light Black Forest gâteau or fruit flan bursting with fruit – both served with cream and costing just 60p. A recent addition is the delightful children's garden, where kids can choose dishes such as sausage and chips or fishfingers and chips from their own special menu.

Salisbury

THE BARON OF BEEF, Endless Street (Salisbury 28937)
Open: during normal licensing hours. Mon-Sun 12noon-2pm, 6-10.30pm

[C] [♫] [P] [S]

The Baron of Beef, opened in February 1978, is a timber and brick transformation of a much older pub. Its lunchtime bar menu includes steak and kidney pie at £1.20, or Cornish pasty at £1, both served with chips and peas, as well as home-made cold dishes such as egg, cheese and onion flan for around £1 and prawn salad for under £2. A ploughman's lunch costs around 65p. The main menu includes excellent home-made soup or pâté as appetisers. Plaice, chicken, lamb or gammon are typical main courses, served with vegetables and trimmings, at around £3 each. Steak dishes are between £3.45 and £4.70. Most desserts are around 75p.

CLAIRE'S RESTAURANT
7-9 The Market Place (Salisbury 3118)
Open: Mon-Sat 11.45am-2.30pm (all year), 6-10pm (Jun-Sep), Wed-Sat 6-10pm (Sep-Jun)

[C] [♫] [P] [S] [♿]

Very handy for shoppers, this is a pleasant rendezvous for a quick break or a substantial lunch. Claire's offers good food at very reasonable prices and (with its children's meals offering two courses including fish fingers or beefburgers at just £1) is excellent for families. Evening dishes include veal provençale (£3.75) and chicken tikka (£2.95).

THE CROSS KEYS HOTEL, Shaftesbury Road, Fovant (Fovant 284)
Open: Mon-Tue, Thu-Sun 12noon-2pm, 7.45-9pm, Wed 7.45-9pm

[P]

The famous highwayman Jack Rattenbury enjoyed the victuals prepared at the Cross Keys. This charming, stone-built hostelry was built around 1485, and can be found in the heart of beautiful countryside. The 20th-century fare is English roasts and home-made sweets, though Elsie and Wendy Thompson have a flair for preparing more exotic dishes such as moussaka. Snacks available in the Buttery Bar include curry or chicken and chips for between £1 and £3, and very modestly-priced ploughman's lunches and freshly-cut sandwiches.

MICHAEL SNELL, 8 St Thomas's Square (Salisbury 6037)
Open: Mon-Sat 9am-5pm

[P] [S] [♿]

No-one should go to Salisbury without trying Michael Snell's superb Black Forest gâteau. In these old, part millhouse premises, the Swiss-trained Mr Snell makes and sells his own chocolate and cakes, besides specialising in the sale of fine teas, coffees, jams, chutneys and local honey. His light lunch menu contains a great variety of dishes, all at under £3, including smoked mackerel fillet with carrot and coleslaw, and cheese flan or home-made pizza with salad. Appetisers include soup for about 50p, and a selection of torten and pastries or speciality sorbets completes a satisfying three-course meal for around £4. Michael Snell is unlicensed. This restaurant has easy access for disabled people, with some tables on street level.

Sherborne

HOUSE OF STEPS, Half Moon Street (Sherborne 2455)
Open: Mon-Sat 9.30am-5.30pm, Sun 12noon-5.30pm

[C] [♫] [P] [S] [♣]

Facing Sherborne Abbey, the mellow, stone-built House of Steps provides a reasonably-priced selection of snacks and more substantial meals. Home-made favourites such as steak and kidney pie, jugged beef and a wide range of salads are available. Traditional Sunday lunch is a speciality. Afternoon cream teas are available and a three-course meal at the cold carvery can be had on a Saturday.

SWAN INN, Cheap Street (Sherborne 4129)
Open: Mon-Sun 12noon-2pm, 6.30-10pm

[C] [P] [S] [♣]

The Swan Inn is to be found through an archway from a pedestrian short cut, leading from the main car park close to the town centre. This quaint hostelry offers a selection of satisfying grills, including scampi (£3.90), half duck and rump steak (both under £5), all served with garni and French fries or jacket potato. Grills may be supplemented with appetising starters (50p-£1.20) such as pâté, whitebait and prawn cocktail, and sweets such as home-made apple pie.

Southampton

GOLDEN PALACE ✕ 17 Above Bar Street (Southampton 26636)
Open: Mon-Sat 11.45am-12mdnt, Sun 12noon-12mdnt

[C] [♫] [P] [S] [♣]

Slap in the middle of Southampton's modern shopping area, this colourful Chinese restaurant oozes Eastern calm. Prettily decked out with coloured lanterns, tiles, high archways and pillars to give a 'palatial' effect, it is immensely popular with the local orientals, and every encouragement is given to Western diners to use chopsticks. Dishes from the Tim Sum menu such as prawns Cheung Fun or meat rolls and duck's webs (available from 12noon-5pm only) prove to be the best loved and are all, unbelievably, around £1.50 each. A three-course à la carte dinner works out at about £5.

LA MARGHERITA, 4-6 Commercial Road (Southampton 22390)
Open: Mon-Sat 12noon-3pm, 6pm-12mdnt

[C] [♫] [P] [S]

A popular nightspot, particularly with theatre and cinema folk from the nearby Gaumont, is Franco Fantini's La Margherita. 'Let's go Margherеating' is the house motto, with a choice of starters ranging in price from about 40p for hot garlic bread to around £2.20 for Parma ham and melon. There are made-to-order pizzas, from £1.40 upwards, and main dishes such as fresh fish, a significant proportion of which, except sole Meunière, cost less than £3.50.

PICCOLO MONDO, 36 Windsor Terrace (Southampton 36890)
Open: Tue-Fri 10am-8pm, Sat-Mon 10am-7pm

[♫] [S]

Very handy for top-of-the-town shopping and the Hants and Dorset bus station, Salvatore La Gumina and Domenico Bibbo's Piccolo Mondo incorporates bakery and snack bar. A good cup of coffee costs about 25p, freshly-baked cheesecakes and cream cakes around 30p, and freshly-cut sandwiches are available. Hot snacks include home-made lasagne alla Romana at around £1.25 and the cooked-to-order pizzas are priced at about £1.40.

PIZZA-PAN, 28A Bedford Place (Southampton 23103)
Open: Mon-Sun 10am-3pm, 6pm-1am

[C] [♫] [P] [S]

The enterprising Signor Strologo's bistro-cum-restaurant has boldly-written outside menus and an eye-catching window display of bottles to tickle the palates of passers-by. Inside (where a personal welcome awaits you), Ercol-style tables and chairs, with check tablecloths, fill the large eating area, whilst attractive chandeliers and a big tank of (edible!) fish complete the furnishings. Most appetisers here tend to be rather expensive (around £1.30), but this is compensated by the pizza prices (*eg*, cannelloni ripieni – £1.85, pizza Napolitana – £1.55). Many steak, fish and poultry dishes are on offer, but if you want a large glass of wine (75p) you'll need to choose carefully to keep within the budget.

THE RED LION, 55 High Street (Southampton 22595)
Open: Mon-Sat 12noon-2pm and normal licensing hours

[♫] [P] [S]

Local tradition has it that, in 1415, Henry V put down a treacherous plot with a hastily-arranged trial in what is now known as the 'Court Room' of the Red Lion. True or not, the room is an impressive one, with its half-timbered walls and stone Tudor fireplace. Charles Waldman's two-course lunch specials for under £2 are an extremely good buy. For the rest, the menu offers good plain English cooking at prices hard to beat for value. The Red Lion is close to the Bargate – opposite Habitat.

SIMON'S WINE HOUSE, Vernon Walk, Carlton Place (Southampton 36372)
Open: Mon-Thu 11.30am-2.30pm, 7-10.30pm; Fri-Sat 11.30-3pm, 7-11pm, Sun 7-10.30pm

[♫] [S]

This simple Simon wine house, with its dark wood, bare bricks and bowls of shiny green palms is located in Southampton's bohemian back-street area. Dishes chalked on a blackboard include home-made pâté or chicken curry at under £2, and Simon's pie (a speciality of the house), with sweets such as gâteau, cheesecake and trifle all for around £1.

VEGIA ZENA, 49 Bedford Place (Southampton 31885)
Open: Mon-Sat 12noon-2.30pm, 7-11.30pm

[C] [♫] [P] [S] [♧]

An eye-catching red awning and brown-glass frontage proclaim the presence of this attractive little Italian restaurant. Inside, the décor is simple, with white, textured walls, low ceiling and red-tiled floor. Brightly-checked tablecloths and pictures of boating scenes add colour and interest. A cold cabinet displays seafood and other delicacies which can be found, in various forms, on the menu. Continental fish dishes are the speciality (at £3-£4), with such delights as fresh clams cooked in wine and herbs with croûtons, stuffed baked trout or fried rings of squid – all around £3-£4. Pasta and pizzas are priced from £2 to £2.50.

Swindon

SHERATON SUITE, East Street (Swindon 24114)
Open: Mon-Sat 12noon-2pm

[C] [P] [S] [♧]

If ornate surroundings are what you look for in a restaurant, you could do no better than to eat in the red and gold dining-room of the Sheraton Suite. Sit back amidst the chandeliers, velvet-upholstered chairs and flock wallpapers and enjoy the table d'hôte lunch, priced at about £3.50. This includes a starter of soup or fruit juice, and eight choices of main dishes such as roasts, steaks, chicken chasseur or fish plus a daily special such as devilled kidneys followed by cheese or a sweet from the trolley. You may, if you prefer, order from the à la carte menu; most dishes obviously fall outside our price range, but three courses such as melon, scampi and gâteau are still within reach. Snacks are available from the bar.

Wareham

PRIORY HOTEL ★★★ Church Green (Wareham 2772)
Open: Mon-Sun 12.30-2pm

[P]

Formerly the 16th-century Priory of Lady St Mary, this charming hotel retains much of its original character and enjoys a magnificent setting amid two acres of beautiful landscaped gardens on the banks of the River Frome. Lunch is served in the traditional dining room where a reasonable choice of high-class cuisine is available at around £5 from the à la carte menu. Be warned – you'll stay within budget only if you choose with care. A sample three-course meal could include avocado 'lounge en ouche' (half avocado cooked in butter with bacon), breast of chicken Algerienne with vegetables of the day and a choice from the sweet selection. Evening meals, served in the Abbot's Cellar, are beyond the scope of this book.

RED LION HOTEL ★ Town Cross (Wareham 2843)
Open: Mon-Sat 12noon-2.15pm, Sun 12noon-2pm, 7-9.15pm

[C] [P] [S]

In the centre of this small country town,

this brick hotel with dormer windows and colourful hanging flower baskets is a find for travellers en route to Bournemouth or Weymouth. Interesting bar snacks are available from 50p-£1 and a good table d'hôte three-course meal can be had in the restaurant for around £4 at lunchtime or around £5.50 in the evening. Choices for lunch could be spaghetti bolognese, fricasée of veal à la crême and strawberry meringue. The dinner menu offers a more imaginative selection of desserts such as profiteroles. A wider choice is available on the à la carte menu, but three courses could break the budget.

Warminster

CHINN'S CELEBRATED CHOPHOUSE
Market Place (Warminster 212245)
Open: Mon-Sat 12noon-2pm, 7-10.45pm (except mid-Oct)

[S]

Rabbits, or rather the lack of them, are the reason that this charming little eating place exists today. The Pickford family had for many years carried on a Butchers' and Fish, Game and Poultry business in Warminster, and if it hadn't been for a devastating outbreak of myxomatosis in 1965, they would still be using these cellars for their once well-established trade in rabbits and rabbit skins which were graded and dispatched from here. Braving their misfortune the Pickfords decided to convert the cellars into a restaurant. So, today you will be welcomed by staff dressed in the traditional straw boaters and striped aprons of that original business. With their knowledge of meats, fish and poultry you are assured a good, reasonably-priced meal. Chops themselves cost around £2.50, whilst all steaks are English and, with the fresh fish, are bought whole to be made ready for the menu at prices ranging from about £2 for haddock to £5 or so for fillet or T-bone steak. Salmon, mackerel and herring, too, are smoked on the spot and all pâtés are home-made (sold as starters at 75p-£1).

Westbury

THE HOT POT, Warminster Road
(Westbury 822551)
Open: Tue-Sun 10am-3pm, Fri-Sat 7.30-12mdnt

[C] [♫] [P] [S] [♤]

Owner Peter Murcott runs this modern corner-sited restaurant at the end of a shopping complex. A starter of home-made soup or fruit juice followed by a hot dish of the day such as steak and kidney pie should set you back under £2, and there's a good variety of fish, poultry and meats to supplement choice. Then try a sweet from the trolley, home-made apple pie or various ices. Coffee and cream awaits you at the finishing line, of course. The children's menu is great value, with fishfingers or beefburgers and chips, ice cream and a soft drink costing only £1.20.

Weymouth

THE CLARENDON RESTAURANT
52/53 The Esplanade
(Weymouth 786706)
Open: Mon-Sun 9am-11pm

[C] [S] [♤]

A seafront restaurant near the shopping area which provides day-long refreshment for flagging shoppers and sunbathers. A variety of 'Shoppers' luncheons' includes cheese omelettes, sausage and egg or fillet of cod with French fries or shepherd's pie as a main course, costing around £1. Starters from around 40p-65p and sweets from the trolley from 65p complement the meal. Alternatively, a three-course lunch for about £2.25 offers a range of starters, grills, roasts and sweets – excellent value! A more ostentatious meal, 'The Clarendon Special' including prawn cocktail and steak, costs around £4.25. An ideal place to take a hungry family of holidaymakers.

Wimborne

HORTON INN, Horton
(Witchampton 840252)
Open: Mon-Sat 12noon-2pm, 7-10pm, Sun 12noon-2pm, 7.30pm-9.30pm

[P]

Good bar snacks are a feature of this attractive 18th-century free house. There's a paved patio where you can savour your food when the sun shines. Dorset pâté or smoked mackerel pâté are tasty snacks, both just over £1, and a range of attractive salads is available at around the £2 mark. The restaurant has an à la carte menu with an interesting selection of main dishes such as Somerset style pork at £3.80, but you may not be able to buy three courses for around £5.

QUINNEYS West Boro'
(Wimborne 883518)
Open: Tue-Sat 9.15am-5.15pm
(lunch served 12noon-2pm)

[S]

Quinneys is a delightful old cottage near to the town's main square and the Minster. Various one-course economy meals include Cheddar cheese with salad (£1.40) and grilled lamb cutlets with three veg (£2.25). The three-course lunchtime meals on offer range from £3.75-£4.50 and examples are roast chicken, lamb and gammon, plus the local speciality – Wimborne trout. Desserts are all around 50p and freshly-ground coffee just 28p.

Winchester

BANNERS RESTAURANT, 18 Little Minster Street (Winchester 67212)
Open: Mon 12noon-2.15pm,
Tue-Sat 12noon-2.15pm, 7-10.15pm

[♫] [🍷]

Banners opened in December 1977. The décor is bistro-style with pine tables and chairs, and the atmosphere is warm and friendly. There is usually a choice of pâtés on offer for around 70p, with a tasty quiche or two in the region of £1.20, as well as salads and a good cold table which includes the likes of roast beef at about £2 and liver sausage (around £1.20). The modestly-priced hot dishes change from day to day and include such dishes as baked potato with cheese filling or chili con carne, both served with salad. Home-made puds are on offer at around 70p. A feature of Banners is the special functions room where lively discos are frequently held and sumptuous buffets are prepared.

MOLES, 53 High Street
(Winchester 4896)
Open: Mon-Sat 9.30am-5pm

[S]

'Moles' is a suitably subterranean name but the place is anything but boring. It's a cheekily imaginative little bistro, sited deep down below a Design and Craft basketware shop in part of what is reputed to have been an ancient tunnel that ran from the Cathedral, beneath the Royal Mint, and thence out of town. With its pine booths, green hessian-lined walls, flagstone floors and subdued lighting, Moles makes a pleasant and convenient meeting place for shoppers and visitors. Both pizza and quiche salads are available for under or around £2. A typical lunch includes a choice of lasagne at around £2.20 or chicken and mushroom pie with vegetables for about £2. The delicious fresh cream gâteau comes at around 60p for a large slice.

MR PITKIN'S WINE BAR & EATING HOUSE, 4 Jewry Street
(Winchester 69630)
Open: restaurant: Sun-Thu 12noon-2pm, 7-10pm, Fri-Sat 12noon-2pm, 7-10.15pm, bar: Mon-Thu 11am-2.30pm, 6-10.30pm, Fri-Sat 11am-2.30pm, 6-11pm, Sun 12noon-2.30pm, 7-10.30pm

[C] [♫] [S] [🍷]

When Tony Pitkin left the hubbub of Fleet Street advertising, he brought a little of the London life to Winchester with him. His wine bar is now one of the busiest rendezvous in the city, with live music (often jazz) five nights a week and a pleasantly trendy, Edwardian-style atmosphere. The long, narrow bar has gas-lamp-style fittings and enlarged prints of wine labels; Mr Pitkin blends into the atmosphere well with his bow tie and colourful shirts. Three courses from the appetising slabs of cold meat and smoked fish, hot dishes of the day (about £1.75) and good range of starters and sweets will cost £3-£4. A chef presides over the bar's Sunday roast and Yorkshire pudding (about £2.50). The upstairs restaurant, elegant and intimate with its marble fireplace and russet walls, serves a daily lunch for around £5, but beware of the enticing items with a budget-breaking surcharge in brackets. Dinner is now less expensive if chosen from the new Menu Touristique, which offers three good courses at £5.95.

SPLINTERS ✕✕ 9 Great Minster Street
(Winchester 64004)
Open: Mon-Sat 11am-2.30pm

[C] [S]

Mike and Fiona Sherret's tastefully Victorian restaurant, with its dark gold wallpaper and 'ball' lights, offers predominantly French cuisine – its à la carte lunches are mainly outside our price range, but it earns a well-deserved place in the guide for the excellent-value lunches served in the brasserie, where soup of the day plus roll and butter is about 80p, quiche lorraine with salad is around £1.50 and a tasty hot dish or two, such as moussaka, crab au gratin, or globe artichokes with butter, is a little over £1.30. Desserts are from around 75p. If the ground floor is full, you can order the brasserie menu upstairs in the restaurant.

THE WYKEHAM ARMS, 75 Kingsgate Street (Winchester 3834)
Open: restaurant: Tue-Thu 12noon-2.30pm, 7-9.45pm, Fri-Sat 12noon-2.30pm, 7-10.15pm, Sun 12noon-2pm, bar: Mon-Sat 10am-2.30pm, Sun 12noon-2pm

[P] [&]

Stroll from the city centre through Cathedral Close to this pub in the shadow of Winchester College. In the bars, the stripped pine, country house atmosphere is complemented by customers from the college, cathedral and cricket pitch. The back room restaurant (à la carte lunch £5 or under, dinner little over £6) is pleasantly like a private living room. The warm welcome from Stanley and Mary Wright adds to this impression. Diners are surprised by a free bowl of salad between starter and main course. Good solid food is elevated from the ordinary – steak and kidney pie, prepared with Guinness or poacher's pie (rabbit and venison in cider). In the bar, try the excellent value nourishing soup (55p), herby cottage pie (90p) or hot tuna and sweetcorn quiche (£1.30). Sweets range from home-made apple pie to gâteau.

Isle of Wight

Arreton

THE FIGHTING COCKS
(Arreton 254/328)
Open: Mon 12noon-2pm, Tue-Sun 12noon-2pm, 7-9.30pm

Built on the site of an inn that had stood for three centuries, and using much of the original stone, The Fighting Cocks boasts a smart restaurant specialising in grills and seafood, but also offers pork chop or grilled gammon at about £3.80. Bar snacks feature at 40p or so, hot dishes at around £1.50 and cold meat salads starting at around £1.90.

Godshill

ESSEX COTTAGE RESTAURANT
High Street (Godshill 232)
Open: Etr-Oct: Tue-Sat (out of season Sat and Sun only) 12.30-5.30pm, 7-9pm

[C] [♫] [P] [S] [&]

Godshill is cream tea country with more tea gardens to the square inch, probably, than any other part of the British Isles. The Essex Cottage does a very good cream tea at under £1, as well as an excellent table d'hôte lunch at around £3. Dinner from the table d'hôte menu will cost only around £4.75 for four courses. The lunch menu is basic English fare including roast pork or lamb, and cherry pie and cream.

Newport

BUGLE HOTEL, 117 High Street (Newport 522800)
Open: during normal licensing hours

[P] [S]

The origins of the Bugle Hotel are a little obscure. It served as the Parliamentary headquarters for the Island meeting between Charles I and the Parliamentary Commissioners. Table d'hôte lunches are around £4, a three-course table d'hôte dinner at about £5 and other meals can be chosen from the à la carte menu which could include mushrooms au gratin, followed by fillet of sole bonne femme, roast lamb and a selection of sweets from the trolley served in the oak-panelled dining room. A three-course, bar buffet lunch costs as little as £1.75.

Shanklin

CLIFF TOPS HOTEL ★★★ Park Road (Shanklin 3262/3)
Open: Restaurant: Mon-Sun 1-2pm, 7-9pm. Coffee Shop: Mon-Sun 10am-6pm (summer only)

[C] [P] [S]

Cliff Tops calls itself the 'good food' hotel and takes great pride in its English and French cuisine. The three-course table d'hôte lunch here costs around £4, the three-course dinner about £5.75, both prices inclusive of service. For dinner, choose from six starters including avocado pear vinaigrette or asparagus in hot butter. A soup course includes consommé and rice. The main course offers hot and cold dishes, a particular delicacy being sweetbreads Valencia with Patna rice. A variety of cold salads are served in the Coffee Shop at prices from £2-£3.

THE TUDOR ROSE RESTAURANT
59 High Street (Shanklin 2814)
Open: Tue-Sun 10am-9pm

[C] [♫] [S] [♣]

A long, mock-Tudor building, originally a bakery and tea-rooms, in which proceedings are supervised by proprietor John Barrymore Simpson. Lunchtime fare consists of mainly traditional English roasts, but fresh salmon, cold meats and flans are also available, and can be followed by a choice from the sweet trolley. With a starter such as pâté or home-made soup, the whole meal is excellent value at less than £4.

Ventnor

THE ROYAL HOTEL ★★★ Belgrave Road (Ventnor 852186)
Open: Mon-Sun 8-9.30am, 12.30-2pm, 7-9pm

[C] [♫] [P] [♣]

The Royal does a limited but reasonably priced à la carte menu, a three-course buffet lunch at around £4 and a four-course table d'hôte dinner at about £5.35 as well as a menu of children's favourites priced below £1. Dinner is a particularly appetising affair, with such dishes as smoked eels or egg Mornay for a starter followed by guinea fowl in Montmorency sauce and then perhaps fresh strawberries for dessert in season.

Yarmouth

THE BUGLE HOTEL ★★ St James's Square (Yarmouth 760272)
Open: Mon-Sun 12.15-2pm, 7.15-9.30pm

[C] [♫] [P] [S] [♣]

The 300-year-old Bugle, with its panelled dining room, complete with ancient stone fireplace, has a great deal of character and charm. The cuisine is international and the menu table d'hôte, with a three-course lunch at about £4 (£4.50 on Sunday) and dinner at around £6. Dinner is an excellent meal, offering a good choice of dishes including prawn cocktail, followed by lamb's kidneys bourguignon with delicious Black Forest gâteau as dessert. The recently-enlarged Galleon Bar, with décor on a nautical theme, has cold meat salads and various snacks available from 50p-£2.

THE GEORGE HOTEL ★★ Quay Street (Yarmouth 760331)
Open: Mon-Sun 8.30-10am, 12.30-2.15pm, 7:30-9.15pm

[C] [P] [♣]

Built by the Governor of the Island, during the reign of Charles II, the George is now a comfortable family-owned and run hotel, popular with yachties and locals. A table d'hôte lunch in the panelled dining room costs around £4.40, but dinner is now a little above our budget. The food is English traditional, with fresh vegetables and is very good. For lunch you can enjoy cucumber salad, nutty fillet of plaice, and apricot trifle. Bar snacks include hot dishes ranging in price from £1.45 for sausage and chips to about £4.50 for steak and salad. Sandwiches and lighter snacks are also available. A large glass of French house wine costs around 70p in the restaurant – a welcome accompaniment to your meal.

'Now I be a rustic sort of chap
My mother lives o'er Thakem,
And my mother she's got
lots more like I,
For her knows how
to make 'em;
Some they calls I Bacon Fat,
And others Turnip Head,
But I tell to you I be no mug,
Because I'm country bred.'

TRADITIONAL

Regional Dishes

Bramley apple pie
Morello cherry jam
Romney Marsh mutton
Selsey crab
Whitstable oysters
Dover sole
Deal plaice and dabs
Ashdown Forest partridge pie
Sussex rabbit pie
Kentish shepherd's pie

The South East

Billingshurst

THE KING'S HEAD, High Street (Billingshurst 2921)
Open: Mon-Wed, Sun 12noon-2pm, Thu-Sat 12noon-2pm, 7-10pm

C P S

This delightful 500-year-old coaching inn in the centre of the village boasts a restaurant extension with a separate entrance from the bar – though you can partake of the cold buffet or snacks there if you are in a hurry. Fresh, home-made fare is the hallmark of the restaurant, where you could start with soup at 45p or pâté at 55p. Main dishes include steak and kidney pie and delicious lasagne and form the basis of the £3 set lunch. In winter good old treacle pudding is 45p, or if you prefer a lighter 'ending', try cheesecake at 55p or home-made fruit pie.

OLD HOUSE, Adversane (Billingshurst 2186)
Open: Mon-Sun 10am-6pm

C P

Manager Jeremy Steward supervises proceedings throughout the day in this quaint, 14th-century restaurant, its two rooms with low oak-beamed ceilings displaying an abundance of antiques – some for sale. Basic English fare includes a special lunch served at any time of the day for around £3.25. Soup of the day, home-made steak pie or home-made quiche and a sweet of the day – fruit pie, ice cream or fruit salad – is a typical menu. The à la carte menu includes grills at about £2.25 and the special Sunday lunch offers three courses for around £5.50 for adults, £3 for children.

Bognor Regis

TUDOR ROSE, 55 London Road (Bognor 23682)
Open: summer: Mon-Sat 10.30am-10.30pm, winter: closed Mon

The restaurant is split into two sections and has olde-worlde wooden-beamed ceiling and walls. A daytime menu offers starters (such as chilled melon) from 35p-£1.25, followed by various fish, roasts and salads at sensible prices (leg of lamb £1.70, fillet of plaice £1.50, farmhouse grill £2.50). In the evening prices rise, but it is still possible to stay within the budget. For example, a grapefruit cocktail plus grilled gammon with cheesecake to finish will cost you £4.25. Of the specials, chicken Maryland is good value at £3. Coffee is 35p per cup.

Brighton

THE CYPRIANA STEAK HOUSE AND GREEK RESTAURANT, 22 Preston Street (Brighton 202661)
Open: Mon-Sun 12noon-3pm, 6pm-1am

C P S

This small, intimate restaurant specialises in Scotch beef and authentic Greek food. English dishes consist of about eleven appetisers, fish, poultry, grills, flambés and omelettes. Greek specialities include as appetisers houmous or taramasalata, both at around £1. Main courses such as moussaka or stifado (beef cooked with shallots and served with rice and potatoes) cost about £3.40. Sweets from the trolley are around 75p. For a real treat, try a Meze – 'a full two-course meal consisting of fourteen delicious Greek dishes to satisfy the most discerning palate'. This is served for two or more people and costs around £4.50 per person.

DANSKE HUS, 163 Western Road (Brighton 202803)
Open: Mon-Sat 9.30am-6pm

C P S

The Danes seem to be renowned in this country for open sandwiches and pastries. You'll find both here, at reasonable prices. It is time to throw your misconceptions about sandwiches being mere snacks to the wind. Try a Dane's delight for around £1 and bite through layers of roast pork, red cabbage, pickled cucumber, orange twist, prune, lettuce and rye bread! Alternatively, for between £2.50 and £4, you can linger over your selection from the Danish smørgasbrød. In addition there is an interesting international menu including baked potatoes or crêpes, stuffed with enticing fillings from about £1.35-£1.85, and various hot meals. Apart from the selection of home-made cakes and pastries, melt-in-the-mouth waffles with various accompaniments for around 55p-80p will threaten your waistline.

MEETING HOUSE, Meeting House Lane (Brighton 24817)
Open: summer: Mon-Sun 8am-6pm, winter: Mon-Sat 8am-6pm

P S

Tom and Sean Wall preside over their modern coffee shop-cum-snack bar with its wooden tables and bench seats, bright décor and counter service. Hot and cold dishes are available, including quiche lorraine and salad or steak and kidney pie at around £2, and there is also a good selection of cold meats. Starters include minestrone or French onion soup for about 40p and you can finish with a delicious Danish pastry or a slice of apfel strudel at about 50p.

TUREEN RESTAURANT, Upper North Street (Brighton 28939)
Open: Tue-Sat 12noon-2pm, 7-9.30pm, Sun 12noon-2pm

C

This unpretentious bistro-style restaurant features a large Japanese tureen in the window and floral-patterned banquettes along the walls. Cuisine is English with French influence and the à la carte menu offers a host of delights. However, we suggest our readers stick with the £3 set lunch, which offers three courses such as salami and tomato vinaigrette, roast shoulder of lamb with apricots, and banana nut sundae. On Sundays a traditional English roast with starter and sweet will cost £5.25.

Broadstairs

THE MAD CHEF'S BISTRO, The Harbour (Thanet 69304)
Open Mon-Sun 10am-3pm, 6-11pm (closed Tue in winter)

C P

Paul Ward is the Mad Chef at this little bistro on the harbour at Broadstairs. The emphasis here is on freshly caught fish and seafood. Lobster and turbot can be expensive but sample the lunchtime Quickies menu which includes crab or cockle and mussel omelettes for around £1.20. The à la carte menu offers other specialities such as pheasant and turkey pie or mixed meat kebabs, both at around £4. Starters include gazpacho, and there is a huge list of tempting sweets. Lovers of Dickensian memorabilia will be interested to note that the Mad Chef's is situated between Dickens' House Museum and Bleak House. Booking is essential on summer evenings.

Camberley

ROBBO'S WINE BAR, 125 London Road (Camberley 21096)
Open: Mon-Sat 11am-2.30pm, Mon-Thu 7-10.30pm, Fri-Sun 7-11pm

C P S

From medical publishing and high-flying with British Airways Robert and Simone Evans have brought to Robbo's a natural flair and enthusiasm for food and good atmosphere despite their lack of previous experience. The emphasis at Robbo's is on relaxed environment where home cooking can satisfy every taste. From cauliflower bolognese at £1, hoppel poppel (a strange sounding potato dish) Vienna steaks and sirloin steak in French bread at £1.75, a typical lunch will cost around £3.60, including wine, sweet and coffee. The evening menu changes into a cosmopolitan affair, with starters such as Alabama prawns and a main course of Robbo's 'veal birds' (veal escalope rolled and filled with Stilton and cream).

Canterbury

ALBERRY'S WINE AND FOOD BAR
38 St Margarets Street (Canterbury 52378)
Open: Mon-Thu 11.30am-2.30pm, 6-10.30pm, Fri-Sat 11.30am-2.30pm, 6-11pm, Sun 6-10.30pm

C P S

A genuine Roman pavement in the basement bar is the talking point of this establishment, where for the price of a steak sandwich you buy a whole evening of entertainment. Jazz, rock and folk musicians often play beneath the arched ceilings. A good selection of wholesome food includes quiche and salad for around £2 and the very popular steak sandwiches served with salad for about £3, with a variety of fresh fruit (such as pineapple and mangoes) for a nourishing last course.

TUO E MIO, 16 The Borough (Canterbury 61471)
Open: Tue 7pm-12mdnt,
Wed-Sun 12noon-3pm, 7pm-12mdnt

C ♫ P S ♣

This cosy Italian restaurant is run by energetic proprietors Raffaele and Patricia Greggio. Unusual dishes such as quails, guinea fowl and pigeon are available on the à la carte menu for about £4 including potatoes, as well as the more predictable veal, chicken and pasta selection – all at around the £3.25 mark. Desserts are all about 70p.

Chichester

THE COFFEE HOUSE, 4 West Street (Chichester 784799)
Open: Mon-Sat 10am-5.30pm
(half-day Thu during winter months)

S

Emphasis here is upon simple, no-nonsense food made from fresh ingredients and cooked on the premises. Plats du jour, including shrimp or chicken salads cost from £1.60 upwards. Three-egg plain omelettes are also available, as is Welsh rarebit at around 65p. The licensed restaurant menu is restricted but it's excellent value, particularly the cold buffet dishes at around £1.60-£2.

JASON'S BISTRO, Cooper Street, off South Street (Chichester 783158)
Open: Mon-Sun 12noon-2pm,
7-10.30pm

♫ S

Tucked away in Chichester's Cooper Street is Jason's Bistro, where a team of staff run by Gerhard and Enid Boesser serve bistro-style lunches and dinners in this spacious and imaginatively-modernised old outhouse building. Starters, including home-made soup with hot garlic bread range from about 60p to £1.50. The 'Chef's Dish of the Day' is usually an excellent buy at around £2; other main courses cost between £1.75 and £4, including vegetables.

Deal

THE HARE AND HOUNDS
Northbourne (Deal 65429)
Open: Mon-Sun 12noon-2.30pm,
6-11pm

C ♫ P

Here's a charming country pub where everyone is catered for; you can have a quick nibble at a bar snack or enjoy a leisurely restaurant meal at a modest price. There are three or four 'specials' which are changed daily, one of which could be home-made soup, boeuf carbonnade and vegetables followed by fresh cherries in brandy, and all for comfortably under a fiver. Alternatively you can sample one of a wide variety of home-made quiches or a succulent steak and kidney pie with vegetables for about £1.50. Finish with a slice of home-made cheesecake or Black Forest gâteau.

Eastbourne

NEW LOUNGE, 4 Cornfield Terrace (Eastbourne 31309)
Open: Tue-Sun 11.45am-2pm

P ♣

Joyce Ellis prepares good, plain English fare in this family-run restaurant. Although at weekends a more exotic, à la carte menu is offered, the workaday table d'hôte lunch offers a choice of soup or fruit juice followed by fish, roasts, steak and kidney pie; liver and bacon or cold buffet. Puddings include home-made fruit pie and custard or various sponges for an all-inclusive price of around £2.40.

Egham

MAGGIE'S WINE BAR, 2 St Judes Road, Englefield Green (Egham 37397)
Open: Mon-Thu 11am-2.30pm,
7-10.30pm, Fri-Sat 11am-2.30pm,
7-11pm, Sun 12noon-2pm, 7-10.30pm

C ♫ P S ♣

If you are energetic enough you can 'do' the Runnymede Memorial, the Kennedy Memorial, the RAF Memorial, and still be in time for Sunday brunch at Maggie's. If you wrongly feel that Sunday brunch at under £2.50 is not filling enough, enjoy a traditional three-course roast meal with a free glass of wine at around £4. Afterwards you can watch Prince Charles play polo at nearby Windsor Great Park, or you could stay with the Sunday papers that are provided. Sue de Barra, a Cordon Bleu cook, creates daily menus which include unusual soups such as egg and prawn at around 70p, home-made pâtés at around £1, moussaka and lasagne at around £2, speciality creole and paella dishes, and for the trencherman, an English sirloin steak platter at around £5. Partner Bob Grahamslaw shares the cooking even after a hard day in London selling an exotic brand of Swedish motor car.

Ewell

THE LOOSE BOX, 3 Cheam Road
(01-393 8522)
Open: Mon-Sat 11am-2.30pm, 5.30-10.30pm

[♫] [P] [S]

This stylish wine bar is a hub of activity in this suburban Surrey village. One attraction is the dazzling array of bargain-priced food – game pie and salad at only around £1.50, a selection of home-made quiches with salad and lasagne both around £1. Cheesecakes, gâteaux or home-made apple pie are all about 60p.

Farnham

SEVENS, 7 The Borough
(Farnham 715345)
Open: Mon-Sat 12noon-2.30pm, 6.30-10.30pm (Fri-Sat 11pm)

[C] [♫] [P] [S] [♧]

Sevens has an intimate atmosphere – from the crowded wine bar at the front to the low-ceilinged bistro at the rear and on the first floor. Starters range from about 65p-£1.30 and include a delicious mushroom pâté. Main courses start at around £2.50 for lasagne or chili con carne to about £4 for rump steak with dishes like coq au vin, barbecued beef and sweet and sour pork in between at around £3.50. Sweets and cheeses are all about 90p. Very popular with students from Farnham Art College, business people and shoppers, it is wise to get to Sevens early!

Faversham

CHIMNEY BOY, Preston Street
(Faversham 2007)
Open: Mon-Sat 11am-3pm, 5.30-11pm, Sun 12noon-2pm, 6-10pm

[♫] [P] [S] [♧]

Husband-and-wife team Jackie and Tony Richards run this pub-cum-restaurant built on a Roman burial ground. They offer four starters and a selection of about eight main courses of the traditional type – steak, chicken, scampi and salads. Meals in the bar consist of grills, burgers, a vast selection of sandwiches, hot dishes of the day, cold buffet and basket meals.

THE RECREATION TAVERN RESTAURANT, 16 East Street
(Faversham 6033)
Open: Mon-Sun 12noon-2pm, 7-10pm

[C] [♫] [P] [S] [♧]

Once a 17th-century, square oast house, this small tavern has been tastefully restored by the present owner. You can choose from a hot or cold buffet including over a dozen salads, meats cut from the bone and a variety of quiches accompanied by salad plus coffee for around £1.50 upwards. You may also be tempted by one of Chef Graham Blackwell's delectable sweets. Interesting hot dishes are always available at under or around £5.

Folkestone

PULLMAN WINE BAR, 7 Church Street
(Folkestone 52524)
Open: Mon-Sat 12noon-2pm, 7-10pm

[♫] [P] [S] [♧]

The Tudor-style building housing Michael and Janet Barnwell's wine bar is thought by some to be the most beautiful in Folkestone. Hot and cold dishes are presented buffet style. Soup is around 60p and a main dish, such as chicken with cider and calvados or pork marengo costs about £3.25. Sweets such as gâteaux and flans are about £1. In fine weather, meals may be enjoyed in the attractive garden.

Godalming

MAIGRETS BISTRO, 78 High Street
(Godalming 29191)
Open: Mon-Sat 12noon-2pm,

7-10pm

[C] [♫] [S] [🍷]

You won't find any trench-coated French police inspector in this quaint olde-worlde restaurant. Maigret, in this case, is the name of the pleasant lady owner and cook, Maigret Bricusse. The interior is a cosy low-ceilinged, beamed and half-panelled room which is all the more romantic in the evening, by candlelight. Bay windows overlook the main shopping street of Godalming. A blackboard menu offers a selection of well-cooked dishes at reasonable cost. A sample meal might include starters of avocado viniagrette or taramasalata at around 85p, main dishes such as chicken Somerset cooked in cider with celery and vegetables for about £2.50 or a selection of salads with prices starting at £1.60. Sweets cost 75p and there's as much coffee as you can drink for 35p.

Guildford

THE CASTLE RESTAURANT, 2 South Hill (Guildford 63729)
Open: Mon-Sat 12noon-2pm, 5.30-11.30pm (last orders 9.30pm) Sun 12noon-2pm

[C] [P]

The older part of this restaurant blends well with the garden effect of the extension, with its stone floor and brick walls. Table d'hôte lunches cost around £4 for two courses or £4.50 for three courses. Seafood pancake is one of eight interesting starters on offer, and of eleven main courses, kidneys with mushrooms in red wine sauce is recommended. The list of sweets is impressive, chestnut ice cream sundae being one of the more unusual examples. Dinner is around £2 extra.

PEWS WINE BAR, 21 Chapel Street (Guildford 35012)
Open Mon-Sat 11.45am-2.30pm, 6.30-11pm

[♫] [S] [🍷]

David Allen runs Pews with flair and a friendly smile. Formerly an old ale house, the building's split-level rooms have dark beams and wood panelling, but are bright with log fires in their proper season and fresh flowers all the year round. The blackboard menu has a choice of hot dishes, from around £2, for example chicken Portugaise and chili con carne and a variety of curries.

YVONNE ARNAUD RESTAURANT
Millbrook (Guildford 69334)
Open: Mon-Sat 12.30-2pm, 6.15-11pm

[C] [♫] [P] [S] [🍷]

You won't go far in Guildford without seeing mention of the Yvonne Arnaud Theatre. A set lunch in the curved Theatre Restaurant costs about £3.60 for two courses and around £4.25 for three. The menu is constantly changing, as a high percentage of patrons are regular play-goers. Evening meals are excellent, but alas, out of our league.

Hastings

CROSSWAYS, Lower Pett Road, Fairlight (Pett 2356)
Open: Tue-Sun 12.30-2.30pm, 7.30-9.30pm

[P] [🍷]

Well-prepared, good-value English cooking is the keynote of this small restaurant, looking very like a modern village home at the crossroads in Fairlight. A three-course lunch costs only about £2.75 and offers such old favourites as home-made steak and kidney or chicken and mushroom pies, roast beef with Yorkshire pud or roast chicken. Sweets, also home-made, include blackcurrant and apple pie or rhubarb crumble. The dinner menu is à la carte and more exotic fare such as rainbow trout with almonds (around £3) is available. With starters ranging from 30p for soup of the day to 90p for prawn cocktail and desserts from 40p, you will still have change from a fiver.

Hayward's Heath

COUNTRY AND WINE, 124 South Road (Haywards Heath 58040)
Open: Mon-Sat 10am-10pm

[C] [♫] [P] [S] [🍷]

This modern bistro specialises in home-cooked fresh food and choice wines and real ale. Décor is rather exotic, with plush wall-to-wall seating, bamboo cane divides, and fresh flowers on every table. Salads and other dishes are on show in a large display cabinet. The menu includes various cold meat salads and a hot dish such as chicken casserole at about £2.95. Home-made soup and pâté are tasty starters at around £1.40 and sweets include huge fresh cream meringues. A thriving take away service also operates.

Herne Bay

LA CHANDELLE, Charles Street (Herne Bay 61126)
Open: Tue-Sat 12noon-2pm, 7-10.30pm, Sun 12noon-2pm

[C] [♫] [P] [🍷]

This French restaurant provides informal eating in the downstairs wine bar, where various hot dishes, pâtés, cheeses and salads are served at about £1.25. Sweets include chocolate brandy cake at around 80p. In the main restaurant the table d'hôte lunch includes a choice of five starters and five main courses, a sweet and coffee for about £4.25.

Horsham

MERRYTHOUGHT RESTAURANT
5 Bishopric (Horsham 4894)
Open: Mon-Sat 9.30am-5pm, Sat 12noon-2.30pm

[🍷]

Michael and Margaret Bance welcome you to their Victorian-style restaurant where snacks are served all day and a comprehensive lunch menu operates from 12noon to 2.30pm. A three-course meal for *two* people may be savoured here for around £5. Soup is only around 30p and main dishes such as boiled ham, beef curry or salads are about £1.50. Puddings such as fruit salad vary in price from 40p-50p. Merrythought is unlicensed, so you will have to wash down your meal with a cup of steaming coffee at 30p.

PILGRIM'S HALT, 24 West Street (Horsham 63281)
Open: Mon-Sat 12noon-2.30pm

[P] [S] [🍷]

A sister restaurant to last year's 'thousandth entry' winner in Maidstone, this first-floor premises in a 13th-century building is run along the same lines as its now-famous twin by Ruth and Dennis Treadaway. Home-made soup or pâté are typical starters at 50-75p, main dishes include Wiltshire gammon or Scotch beef goulash at around £2.60. Fruit salad laced with muscatel is a must at 85p.

Lewes

PAUL'S WINE BAR, 53 High Street (Lewes 4676)
Open: Mon-Fri 10am-2.30pm, Sat-Sun 10am-6pm

[♫] [P]

Original oak beams in this 400-year-old building lend atmosphere to the wine bar which operates on two floors. The printed menu offers budget grills – sirloin or rump steak is only about £2.50 and lamb cutlets £2. The cold buffet includes smoked mackerel or turkey at around £1. Chef's Daily Specials are highly recommended and veal and mushroom pie at around £1 or beef goulash at £1.20 are examples. Gâteaux, fruit salad and ice cream are some of the sweets available. In the evening you may savour your food to the sound of the guitar.

Maidstone

THE PILGRIM'S HALT, 98 High Street (Maidstone 57281)
Open: Tue-Sat 12noon-2.30pm, 7-10.30pm, Sun 12.30-3pm

[C] [♫] [S] [🍷]

Winner of our 1981 thousandth entry competition, The Pilgrim's Halt remains excellent value for those who will join the search for imaginative meals served in pleasant surroundings throughout the coming year. Daily specials such as old English casserole represent best value for money, but fillet of North Sea plaice or Wiltshire gammon won't break the bank at under £2.50. Finish with vanilla ice cream with hot chocolate fudge sauce.

Nutbourne

CEDAR TREE RESTAURANT
On A27 near Bosham (Bosham 573149)
Open: Tue-Sun 12noon-2.30pm, 7-10.30pm

S

David and Sue Ullah have successfully converted a one-time transport café, on the main Emsworth-Chichester road, into a thriving little restaurant. Set lunches are £1.75 and include roast of the day and home-made steak and kidney pie, plus salads as a lighter option. During the evenings prices go higher, but it's still possible to eat well for around £4.50. A large coffee is around 40p a cup.

Petworth

THE LICKFOLD INN, Lodsworth, 3 miles west of Petworth off A272 (Lodsworth 285)
Open: normal licensing hours

P

Real ale fanatics will feel at home at this old hostelry and free house, serving a wide selection of beer from the wood. To soak up their liquid intake, they might also be interested in the lunchtime menu of home-made steak and kidney pie, moussaka and other hot dishes, plus a good range of snacks and sandwiches for under £2. Evening meals include a wide table d'hôte selection for around £4, in which Mexican lamb cutlets, halibut mornay and mignon of beef chasseur might figure. Add a starter (whitebait?) and a sweet such as chocolate rum crunch to make a really memorable meal.

Reigate

HOME MAID, 10 Church Street (Reigate 48806)
Open: Mon-Sat 6.45am-6pm, Sun 10am-3pm

As the name suggests, the atmosphere is homely, the food simple. The staff have a warmth and courtesy that is almost old-fashioned. Black beams offset cool white walls and checked tablecloths. Two three-course lunch menus, served from 11.30am, at £2.15 or £3.75 are of the grill, roast or fried variety, with fresh vegetables when available. Traditional puds follow, including steamed sponges and rice pudding. Individually-priced grills and snacks are also available throughout the day, giving a café-style service, although Home Maid is licensed.

Sandwich

16TH CENTURY TEA HOUSE, 9 Cattle Market (Sandwich 612392)
Open: Mon-Sun 9am-6pm, 7-11pm

P S

Set in the market square of the picturesque old town is this historic 16th-century building with a quaint, beamed restaurant. A three-course lunch is served here for around £3.75. Appetisers include Normandy pâté with toast or hors d'oeuvres. Home-made steak and kidney pie or sweet and sour chicken with special fried rice are two of the five main courses on offer, and desserts such as chocolate nut sundae or baked lemon curd roll complete the meal. A suggested evening dish is grilled gammon steak Hawaian style which, with starter and sweet costs around £4.80.

Seaford

REGENCY RESTAURANT, 20 High Street (Seaford 895206)
Open: summer Tue-Sun 12noon-2.15pm, 6.30-9.30pm, winter: 12.30-2.15pm, 6.30-9.30pm, Sun 12.30-2.15pm

S

Head for the daily special three-course menu served on the ground-floor of this two-floor restaurant, and you'll be well within budget. Upstairs, the menu's more elaborate and a bit out of our range. All the cooking is masterminded by Andrew Robertshaw, the restaurant supervised by his partner Eric Molton. Special main courses may include plaice or cod, home-made steak and kidney pie, roast chicken or chicken leg cooked with wine and mushrooms, all served with fresh vegetables. The set price of £3-£4 includes soup or fruit juice starter and choice of sweet.

Tunbridge Wells

BRUINS, 5 London Road (Tunbridge Wells 35757)
Open: Mon-Sat 12noon-3pm, 7-11pm

[C] [♫] [P] [S] [🍷]

Good food, good wine, good ale and great company are what Randy and Gill Brown, owners of Bruin's, view as life's '*bear necessities*'. All three are taken care of in this bistro-style restaurant, decorated in shades of brown and adorned with an assortment of teddy bears that give the restaurant its name. Choices from the long and varied menu include starters such as home-made French onion soup at around 70p, and main courses like whole baby chicken provençale (around £4) or Bruin's casserole at about £3. Dessert choices for around 85p include pancakes, apple crumble and ices. Bruins burgers (100% beef) make a cheap and satisfying main course at around £2, including French fries, salad and relish. A range of bar snacks are available on the ground-floor dispense bar.

Westerham

THE HENRY WILKINSON, 26 Market Square (Westerham 64245)
Open: Mon-Thu 12noon-3pm, 7-10.30pm,
Fri-Sat 11.30am-3pm, 7-11pm

[S]

This new wine bar has a pleasant restaurant with pine tables and a good choice of home-made casseroles and soups, fresh salads, savoury flans and pies. The blackboard menu displays the special hot dish of the day for lunch and supper, which is usually served with potatoes or rice and a green salad. Desserts include meringue glacée and a pudding of the day for around 75p and a three-course meal may cost from £4.50 upwards.

Worthing

HAPPY CHEESE, Liverpool Buildings, Liverpool Road (Worthing 201074)
Open: Mon-Sat 8.30am-5pm

[♫] [S] [🍷]

Two floors are devoted to this modern eating place and bar. A wallboard menu offers such dishes as home-made soup, roast chicken with vegetables, pizzas and salads. A three-course meal with coffee and wine need not cost more than £5 and there's plenty of choice.

'And not a girl goes walking
Along the Cotswold lanes
But knows men's eyes in April
Are quicker than their brains.'

JOHN DRINKWATER

Regional Dishes

Brown Windsor soup laced with Madeira
Poached salmon from the River Severn
Marrowbones with toast
Aylesbury duckling with sweet Oxford sauce
Double Gloucester cheese

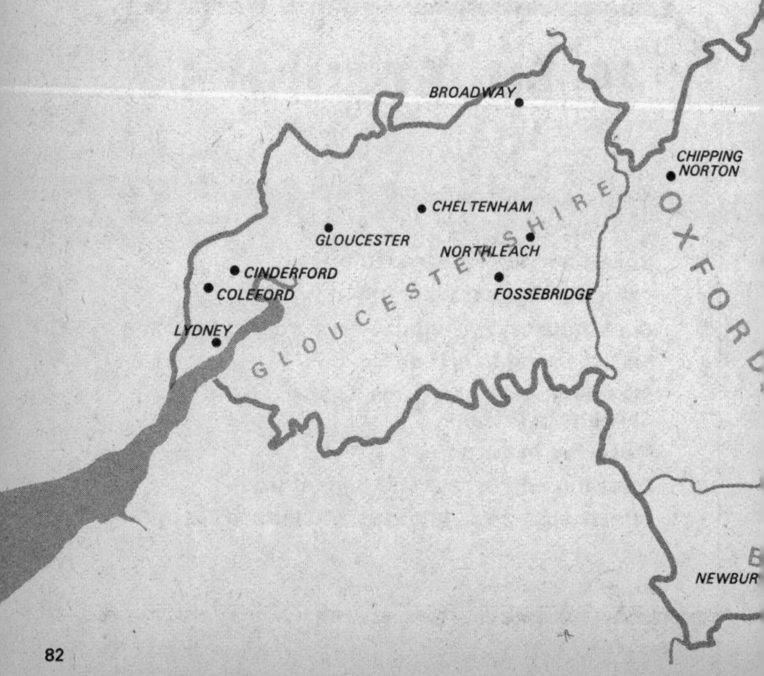

Cotswolds and Chilterns

4

Amersham

BEAR PIT BAR AND BISTRO
Whielden Street (Amersham 21958)
Open: Mon-Sun 12noon-2.30pm, Sun-Thu 7-10.30pm, Fri-Sat 7-11pm

[C] [♫]

A bear-baiting pit can still be seen inside this delightful, period bistro which is almost concealed in the courtyard of the 16th-century Saracen's Head pub. 'Beginnings' include 'Bloody Mary' soup (70° proof – B. marvellous!) or grilled smoked mackerel, both around £1. Main courses are from around £2. Particularly recommended is a spicy chili con carne served with a crisp salad and hot pitta bread. The French dressing is outstanding. Alternatives include marinated beef kebab, gammon, trout, steak, crab salad Louis or Bear Pit Burgers. 'Endings' offer a good choice and chocolate gâteau with whipped cream is about £1.

THE ELEPHANT AND CASTLE, High Street (Amersham 6410)
Open: summer: Mon-Sun 12noon-2pm, 7-9.30pm

[C] [P] [⚘]

This historic pub, covered with climbing roses, offers good-value, well-prepared meals for the hungry public. Steak pie and two veg or Spanish omelette are popular choices costing around £2 and £2.25 respectively. You can take lunch in any part of the low-beamed, olde-worlde pub that takes your fancy, and in addition, there's a small-budget à la carte menu offering mostly grills. Children are welcome in the pleasant beer garden.

THE HIT OR MISS INN, Penn Street Village (High Wycombe 713109)
Open: Mon-Sun 12noon-2pm, 6.30-10pm. Closed: last week in Jul, first week in Aug

[P]

Within range of six from its own cricket ground across the road – any customer can join the club and play – this aptly-named wisteria-covered 17th-century inn is a big hit with the locals and visitors alike. In the Cricketers Bar, they can also enjoy an excellent selection of home-cooked fare available every day for lunch or dinner. Chef's pâté and toast is about £1, spaghetti bolognese around £1.70, and strawberries when in season about 45p, or try a 'steak butty' – sirloin steak grilled with onion and garlic, sandwiched in French bread and costing around £2. In addition, the restaurant serves an excellent three-course budget menu at lunchtime for about £5. Choice is wide – prawn and tomato medley, sauté of beef paprika and peach fool is a good example.

PAUPERS, 11 Market Square (Amersham 7221)
Open: Mon-Sun 12noon-2pm, 7-10pm

[C] [P] [⚘]

Situated close to the parish church of St Marys, Paupers is housed in an attractive cottage with its black and white Tudor-style exterior gaily decorated with brass coach lamps and striped awnings. Inside is a warm 17th-century room which retains much of the period atmosphere with an inglenook fireplace, exposed beams, polished oak tables and pew seating. The menu offers two set dinners, two courses for less than £5 and three courses for just over £6. Appetisers include mushroom pâté or prawn salad with seafood sauce and a choice of six main dishes includes lemon chicken or baked bream. Finish with a home-made sweet and a cup of freshly-ground coffee.

Aylesbury

THE BODEGA WINE BAR, The Market Square (Aylesbury 27582)
Open: Mon-Sat 10am-2.30pm, 6.30-10.30pm, Sun 7-10.30pm

[♫] [P] [S]

The Bodega from the 18th century is all that remains from the days of the historic George Hotel, which boasts a tunnel, used by Roundheads, under the Market Square. This sophisticated, well-decorated wine bar offers food cooked to perfection. A blackboard lists a hot dish of the day such as chili con carne, lasagne or beef curry at around £1.50 and cold meats such as turkey breast or ham off the bone with salad at around £2, topside of beef for about £2.50 (including kouskous or coleslaw) and American cheesecake for around 65p. The 1982 menu will include some German dishes.

THE HEN AND CHICKENS AT AYLESBURY, Oxford Road (Aylesbury 82193)
Open: Mon-Sat 12noon-2pm, Tue-Sat 7-10pm

[C] [P] [S] [⚘]

This popular pub with its attractive ship-boarding stands on the Oxford Road roundabout close to the original

'Aylesbury duck' pond. Norman Haggan, the genial landlord welcomes you to the pleasant restaurant, tastefully furnished with pinewood tables and dresser and adorned by candles on the tables. Starters include delicious smoked mackerel (about 80p) and among the interesting main courses are pork chops in honey sauce at around £2.70, Aylesbury duckling at about £4 and speciality mixed grill (around £3.50). Traditional English Pudding of the Day costs about 60p.

Baldock

THE VINTAGE WINE BAR, 3 Hitchin Street (Baldock 895400)
Open: Mon-Sun 12noon-2.30pm, 7-11pm

C ♣

This old timber-frame house near the centre of Baldock has been converted into an attractive wine bar. Husband-and-wife team Barbara and Peter Clarke cook and wait at table, preparing at least two hot dishes a day. You could start with stuffed cucumber at 40p, followed by pork in spicy orange sauce or trout stuffed with prawns and cooked with garlic at £2.30. Sweets such as pears in chocolate sauce and home-made cheesecake run from 60-70p. An attractive children's room is available.

Bedford

GREEK VILLAGER RESTAURANT
36 St Peters Street (Bedford 41798)
Open: Mon-Tue 6pm-1am, Wed-Sat 6pm-2am, Sun 6-11.30pm; Closed: last two weeks in Aug

♫ P S

Bursting with authentic atmosphere and cuisine, this taverna is a fun restaurant not to be missed. As well as the usual taramasalata, tsatsiki and houmous, starters include delicious horiatiki salata topped with crumbly fetta cheese and olives (about £1). You are spoiled for choice with main dishes. Dolmades for around £3 is particularly full of flavour. Greek sweets include baklava, siamali and kateifi and are about 80p each.

Berkhamsted

PATRICIA'S RESTAURANT
40a Lower Kings Road
(Berkhamsted 2048)
Open: Mon-Sun 12noon-3pm, 7-9pm Closed: Wed

C ♫ P

This warm, friendly and comfortable restaurant is a family-run business with father and daughter doing the cooking and Patricia attending to the diners' needs in the restaurant. Emphasis is on English food, and table d'hôte lunch and dinner menus are offered from as little as £3 or £4. Traditional Sunday lunch is available. The à la carte menu offers all the good basic meat and fish dishes. Prices range from around £4 for roast beef or roast pork to about £6 for mixed grill.

Bishop's Stortford

THE SWAN RESTAURANT
88 South Street
(Bishop's Stortford 52007/59439)
Open: Mon-Sat 9am-9.30pm, Sun 12noon-2.30pm

C ♫ P S ♣

A delightful Regency-style frontage with attractive half curtains on brass rails tempts you to explore further into this restaurant. On the à la carte menu, the home-made soups and selection of omelettes are to be recommended, although more exotic dishes such as melon liqueur and Porterhouse steak garni are offered at prices coming close to our limit. A daily lunch menu costs around £3 for three courses plus coffee, with Sunday lunch at around £4.50 for adults, half price for children.

Broadway

COTSWOLD CAFE AND RESTAURANT, The Green (Broadway 853395)
Open: summer Mon-Fri 10am-6pm, Sat-Sun 10am-8pm, winter: Mon-Sat 10am-5.30pm, Sun 10am-6pm

The Cotswold Cafe and Restaurant has counted amongst its customers John Wayne and the pop group Genesis. Delicious home-made ice creams are for sale, a speciality of Mrs Susan Webb's family since 1945. The restaurant serves snacks and three-course à la carte meals throughout the day, with prices varying from about £2 for roast chicken, fresh vegetables and two kinds of potato to around £4 for sirloin steak.

THE GALLERY RESTAURANT
North Street (Broadway 853555)
Open: Tue-Sun 11am-9pm. Closed: Jan

P

A former 16th-century coach house, this restaurant's white-painted interior has a wealth of black timbers supporting the barn-type ceiling and a minstrel's gallery at the far end. A special three-course lunch includes fresh orange juice, roast beef and Yorkshire pudding and a choice of desserts such as lemon meringue pie, sherry trifle or gâteaux for around £3. Lunchtime specials offered include home-made steak and kidney pie, fried chicken or cod – all for around £1.50.

GOBLETS WINE BAR, High Street (Broadway 852255)
Open: Mon-Sun 12noon-5pm, 6-9.30pm

C P S

Dating back to 1631, this stone-built one-time inn is now a thriving wine bar. A stone-flagged floor with scatter rugs, and black and white half-timbered walls adorned by tapestry panels make an ideal setting for the numerous antiques. Imaginative home cooking and a warm welcome have made Goblets very popular with the locals. Appetisers include home-made mackerel and apple pâté at around £1 and Andalusian gazpacho (chilled tomato soup with garlic, onions and peppers). Chicken à la Indienne (strips of chicken in mild curry and peach sauce) is about £2.50, with honeyed pork or beef and prune casserole in the same price bracket. Desserts include Goblets gâteau and home-made coffee and walnut ice cream.

Buckingham

THE OLD MARKET HOUSE
The High Street (Buckingham 2385)
Open: Mon-Sun 12noon-2.15pm, 7–9.15pm. Closed: Sun and Mon pm

[♫] [P] [S] [♣]

The delightful, beautifully restored 14th-century half-timbered building immediately commands attention. The superb restaurant offers outstanding value for money. You can spend as much, or as little as you like at lunchtime, but with roast beef, two veg and two kinds of potato at £2, and plaice chips and peas at only £1.50 you'd be hard put to break the bank. The dinner menu is also extremely reasonable with an exciting choice for all courses. Potted shrimps, trout in almonds and sherry trifle 'with a difference' (the sherry bottle is brought to your table – all you have to do is say 'when') are typical examples at around £5. As a bonus, Bernard the saucy chef-cum-manager will tell you a tale or two.

Cheltenham

COTSWOLD HOTEL, 17 Portland Street (Cheltenham 23998)
Open: Mon-Sat: 12noon-2pm

[C] [P] [S] [♣]

What the Cotswold Hotel would be like without Con Carroll is anybody's guess. For over fifteen years he has presided over this ground floor bar, earning it an enviable name for superb lunchtime bar snacks. Centrepiece of the lunch operation is the carvery, offering hot roast beef, turkey and home-cooked ham with salad or vegetables, as well as smoked or fresh salmon with salad. A dish of the day is offered at £1.

FORREST'S WINE BAR
Imperial Lane (Cheltenham 38001)
Open: Mon-Sat 10.30am-2.30pm, 6-10.30pm

[♫] [P] [S]

Forrest's is tucked away in Imperial Lane just behind Habitat and is a useful venue at lunchtime or during the evening with the cinema nearby. The large, high-ceilinged ground-floor premises was formerly a bakery but has been cleverly adapted, with low-slung pendant lights and intimate eating areas cordoned off by waist-high walls. There are over twenty wines sold by the glass here at prices from about 60p to 90p. The menu changes daily but a typical one might well include a choice of soups at around 40p, a continental ploughman's (with sausages) or a pizza with tossed salad, both at about £1 and a choice of three enticing plats du jour such as beef casserole with red wine and mushrooms, or grilled rump steak from just £2 to around £4.80.

MISTER TSANG ✕ 63 Winchcombe Street (Cheltenham 38727)
Open: Mon 7-11.30pm, Tue-Fri 12noon-2pm, 7-11.30pm, Sat 12noon-12mdnt

[C] [S] [♣]

Food 'to indulge the palate and encourage good health' is what Mister Tsang and his family aim to provide. We were impressed by the nutritious and tasty house hors d'oeuvres at about £1.60, beef in black bean sauce (around £2.70) and king prawns with ginger and spring onions. To keep within the budget and do justice to the extensive menu, go with a friend or three! The seafood pot (a secret recipe, costing about £4.50) is very tasty, and Mister Tsang's 'Introduction to True Cantonese Cuisine' for two or more people works out at about £4 a head for a good variety. Desserts include Chinese toffee apples and are around £1.

MONTPELLIER WINE BAR AND BISTRO, Bayshill Lodge, Montpellier Street (Cheltenham 27774)
Open: Mon-Sat 12noon-2.30pm, 6-10.30pm (11pm Fri-Sat), Sun 6-10.30pm

[C] [P] [S]

This imposing Regency building behind the Montpellier Rotunda has been converted from a long-established grocer's shop into a ground-floor wine bar and cellar bistro. You can buy ten or so wines by the glass for about 50p upwards. Notice boards display the daily menu, which includes hot soup at around 50p among the dozen or so starters, a hot speciality dish of the day, a variety of pies, smoked meats and fish from around £1.50 to £2.50, interesting salads, and tempting sweets from 75p.

Chipping Norton

BEAN FEAST, 7 Horse Fair (Chipping Norton 2320)
Open: Mon-Wed, Fri-Sat 10am-2.30pm

[P] [S]

This pretty, whitewashed cottage houses a delicatessen and wine bar, both of which specialise in home-made, unusual food. You could try the French onion soup with toasted cheese croûtons at around 50p and move on to scrumptious spinach and cottage cheese roulade at only £1.30, followed by a delicious sweet such as lemon fluff with shortbread, black cherry and almond frangipan or strawberry tartlets. Or you could head straight for the salad counter, where mixtures such as cracked wheat with mint, lemon juice, parsley vinaigrette and diced cucumber costs a mere 25p a portion.

MARKET HOUSE, 4 Middle Row (Chipping Norton 2781)
Open: Mon-Wed, Fri-Sun 10am-6pm (Fri-Sat 8pm summer)

[P] [S]

A peep through the dimpled bow windows is likely to reveal tempting desserts such as chocolate fudge gâteau on display; be assured it tastes as good as it looks. We tried fried fillet of plaice served with crisp golden chips and garden peas (£2.20) and noticed the colourful fresh salads being served to other diners. Apart from the chocolate gâteau we could have tried banana split, pineapple meringue glacé, peach melba and a few others for around 80p. Sandwiches, scones and snacks are served throughout the day.

Cinderford

THE WHITE HART HOTEL RESTAURANT AND BISTRO
St White's Road, Ruspidge (Cinderford 23139)
Open: Mon-Sun 12.15-2pm, 7.30-9.45pm

[C] [P]

Meals can be taken in the restaurant or bistro. An extensive à la carte menu features the popular Forester's Grill for around £3.30. Dishes such as pork tenderloin, steaks and chicken Kiev are about £4.75, so if you want a starter and a sweet you will have to choose carefully to stay around £5. The cold table in the bistro has meats and interesting salads which you serve yourself – as much as you want for around £2. A snack menu includes Californian salad (chicken, sweetcorn and home-cooked ham with lightly curried mayonnaise) at about £2.20 and hot dishes such as chili con carne at £1.50. Traditional Sunday lunch is served at around £5.

Coleford

WHITE HORSE INN, Staunton (Dean 33387)

Open: Mon-Sat 12noon-2pm, 7-10pm, Sun 12noon-1.15pm, 7-10pm

[P]

This early Victorian pub, strategically sited 'twixt Coleford and Monmouth on the A4136 in the beautiful Forest of Dean, was built on top of a much older hostelry which now forms the inn's Cellar Restaurant. Prices are a little above our limit here, but the Saddle Room Grill, complete with beams and stable paraphernalia, offers well-prepared food which is both economical and interesting. Home-made liver pâté is about £1 and home-made soup 50p. Smoked mackerel or local trout served with vegetables are both around £3. Dish of the day could be lasagne, coq au vin or home-made chicken and mushroom pie at around £1.50.

THE WYNDHAM ARMS ✕ Clearwell (Dean 33666)
Open: Tue-Sat 12noon-2pm, 7-10pm, Sun 12noon-2pm, 7-9.30pm

[C] [P] [♧]

Built in 1340, in the centre of the ancient Dean Forest village of Clearwell, this picturesque inn has long been renowned for the excellence of food served in the à la carte restaurant. The Wyndham Arms has also gained an enviable reputation for satisfying bar snacks and for appetising meals in the Grill Room, whitebait or mushrooms tartare cost about £1.95 in the bar, while egg and prawn mayonnaise or chicken liver pâté are a few pence less. An extensive range of grills includes fresh local trout, pork chop, gammon steak and fillet steak, served with all the trimmings and costing from around £4-£6. Home-made desserts are around £1.

Datchet

THE UPPER CRUST WINE BAR
Country Life House, Slough Road (Slough 49314)
Open: Mon-Thu 11am-2.30pm, 6-10.30pm,
Fri-Sat 11am-2.30pm, 6-11pm

[C] [♫] [♧]

Despite its name, Mrs Diana Vernon-Smith's wine bar offers good home-made food at anything but upper-crust prices. French cane stools and polished-topped tables, plus several modern pictures, all blend well with the modern décor. A typical bar meal displayed on the daily-changing blackboard menu is quiche with salad (£1.50), fresh cream gâteau (90p) and coffee (35p). There's live music here every Friday and Saturday night.

Eton

THE ETON BUTTERY, 73 High Street (Windsor 54479)
Open: Mon-Sun 9.30am-7pm

[C] [♫] [S] [♧]

Alongside the Thames and next to the bridge joining Windsor to Eton is this bright, modern buttery with its smart French cane chairs and elegant pot plants. Take a tray and make your choice from the cool and colourful salads, cold meats and poultry on display, or try a hot dish such as chicken and ham vol au vent at around £2.75. Find a window seat and watch the boats on the river below, with Windsor Castle in the background.

ETON WINE BAR, 82-83 High Street (Windsor 55182/54921)
Open: Mon-Thu 11.30am-2.30pm, 6-10.30pm, Fri-Sat 11.30am-2.30pm, 6-11pm, Sun 12noon-2pm, 7-10.30pm

[S]

Within earshot of the famous College, this attractive wine bar is the place to go for good wholesome food and a folksy atmosphere. Décor is simple, with scrubbed wooden floors, church-pew seating and stripped-pine furniture. Alternatively you can sit out in the small garden. Mike and Bill Gilbey and their wives do the cooking, producing such delights as pâté village au poivre vert at around £1.35, chicken liver, bacon and egg mousse at £1.65 and chili pork at around £3.50. Desserts include Victorian Brown Bread ice cream.

Fossebridge

FOSSEBRIDGE INN ★★
(Fossebridge 310)
Open: Mon-Sun 12noon-2pm (Sun 1.30pm), 7-9.30pm

[P]

Ideally-placed in a wooded valley and beside a small river is this part-Georgian, part-Tudor inn, with its roaring log fires, stone walls and beautiful antiques. At around £1 you can sample starters such as mushrooms à la Grecque or spicy crab pâté, and a main course of home-made cottage pie or fresh local trout costs from around £2 upwards. The selection of home-made sweets may include a light and fluffy lemon meringue pie or a crispy bread and butter pudding.

Gloucester

THE COMFY PEW, College Street (Gloucester 20739)
Open: Mon-Sat 9am-5.30pm

[S]

On the main approach to the cathedral, The Comfy Pew lives up to its name with some entirely appropriate seating. Michael Edgington's food is home-cooked and wholesome; it's reasonably priced too, with soup, roll and butter at around 60p, a variety of meat or fish salad platters from £1.75, pâtés with salad and toast, curried prawns and snacks on toast all under £1.50.

TASTERS WINE BAR, 22 London Road (Gloucester 417556 and 23536)
Open: Mon-Thu 12noon-2.30pm, 7-10.30pm, Fri-Sat 12noon-2.30pm, 7-11pm, Sun 12noon-2pm

[P] [S]

This cheerfully decorated bar, close to the city centre features mainly cold dishes such as Stilton and spring onion quiche or mackerel pâté (at about 75p) but cider-baked gammon or Normandy pork may be the hot dish of the day, both at around £2 and extremely tasty. Boston aubergines or curried prawn and melon balls cost around £1. Crisp, fresh salads and potato dishes are in demand and sweets cost 60p-£1.

Hatfield

CORKS AND CRUMBS
23 Park Street, Old Hatfield (Hatfield 63399)
Open: Mon-Sat 10am-11pm

[C] [♣]

This wine bar and coffee house, with pretty patio and terrace, in the old part of Hatfield, is run by a husband-and-wife team. It's small, attractive, and imaginative, with a menu to match. Corks and Crumbs wins points for offering a vegetarian pie, hot cheesy pepper, or courgette and tomato gratin (none much over £1). For the meatier-minded, the daily special main courses from £3-£5.50 may feature Mexican lamb with savoury rice and vegetables, or kidneys in red wine sauce. Wines are imaginatively chosen too, the restaurant is not afraid to offer lesser known varieties from Chile or Argentina.

Hemel Hempstead

THE OLD BELL HOTEL, High Street (Hemel Hempstead 52867)
Open: Mon 12noon-2pm, Tue-Thu 12noon-2pm, 7-9pm, Fri-Sat 12noon-2pm, 7-10pm

[C] [P] [S]

Built in 1580, and an inn since 1603, the Old Bell is a fine example of a 17th-century hostelry. Here you can dine by candlelight in the original Tudor dining room with its intriguing 19th-century French wallpaper. Appetisers include melon with orange segments and curaçao for just over £1. Main courses include lamb kebab at around £3 or pepper steak, cooked in butter and finished with brandy and cream at £4.

Hertford

THE WENDY HOUSE & PETER PAN'S PANCAKE PARLOUR, 3 St Andrews Street (Hertford 50582)
Open: Wendy House: Mon-Sat 10am-3pm Pancake Parlour: Thu 6.45-10pm, Fri-Sat 6.45-11.15pm

[♣]

Just as you might expect in Never Never Land, there's a touch of magic about this two-in-one restaurant. Wendy herself runs the low-profile daytime business, serving a good selection of simple home-cooked snacks, salads, daily specials such as pork casserole (£1.75), and afternoon teas. Then, come Thursday evening, you're plunged into the altogether brasher, more adventurous world of Peter Pan's Pancake Parlour. The pancakes, stuffed with chicken, pork, cheese, minced beef or fish-based mixtures, come with a 'monster' salad. The £5 set price covers starters like stuffed mushrooms and sweets such as Wendy's date and walnut meringue kisses.

Leighton Buzzard

THE CROSS KEYS ✕ The Market Square (Leighton Buzzard 373033)
Open: Mon 10am-2.30pm, Tue-Sat 10am-2.30pm, 7-10pm, Sun 12noon-2.30pm

[C] [P] [S] [♣]

Opposite the famous 15th-century Market Cross, this pub food bar serves a selection of hot and cold snacks at budget prices. On fine days you can bring the children and enjoy food on the paved forecourt. A special children's menu operates – including egg salad at 50p to half-portion scampi and chips at about 70p. Hot snacks for adults are either served with chips or vegetables and potatoes – plaice, curried chicken, veal escalopes or hot dish of the day such as hot-pot or beef stew are examples, all in the £1-£1.50 range. Cold buffet meats, fish, pâtés and salads are reasonably priced and desserts such as gâteaux with fresh cream cost 60p.

Little Chalfont

THE COPPER KETTLE, Cokes Lane
(Little Chalfont 3144)
Open: Tue-Sat 9.30am-5pm

[P]

Simplicity is the keynote here, with polished tables and wheel-backed chairs for about twenty people. The lunch is home-cooked, just as mother used to make it and, astonishingly, below £3 for three courses. Soups or fruit juices are offered as appetisers. Main dishes served with a variety of fresh vegetables include steak or chicken and mushroom casseroles, roast pork and apple sauce or home-baked pies or flans. Cherry and apple sponge is a typical sweet.

Lydney

THE OLD SEVERN BRIDGE HOTEL
Purton (Dean 42454)
Off A48 between Lydney and Blakeney
Open: Mon-Sat 12noon-2.30pm, 6-11pm (10.30pm in winter), Sun 12noon-2pm, 6-10.30pm

[C] [S] [🍷]

It is said that Sir Walter Raleigh did his courting here – and small wonder – for the pleasant rural scene encompasses the River Severn and the Cotswold Hills. Now parts of this country inn date back only to 1835, but the setting is as romantic as ever; with lawns and terrace laid out with umbrella'd tables – and a fish pond. A small but tasty bar menu (beef casserole £1.30, lasagne £1.15) is supplemented by seasonal fresh fish (local trout £1.75), and fresh vegetables whenever possible.

Maidenhead

THE BACCHUS WINE BAR AND RESTAURANT, St Mary's Walk
(Maidenhead 36638)
Open: Mon-Sun 12noon-2.30pm
Tue-Sat 7-10.30pm

[C] [♫] [P] [S] [🍷]

If you are after something completely different, sample a Swiss cheese fondue in this tasteful wine bar, with its brick walls, stone floor, chunky wooden tables and candlelight. Slightly more expensive, at £3.75, are almond or mushroom cheese fondues. They are all served with a fresh potato dish of the day and a natural salad. Meat fondues are £5.25, so if you are an inveterate meat-eater you will have to forego the other courses. Starters include delicious pâté with cranberry sauce at around £1.65, seafood platter and avocado Bacchus, both £1.85. Desserts include Swiss chocolates and petits fours for 85p. If fondues are not your style, there is an excellent buffet lunch including fish, meat and cheese salads, and raclette (the house speciality) for around £2.50.

BUMBLES, Bridge Avenue
(Maidenhead 36724)
Open: Mon-Sun 12noon-2.30pm,
7-10.30pm

[C] [S]

Maidenhead's 'first American restaurant' is a friendly place with a bright attractive décor. An imaginative list of grills and burgers grace the menu and starters include Iowa corn chowder soup and spare ribs with barbecue sauce, both around £1. Spare ribs are also served as a main course (with a finger lickin' good Bumbles special sauce) for about £2.60 or, for the same price you might prefer a cadillac – a 6oz beefburger served on a bun with crisp back bacon and deep fried onion. Sweets include pan-fried pancakes with maple syrup at around 85p.

Marlow

BURGERS, The Causeway
(Marlow 3389)
Open: Mon 9am-12noon,
Tue-Sat 9am-5.45pm

[P] [S]

Opposite Marlow Park, this 17th-century building has been in the Burger family since 1942. The restaurant is on two levels. A simple, homely menu offers well-cooked food at very reasonable prices. Dishes include liver pâté or egg mayonnaise as a starter, steak and kidney pie or chicken and ham vol-au-vents with potatoes and vegetables, plus walnut torten or Black Forest gâteau and cream to finish. A three-course meal costs around £3.20.

Newbury

CROMWELL'S WINE BAR, 20 London Road (Newbury 40255)
Open: Mon-Sat 10.30am-2.30pm,
6-10.30pm (11pm Fri-Sat),
Sun 7-10.30pm

[C] [P]

Though a Courage Brewery-owned wine bar, Cromwell's avoids any big business anonymity, thanks to friendly table service from Mike and Jenny English, and a relaxed, warm interior. Bare floorboards, pew seating and checked tablecloths are the setting for 'no frills' fare. There's a good selection of hot and cold dishes on display, including pizza and salad (£1.40), daily specials from £1.40, and grilled local trout with salad (£3). A choice from the sweet flans and gâteaux or cheeseboard, will keep you well within budget.

THE HATCHET, Market Place
(Newbury 47352)
Open: Mon-Sat 12.30-1.45pm,
6.30-9.45pm, Sun 7.30-9.45pm
Newbury Race Days: Opens 12noon

[C] [P] [S]

By the Corn Exchange in this attractive market town, you'll discover this interesting restaurant, with its unique ceiling of wattle sheep-pen fencing. Emphasis is on grills and roasts at competitive prices. Rump steak is around £4, lamb cutlets or shallow-fried rainbow trout about £3. A good selection of starters includes seafood cocktail and there are tempting sweets from the trolley to complete the meal.

THE SAPIENT PIG, 29 Oxford Street (Newbury 44867)
Open: Mon-Fri 12.30-2pm, Tue-Sat 7.30-10pm

[C] [♫] [P] [S] [♣]

This sophisticated bistro is steeped in Laura Ashley. The cosy atmosphere is an ideal setting for the delicious home-cooked fare. Hot dish of the day is around £3 and could be anything from sauté of pork provençale to Olde English steak and kidney pie – both served with three vegetables. Coronation chicken is an appetising cold dish costing around £2 and salads are available from 40p. Desserts, including such delights as strawberry Pavlova or apfel strudel cost around £1.

Northleach

COUNTRY FRIENDS ✕ Market Place (Northleach 421)
Open: Tue-Sat (lunch by appointment only) 7-9.30pm, Sun 12.30-2pm

[C] [P]

The table d'hôte at this charming Cotswold-stone restaurant is excellent. For around £4.75 on weekdays and about £5.75 on Sundays, you can enjoy an imaginative meal which offers a choice of starters – a soup, perhaps a fish pâté – and a main course served with potatoes and fresh vegetables. On Sunday the choice of main course includes a roast, and weekday menus include such things as gingered pork chops, or seafood pancake; sweets might include chocolate roulade.

Olney

THE OLNEY WINE BAR, 9 High Street South (Bedford 711112)
Open: Mon-Sat 12noon-2pm, 7-10.30pm (Fri-Sat 11pm)

[P] [S]

The charming Georgian shop front of this wine bar leads into a room with an attractive open fireplace. The original bakehouse ovens are still to be seen in the back room. Bill of fare is on a blackboard and includes hot burgundy mushrooms and taramasalata, both at around £1.20, and Swedish chicken for around £1.50. Pork fillets in tarragon and mushroom sauce and Westmorland tart are specialities.

Oxford

BURLINGTON BERTIE'S RESTAURANT AND COFFEE HOUSE
9a High Street (Oxford 723342)
Open: Mon-Sun 10am-12mdnt

[S] [♣]

Look above the covered market in Oxford High Street, and there's Bertie's – all plants, pub mirrors, cane-bottomed chairs and highly-polished tables with wrought-iron pedestals. You can get a meal or any kind of drink here at any time. The cuisine is English and Continental, the service fast and efficient, the welcome warm and friendly. Salads are priced at under £3, spaghetti and pasta dishes at under £2.50, and meat and fish main courses at under £5. Desserts include 'specials' such as pancake surprise for around £1.

MAXWELL'S, 36 Queen Street (Oxford 42192)
Open: Mon-Sun 11.30am-12mdnt

[♫] [S] [♣]

A bright and breezy first-floor restaurant where the high ceiling, iron girders and steel supports give an aircraft-hangar effect. American-style food is efficiently served in an informal atmosphere. Specialities such as lamb kebab, chili and chicken (around £2.75) supplement the hamburgers, which come with French fries, tossed salad and a choice of dressings. Ice cream sodas and milk shakes continue the American theme.

THE NOSEBAG, 6-8 St Michaels Street
(Oxford 721033)
Open: Mon-Sat 10am-5.30pm
(Fri-Sat 6.30-9.30pm),
Sun 12noon-5.30pm

[♬] [S]

Inelegant its name may be, but this upstairs, split-level restaurant, with its oak-beamed ceiling and bright and homely décor, has a certain charm all of its own. The lunchtime hot dish of the day for around £1.70, is likely to be moussaka, chicken à la crème or herrings in oatmeal. A tempting choice of original salads (as much as you like) costs around 80p. With soup at about 60p and hot garlic bread at about 40p, the three-course lunch must be a bargain, even after ordering delicious home-made ice cream or sorbets. And on Friday and Saturday evenings the Nosebag offers an excellent three-course meal for just under £5 with exciting main courses such as mackerel with gooseberry sauce.

OPIUM DEN ✕ 79 George Street
(Oxford 48680)
Open: Mon-Sat 12noon-2.30pm,
6-12mdnt, Sun 1-2.30pm, 6-12mdnt

[C] [♬] [P] [S]

Don't let the name discourage you, the only addictive thing sold at the Opium Den is the food. Cantonese with a few Pekinese dishes, the specialities of the house are the sizzling dishes brought piping hot to your table on wooden platters. Lunchtimes are always busy, with a table d'hôte menu available at around £2.50. The à la carte is extensive, with prices to suit all pockets. Set dinners are particularly reasonable at around £6-£7 for two people.

Reading

BEADLES WINE BAR, 83 Broad Street
(Reading 53162)
Open: Mon-Sat 10.30am-2.30pm,
5.30-10.30pm

[C] [♬] [S]

This popular basement wine bar is situated on the one-time site of Simmonds Brewery and the original globe lights are still a splendid feature. An interesting selection of food includes 'snacks for the peckish or starters for the starving' such as taramasalata at around £1.30. Main courses served with salad could be roast beef, turkey, chicken, dressed crab or prawns, depending on their availability or a hot dish such as prawn risotto (£1.30) or pork in a cream and mushroom sauce, served with courgettes and potatoes at around £1.75. Delicious home-made sweets follow.

THE GEORGE HOTEL ★★ King Street
(Reading 53445)
Open: Mon-Sun 12noon-2.30pm,
6-11.30pm (Sun 7-11pm)

[S] [♧]

The historic, timbered George Hotel complete with cobbled courtyard and stagecoach has obscure origins, but appears in a rent roll dated 1578. Today it boasts four steak bars of distinctive character. The Cocked Hat, Pickwickian and Cavalier Grills and Rib Room offer an excellent selection of grills and roasts. Half a roast duckling with apple sauce and jacket potatoes is very good value at around £5.50-£6 – this includes a choice of sweets or cheeses.

HEELAS RESTAURANT, Broad Street
(Reading 55955)
Open: Tue-Sat 9.30am-5pm
(6.30pm Thu, 5.30pm Sat)

[P] [S] [♧]

Still a haven in one of Reading's most popular department stores, but now relocated and newly built on the second floor, Heelas' restaurant offers a relaxing break from the hustle of a busy day's shopping. Predominantly green and white décor with lots of leafy green plants is complemented by the classy contemporary prints which line the walls. Smart waitresses provide swift service and the food tastes all the better for being served on modern Wedgwood bone china. There are meals to suit everyone, from a half portion of fish and chips for children and a Danish open sandwich, piled high with meat or cheese and salad, for the weight-conscious to the Chef's choice roast beef and Yorkshire pudding. This meal is the most expensive but even with three courses and coffee you could still have change back from £5.

MAMA MIA, 11 St Mary's Butts
(Reading 581357)
Open: Mon-Fri 12noon-2.30pm, 6-9.30pm
(Fri 10pm) Sat 12noon-10pm

[C] [♬] [P] [S] [♧]

The trattoria Mama Mia serves only Italian food and wines in an almost operatic setting of rough-cast, white-painted walls, crowned by rafters hung with clusters of Chianti bottles and strings of onions and other vegetables. Home-made soups at around 85p, pastas and pizzas from around £1.90, offer excellent value, although penny- and weight-watchers are advised to resist the entrées.

SWEENEY AND TODD, 10 Castle Street (Reading 586466)
Open: Mon-Sat 11am-3pm, 5.30-10.30pm (Fri-Sat 11pm)

[P] [S] [♧]

Through the Victorian pie shop, up sawdust-strewn steps, is this small saloon-type restaurant, with church pew seating, copper rail curtains and gilt globe lighting. Lunchtime specials such as roast suckling pig cost around £2.20, with fresh vegetables at 40p. Imaginative home-made pies (about £1.10-£1.40) include steak and oyster, kidney and fennel and poachers (mixed game). 'Vicars' lunches consist of a plate of cold meat with French bread, pickles and salad and they set you back around £2. Home-made treacle tart, apple pie and crumble and fresh fruit with cream are some of the home-made desserts on offer for 65p-80p.

TRUNKWELL HOUSE, Beech Hill (Reading 883754)
Open: Mon-Sat 12.30-2.30pm, 7.30-10.30pm (Fri-Sat 7.30-11pm), Sun 12noon-2pm, 7.30-10pm

[C] [♫] [P] [♧]

Hard to find, but well worth the effort, this imposing Victorian house is hidden 300 yards down a single-vehicle-width road. Owner Isidro Rodriguez does the cooking, while his all-male Spanish staff wait at table. The food is superb, with a businessperson's lunch of chicken, veal, pork chop, steak (all in gorgeous sauces) or an enormous trout with crisp vegetables, starter, sweet and coffee for about £5. On summer days a cold buffet with smoked salmon or cold meats is served in the garden for £4.

Redbourn

AUBREY PARK HOTEL ☆☆☆
Hemel Hempstead Lane, Redbourn, St Albans (Redbourn 2105)
Open: Ostler's Room: Sun-Sat 12.30-2pm, 7-10pm (Sat 7-10.30pm)

[C] [♫] [P] [♧]

The warmly-glowing Ostler's room, with its glazed brickwork and low-beamed ceilings, is dedicated to the serving of traditional English dishes in an atmosphere of medieval jollity. A wholesome three-course meal can be picked from a choice of kitchen-garden broth or Whitby mix (prawns, crabs and mussels in a cocktail sauce), followed by deep dish steak and kidney pie, braised beef in stout, or Studham spatchcock (whole baby chicken in a piquant sauce) and finishing with pastries and puddings from the cook's pantry.

Rickmansworth

THE CHEQUERS RESTAURANT
21 Church Street (Rickmansworth 72287)
Open: Mon-Sun 12noon-2pm, 7-10.30pm

[C] [♧]

The Chequers Restaurant, built in 1580, is the oldest building in this old town. Another Four Pillars Group venture, the menu and prices are comparable with those at the Pinner restaurant, though during any particular week the actual dishes available are different. There is a separate, more expensive steak menu. A table d'hôte lunch is available at about £2.25 a head.

St Albans

BLACK LION HOTEL, Fishpool Street, St Michaels Village

(St Albans 51786/64916)
Open: Mon-Fri 12noon-2pm, 7-10pm, Sat 12noon-2pm, 7-10.30pm, Sun 12noon-2.30pm

[C] [P]

Modernisation has not stripped the interior of its character and old beams and brickwork abound. In the bar an impressive cold buffet is on display for £2.50 and a hot dish of the day such as Irish stew costs around £2. A table d'hôte menu in the restaurant is priced by the main dish – from about £5 for lamb sweetbreads with banana or fillet of plaice bonne femme to nearly £6 for escalope of chicken Viennoise or roast pork. Appetisers include corn on the cob, ham and cottage cheese coronet and a selection of home-made soups. Choice from the sweet trolley is good.

TUDOR TAVERN, 28 George Street (St Albans 53233)
Open: Mon-Sun 12noon-2.30pm, 6-11pm

[C] [P] [S]

The special thing about Berni is that it restores and preserves some of this country's most attractive old buildings. The Tudor Tavern is the oldest complete half-timbered building in the ancient city of St Albans. Many main-dish prices here include tomato soup to start, roll and butter, and ice cream or cheese and biscuits to follow, so an 8oz rump steak with chips, tomato and peas at about £5 is just in our price range.

Thame

THE COFFEE HOUSE, 3 Buttermarket (Thame 6302)
Open: Mon-Tue, Thu-Sat 10am-5pm

[P] [S]

This charmingly decorated restaurant with its pine furniture, white walls, large open fireplace and green plants was opened in 1979. Appetisers include home-made pâté with brandy, served with French bread (the most expensive starter at around £1.50), main courses include spaghetti bolognese made with wine, pizza salads and a daily special such as cottage pie or chicken and ham pie all for around £2.50. Desserts include chocolate rum mousse for around 85p.

Theale

RED PEPPERS, 21 High Street (Reading 303408)
Open: Tue-Sat 12noon-2pm, 7-10pm

[C] [S]

We had a very enthusiastic report from the AA inspector who visited Red Peppers. Things start looking good from the moment you sit down and are offered crudités. The atmosphere created by proprietors Guy and Lynne Symons is spontaneous and warm, the food is freshly cooked, home-made and generously apportioned. There's something about a well-prepared Lancashire hotpot (£2.95) that beats any fancy foreign dish. Savoury pancakes filled with fresh ham, sweetcorn and béchamel sauce (£2.75) fill you up only too easily, but do save space for the rather special Knickerbocker Glory (£1) or choice from the selection of pies and puddings (75p).

Waltham Cross

SOUR GRAPES, 41b High Street (Lea Valley 718633)
Open: Mon-Thu 11am-2.30pm, 7-10.30pm, Fri-Sat 11am-2.30pm, 7-11pm, Sun 7.30-10.30pm

[P] [S]

Situated close to the 'cross', this attractive wine bar has maps of French vineyards on the walls and distinctive wooden tables and chairs making it a relaxed and casual rendezvous for lunch or dinner. The blackboard menu offers a hot 'dish of the day' for around £1.65, pizzas about £1.20 salads at around £1.70 and apple pie and ice cream for about 70p. Service is friendly and efficient and in fine weather you can enjoy your food in the peaceful garden at the rear.

Welwyn Garden City

TOBY FOOD AND WINE BAR
49 Wigmores North
(Welwyn Garden City 26663)
Open: Mon-Sat 11.30am-2.30pm, Wed-Sat 6.30-11pm

[C] [♫] [P] [S]

Striking artwork and an attractive brown awning identify Toby's, where Eric and Elsa Norris both do the cooking for their popular wine bar. Dishes may include smoked mackerel at about £1.25, beef casserole for around £2 and home-made apple pie and fresh cream for about 75p. The Victorian décor of this first-floor, split-level bar, with its genuine mahogany bar front is an ideal background for enjoyment of both food and excellent wine. Downstairs, the Toby Grill serves breakfast.

Windsor

THE DRURY HOUSE RESTAURANT
4 Church Street (Windsor 63734)
Open: Tue-Sun 12noon-5.30pm

[♣]

In this charming 17th-century setting, within a stone's throw of the guardsmen at the gate of the Castle, Joan Hearne serves good, plain English food at no-nonsense prices, with a choice of salads from around £2.50 and of main dishes from £2, for grilled lamb's liver and bacon, to around £4.50 for three courses. Omelettes cost around £1.50. Home-made gâteaux are on sale.

LONDON STEAK HOUSE
10 Thames Street (Windsor 66437)
Open: Mon-Sat 12noon-3pm, 6-11pm, Sun 12.30-3pm, 6.30-10.30pm

[C] [S] [♣]

Handily placed for a visit to Windsor Castle, this busy restaurant, although small, has refreshingly uncluttered floor space. Traditional-style wall-lights interspersed with framed prints make for a pleasant enough décor. A well-cooked meal such as consommé printanier (55p), lamb cutlets (£2.60) and ice-cream (50p) sounds reasonable, but you'll need to add about £1 for veg.

Wingfield

THE PLOUGH INN
On the A5120 near Toddington
(Toddington 3077)
Open: Mon-Sat 12noon-2pm, 6-10.30pm, Sun 12noon-2pm, 7-10.30pm

[♫] [P]

A good place to stop when the weather's good, this Whitbread pub dating from the early 17th century is in pleasant countryside between Houghton Regis and Toddington, and has a garden. A fairly conventional choice of lunches is available (roasts, steak, fish, etc), but excellent value. Apart from peas, only fresh, local vegetables are served. Interesting specialities such as humble pie make filling main courses.

Winslow

THE BELL HOTEL, Market Square
(Winslow 2741)
Open: Mon-Sun 11.30am-2.15pm, 6-10.15pm (Sun 7-10.15pm)

[C] [♫] [P] [S] [♣]

Musical church bells provide an authentic background to the peaceful, historic atmosphere of the heavily-timbered and balustraded Claydon Restaurant of this 17th-century hotel. The table d'hôte menu in the restaurant offers three courses plus coffee for around £4. Tournedos Val Prais is an enterprising main course, and fresh strawberries and cream are served as a dessert when in season. The Wineslai Bar serves a good selection of grills including steak garni at about £3.25 or lamb chop, pork chop or plaice for around £2.50. French fries and chips are included. A lunch special with vegetables of the day costs about £1.75.

Woolhampton

THE ROWBARGE, Station Road
(Woolhampton 2213)
Open: Mon-Sun 12noon-2pm, 7-9pm

[♫] [P] [♣]

Character actor Lawrence Naismith presides over this low-ceilinged inn. The menu changes every day, but excellent examples are home-made rissoles in wine gravy with sauté potatoes at about £1.50 or haddock Monte Carlo (served with parsley and egg sauce, poached egg and sauté potatoes) at around £2.20. Also on offer is cheese and bacon flan at about £2.

'Oh, London is a fine town,
A very famous city,
Where all the streets are paved with gold,
And all the maidens pretty.'

GEORGE COLMAN

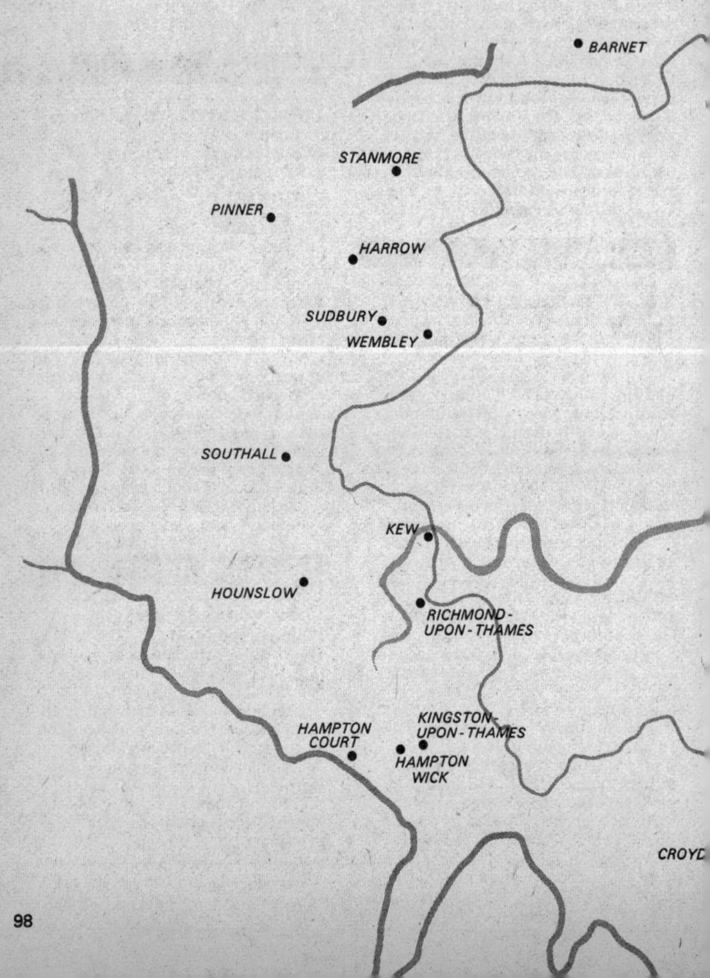

Greater London

Regional Dishes

Boiled beef and carrots
Bangers and mash
Roast beef and two veg
Steak and kidney pudding
Cockles, winkles and mussels
Jellied eels

5

FIELD

ILFORD

UPMINSTER

BARKING

dex to Inner London
tries shown overleaf

BROMLEY

Greater London Index

E1

DICKENS INN, St Katherine's Way, St Katherine's Dock (01-488 2208)
Open: Mon-Sat 12noon-2.30pm, 7-10pm, Sun 12noon-2.30pm

This old brewery dates back to around 1780 and the fact that the building was at one time moved several hundred feet is reflected in the huge oak pillars and beams supporting it. The Tavern Room on the first floor offers a good cold collation specialising in seafood and including cockles at about 70p, prawns for around £1.20, ploughman's at around £1.25 and cold meat salad for about £2.20. This restaurant is conveniently-placed for holiday-makers making a tour of the Tower or viewing the old Thames sailing barges in the nearby marina.

GRAPESHOTS, 2-3 Artillery Passage (01-247 8215)
Open: Mon-Fri 11am-3pm, 5-7pm

C P S

For a wine bar in Artillery Passage Grapeshots is an appropriate name, but put out of your mind the fact that grapeshot was produced by dropping lead from a height into water – the grapes here are of a more fruity variety. This Davys of London wine bar, on the ground and basement floors of a building round the corner from Petticoat Lane, is rather on the small side but with an intimate, relaxed atmosphere. The menu is limited and largely cold but good value at around £2 for an enormous helping of cold meat, with a mixed salad at 60p. Game, salmon and strawberries are sold in their proper seasons.

EC1

THE COFFEE SHOP AT THE WHITBREAD BREWERY
Chiswell Street (01-606 4455)
Open: Mon-Fri 8.30am-5.30pm, Sat 9am-4pm

The large brewery complex houses this bright little restaurant with its country-kitchen atmosphere and quaint cobbled courtyard. Simple food is served here, with at least one hot dish such as chicken à la king (around £1.50) available daily to supplement the many salads, which cost between £1-£1.30. Finish with a no-nonsense pud such as jam roly-poly and a cup of coffee.

EC2

BALLS BROS, 6-8 Cheapside (01-248 2963)
Open: Mon-Fri 11.30am-3pm, 5-7pm

[C] [P] [S]

This is a typical Balls Bros City outlet, with food at lunchtimes only, but an excellent wine list including some very reasonable half-bottles. The ground floor bar and basement restaurant serve satisfying snacks and sandwiches, a range of good salads and one hot dish daily, all from around £2-£3.50. This is a friendly and comfortable little bar, with a faithful following among City folk.

BALLS BROS, Moor House, London Wall (01-628 3944)
Open: Mon-Fri 11.30am-3pm, 5-7.30pm

[C] [P]

Don't look for an evening meal here, because you won't find it. The lunchtime menu is a typical one for the Balls Bros chain, with hot and cold dishes from around £2.85, as well as sandwiches and salads. Portions are generous, and service excellent, and the atmosphere very friendly. As with all the BB outlets, the long-staying staff know their customers and it's nothing to see a City gent waiting for 'his own' waitress to be free to serve him.

BALLS BROS, 42 Threadneedle Street (01-283 6701)
Open: Mon-Fri 11.30am-3pm, 5-7pm

[C]

This is the smallest Balls Bros wine bar and (at the time of writing, at least) the only licensed premises in Threadneedle Street. Very popular with stockbrokers, this intimate little wine bar has only sixteen covers and offers a very limited menu and sandwiches, but what there is is good. No food after 3pm.

THE CITY BOOT, 7 Moorfields High Walk (01-588 4766)
Open: Mon-Fri 11.30am-3pm, 5-8.30pm

You can buy extremely fine sandwiches here from around 95p, as well as the usual range of Davys of London salads and cold meats for about £2.50 a sizeable portion. The food side of the operation (lunchtime only) is small and simple but very good. One Davy's treat is the serving of grouse, partridge, pheasant and Scotch salmon when in season. Polished wood and candles help to create a serene atmosphere.

THE GEORGE AND VULTURE
3 Castle Street (01-626 9710)
Open: Mon-Fri 12noon-3pm

[C]

Charles Dickens stayed at The George and Vulture and made it famous in his 'Pickwick Papers'. But even without Dickens it has a claim to fame as probably the oldest tavern in the world, for it is known to have existed in 1175 although only one wall remains of the old structure. The present building retains the Pickwickian aura and is almost a museum in its own right. You can't stay there now, but you can have a substantial lunch at a very reasonable price. There is a good selection of starters, most of them around £1. Fish and main courses (a good mixed grill, for example) are from £2.50, with vegetables extra. For a sweet there is, in season, fresh strawberry flan, and a variety of other items. Stilton cheese is recommended, but there is plenty of choice from the cheese board. The restaurant is available in the evening for private functions – just telephone for menu details.

EC3

CITY FLOGGER, 120 Fenchurch Street (01-623 3251)
Open: Mon-Fri 11.30am-3pm, 5-7pm

[C] [S]

Although it is in the basement of a modern office development, this Davys of London wine bar next door to Mappin & Webb has the Group's usual 19th-century décor, with sawdust on the floor, hessian-covered walls and wood panelling. A special plate of prawns at £1 is particularly recommended as are seasonal game dishes. There are French-bottled house wines from 90p or so a glass. Don't just turn up and expect to get in, for the place is usually jam-packed with people from Lloyds and the City banks who have their lunch at the City Flogger every day.

EC4

BOW WINE VAULTS, 10 Bow Churchyard (01-248 1121)
Open: Restaurant: Mon-Fri 12noon-3pm, Wine bar: Mon-Fri 11.30am-3pm, 5-7pm

The minimum charge of £4 for lunch at the Bow Wine Vaults would buy you baked Scotch salmon with mayonnaise or perhaps you would prefer smoked chicken salad for around £2. Starters are priced from 80p for chilled watercress soup to £1.50 for smoked salmon mousse. Main courses include daily specials at around £2.90-£3.90 and for a sweet you might choose chocolate truffle or strawberry fool, at £1 or so. The restaurant is a converted warehouse with whitewashed walls, but a Victorian atmosphere is created by the furnishings and bric-à-brac.

CORTS, 33 Old Bailey (01-236 2101)
Open: Mon-Fri 11.30am-3pm, 5-8.30pm

[C] [♫] [S]

Rub shoulders with lawyers (and possibly criminals too!) in this comfortable wine bar near the Central Criminal Court. Maybe, though, you'd be more interested in the young and pretty waitresses. Food at lunchtime is straightforward and enjoyable, with soup at about 80p, a selection of quiches, pies and cold meats for around £2 (potatoes and salad could add about £1), and cheesecake, chocolate gâteau or apple pie at £1 or so.

MOTHER BUNCH'S WINE HOUSE
Old Seacoal Lane (01-236 5317)
Open: Mon-Fri 11am-3pm, 5.30-8.30pm

[C] [P] [S]

Under the railway arches in Old Seacoal Lane, hard by Ludgate Circus, this Davys of London wine bar does a nice line in Buck's Fizz at £2.50 a tankard. Food (do book for the place is extremely popular) is mostly cold but very tasty and good value. A generous plate of finest ham off the bone or game pie with mixed salad or hot potatoes can be had for under £2.50. Seafood is a speciality here.

OODLES, 31 Cathedral Place
(01-248 2559)
Open: Mon-Fri 11.30am-7pm

[P]

Although it's in a new building, this Oodles has succeeded in retaining the character of all the others, even though this branch is unlicensed. See under Marble Arch W2 for full description.

OODLES, 3 Fetter Lane, Fleet Street
(01-353 1984)
Open: Mon-Fri 11.30am-3pm

In the heart of the newspaper world, this Oodles offers identical menu and atmosphere to the branch described under Marble Arch W2. But it's open for only 17½ hours in the week.

SLENDERS WHOLEFOOD RESTAURANT AND JUICE BAR
41 Cathedral Place (01-236 5974)
Open: Mon-Fri 8.30am-6.15pm

[♫] [P] [S] [🍷]

Situated in a quiet backwater of the City, and with an equally quiet décor of natural brick, wood and hessian, Slenders is tremendously popular. There is seating for over 100 in separate booths. At lunchtime it is extremely busy. The menu is vegetarian and you can obtain a good wholesome meal for about £1.80. Everything is prepared on the premises, including the wholemeal bread. A good mixed salad or a hot dish such as vegetable and cheese flan or stuffed peppers costs about £1.10 for a portion, and sweets – chocolate mousse or fresh fruit salad are around 65p each.

N1

GRAPES WINE BAR, The Mall, Camden Passage, Islington
(01-359 4960)
Open: Mon-Tue, Thu-Fri 12noon-3pm, 6pm-1am, Wed and Sat 12noon-1am

[♫] [P]

This sophisticated wine bar spills out on to a pretty verandah and subtle décor including cushioned 'milk churns' make it a most original haunt. On Saturdays you can enjoy live folk music or even a Noël Coward evening! Original dishes include aubergine Charlotte at around £2, chili con carne garnished with fresh apple for about £2, home-made desserts such as cheesecake and summer pudding.

N6

THE FLASK TAVERN, 77 Highgate West Hill, Highgate Village (01-340 3969)
Open: normal licensing hours

[C] [P] [S] [♲]

Built in 1663, The Flask Tavern has been the haunt of many interesting characters, including the legendary highwayman Dick Turpin and distinguished painters Hogarth, Morlane and Cruickshank. During the summer the natural wood tables, set out in the large stone courtyard, are constantly in use. You may eat a snack in one of the three popular bars, but if something more substantial is preferred, a good three-course meal can be had in one of the bars for around £3. Starters include soup or grapefruit, main course sauté kidneys, fried plaice, fried rock salmon or cod and shrimp Mornay. Dessert is a choice of ice creams or banana fritters.

N8

LA CRESTA RESTAURANT, 18 Crouch End Hill (01-340 4539)
Open: Mon-Fri 12noon-3pm, 5.30-11.30pm, Sat 5.30-11.30pm

[P]

A family-owned-and-run restaurant, where a warm welcome is assured. The menu is mainly Italian, with a few English fish and steak dishes thrown in for good measure. Highly recommended is the house speciality of veal escalope valdostana – a marvellous concoction of ham, cheese, spaghetti and veal at about £3, and the freshly-baked poppy seed bread which comes free with the main course.

NW1

FAMAGUSTA TAVERN, 3 Camden High Street (01-387 3391)
Open: Mon-Sun 12noon-3pm, 6pm-12.30am

[♫] [P] [S]

Be sure to have plenty of room under your belt when you visit Famagusta, for the delicious Greek cuisine, produced by proprietor Ioannas Louca, is served in very generous portions. There is always a choice of more than three 'Famagusta Specials', main courses served with potatoes or rice, and salad; and all but one are around £2.75. Hors d'oeuvres start at 65p with a choice of ten interesting Greek dishes such as kalamari – squid cooked in a wine sauce. Charcoal grills are also reasonably priced – try quails at about £1.50 each. Three courses, such as hors d'oeuvres, kebabs and sweet, plus coffee and wine may only cost around £5. The simple but effective décor is conducive to good eating, particularly in the evening when candlelit tables reflect a warm glow from the red tablecloths. Reproduction carriage lamps are the main form of lighting.

SEA SHELL, 33-35 Lisson Grove (01-723 8703)
Open: Tue-Sat 12noon-2pm, 5.30-10.30pm

Here is a fresh fish restaurant par excellence, where portion control has been abandoned in favour of customer satisfaction. A Rolls-Royce parked outside while its owner queues for a take-away cod and chips, or enjoys a quick sit-down meal in the small restaurant, is not an uncommon sight. Apart from the fried chicken, the menu is devoted entirely to fish such as plaice, cod, halibut, skate, lemon sole and Dover sole. An extremely satisfying meal can be had for around £3.50, including soup and sweet.

NW3

COSMO, 45-46 Northways Parade, Finchley Road (01-722 1398)
Open: Restaurant: Mon-Sun 12noon-11.30pm,
Coffee shop: Mon-Sun 8.30am-11pm

[S]

Mainly Hungarian, German and English food is served at this uncluttered restaurant with its large shop-front window. Try chilled fruit soup with macaroons for starters, then move on to Hungarian beef goulash with continental dumpling, or sweet and sour braised beef in raisin sauce with red cabbage. The unadventurous might be relieved to know you can get good old egg, sausage and chips here too. Sweets include Viennese apple strudel with whipped cream or creme caramel chantilly.

PEACHEY'S, 205 Haverstock Hill (01-435 6744)
Open: Mon-Fri 11am-3pm, 5.30pm-12mdnt, Sat 5.30pm-12mdnt, Sun 12noon-3pm, 7-11.30pm

C P

Down the road from the Post House and directly opposite Belsize Park tube station is this small wine bar and restaurant. Unusual décor features cigarette card sets in frames, Victorian prints, stuffed pike and trout in glass cases, a stag's head and numerous other exotic items of bric-à-brac. Ferns in hanging baskets add colour to the scene. The food selection, chalked up on a wallboard, changes daily but the standard menu remains constant. Starters such as kalamari are about £1.20. Hot dish of the day is from £2.50-£4 and a particularly delicious example is thinly sliced fried liver, covered with avocado slices and pieces of gammon. Chicken curry with peaches and rice is about £3.

PIPPIN RESTAURANT
83-84 Hampstead High Street
(01-435 6434)
Open: Mon-Sun 11am-12mdnt

C P

An enticing selection of vegetarian specialities in the shop window draws you into this interesting restaurant. Self-service operates – just collect a tray and have it laden with your choice from the list of items displayed on the wall menu. Everything is reasonably priced – salads, hot risotto and cauliflower cheese are all about £1.15, delicious nut roast around £1.15 and fresh fruit salad about 75p.

NW5

EDWARD'S BISTRO, 323 Kentish Town Road (01-267 6956)
Open: Mon-Sat 6.30-11pm

C P S

Edward's Bistro was built around an old shop and the old shop front has been preserved inside the entrance. Wood panelled walls hung with paintings, a dark ceiling and gingham-covered lamps hanging over each table complete the effect. Dinner here is pricey but excellent value, including specialities such as pork and pineapple kebabs, ragoût of beef and pepper or garlic steak. An imaginative three-course dinner can be enjoyed for about £5. All desserts are served with lashings of cream.

SE1

THE BOOT AND FLOGGER
10-20 Redcross Way (01-407 1184)
Open: Mon-Fri 11am-3pm, 5.30-8.30pm

Just off Southwark Street is an old ham-curing warehouse, part of which is the John Davy Free Vintner wine bar. One of the smaller Davy outlets, it offers one of the finest wine lists in the whole of London, including vintage ports going back to 1837. Dark wood, glazed partitions and comfortable seating lend a cosy air, and the bill of fare includes game pie at around £2 and plates of cold meats at around £1.80; a 'special' is a dish of prawns at about £1.20. There is an excellent cheesecake or you may care to finish with a couple of toasted fingers with anchovy or sardine.

ROYAL FESTIVAL HALL CAFETERIA
South Bank
(01-928 3246/2829)
Open: Mon-Sun 12noon-2.30pm, 5.30-8pm

P

Good places to eat are few and far between once you're south of the river, so it's worth knowing that you can use the Festival Hall cafeteria whether you're attending a performance or not. Quite near to Waterloo Station and not far from Waterloo Bridge, the South Bank complex is aesthetically pleasing even to those who are not too keen on modern architecture. The uncrowded cafeteria overlooks the busy and perennially interesting Thames, and provides a pleasant place to relax and enjoy a meal. Each day there are two hot dishes costing around £2.50 as well as cold meats and salads, and home-made sweets and good coffee are served.

RSJ, 13A Coin Street (01-928 4554)
Open: Mon-Fri 12noon-3pm, 7-11.30pm, Sat 7-11.30pm

C P

Once a stable but for the last thirty years a cycle warehouse, this newly-converted restaurant occupies prime position near to the West End and Covent Garden. Decorated in smart brown and white, it is deservedly popular with business-people from the nearby offices. Starters include watercress soup and haddock mousse (under £2) and main courses offer cold salmon-trout and calf's liver with avocado at around £3.25. Dutch apple pie, strawberries and cream and various sorbets provide the basis of the sweet selection.

SKINKERS, 40-42 Tooley Street
(01-407 9189)
Open: Mon-Fri 11am-3pm, 5.30-8.30pm

[C]

Built into the railway arches under London Bridge, next door to the London Dungeons horror museum, Skinkers is beautifully cool in summer, very spacious and relaxed, and enormously popular with City folk and local business people. Décor, menu and wine list are in Davy tradition. The buffet offers starters from about £1, a plate of finest smoked ham, roast beef or game pie (all at around £2), with a mixed salad at 60p or so. If you're going on the off-chance, get there early.

SE3

THE BARCAVE WINE BAR
7-9 Montpelier Vale, Blackheath
(01-852 0492)
Open: Mon-Sat 12noon-3pm, 5.30-11pm, (Fri-Sat 12mdnt)
Sun 7-10.30pm

Special feature of this wine bar is the pretty walled terrace garden on two levels with fountains, a fish pond and hanging plants – very restful on a summer evening. Listed on a blackboard are Today's Specials such as minute steak with chasseur sauce and new potatoes at £2.95, curry or cold chicken and salad at around £2.90. A printed menu offers a choice of eight starters from melon (about 60p) to pâté maison (about £1). Cold buffet includes excellent rare roast beef for around £1.70. Quiche or lasagne are examples from the hot buffet at about £1.50. Cheesecakes, gâteaux, trifles or fresh fruit salad are served, and cost from 90p.

KATE 2 BISTRO, 121 Lee Road
(01-852 3610)
Open: Tue-Sat 7-10.30pm

The food at this simple bistro presided over by Kate Lee and Diana Willis was described as the 'most enjoyable meal tasted in over thirty years of eating out' by one of our inspectors. A varied menu includes mackerel fillets in sherry sauce as an appetiser at about £1.20, home-made quiche and mixed salad for around £3, scampi served with mixed salad at £3.85, or steak pizzaiola at around £1.60 as main courses, and a selection of delicious desserts which change daily as shown on the blackboard. Special portions are offered for children.

SE9

BISTRO 22, 1 West Park, Mottingham
(01-851 2233)
Open: Tue-Sun 7-11.30pm

[C] [S]

French posters, bright tablecloths and candles lend an authentic air to this unpretentious bistro, where the menus are written in French and English. A host of interesting dishes are on offer, but care will be needed if you are to pick three courses for around £5, since vegetables are individually priced. Try prawn cocktail at less than £1, hot garlic bread (only about 20p), cocktail de fruits de mer – seafood in wine and cheese – around £3.60 *with* vegetables and syllabub au citron – about 80p.

MELLINS WINE AND FOOD, 90 Eltham High Street, Eltham (01-850 4462)
Open: Mon-Sat 12noon-2.30pm, 7-11pm, Sun 7-10.30pm

Mellins the apothecary stood here for

about 200 years and the wine bar has retained the signs, labels and display cases. An interesting menu offers hot or cold platters such as ham ratatouille or fish pie for under £2, chili con carne or moussaka for about £2.15, and goulash, chicken basquaise or pork'n peppers for close on £3.50. Banana mousse is one of the many tasty desserts.

SE10

BAR DU MUSEE, 17 Nelson Road, Greenwich (01-858 4710)
Open: Mon-Sat 12noon-3pm, 6.30-11pm, Sun 12noon-2pm, 7-10.30pm

[C] [♫]

This wine bar is on two levels with a cellar bar reached by a spiral staircase. Coats of arms and Dickensian prints enhance the décor. There's a good choice of starters but try the soup of the day, with French bread, at around 80p. Hot dishes such as pizza and salad (around £1.70) or a 6oz pure beefburger with salad and French fries (about £1.80) are recommended. Beef or ham salads at around £2.60 are particularly good. Desserts include cheesecakes, gâteaux and profiteroles.

DAVY'S WINE VAULTS
165 Greenwich High Road
(01-858 7204)
Open: Mon-Fri 11.30am-3pm, Mon-Thu 5.30-10.30pm, Fri 5.30-11pm, Sat 12noon-3pm, 7-11pm

[C] [P]

Under Davy & Co's head office building in Greenwich the old wine cellar is now used as a wine bar and eating house. Victorian touches add to the out-of-the-past aura and help to make this a most popular place. Davy's offer 'fine foreign wines' and 'rare ports of the finest vintages' to wash down their specialities such as avocado pear with prawns at just over £1.30, cold chicken cooked in red wine and spices at about £3.80, or the tempting fresh salmon salad at around £5.80. If you're looking for something slightly less expensive, why not try the cold buffet?

DIKS, 8 Nelson Road, Greenwich (01-858 8588)
Open: Mon, Wed-Sat 12noon-2pm, 7-11pm, Sun 12.30-3pm

[C]

Value for money is guaranteed at this delightful restaurant. Proprietor Dik Evans cooks all the food, even the bread rolls and mint fudge served with the coffee. The soup and pâté are served in terrines from which you help yourself to as much as you like. At lunch, three courses are priced by the main dish – veal scaloppini Viennoise with fruit juice and meringue glacé is £3.50.

GACHONS, 269 Greek Road, Greenwich (01-853 4461)
Open: Wed-Mon 10.30am-5pm, Thu-Sat 7-10.30pm

[♫] [P] [S] [♣]

Young chef/proprietor Marc Gachon-Dyer says his cooking has been greatly influenced by his French mother, and he produces a Cordon Bleu Chef's Special (such as kidney sautéd in wine with fresh vegetables) every day to prove it. In fact, this quaint little coffee house, with its bright pine furniture, caters for the majority of tastes by offering a selection of pastries and salads (about £1.75) to supplement the substantial hot meals, such as home-made quiche and chicken vol-au-vent.

THE SOURCE, 106 Blackheath Road (01-691 1010)
Open: Mon 12noon-3pm, Tue-Sat 12noon-3pm, 7-11pm

[♫] [♣]

Enthusiastic vegetarians, Keith and Norma Perry ensure that you enjoy wholesome, unadulterated food in pleasant surroundings – pine tables, a Welsh dresser and an old kitchen range set the scene for a gastronomic experience in healthy eating. Appetisers include stuffed vine leaves or mushrooms à la Greque, both around 95p. The list of main dishes is no less interesting, with stuffed pepper and ratatouille costing about £2.50 and quiche with salad and potatoes at around £2. All the desserts, such as cinnamon apple cake, are under £1 and are served with fresh cream or yoghurt.

SE19

JOANNA'S, 56a Westow Hill, Upper Norwood (01-670 4052)
Open: Mon-Fri 12noon-2pm, 6-11.15pm, Sat 6-11.15pm

[♫] [P] [S] [♣]

Very appealing décor, with hanging plants, large photographs of film stars and smart check tablecloths, is complemented by an atmosphere kept fresh by two huge ceiling fans. Burgers are a speciality of the house – 100% beef served in a toasted sesame bun plus potatoes and fresh salad. There are eight varieties – 'Gourmet' is dressed in wine and mushroom sauce. You can have a

6oz burger for around £2.45. Grills and dishes such as chili con carne (served with side salad and hot pitta bread for about £2.50) are also on offer as are starters and delicious desserts such as 'Joanna's Special' – hot waffle with maple syrup and whipped cream or chocolate fudge cake both about 90p.

SW1

THE GREEN MAN, Harrods, Knightsbridge (01-730 1234)
Open: Mon-Sat 11.30am-3pm

P S

They say that there's nothing you can't buy at Harrods – at a price, and that's true even when it comes to finding a tasty meal. Located next to the Men's Department, the air is distinctly pubby and masculine in the Green Man restaurant. Pleasant and fast service is one bonus to the excellent food, with seafood platter at around £5.25 the most expensive item on the menu. A cold buffet displays a choice of salads, cold meats and a very good game pie for about £3.90. Apple pie or cheesecake are examples of desserts.

THE SCALLOP RESTAURANT
Central Hall, Westminster
(01-222 3222)
Open: Mon-Sat 12noon-2.30pm, 3.15-5.30pm

Occupying the whole of the basement under the vast Central Hall, The Scallop caters for large numbers yet manages to present well-cooked, appetising food at modest prices. The à la carte menu includes grills and omelettes, all (except steak) priced around £2, fish and chips or salad for under £2, and a selection of sweets priced around 60p. The special lunchtime menu offers soup or fruit juice at around 40p, a choice of five main courses such as a roast, steak and kidney pie or a pasta dish (costing in the region of £1.60), and a sweet at about 40p. There is also a three-course set lunch for around £3 which is very good value.

STRIKES, 124 Victoria Street
(01-834 0644)
Open: Mon-Sun 11.30am-11.30pm

C ♫ S

Just why a group of American-style eating houses should be named after a British general strike is hard to fathom, but arrive at Victoria Station feeling hungry and you may be glad to see a Strikes restaurant opposite the main exit. Inside you'll find a long narrow room with tables along one side, decorated with pictures of the 1926 strike, and there's a staircase twisting down to a second dining area. Starters vary from soup at 45p to avocado pear and prawns at £1.45 and you may choose a main course from a wide selection of hamburgers (£1.45-£2.80), platters (fish and chips at £1.40 to minute steak, egg, baked beans and chips at £2.95), steaks (up to £4.50), salads (£1.95 for tuna, or cottage cheese with whole peach, or prawn). Whichever you choose you'll be offered a choice of relishes and sauces at your table. Desserts are all variations on the theme of ice cream, and magnificent concoctions some of them are – as they should be when they cost up to £1.85! Amongst other beverages are Strikes Shakes at 65p.

SW3

BISTRO D'AGRAN, 1a Beauchamp Place, Chelsea (01-589 3982)
Open: Mon-Sat 12noon-2.45pm, 7-11.30pm

C S

If you are looking for a good place for an inexpensive meal and a glass of wine then the Bistro d'Agran is the place for you. This French-style bistro has pink walls and mahogany booths made from benches from an 1840s coffee house. The lunch menu includes a number of low-priced main dishes such as liver cooked in butter, onions and red wine, at about £2.20 or spaghetti bolognese at a little over £1. Even steak Diane is only about £3.75, as is salmon steak Danoise. Prices include vegetables, but you might like to add hot garlic bread at 35p. Starters average about 75p, sweets cost from around 50p for cream caramel to 70p for banana split. There is a minimum charge for dinner of £2.60, which would buy you fried chicken Southern style.

LE BOUZY ROUGE, 221 King's Road Chelsea (01-351 1607)
Open: Mon-Sat 11.30am-3pm, 5.30-11pm, Sun 7-10.30pm

♫ S

A wine and spirits shop on the ground floor and a wine bar in the basement is an excellent combination, and a useful place to find a few yards from Chelsea Antique Market (if you've any money left). Simple foods, such as pork sausage and butter beans and navarin of lamb, are served in ample portions for around £1.80, and salads are available, too.

There is a good variety of wines, of course, with the house wine costing from 55p a glass. Large bags hanging from brass rods provide comfortable backrests to the bench seating. A welcome change is the background of classical music – piped, certainly, but nevertheless a soothing change from the roar of London's traffic.

CARAVELA, 11 Beauchamp Place, Chelsea (01-581 2366)
Open: Tue-Sat 12noon-2.30pm, Tue-Sun 7pm-1am

[C] [♫] [P] [S] [♨]

Delicious squid is served at this simple, semi-basement Portuguese restaurant, so if you're adventurous – or Portuguese – you'll enjoy such novel dishes as grilled squid or highly spiced pork chops, each for about £3.50. But there are less exotic dishes to choose from in a warm cosy atmosphere, with varnished wood slats cladding the ceiling, walls and arched alcoves. A fine model galleon on the bar, and pictures, continue the theme of ships and the sea. Victorian gentlemen would have loved the continually-changing view through the window, which is at ankle-level to the street. Watch the prices, too – vegetables are sometimes charged extra and there's a cover charge of 65p – but it's not expensive for this part of London and it may be useful to know somewhere which is open until 1am every day of the week.

CHEYNE WALK WINE BAR, Pier House, 31 Cheyne Walk (01-352 4989)
Open: Mon-Sat 11.30am-3pm, 6.30-11pm, Sun 12noon-2pm

[C] [♫]

Behind the graceful statue of David Wynn's 'Boy on a Dolphin' is a wine bar where you can eat until late evening (and drink until midnight) to the accompaniment of live piano music. The Victorian-style interior in shades of brown and hung with carriage lamps and old prints overlooks a splendidly romantic night view of the illuminated Albert Bridge. Two Cordon Bleu cooks provide tantalising starters, main courses of steak and kidney or chicken and mushroom pie with vegetables for under £3, a range of salads and cold meats, and at the higher end of the price scale, fresh lemon sole for £3.75.

SW6

CROCODILE TEARS, 660 Fulham Road (01-731 1537)
Open: Mon-Sun 11.30am-2.30pm (2pm Sun), 6.30-10.30pm

[C] [S]

This is no run-of-the-mill wine bar; the décor is original – with a stuffed crocodile dangling from the ceiling, and the food likewise. For an adventurous meal try the carrot and orange soup or gazpacho, both around 85p, seafood kebab at about £2.75 and finish with ice cream gâteau or hot treacle tart with cream – a sweet sensation for around £1.25. All this will be served by pleasant waitresses who will bring you a freshly-ground coffee at 50p or so per cup. If you come here for the wine you won't be disappointed – there are fifteen varieties served by the glass.

SW7

DAQUISE, 20 Thurloe Street, South Kensington (01-589 6117)
Open: Mon-Sun 10am-12mdnt

[S]

Full meals can be obtained here at any time between midday and midnight, so if you fancy goulash for tea you can have it. You can buy a selection of other dishes at this Polish restaurant, from Polish zrazy at £2.80 to chicken à la Vienna at £2, as well as straightforward salads and omelettes costing around £1. Vegetables will add another 50p or so, and soup will cost about 40p. Ice cream and pastries are available if you want a sweet to finish the meal. From noon until 3pm, set-price two-course lunches are served. Soup, followed by meatballs kasza or stuffed aubergine, for instance, costs around £1.80. Desserts are mainly gâteaux (from 60p-£1). Downstairs there is a small licensed restaurant where the atmosphere is cosily intimate.

SW8

ATUCHACLASS, 24 Queenstown Road
Open: Mon-Sat 6.30-11.30pm

[♫] [P] [S]

An offshoot of the up-market 'Alonso's' (next-door-but-one), this intimate bistro certainly has a touch of class, from its quarry-tiled floor and subdued lighting to its imaginative international cuisine and the excellence of its fresh vegetables. The prices are just about within our limit, which for this type of establishment is surprising in itself. How about this for a meal: chicken liver pâté with herbs, spinach and chutney; Indonesian lamb in pastry (pieces of lamb, prawns, rice, raisins, mushrooms, chutney, light curry sauce) served with a selection of fresh vegetables; raspberry sorbet and coffee.

SW11

ANGELA AND PETER, 300 Battersea Park Road (01-228 6133)
Open: Mon-Sat 12noon-3pm, 7-11pm

[♫] [P] [glass]

The décor of this wine bar-cum-bistro is enhanced by interesting relics from the former antique shop. Excellent home-made fare includes cream of cucumber soup (about 60p) or tuna pâté (around £1.25) as starters, chicken with almonds in white wine and cream sauce (around £3), lamb cooked in white wine sauce with garlic (about £3.50) or rump steak (around £4) as main courses, and delicious sherry syllabub at around £1.

JUST WILLIAMS, 6a Battersea Rise (01-223 6890)
Open: Mon-Sat 12noon-3pm, 5.30-11pm, Sun 12noon-2pm, 7-10.30pm

[C] [♫] [P] [S]

This intimate wine bar, with its pine display counter, colourful check tablecloths and rear garden for the summer months is enthusiastically managed by ex wine merchant Michael Walker. The blackboard menu lists interesting starters such as taramasalata, served with pitta bread for about £1. Hot dishes of the day include goulash and boeuf bourguignon at around £2. Desserts include cheesecakes and gâteaux such as passioncake – a delicious fantasy of walnuts, apples and cream – about 75p.

SW15

LA FORCHETTA, 3 Putney Hill (01-785 6749)
Open: Mon-Thu 12noon-2.45pm, 6.30-11.15pm, Fri-Sat 6.30-11.30pm

[C] [♫] [P] [glass]

You'll find this bright little Italian restaurant at the bottom of Putney Hill. You can buy a cheap pasta dish here for around £1.60. A more elaborate meal could exceed budget but won't if you take care. Starters range from soup at about 80p to Parma ham and melon at around £2.20. Similarly, you could choose scampi alla provinciale at about £4 or piccatina al Marsala (veal escalope in Marsala) at about £3.20, or steak dishes at £3.70 or so. Vegetables add about 60p, and you can choose a sweet from the trolley or try zabaglione al Marsala – good value at around 90p. There is a cover charge of 50p. A good place for a tête-à-tête dinner.

MR MICAWBER'S, 147 Upper Richmond Road, Putney (01-788 2429)
Open: Mon-Fri 12noon-3pm, 5.30-11pm, Sat 12noon-3pm, Sun 7-10.30pm

[♫] [S] [glass]

There's sometimes a queue for food, but you won't have to wait too long for something to turn up in Mr Micawber's wine bar. You should be able to heed Mr Micawber's maxim about annual expenditure too, for food is very reasonably priced. Choice is limited, but there are hot casseroles, chili con carne and quiches as well as cold meats, pies and salads.

SW16

MR BUNBURY'S BISTRO, 1154 London Road, Norbury (01-764 3939)
Open: Tue-Sat 12noon-2.30pm, 7-11pm (Sat 11.30pm)

[C] [♫] [S] [glass]

A small bistro with Victorian décor and a cosy atmosphere enhanced by the oil lamps and old photographs and prints.

Susan Williams looks after the diners while husband Kenneth keeps busy in the kitchen preparing such delights as Bunbury pie (a large individual pie filled with lean chunks of beef, mushrooms, onions, and carrots topped with flaky puff pastry). The set lunch at around £5 is excellent value. Vegetables are plentiful and served in separate earthenware dishes; the puddings (always generous helpings) are home-made.

RINO'S RESTAURANT
82/84 Streatham High Road, Streatham (01-769 7916)
Open: Mon-Sun 12noon-3pm, 6pm-12mdnt

[C] [♫] [S]

A large regular clientele haunts this very busy Italian trattoria – and not just because Salvatore Polumba, one of the proprietors, otherwise known as Rino, is always chatting with the diners. The menu is very extensive – fourteen starters and five soups offer an interesting choice including snails, tunny fish and Italian hors d'oeuvres. Pastas, pizzas and omelettes are around £1.50 and Rino's specialities, served with two vegetables of the day, include pollo principessa (chicken with white wine, cream and asparagus tips) or piccatina al Marsala (veal escalopes cooked in butter and Marsala wine) priced from around £2.95. Sweets such as zabaglione al Marsala (about £1), crêpes Suzette (around £2) or lemon sorbet (about £1), complete a very substantial meal. This restaurant does a roaring late-night trade.

SW19

THE CROOKED BILLET, 15 Crooked Billet, Wimbledon Common (01-946 4942)
Open: Mon-Thu, Sun 12noon-2.30pm, 7.30-10pm, Fri-Sat 12noon-2.30pm, 7.30-10.30pm

[C]

A building which started life as a barn way back in the 15th century, is now an olde worlde restaurant, retaining some of the bygone features such as timbered beams and pillars. Fare is varied and at sensible prices. Starters range from 50p-£1.20, featuring egg mayonnaise and Swedish herring. Of the main dishes, beef curry or steak pie with two veg are both good value at around £1.50, whilst huge egg or cheese salads are a snip at around £2. Home-made apple pie and Black Forest gâteau make delicious desserts from 75p.

DOWNS WINE BAR, 40 Wimbledon Hill Road (01-946 3246)
Open: Mon-Sun 12noon-3pm, 7pm-2am

[C] [♫] [S]

Unobtrusive décor gives an atmosphere of intimacy and informality, both in the cosy cellar bar, with its alcoves and dance floor, and in the ground floor bar, where one can take a quieter meal. The menu is changed daily, but there's always a good selection of both hot and cold dishes. Pâté maison comes at around £1.15 while a variety of quiches and cold meat salads cost slightly more. Hot dishes, such as burgundy beef, pork paprika or tarragon chicken in cream and lemon sauce are around £3 but extremely tasty. House special is seafood chowder served with garlic bread at around £3.

W1

L'ARTISTE MUSCLE, 1 Shepherd Market (01-493 6150)
Open: Mon-Sat 12noon-3pm, 5.30pm-12mdnt, Sun 7-11pm

[♫] [S]

In the heart of the Shepherd Market lies L'Artiste Musclé, a French wine-bar-cum-bistro in a 19th-century building which at first sight appears to be a well-populated junk shop. Closer inspection discloses that people are actually eating and drinking inside, though with a minimum of ceremony as they rub shoulders with anything from old chests to chamber-pots while doing so. The menu is short, but has a real French-peasantish flavour, with items such as jambon and quiche. Typical prices are about £2.30 for côte de porc or ragout d'agneau.

THE CHICAGO PIZZA PIE FACTORY
17 Hanover Square (01-629 2669)
Open: Mon-Sat 11.45am-11.30pm

[♫] [S]

This popular pizza restaurant has a very informal atmosphere, the walls lavishly decorated with Chicago memorabilia. The deep-dish Chicago-style pizza is new to this country: it has a thick crust and rich filling based on mozzarella cheese. Don't go alone however, as the smallest serves two – and is priced accordingly (around £3.50). If you think you can tackle more than a pizza, start with savoury stuffed mushrooms with sherry and garlic and finish with a delicious cheesecake. Owner Bob Payton's great passion, second after pizzas, is music and a sophisticated stereo system keeps his customers entertained while they wait the customary thirty minutes for their culinary masterpiece to appear from the kitchen.

DOWNS WINE BAR, 5 Down Street (01-491 3810)
Open: Mon-Sat 12noon-3pm, 5.30pm-1am, Sun 12noon-3pm, 7-12.30am

[C] [♫] [P] [S] [🍷]

A wine bar situated in an 18th-century backwater of Mayfair might be expected to price itself into the millionaires-only class, so it is a pleasant surprise to find that a dinner for £5 is eminently possible at Down's. True, one could choose a more expensive meal, but with a starter of smoked mackerel at about £1 or rough country pâté at £1.50, a daily special (chicken chasseur for instance), or trout costing about £3 with vegetables and a sweet such as cherry cheesecake averaging 85p, even the addition of the 10% service charge does not take us over the top. There is also a well-stocked 'downstairs' cold table.

GARFUNKELS, 57/61 Duke Street (01-499 5000)
Open: Mon-Sun 12noon-11pm

[S] [🍷]

Shopping in Oxford Street needn't be a chore when you have the pleasure of a meal at Phillip and Reginald Kaye's luxurious restaurant to look forward to. The soft brown, beige, cream and amber interior and the profusion of palms and other greenery provides a restful haven just far enough from the milling crowds. For a light refresher you might choose the salad bar where you can help yourself to heaps of fresh salad from £2.60 for a main course, or you might prefer a hot meal such as veal escalope with spaghetti neopolitan for £3.30 or, at about £2.25, chili con carne with baked potato. A starter of vegetable soup at 70p, a dish of Garfunkel's American ice cream at 70p for dessert and coffee at 35p completes your meal.

GRANARY, 39 Albemarle Street (01-493 2978)
Open: Mon-Fri 11am-6.50pm, Sat 11am-2.30pm

[S]

Baskets of ferns and air-conditioning create a fresh, cool atmosphere in which to enjoy your meal in this delightful restaurant. Choose what you fancy from the tempting array of food on display, and one of the heart-throb waiters will carry it to your table. The menu is chalked up and is sure to include a choice of nine main dishes, all at around £2-£2.30. Prawn provençale, beef Stroganoff and steak and kidney pie are likely choices. Salads are less than £1, and there is a really delicious array of sweets priced at about 85p.

IKAROS, 36 Baker Street (01-935 7821)
Open: Mon-Sat 12noon-3pm, 6pm-12mdnt

[C] [♫] [S] [🍷]

This small Greek restaurant has an authentic air. The charcoal grill wafts the most delicious smells to the diner and gives a flavour to the food not found in normal cooking. An interesting Greek starter such as taramasalata or longaniko sausage costs around 85p, and main dishes include doner kebab at around £2.50 and moussaka at £2.95. Vegetables cost about 60p a portion and sweets come from 60p. This is another restaurant where it would be all too easy to exceed the £5 limit, but for central London the prices are not unreasonable.

KNIGHTSBRIDGE SPAGHETTI HOUSE, 77 Knightsbridge (01-235 6987)
Open: Mon 12noon-3pm, Tue-Fri 12noon-3pm, 5.30-10.30pm, Sat 12noon-3pm, 5.30-11pm

[♫] [P] [S] [🍷]

This is the most famous of the Spaghetti Houses – six Italian restaurants specialising in pasta dishes. The menu is nearly the same throughout the group, with all the pastas and pizzas costing about £1.50 a portion. Also on the menu are fish and meat dishes, served with potatoes and another vegetable, or spaghetti, or rice, or salad. There's a good selection of starters, sweets and cheeses.

LORD BYRON TAVERNA, 41 Beak Street (01-734 0316)
Open: Mon-Sat 12noon-3pm, 6pm-3.30am (closed Sat lunch)

[C] [♫] [S]

'You have to kiss a helluva lot of frogs before you find Prince Charming'. This is just one of the thousands of comments that decorate the walls and ceiling of this Greek taverna. Hardly Byronic, but most of the graffiti are quite amusing, and if you can think up something better you are welcome to add your piece. The restaurant premises were once lived in by Caneletto, the Venetian painter, and there is a blue plaque to commemorate this above the entrance. Food is almost entirely Greek, starters including a special variety of taramasalata and avgolemono (chicken soup with egg, lemon juice and rice), either costing about 70p. Most of the main course dishes are priced around £2 but salad and other vegetables are charged extra.

RASA SAYANG, 10 Frith Street (01-734 8720)
Open: Mon-Sat 12noon-3pm, 6pm-12mdnt

[C] [♫] [S]

Attentive waiters at this cool, airy South East Asian restaurant, with its tasteful wood and wicker décor, will help you to select dishes from the intriguing menu. Starters include a variety of soups and a host of main courses is offered – seafood, chicken, beef, pork and vegetarian dishes. Speciality of the house is 'satay' – tender skewers of chicken and beef marinated in Malaysian spices, gently grilled and served with fresh cucumber, rice cakes and a rich savoury peanut-based sauce – all this for around £2. Desserts costing from 80p-£1 include kolak pisang – banana slices in coconut milk sweetened with brown sugar or seasonal fresh fruits. Side dishes are extra, so you will have to select with care to remain within the budget.

RISTORANTE ALPINO, 42 Marylebone High Street (01-935 4640)
Open: Mon-Sat 12noon-11.30pm

[C] [♫] [S] [🍷]

A typical Alpino this, with décor in the chalet style; skis on the wall, and the standard Alpino menu including scampi and escalopes of veal cooked in Marsala, both at just over £3. A very friendly little restaurant, managed with Italian flair and Italian charm. An accordionist plays light music to aid the digestion of the supper trade. Madame Tussaud's is close by.

RISTORANTE ALPINO, 102 Wigmore Street (01-935 4181)
Open: Mon-Sat 12noon-11.30pm, Sun 7-11.30pm

[C] [♫] [P] [S] [🍷]

This is the Alpino for Oxford Street shoppers, with a small front section for afternoon teas, a main restaurant of about sixty covers and a side rear room with fifty more. The gâteaux for all the Alpinos are made in the patisserie beneath this particular restaurant and very good they are. 'My Black Forest gâteau is the best in London' the pastry cook has been known to boast, and no one – but no one – argues with a Sicilian pastry cook.

THE ROSE RESTAURANT, Dickins and Jones, Regent Street (01-734 7070)
Open: Mon-Sat 11.30am-3pm, 3.15-5.15pm

[C] [♫] [S] [🍷]

Judging by the starched linen tablecloths, heavy cutlery, thick carpets and cool, green plants hanging in baskets from the elegant supporting pillars, Dickins and Jones work hard to maintain the old traditions. There is both a cold carvers table at around £4.95, and a hot carvers table for £5.25. Ask your waitress for a voucher, and choose what you fancy from roast rib of beef and veg, fish and salads. In addition, there are the hot dishes of the day such as chicken kebab (£4.65) or fillet of plaice with French fried potatoes for around £3.65, or a choice of grills such as Scotch entrecôte or lamb cutlets, with a mouth-watering selection of gâteaux, trifles and pastries on the buffet, and a good range of ice cream-based sweets – none more than £1.10.

RENDEZ-VOUS, Swiss Centre, Leicester Square (01-734 1291)
Open: Mon-Sun 11.30am-12mdnt

[C] [P] [🍷]

Walking into a bit of Switzerland in the heart of London saves a lot of money in air fares. The Rendez-vous menu is inspiringly continental and within the means of the British pocket. You won't be indulging yourself amongst the open sandwiches, smoked meat and Appenzeller cheese alone, though – the Swiss Centre's a popular place. Even the humble beefburger – or Toggeburger – is elevated to new gastronomic realms when called Alpenrose, and served with peach and spicy butter (£2.90); fried egg, too, when served with housebread soaked in white wine and topped with Emmenthal cheese (£2.30). Salads intriguingly marry sweet and sour – try a fillet of herring with grapefruit and apple in sour cream (£1.90). Luscious Swiss sweets range from 80p to £1.50 and promise similar ascents into alpine ecstasy.

SWISS CENTRE RESTAURANT
10 Wardour Street (01-734 1291)
Open: Mon-Sun 11.30am-12mdnt

[C] [♫] [P] [S] [🍷]

There are four separate restaurants at the Swiss Centre, each with its own décor and menu. Of these only The Chesa prices itself out of this book. The other three are predominantly Swiss in style from the three different regions and all offer regional specialities, most of which are well within our price-range. Of special interest are the fondues, hors-d'oeuvre (which may be ordered either as an appetiser or as a main dish) and herrings or perch cooked in a number of intriguing ways. The speciality of the house is the range of sausage meats, bread, ice cream, gâteaux and chocolates, all freshly-made on the premises. Rum sponge with marzipan at around 60p and Matterhorn Ice Firn (sponge, ice cream, curacao soufflé and candied fruits made into an ice pie and glazed in the oven) at about 90p are just two of these.

W2

THE GYNGLEBOY, 27 Spring Street (01-723 3351)
Open: Mon-Fri 11am-3pm, 5.30-9pm

[C] [S]

The 'Gyngleboy' was a leather bottle, or black jack, lined with silver and ornamented with little silver bells 'to ring peales of drunkeness'. So now you know. Conveniently close to Paddington Station, this is a very superior wine bar offering a substantial choice of cold dishes – even the game pie is cold. So are the smoked chicken and smoked salmon specials, as well as the home-baked apple pies and puddings. But try the soup – that's piping hot. The cellar is extensive and there's a sophisticated range of château bottled vintages.

OODLES, 128 Edgware Road, Marble Arch (01-723 7548)
Open: Mon-Sat 11am-9pm, Sun 12noon-8pm

[S] [♣]

You've got to hand it to Oodles Ltd. The name over its restaurants conjures up visions of plenty. And that's just what it offers – large helpings of nourishing country-style dishes, just like Mother used to make them. Casseroles, beef stew, chicken curries, steak pie, are all under £2, which with a modestly priced wholesome sweet and starter selection will keep the bill to under £5. This Oodles is the most recently opened of the five branches in London, and each has the same simple décor – rough wooden tables, bench seats, white stucco walls hung with wooden advertising plates such as used to be seen on horse-drawn delivery carts. See listing under EC4 and WC1 for details of other branches.

TAORMINA, 19 Craven Terrace (01-262 2090)
Open: Mon-Sun 12noon-1am

[C] [♫] [♣]

As in most London restaurants, you have to choose rather carefully when ordering your meal here. The Taormina's motif is a wheel, the window area being taken up by two large cart wheels, with the theme repeated on the cover of the menu. White stucco walls relieved by paintings and ornaments, and a false ceiling of polished beams make the interior light and pleasant. Food is authentically Italian, with soups at about 70p, freshly-made pizzas (you'll have to wait while yours is cooked), pasta and rice dishes from £1. And then there's squid (around £4) which is cooked in tomato purée with garlic and parsley – delicious. Sweets start at 40p or so.

W3

NORTH CHINA, 305 Uxbridge Road, Acton (01-992 9183)
Open: Mon-Thu, Sun 12noon-2pm, 5.30-11.30pm, Fri-Sat 12noon-2pm, 5.30-12mdnt

Proprietor Lawrence Lou specialises in Peking cuisine – particularly in Peking Crispy Aromatic Duck – a rare delight which can be enjoyed whole (around £11) or in portions (the smallest is about £3). Special dinners are on offer for two people at around £5.75 each – mixed hors d'oeuvres, spare ribs, Peking duck, prawns in chili sauce or sweet and sour pork, shredded beef, diced chicken with cashew nuts in yellow bean sauce and Chinese-style toffee apple or banana is one example. The usual baffling à la carte menu with hundreds of dishes is also astonishingly reasonable.

W4

FOUBERTS WINE BAR, 162 Chiswick High Road (01-994 5202)
Open: Mon-Sat 12noon-3pm, 7-11pm

[♫] [S] [♣]

This is a small basement wine bar which uses both wooden and cast-iron furniture to give a slightly Bohemian air. Italian dishes such as lasagne (about £1.80) are good here, or if you prefer English no-frills food you can get steak and chips for around £3.50. Soup with roll and butter costs 50p or so. A large selection of wines includes several which can be bought by the glass for around 55p. Italian, German, French and Portuguese varieties prove popular with cosmopolitan visitors.

W5

CRISPINS WINE BAR, 46-47 The Mall, Ealing (01-567 8966)
Open: 12noon-2.30pm, 6-8pm and normal licensing hours.

[S]

The unusual exterior is reminiscent of an old railway station, with its cast-iron-and-glass portico forming a protected area where ironwork tables and chairs are available for patrons. There is a similarly-equipped garden at the back for rain-free days. The bar itself is reputed to be the largest in London, stretching almost the full depth of the premises, with cast iron tables and chairs arranged along one side. In spite of its size it gets very crowded on Friday and Saturday evenings. The interior is French bistro-style, the décor somewhat barn-like with natural wood beams and panels and a quarry-tiled floor. Food is cheap and good. At lunchtime around £2 buys a hot dish such as moussaka, curry or hotpot with accompanying vegetables, and cold food such as quiche with salad is available at lunchtime or in the evening at similar prices. Desserts are about 50p a portion. There is another Crispins at 14 The Green, Ealing.

CRUSTS GAFF, 17 The Green, Ealing (01-579 2788)
Open: Mon-Thu 12noon-11.30pm, Fri-Sat 12noon-12mdnt, Sun 12noon-10.30pm

[♫] [P]

An abundance of natural wood comes in handy for hanging numerous knick-knacks including a spinning wheel, steel helmets and statues. Walls covered with old prints and mirrors complete the individual décor of this popular bistro. Emphasis is on good, wholesome food. Starters include soup at around 90p or pâté at about £1. Main dish specialities such as lasagne are on offer at around £3.50, spare ribs at about £3. Meat and cheeseburgers are rock bottom budget items and there is a selection of competitively-priced salads. Sweets include apple pie and crème caramel for around 80p-£1.

W8

THE ARK RESTAURANT, 122 Palace Gardens Terrace (01-229 4024)
Open: Mon-Sat 12noon-3pm, 6.30-11.30pm, Sun 6.30-11.30pm

[C] [S]

You won't need to walk into The Ark two by two, but it is advisable not to arrive with a large family party unannounced. The Ark is a small, intimate bistro in the true French tradition. It has plain tables and a warm, friendly staff. The plat du jour, though not entirely French, ranges from crevettes rosés (a shrimp concoction at around £1), to moules marinières at about £1.25 for starters. For the main course, coq au vin (only around £2.50) or foie de veau à l'ail (calf's liver with garlic) linger in the memory – and on the palate. Follow on with profiteroles, or a gigantic portion of sorbet and, surprise, surprise, at lunchtime you may still have some change from your £5 note.

W9

ELGIN LOKANTA, 239 Elgin Avenue (01-328 6400)
Open: Mon-Sun 12noon-12mdnt

[C] [S]

The grill-kitchen of this Turkish restaurant is at the front and takeaway kebabs are a favourite of the locals. Mezeler (starters) include deliciously flavoured calves' livers at about 90p and there are over twenty more starters on the menu. Main courses are from around £2.25-£3.75 and are all served with pilaf rice. Try one of the lamb specialities such as sis saslik (skewered lamb with mushrooms and onion slices). Honey and walnut baklava (75p) is a tempting dessert from the trolley with which to complete your meal. There is a nominal cover charge for which you receive butter, hot pitta and black olives.

W11

FINCH'S WINE BAR, 120 Kensington Park Road (01-229 9545)
Open: Mon-Sat 11am-3pm, 6-11pm

[C] [P] [S]

Only a stone's throw from the Portobello Road antique market is this neat little basement premises, with its plain white walls and pillars forming intimate alcoves. Hot dishes include a quiche or pie from £1.75 or lasagne or moussaka from £1.55. The cold collation offers such tempting delicacies as fresh prawns for around £1.50, pâte (about £1.20) and porc encroute.

KLEFTIKO, 186 Holland Park Avenue, Holland Park (01-603 0807)
Open: Mon-Sat 12noon-3pm, 6-11.30pm

[C] [♫] [P] [🍷]

Michael Hagisoteri opened the Kleftiko as an offshoot of his nearby hairdressing establishment on the Holland Park Avenue corner of Shepherds Bush roundabout. And very bright and cheerful it is, with natural brick walls, trellis-work ceiling, red and white cloths and fresh flowers. If you really want to go to town, book in advance and order Meze – a six-course evening meal at about £5 a head during which you can sample authentic Greek dishes. Starters cost about £1 and include houmous, taramasalata and tambouli. Main dishes are served with rice and salad and include the lamb speciality kleftiko or afelia, either of these costing around £3. Any two or three items may be combined and they then cost about £3 a helping. Sweets are about 60p, fresh fruits in season around 85p. Greek coffee is about 35p a cup.

TOOTSIES, 120 Holland Park Avenue
(01-229 8567)
Open: Mon-Sun 8am-12mdnt
(Sun 11.30pm)

[♫] [S] [🍷]

The menu at Tootsies offers 'Eye Openers': orange juice with raw egg 'for those who did and wish they hadn't' and a full English breakfast 'for those who didn't and wish they had'. This is primarily a hamburger house – a dozen varieties are listed costing from about £1.30 to about £1.80, all prices including chips (except in the case of the 'calorie counter' version, where bun and chips are replaced by pineapple and cottage cheese) and a selection of relishes. You can get a number of other dishes here – steak, salads, quiches, for example, at very reasonable prices, and there are delectable cakes and ice-cream specialities.

W12

SHIREEN TANDOORI ✕
270 Uxbridge Road (01-749 5927)
Open: Mon-Sat 12noon-3pm, 6-11.30pm, Sun 6-11.30pm

[C] [♫] [T] [S] [🍷]

You can drink an aperitif and nibble spicy Indian nuts at the bar and seating area at the far end of this smart little restaurant, just ten minutes' walk from Shepherds Bush roundabout. Attractive Indian prints are displayed against matt black walls, and the natural wood of the ceiling is echoed in the herringbone-patterned latticework which screens diners from the main road. Main course prices range from about £2.50 (for Tandoori chicken) to around £4 (for Jhinga tandoori, a prawn speciality). The addition of vegetables (about £1.20), coffee (around 45p) and wine (bottles only) could bring the total over £5 even without a sweet. But if you appreciate the art of Tandoori cooking you will enjoy your meal.

WC1

OODLES, 113 High Holburn
(01-405 3838)
Open: Mon-Fri 11.30am-9pm, Sat 11.30am-2.30pm

[S]

Apart from staying open more hours in the week than the others, this branch of Oodles is no different from any other, but catch the flavour of its menus by reading the description in the entry under W2.

OODLES, 42 New Oxford Street
(01-580 9521)
Open: Mon-Fri 11am-9pm, Sat 11am-8pm, Sun 12noon-7pm

[S]

The frontage may be reminiscent of 'Ye Olde Tea Shoppe', but inside this eating house is unmistakably Oodles. No time to linger over evening meals, but a glass of wine can be had here. See under W2.

WC2

CORTS, 84-86 Chancery Lane
(01-405 3349)
Open: Mon-Fri 11am-3pm, 5.30-8pm

[C] [♫] [S]

You are less likely to meet criminals here than in the Old Bailey Courts, but lawyers abound as the wine bar is handy for the Strand Law Courts and is not far from the various Inns of Court. Here you will find an air-conditioned basement self-service bar and a ground-floor restaurant in which olive green and red blend with polished wood to create a warm *ambience* which is matched by the pleasant and helpful waitresses. Food is on the same lines as the original Corts (see under EC4) and starters include items such as smoked mackerel or avocado pear vinaigrette at around £1.30, or potted shrimps. Followed by a main course of duck and walnut pie (£1.80) and a sweet or fruit and cheese (about £1.20), a three-course meal should cost about £4.30. Food is served at lunchtime only.

HOBSON'S WINE BAR
20 Upper St Martin's Lane

(01-836 5849)
Open: Mon-Sat 11am-3pm, 5.30-11pm, Sun 7-10.30pm

C P

This eaterie, close to Covent Garden, is located below-ground and is on the whole candlelit with the occasional modern discreet light. There's bags of equine atmosphere here with wood-panelled walls, a 'Horse-Box' window and even sawdust. Of the various starters, spicy chicken and wine pâté (£1.40) is highly recommended. Main course options are fish-biased and include smoked trout (£2.50) and lemon sole (£2). If you fancy spoiling yourself with some wine, on this occasion you'll find Hobson's choice from the wine cellars immense.

PLUMMER'S RESTAURANT
10a James Street, Covent Garden
(01-240 2534)
Open: Mon-Sat 12noon-3pm, 5.30pm-12mdnt

S

Victoriana epitomised by old photographs, prints and large mirrors, characterises this eating house, one of the original of the 'new wave' of restaurants in Covent Garden. Dishes include home-made steak and kidney pie, Californian chili served with Chef's salad (both around £3) and Plummer's Superburgers (8oz 100% pure Scottish beefburgers topped with bacon, egg and melted cheese).

SOLANGE'S WINE BAR, 11 St Martin's Court (01-240 0245)
Open: Mon-Sat 11am-3pm, 5.30-11pm

C ♫

A great attraction of this large, unpretentious wine bar is the excellent food, which is prepared in the famed neighbouring two knife and fork restaurant, Chez Solange. The four rooms can accommodate 200 people and more on the white-painted garden furniture outside. The menu changes daily, and is written on a blackboard. As an appetiser you could sample one of about a dozen cold dishes – champignons à la Greque at 65p, pâté maison or ratatouille at 85p are tasty examples. Hot dishes of the day cost less than £2 and might include coq au vin, veal or spare ribs – delicious with a serving of cauliflower cheese at 45p. Desserts such as fruit salad or cheesecake are in the 65p-80p range.

TUTTONS, 11-12 Russell Street
(01-836 1167)
Open: Mon-Fri 9am-12mdnt, Sat 11am-12mdnt, Sun 12noon-10.30pm

C S

This cream-decorated brasserie with plain pine furniture offers a good range of snacks and salads, and some unusual main dishes such as vegetables and spices wrapped in pastry and baked at around £2.70 or smoked chicken and avocado salad at about £3. You are welcome to drop in for a late breakfast, or perhaps just a coffee.

VECCHIA PARMA, 149 Strand
(01-836 3730)
Open: Mon-Sat 12noon-3pm 5.30-11pm

C ♫ P S

In the best traditions of Italian restaurateurs, the Ronchetti family do a grand job in running this restaurant close to London's theatreland – Signor Ronchetti is the barman and his wife is also behind the bar. Of their two sons, Sergio cooks and Silvano produces the 'service with a smile' of which they are so proud. Apart from the usual pasta and pizza dishes, mostly around £1.45, there are several tasty grills, omelettes, fish and salad choices, many of them costing not much more than £2.50 and served with potatoes and vegetables.

Barking

THE SPOTTED DOG, 15 Longbridge Road (01-594 0228)
Open: Mon-Sun normal licensing hours

C S

Genuine East London atmosphere abounds in the Spotted Dog, one of Davy & Co's original enterprises (near Barking tube). The ground floor 'doghouse' offers good old steak and kidney pie with vegetables and potatoes for under £3, but a steak or a mixed grill will be more pricey (around £4.50 with vegetables). Bar snacks such as sandwiches, filled rolls and toasted fingers are also available. An enormous antique fireplace dominates the room. Downstairs, you find yourself in the 'clink' – a dungeon-like place complete with an ill-looking skeleton. No bread and water here, but plaice or scampi and chips at around £3.50.

Barnet

FRANCO AND GIANNI, 45 High Street (01-449 8300)
Open: Tue-Sat 12noon-3pm

C S

This attractive little Italian restaurant is somewhat out of our league in the evenings but at lunchtimes a typically Italian table d'hôte menu prevails, offering such dishes as cannelloni or lasagne for starters, medaglioni di manzo (thin fillet steak in red wine and mushroom sauce) with cauliflower and potato to follow, gâteau of the day plus coffee – all for around £4.50.

THE TWO BREWERS, 64 Hadley Highstone (01-449 3558)
Open: Mon-Thu 10.30am-2.30pm, Fri-Sat 10.30am-2.30pm, 5.30-11pm, Sun 12noon-2pm, 7-10.30pm

P

A one-time 'Pub of the Year'; this superb Tudor-style building is well-known to the locals, and they take full advantage of the high standard of cooking. Meals are eaten in the restaurant which echoes the Tudor theme, with warm red curtains and carpet. A daily-changing menu offers traditional Old English dishes such as grilled gammon and pineapple, cod and chips or home-made steak, kidney and mushroom pie all around £3.50. With starter, sweet and coffee you will feast for around £5.

Bromley

HOLLYWOOD BOWL, 5 Market Parade, East Street (01-460 2346)
Open: Mon-Thu 11.30am-2.45pm, 6-11.15pm (Fri-Sat 6-11.45pm), Sun 6-11pm

♫ P S

Old enamelled bill posters and hanging plants decorate this popular hamburger restaurant. There are nine burgers to choose from, all with interesting names; for example, the 'hen house' has a fried egg topping and the 'Bronx boiger' is 'overflowing with spicy baked beans'. The star of this show is 'Hollywood Bowl's de-luxe cheeseburger' – a hunky half-pounder with a generous topping of melted cheese, lettuce, tomato and pickles smothered in thick mayonnaise. All of them are served in a toasted sesame bun with French fries. A rump steak at around £3.90 with a choice of three salads around £2.20 each are alternative main courses. Fresh home-made apple pie is a tasty dessert at around 60p.

Croydon

FUSTO D'ORO PIZZERIA, Leon House, 237-239 High Street (01-688 4869)
Open: Mon-Sat 11am-3pm, 6pm-12mdnt

C ♫ P S

If pizza's your dish you'll be quite spoiled for choice at this popular Italian pizzeria in the heart of Croydon. There are twenty-two varieties. For the quickie meal, eat your pizza in the busier section of the restaurant where the décor is simple, with formica-topped tables. When you want to linger and enjoy a more romantic atmosphere, dine by candlelight in the other section. Wherever you eat the food is the same, with pizzas from the basic Margherita to an elaborate Mediterraneo with seafood and tomatoes, pasta dishes, salads and steaks. For dessert there's a choice of either 'dolci', including such tempters as rum baba, zabaglione or cheesecake.

SNIFTERS WINE BAR, 71 High Street (01-686 8480)
Open: Mon-Thu 11am-3pm, 5.30-10.30pm, Fri 11am-3pm, 5.30-11pm, Sat 11am-3pm, 7-11pm Sun 7-10.30pm

C ♫ P S

Art nouveau décor and a mezzanine floor with balcony are unique features of this attractive wine bar. The menu is excellent, with a choice of seven interesting appetisers such as egg mayonnaise with anchovy at about 70p and pâté with wholemeal bread for around 90p. Cold buffet offers fine ham off the bone or roast beef (both about £1.50), quiche (around 95p) or smoked mackerel (about £1.20). Hot buffet includes pastas at around £1.60 and veal escalopes for about £1.85. Additionally, the blackboard lists daily specials such as lamb cutlets in rosemary or chicken supreme for around £1.95. An excellent choice of desserts such as home-made apple pie and cream (about 75p) makes the three-course meal complete.

THE WINE VAULTS
122-126 North End
(01-680 2419)
Open: Mon-Sat 11am-2.30pm, Mon-Thu 5.30-10.30pm, Fri 5.30-11pm, Sat 7-11pm

C P S

Another Davy & Co outlet this, with solidly Victorian décor and sawdust on the floor in true Davy fashion, in basement premises on Croydon's busy High Street close to the railway station and next door to Marks & Spencer. Toasted fingers cost about 20p each here, or £1 for a plate of six, but otherwise the menu and prices are fairly typical of the company. A popular meal is charcoal grilled ribs of prime beef with a tossed mixed salad, but this will cost about £4.50 without other courses.

Enfield

DIVERS WINE BAR, 29 Silver Street (01-367 2549)
Open: Tue-Fri 12noon-2.30pm, Mon-Sun 7.30-10.30pm (11pm Fri and Sat)

♫ P S

The smart brown awning of this little wine bar picks it out in the tree-lined street. The blackboard menu offers daily specialities such as chili con carne, goulash or roast chicken. Pizzas, quiches and ploughman's are always available for around £1 and desserts include a delicious chocolate cherry gâteau for around 75p. A dazzling selection of wines and good background music make this a popular mealtime haunt. Summer visitors may like to eat in the sheltered, paved garden to the rear of the restaurant.

Hampton Court

CARDINAL WOLSEY, The Green (01-979 1458)
Open: Mon-Sun 12.30-3pm, 7-10.30pm

C P

This charming inn, pleasantly sited close to Hampton Court, offers sound home-made English fare for the footsore and famished foreign tourist's enjoyment – and British visitors are equally welcome. A three-course table d'hôte meal, changed daily, but always providing interesting choices, costs around £5. Portions are very generous and old favourites frequently featured include Chef's stock pot soup, home-made pâté, roast beef and Yorkshire pud, steak and kidney pud, apple pie and peach Melba – a taste of old England at its best.

Hampton Wick

GENZIANI RESTAURANT
35 High Street (01-977 4895)
Open: Mon-Thu 12noon-2.30pm, 6.30-10.30pm, Fri-Sat 12noon-2.30pm, 6.30-11pm

C P

The Genziani family run this intimate Italian restaurant – Dino prepares the food and his wife Dora attends to the needs of the diners. Apart from conventional Italian cuisine, fish, omelettes, salads and grills are also served. Hors d'oeuvres include home-made pâté and antipasta della casa for about £1. Minestrone soup, home-made and thick, with fresh vegetables is a meal in itself for around 85p. Spaghetti della casa is a speciality – a version of bolognese with sliced ham and melted cheese – and is yours for about £2.65. A selection of desserts includes hot zabaglione – a serving for two people costs around £1.50.

Harrow

PLATO'S, 294 Preston Road
(01-904 8326)
Open: Mon-Sat 12noon-3pm, 6-11pm

[S]

This Greek restaurant is furnished in the modern style and specialises in French and English as well as Greek cuisine. Theo Vazanias is always on hand to ensure your enjoyment of his food. The à la carte menu offers a dazzling choice of over twenty starters, more than thirty main courses and about twenty sweets. You could break the bank by going for all the most expensive items, but there is still a wide choice awaiting you. An all-Greek meal could include tsatsiki as an appetiser at around 80p, with dolmades or afelia as your main dish for about £3.10 and baklava or kateifi as delicious desserts at around 80p. Vegetables are extra and there is a cover charge for bread and butter.

Hounslow

THE TRAVELLERS FRIEND
480 Bath Road (01-897 8847)
Open: Mon-Fri 12noon-2.30pm,
Fri-Sat 7-9.30pm

[C] [P]

Tudor architecture is reflected in the oak beams, pillars, plain brick and stone walls and olde worlde furnishings of the charming restaurant in this hostelry. Cuisine is basically English with the odd French dish to vary the pace. Starters include soup at around 60p, pâté maison at about £1.20 and prawn cocktail for around £1. Main courses include fish (from £2.50-£5.50), grills (from £2.20 for lamb cutlets to £4.50 for fillet or T-bone steak) and entrées such as escalope of veal cordon bleu. Vegetables are 50p extra. Various gâteaux cost around 60p.

Ilford

HART'S, 545 Cranbrook Road
Gants Hill (01-554 5000)
Open: Mon-Thu 12noon-3pm,
6-10.30pm, Fri-Sat 12noon-3pm,
6-11pm, Sun 7-10.30pm

[C] [♫]

Leonard and Alan Hart's wine bar specialises in good home-made cooking ideal for businesspeople and travellers alike. Start with home-made cabbage soup (about 70p) or crab cocktail at £1.35, then sample lasagne (about £1.80). Freshly caught trout from Hanningford or Australian Pacific prawns cooked with garlic may stretch the budget but are good value. Hard-to-resist desserts include hot black cherries with port and ice cream (about £1). In fine weather you can enjoy your meal on the tree-lined terrace to the rear.

Kew

LE PROVENCE, 14 Station Parade,
Kew Gardens (01-940 6777)
Open: Tue-Sat 6-9.15pm,
Sat 12noon-3pm

[P]

This traditional French restaurant, tucked away under the oak tree-lined parade at Kew Gardens, offers honest French cooking at no-nonsense prices. Daily specials are excellent value – fresh artichoke vinaigrette is around £1.20, risotto du chef around £1.25 and foie saute à la Venitienne (sliced liver cooked in butter with sherry and sliced onions, served with a selection of vegetables) at about £3.30 are typical examples. Main courses, all served with vegetables, range in price from around £1.50 to nearly £3.50. The desserts are a delight – real fruit sorbet (usually raspberry) or meringue glacé Chantilly (around 90p) are both superb. Booking is essential.

Kingston-upon-Thames

CLOUDS, 6-8 Kingston Hill
(01-546 0559)
Open: Mon-Sun 11am-11pm

[P] [S] [🍸]

This busy, friendly restaurant operates on two floors. The first floor is a cocktail bar, where a limited menu of filled jacket potatoes is usually available. The ground floor menu offers stuffed mushrooms among other appetisers, quiches, spaghettis, hamburgers, spare ribs or salads as a main course (from £2-£3) and gâteaux, cheesecakes or fantastic ice creams for dessert. Children's portions come at £1.

COUNTRY KITCHEN RESTAURANT
20 Vicarage Road (01-549 4774)
Open: Mon-Fri 9.30am-5pm,
Sat 9.30am-6pm

[P] [S] [icon]

Decorated in the style of a country kitchen, this small restaurant has white-painted walls, red tile-patterned floor and scrubbed wood tables and chairs. Hanging baskets and green potted plants add to the rustic atmosphere. Good, basic food is available all day, from fried 'brekkers' for around £1.10 to a three course lunch or early dinner. Home-made soup of the day, dish of the day such as chicken casserole served with spring greens and new potatoes and lemon meringue pie will cost around £2.65. There is a huge range of snack food available including a daily 'supa-snack' such as sardines with tomato and onion salad at about £1. Lemonade shandy is the nearest you'll get to alcohol, since the Country Kitchen is at present unlicensed, though this may be rectified soon!

STONEWALL, 14 Kingston Hill (01-549 5984)
Open: Mon-Sun 12.30-2.30pm, 7-11pm

[C] [icon] [P] [icon]

There is a continental air about the rustic wood-and-house-plant décor of this restaurant. Its windows overlook the wide tree-lined pavement of Kingston Hill, on the outskirts of an old market town which is now almost part of London. Food is imaginative and not overpriced though one could exceed the limit when choosing from the à la carte menu. Mushroom Dijonaise followed by chicken farci and Grand Marnier pancakes comes to around £5.75 and there is a 40p cover charge. A traditional three-course Sunday roast costs around £5 a head.

Pinner

THE OLD OAK, 11 High Street (01-866 0286)
Open: Mon-Fri 12noon-2pm, 7-10.30pm, Sat 12noon-2pm, 7-11pm, Sun 12.30-2.30pm, 7.30-10pm

[C]

The set price for a three-course lunch is only about £3 here, including service charge. Businessperson's lunch starters include delicacies such as avocado and grapefruit salad, Waldorf salad (apple, celery and walnuts in sour cream) or crevettes aioli (peel-yourself prawns and garlic mayonnaise). There is a wide choice of main dishes: meat which could be pork in an apple, sage, cider and cream sauce, or a spicy dish such as chili con carne or curry de volaille aux bananes. To finish a satisfying repast, sweets include rum and coffee mousse and Old English flummery, or you might prefer Brie or Camembert to keep the meal memorably continental.

Richmond-upon-Thames

MRS BEETON'S, Hill Rise (01-948 2787)
Open: Mon-Sun 10am-5.30pm, Wed-Sun 6.30pm-12mdnt

[S] [icon]

This village-style restaurant has a craft shop in the basement selling local crafts and kitchen items. The informal restaurant is run by a co-operative of women who are each allocated a day to prepare and serve the food, which is home-made and excellent value for money. Starters include minted cucumber soup or liver pâté with toast for around 60p. Cheese and courgette quiche is about £1 with a salad, fricassée of chicken and mushrooms with rice or lasagne are both around £1.60. A huge choice of desserts includes a very light chocolate layer cake – a very large portion costs about 60p.

Stanmore

PEKING DUCK, 35 The Broadway (01-954 4050)
Open: Mon-Sat 12noon-2.30pm, 6pm-12mdnt
Sun 6pm-12mdnt

[C] [S]

For those who understand the language, the extensive Peking Duck menu is in Chinese as well as English. The westernised Chinese dishes, familiarised by a thousand take-aways are there, but supplemented by more convincingly eastern-sounding dishes such as Gota fish with garlic and ginger (£2.10), or crab meat with straw mushroom (£1.55). A lunchtime special menu, with six choices of main course costs under £2, and the restaurant specialises in meals consisting of six to eight dishes ranging from £3.80 to £7.35 per person. The décor of the first-floor restaurant is pleasantly muted, coloured in shades of cream and brown, with modern Chinese prints on the walls and wicker-shaded lights hanging low over the tables.

Sudbury

TERRY'S RESTAURANT AND BANQUETING SUITE, 763-765 Harrow Road (01-904 4409)
Open: Mon-Fri 12noon-2pm

[P] [icon]

The main operation here is catering for large parties, but on weekday lunchtimes the reception area is utilised for serving what could be one of the cheapest three-course lunches in London. For around £1.50 you get a choice of starters which include items such as melon cocktail and egg mayonnaise, a choice of four main dishes such as roast or meat pie with a good selection of the appropriate, well-cooked vegetables, tasty omelette, or cold meat salad, and a choice of four mouth-watering sweets or cheese and biscuits with which to round off the meal.

Upminster

THE MILL, Roomes Department Store, Station Road (Upminster 50080)
Open: Tue-Thu 9am-5pm (Fri-Sat 5.30pm)

[S] [icon]

Recently modernised, this pleasant restaurant, with its attractive wall mural and soft lighting is on the second floor of Roomes department store. Service is personal and friendly and good, no-nonsense food is excellent value for money. The menu changes every day, but particularly recommended is the home-made steak pie, bursting with meat and served with two veg. With a starter and sweet, the meal is likely to cost about £2.50. Children's portions cost about 50p to £1.

Wembley

PEKING CASTLE RESTAURANT
379 High Road (01-902 3605)
Open: Mon-Sun 12noon-2.30pm, 6-11.30pm

[S]

Apart from the à la carte menu, this quiet haven from the rush of the High Road traffic, where hanging Chinese lanterns and a dragon motif evoke the East, offers special dinners for two or more people at about £4.50 a head for seven items or around £5.50 a head for nine items. If you fancy a meal composed of soup, crispy duck, chicken in yellow-bean sauce, prawns in chili sauce, vegetables, fried rice and toffee apple, £4.50 is not overmuch to pay for it. The main menu includes the usual array of fish, poultry and meat dishes, the cuisine is the upper-class Peking style. Economy-minded diners would be well advised to skip wine with their meal, instead drinking china tea, which will be served ad infinitum. Drivers please note!

'Said I to Sally, come, said I, and eat along of me.
For supper a bit of meat, a pie of veal, some ham and tea.
For O, my dear, my heart is yours, O can't you care for me?'

TRADITIONAL

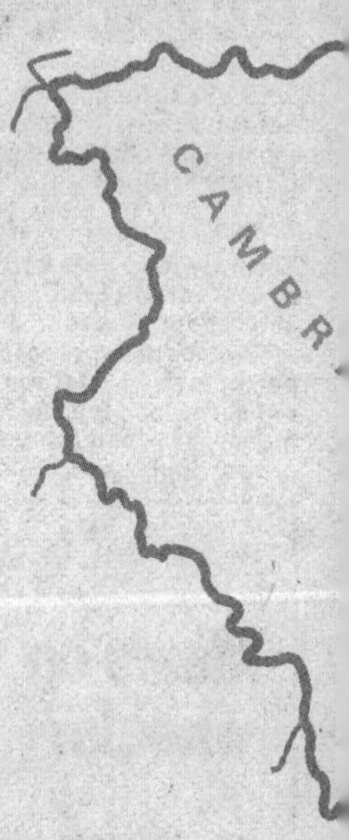

Regional Dishes

Suffolk bacon in beer and treacle
Mutton, lamb or dab with samphire (fleshy-leafed vegetable)
Norfolk turkey with wild, shoreline asparagus
Stewky Blues (grey-blue cockles from Stiffkey)
Cromer crabs
Wells whelks
Brightlingsea oysters
Herrings with dumplings

East Anglia

FAKENHAM
NORFOLK
NORWICH
GREAT YARMOUTH
DOWNHAM MARKET
LOWESTOFT
HARLESTON
BOTESDALE
BURY ST EDMUNDS
SHIRE
MBRIDGE
SUFFOLK
IPSWICH
SAFFRON WALDEN
FELIXSTOWE
COLCHESTER
BRAINTREE
ESSEX
CHELMSFORD
MALDON
BRENTWOOD
SOUTHEND-ON-SEA
SHOEBURYNESS

6

Botesdale

HAMBLYN HOUSE, Rickinghall (Botesdale 292)
Open: Mon-Sat 12noon-2pm, 7.30-10pm (closed Mon pm)
Sun 12noon-1.45pm

[C] [P] [ ]

Run by joint owners Geoff Lazell and Nigel and Judith Philpin, this delightful beamed restaurant forms part of a fine 16th-century property. Imaginative meals, from bar snacks through to the elaborate à la carte, are enhanced by fresh vegetables grown in the garden and prepared by chef Nigel. A typical bar snack would be smoked mackerel and horseradish quiche with salad for around £1.35 or, for slightly less, there's the hot dish of the day – a curry or steak and kidney pie, perhaps. The table d'hôte lunch at about £3.95 might be half a fresh grapefruit, followed by devilled breast of chicken, with rhubarb syllabub for dessert. For around 30p extra the Sunday lunch offers a choice of traditional roasts. Although the à la carte menu is a little more expensive, a meal including braised pork in cider (around £3.95) or Suffolk duckling in a black cherry and Madeira sauce could be yours with careful selection of additional courses.

Braintree

TUDOR ROSE, Little Square (Braintree 45349)
Open: Mon 12noon-2.30pm, Tue-Thu 12noon-2.30pm, 7-10.30pm, Fri-Sat 12noon-2.30pm, 7-11pm, Sun 12noon-3pm

[S]

This attractive 17th-century restaurant is situated in the oldest part of town, in a particularly historic area with 'Cromwell's Court' nearby. Original beams, inglenook fireplace and wooden wheelback chairs give the room an atmosphere of history. A full à la carte menu is available, but for the budget-conscious the set three-course lunch offers an excellent choice of dishes at around £3.50 each. The business person's lunch at £3 might consist of grapefruit, steak and kidney pie, sweet and coffee, and a three-course meal including lasagne or other 'special' pasta dishes will be about £4.50. A three-course traditional roast lunch is about £4 – try the roast duck with 'heavenly' sauce.

Brentwood

THE EAGLE AND CHILD
13 Chelmsford Road, Shenfield (Brentwood 210155)
Open: Mon-Sun 12noon-2pm, 7-10pm

[♫] [P]

This popular Tudor-style pub houses a carvery restaurant which has wood-panelled décor reminiscent of a private club. Value for money is self-evident with modestly priced starters such as pâté at about 80p, followed by a choice of meats carved to your liking. Fresh roast legs of lamb and pork, topside of beef and whole turkeys are on display and James or Keith, the waiters, will only stop filling up your plate when you say so. All this plus generous portions of vegetables for about £4. Alternative main courses include home-made steak pie or salad selection for £2. A choice of sweets is also included in the price. On fine days, a salad bar operates in the attractive garden and if you're lucky you may see a display of Morris dancing.

Bury St Edmunds

THE BEEFEATER STEAK HOUSE
27 Angel Hill (Bury St Edmunds 4224)
Open: Tue-Sun 12noon-2.30pm,

6-12mdnt

C ♫ P S ♣

Don't let the name mislead you, this is a Greek restaurant typical of any to be found on the Greek islands – the weather being the only difference! However, you'll hardly miss the sun as you sit amidst the fishing nets and Greek bric-à-brac enjoying the traditional moussaka, kleftiko or dolmadakia. The cost of a three-course meal is a bit over the budget at £6.25, but qualifies, as a glass of wine is included. Go for a Greek dish such as fresh squid or octopus with rice and salad, rounding off with traditional Greek coffee. The less adventurous may have to pay more for the conventional English dishes (about £6.70); the charcoal-grilled steaks are a credit to proprietor Andreas Kyriakou and his family.

PEGGOTTY'S CARVING ROOM
30 Guildhall Street
(Bury St Edmunds 5444)
Open: Tue-Fri 12noon-2pm, 6.45-10pm, Sat 12noon-2pm, 6.30-10.30pm, Sun 12noon-2.30pm

C S ♣

Notice the Dickensian-type exterior with eye-catching red canopies over the windows. Inside, the heavy wooden tables, tapestry-upholstered chairs, brick pillars and sand-coloured walls lined with prints create a cottage-like atmosphere. Starters are served to your table, then, in the carvery style, you take your pick from an array of hot or cold roasts, carved for you by the chef, or proprietor Luigi, and add to this your own selection of vegetables or salad. Roll and butter and sweet are included in the price of the main course with starters and coffee additional, totalling under £5. After a good lunch at Peggotty's why not take time to explore Bury Cathedral or the Athenaeum, where Dickens gave two readings.

Cambridge

EROS, 25 Petty Cury (Cambridge 63420)
Open: Mon-Fri 12noon-3pm, 5.30-11pm, Sat-Sun 12noon-11pm

C ♫ S ♣

Eros has the atmosphere of a taverna, complete with Greek music, despite very English décor with college arms on panelled walls. The menu is enormous, with fish, omelettes, roasts, grills, salads and a formidable variety of steaks, not to mention Greek, Cypriot and Italian dishes by the dozen. For a satisfying three-course Greek meal, start with taramasalata, followed by sousoukakia and round it off with Grecian-style gâteau – all this for around £4 or so.

THE PENTAGON, The Arts Theatre, 6 St Edwards Passage
(Cambridge 59302)
Open: Mon-Sat 12noon-2pm, 6-10.30pm

C ♫ S

The majority of the dishes are chosen from an attractively displayed buffet of turkey, ham, beef, salmon, quiche and assorted salads. A daily menu of at least three hot dishes such as steak and kidney pie, pork chops or fillet of plaice meunière at around £2.45 is also available. A special theatre-and-supper deal is offered to parties of ten or more.

THE ROOF GARDEN, The Arts Theatre, 6 St Edwards Passage
(Cambridge 355246)
Open: Mon-Sat 9.30am-8pm

C S

This 200-seater self-service restaurant over the Arts Theatre is one of the busiest rendezvous in the city. The main dining area is light and airy but in fine weather many customers prefer to sit outside on the roof. You can eat here from early morning when a full English breakfast is served, through to the 'theatre supper' of hefty ploughman's, cottage pie, fried chicken in a basket and the like. A three-course lunch of melon, Chef's Special dish and home-made sweet with coffee and wine will cost around £3.50. A special item is a two-course lunch for about £1.50, the courses changing every day.

UNIVERSITY ARMS HOTEL ★★★★
Regent Street (Cambridge 51241)
Open: Mon-Sun 12.30-2pm, 7-9pm

[C] [♫] [P] [S] [🍷]

Close to the centre of Cambridge, and overlooking Parker's Piece – a 25-acre park – stands this imposing hostelry which has been the leading hotel here since 1831. It has been owned by the Bradford family since 1891. The large ground-floor restaurant overlooks the park through windows which depict the arms of the colleges in stained glass. Only by sticking to the two-course table d'hôte menu will you be safe on the budget as an à la carte meal plus wine would be well over £5. For about £5.40 you can choose from a menu of traditional dishes such as fried lemon sole, roast leg of pork with apple sauce, or cold ham salad plus a sweet. A simpler lunch may be chosen from the buffet set up in Parker's Lounge, where sandwiches and simple salads cost as little as 70p, and a selection of cold meats, savouries and salads will set you back about £3.

VARSITY RESTAURANT
35 St Andrew's Street
(Cambridge 56060)
Open: Mon-Sun 12noon-3pm, 5.30-11pm

[S]

This two-storey Greek restaurant is housed in one of Cambridge's many listed buildings in one of the city centre's not-so-busy streets. The atmosphere is very authentic, with Greek pictures scattered on white-washed walls, an effect which is emphasised by black wooden beams and doors. A good three-course meal, including wine and coffee, can be enjoyed for around £3.50. Food is basically Greek with some French and English dishes. Kebab of the house – two skewers of tenderloin, served with Greek salad and fetta cheese, is one of four speciality dishes. Service is quick and friendly despite the fact that the restaurant seats 105.

WILSON'S RESTAURANTS
14 Trinity Street (Cambridge 356845)
Open: The Carvery: Mon-Thu 12noon-3pm, 6-11pm,
Fri-Sat 12noon-3pm, 6pm-12mdnt
The Granary: Mon-Sat 10.30am-10.30pm,
Sun 10.30am-6pm

[P] [S]

Wilson's is a fine black and white, 16th-century building housing three restaurants. The Carvery, on the first floor, retains the Tudor style. There is a good choice of starters and desserts served by waitresses, but the interesting feature is the help-yourself carvery table, where the chef will carve beef, roast pork or poultry to your choice and you select your own vegetables. Three courses will cost around £5. For a quicker, less expensive meal, try The Granary. A separate entrance takes you into the original cellars and here up to ten hot dishes are on display. Beef casserole, curried chicken and sweet and sour pork are all about £1.80, while a selection of hot quiches are on offer for around £1. Fresh cream desserts are available for about 80p. Trinity Street Restaurant on the second floor offers a more traditional à la carte menu which is a little above our limit.

Chelmsford

CORKS, 34a Moulsham Street
(Chelmsford 58733)
Open: Mon-Sat 12noon-2.30pm, 6-11pm, Sun 7-10.30pm

[C] [♫] [P] [S]

Situated opposite the AA office, this trendy wine bar is a popular place for a good meal or informal drink and chat. A brown-painted window front and the Tudor beams beyond entice you over the threshold, where a tempting menu chalked on the ubiquitous plât du jour blackboard announces moussaka and salad, at around £1.75, or turkey pie and pâté (about £1). The competent staff is led by Michael Dunbar who is always on hand to extend a friendly welcome to his guests.

PIZZA AND PASTA, 44 Moulsham Road (Chelmsford 352245)
Open: Mon-Sat 12noon-2.30pm, 6-10.30pm

[C] [S] [🍷]

A decorative brown awning and Venetian blinds adorn this highly original-looking Italian restaurant and garden terrace. The simple but appetising menu specialises in the pizzas and pastas anticipated. Starters include Spanish gazpacho and minestrone soup at about 95p. An imaginative pizza is napoletana, with mozzarella cheese, tomatoes, capers, anchovies and olives for around £2. Pastas include delicious fetuccine matriciana (noodles with tomato, onion and bacon) at about £2. Selection of sweets is good with home-made cheesecake and strudel at around £1.

Colchester

BISTRO 9, 9 North Hill
(Colchester 76466)
Open: Tue-Sat 12noon-1.45pm, 7-10.45pm

[C] [S] [☙]

This small bistro has a short menu of home-made dishes served with fresh vegetables and home-made bread. It will be easier to keep within the £5 limit in the basement, where substantial 'snacks' are served. Home-made soup and bread, the hot dish of the day (such as moussaka or chili con carne), and a pudding from the à la carte menu – try the brown bread ice cream – will cost about £3.50. With quiche and salad as a main course, you'll spend less than £3. The Bistro always offers a vegetarian dish of the day at under £3 and on Saturdays a set lunch of two courses and coffee for £3.75. The service by friendly waitresses is guaranteed to please, as is the pleasantly informal atmosphere, the large refectory tables (you may have to share), and pretty country décor.

Wm SCRAGG'S ✕✕ 2 North Hill
(Colchester 41111)
Open: Mon-Sat 12noon-2.15pm, 7-10.30pm

[C]

This elegant seafood restaurant bears the name of the journeyman bricklayer who bought the premises in 1832, and lived there peacefully until the ripe old age of seventy-eight. Many of the appetising dishes come dangerously near to our limit, a couple of the cheaper ones being baked trout and grilled mackerel, both under £4. However, a fine selection of bar snacks is available; fish pâté at £1.40, seafood flan with salad or smoked mackerel at around £2.25, and a good choice of inexpensive sandwiches such as prawn and lettuce or fish pâté and cucumber. A sweet may be chosen for about £1.

Downham Market

CROWN STABLES, CROWN HOTEL
(Downham Market 2322)
Open: Mon-Sun 10am-10pm

[C] [P] [☙]

This 300-year-old coaching inn has always been a popular haunt of locals in the quiet town of Downham Market. However, since the spring of 1980, the old stables have been converted into a slick grill room and buttery with natural wood tables, tiled floor, brick walls and horsey bric-à-brac creating a clean and simple atmosphere. Here, a very reasonably-priced cold buffet comprises home-cooked cold meats and hand-raised pies, quiches, pâtés and flans with a selection of salads at under £2. Charcoal grill steaks or kebabs will push up the price, but ploughman's platter, pizza or a steak sandwich are tasty alternatives at the other end of the price-scale. Home-made gâteaux and flans are around 80p.

Fakenham

THE CROWN HOTEL Market Place
(Fakenham 2010)
Open: bars: Mon-Wed, Fri-Sun, licensing hours, Thu 10.30am-4.30pm, 5.30-11pm, restaurant: Mon-Sat 12.15-2pm, 7.15-9.15pm, Sun 12.15-2pm

[C] [♫] [P] [S]

In the restaurant, dark oak beams and panelling are offset by gold tablecloths and napkins, a red carpet and red-globed oil table lamps. A three course table d'hôte lunch is only around £3.50 and offers a good choice for all courses. Sardine and tomato salad, Florida cocktail or ravioli are examples of starters, a selection of roasts make up the main course and sweets from the trolley include cheesecake, fruit and cream or éclairs. A slightly extended menu operates for a three-course dinner at about £4.50. A three-course Sunday lunch for about £3.75 is good value. The à la carte menu offers more exotic dishes – still reasonably priced at between £2-£6.50 including fresh vegetables.

THE LIMES HOTEL, Bridge Street
(Fakenham 2726)
Open: Mon-Fri 12noon-1.30pm, 7-9.30pm, Sat 12noon-1.30pm, 7-10pm, Sun 12noon-1.30pm

[P] [S]

This friendly free house was only created in 1975, but already it has an excellent reputation for fresh, home-cooked food. The 'Summer Special' three-course lunch costs £3.75, and the choice is good for each course – you could choose Florida cocktail, rainbow trout and sherry trifle. The 'Winter Special' offers warming starters and sweets. A cold lunch buffet is on offer in the conservatory for £1.70 – and all the meats are home-cooked. À la carte dinner by candlelight offers a very wide selection, with a dozen appetisers, including whitebait at 90p or smoked salmon at £1. Entrées vary in price, but gammon steak with peaches or pineapple or deep fried southern style chicken, both served with vegetables of the day, are less than £3. Sweets such as sorbets are from 70p.

Felixstowe

BUTTERY BAR, ORWELL MOAT HOUSE ★★★★ Hamilton Road (Felixstowe 5511)
Open: Mon-Sat 12noon-2pm, 6-9.15pm (Sun 12noon-2pm summer only)

[C] [P] [☘]

This elegant buttery with its dark oak panels and richly-ornamented ceiling offers you all the comfort and luxury of a four-star hotel without the prices. Home-made soup of the day could be followed by smoked Scotch salmon, Norfolk turkey, ox tongue or other cold meats all served with salads, pickles, and a roll and butter. Finish with home-made fruit pie and cream and you'll still be within the budget. In the restaurant, table d'hôte lunch is around £5.25 and dinner about £5.75.

Great Yarmouth

MOMENTS, 149 King Street (Great Yarmouth 2967)
Open: Mon-Sun 12noon-2pm, (Sun 1.30pm), 6.30-11.30pm

[C] [♫] [P] [S] [☘]

Originally two merchants' houses, this modern grill restaurant features particularly attractive décor, with wood-clad walls, polished wood floor and tables, high-backed banquettes and pendant copper-shaded lamps over each table. The 'Daily Economiser' menu offers excellent value at around £2.25, all in with a daily changing main course, plus sweet of the day. There is a good choice of starters, fish, salads, grills and sweets on the à la carte menu which qualify for this Guide.

Harleston

THE DOVE, Wortwell (Homersfield 315)
Open: Tue-Sat 11am-2.30pm, 7-9.30pm, Sun 12noon-3pm (evenings reservations only)

[P] [☘]

Freshly-prepared food and friendly service are the watchwords at John and Pat Oberhoffer's tiny restaurant. Once a pub and smithy, it is conveniently placed at the junction of the A143 and B1062 for travellers in need of refreshment on their way to and from the coast. The limited lunch menu offers a three-course meal for between £2.50-£3.50, but the more extensive dinner menu costs considerably more and care is required when choosing a budget meal. You could choose ratatouille, served hot or cold, as a starter for around 75p, followed by truite almandine (pan fried trout served with almonds) and fresh vegetables at about £3.90 with chocolate eclairs for dessert at 50p or so, and still have change from £6. The Dove can offer you a mouthwatering cream tea of fresh cream gâteau with coffee.

Ipswich

GREAT WHITE HORSE ★★
Tavern Street (Ipswich 56558)
Open: Buttery: Mon-Sat 11am-9.30pm Carving Table: Mon-Sun 12.30-2pm, 7-9.15pm

[C] [S] [☘]

A leading inn in Ipswich since the 16th century, the Great White Horse was once the haunt of Charles Dickens when the author was employed as a reporter on the Ipswich Chronicle and it was to receive a mention in his *Pickwick Papers*. A wood-panelled buttery offers a wide range of food from toasted tea-cakes to omelettes and grills served all day at prices well within our budget (there is even a special menu for the under 12s). A more elegant meal may be enjoyed within the plush deep red and copper surrounds of the Carvery. The à la carte menu here is rather over the top, but an excellent table d'hôte Carving Table menu gives a choice of five starters including prawn cocktail; prime rib of beef, selected hot roasts with traditional accompaniments or cold roast with salad; sweet from the trolley or cheeses plus coffee with cream for an all-inclusive price of £5.95.

HENEKEY'S HOTEL ★★
Westgate Street (Ipswich 58506)
Open: Mon-Sun 12noon-2.30pm, 6pm-10.30pm (Fri-Sat 11pm)

[C] [♫] [P] [S] [☘]

Behind an ornate gothic, stone façade, this Trusthouse Forte concern has been completely modernised and refurbished. There are two comfortable restaurants, the Grill and the Sherry Restaurant, the latter being slightly more expensive. Although described as 'Henekey's Steak Bars', plaice (about £3.50), Barnsley chop (about £4) and chicken cordon bleu (£4.20) are also available and the prices include sweet or cheese. Appetisers are around the £1 mark, and include whitebait and smoked mackerel.

MARNO'S, 14 St Nicholas Street (Ipswich 53106)
Open: summer: Mon-Wed 10am-2pm, Thu-Sat 10am-2pm, 7.30-10pm, winter: closed Wed pm

[♫]

A vegetarian restaurant with dishes imaginative enough to tempt the most confirmed meat-eater. The lunch menu includes savoury flans, bean hotpot, nut rissoles, freshly-made salads and fruits for about £3.70. The much more extensive evening menu averages around £5.25 for three courses such as mushroom pâté, Cheshire cheese and herb pie, pashka (a Russian mixture of curd cheese, butter, cream, raisins and brown sugar), followed by herbal tea. Live music is provided by local folk musicians at weekends.

NOBLE ROMANS, 9 Buttermarket (Ipswich 219376)
Open: Mon-Sat 10am-11pm, Sun 5.30-10.30pm

[♫] [S] [🍷]

Claudius and Tiberius are among the fourteen noble Romans whose names are taken in vain for the pizzas in this trendy Italian restaurant. A 'Claudius' has mozzarella cheese with tomato and costs about £1.20 while a 'Tiberius', at the top of the range, has tuna, sardine, anchovy, onion, lemon, olives, capers, mozzarella and tomato for around £1.75. A full three-course meal here need only cost about £3, with appetisers such as melon for around 75p and most desserts costing around 70p – try Black Forest gâteau or lemon sorbet. All this and décor in oatmeal, fawn and brown with basket-weave chairs has attracted a regular clientèle.

Lowestoft

VICTORIA BAR BUTTERY, VICTORIA HOTEL ★★★ Kirkley Cliff (Lowestoft 4433) Open: Mon-Sat 12noon-2pm

[C] [P] [🍷]

A well-stocked cold buffet table holds roast Norfolk turkey, ox tongue, beef, ham and prawns in cocktail sauce, which with a serve-yourself salad average at about £2 a head. Hot meals often include grilled minute steak, breaded scampi or fillets of Lowestoft plaice, but the Chef's special (changed daily) is warmly recommended. At the cheap end of the scale are sandwiches, a ploughman's lunch or hamburger with salad garnish. Sweet and a starter add around 50p.

Maldon

MANN'S BISTRO, 46 Market Hill (Maldon 57752)
Open: Mon-Sat 7-10.30pm (11pm Fri & Sat)

[♫] [S] [🍷]

Wooden tables and benches, bathed in candlelight and the live music of soft guitars (some evenings) enhances the bistro-like atmosphere at Mann's. Situated close to the boating yards and moorings, this intimate little haunt offers first-class respite for the sailing fraternity, and anyone else besides. The imaginative menu is changed regularly and leaves you spoiled for choice with such delights as Cornish chicken, pork stuffed with apricots and prunes and ragout of beef. An unusual vegetarian dish is included in each menu at around £2.50 for sweet and sour red beans or Neapolitan quiche. With an appetiser such as grapefruit and mint and a sweet from the trolley, a most appetising meal and coffee should cost you less than £5.

Norwich

LE BISTRO, 2a Exchange Street (Norwich 24452)
Open: Mon 11.30am-2pm, Tue-Fri 11.30am-10pm, Sat 11.30am-2.30pm, 5-10pm

[C] [♫] [P] [S] [🍷]

Table d'hôte at Le Bistro is very good value, an English lunch costing around £2.30 and dinner – with some French dishes – about £4.40. You could choose a good meal from the à la carte menu for less than £6, too. Veal Maison is a popular choice; other favourites include sole Normandy and duck with orange sauce. The first and second floor restaurants are pleasant and comfortable (once the stairs are negotiated), with dried-flower arrangements set against brocade-patterned wallpaper and brown check cotton cloths.

MANO, 72 Prince of Wales Road (Norwich 613143)
Open: Mon-Sat 7-11.30pm

S

The bright orange and white exterior of this bistro proclaims its presence on the corner of Prince of Wales Road and Cathedral Street. As a striking contrast the interior is a faithful reproduction of a Parisian café with dark red paintwork, red velvet café curtains on brass rails and French posters. Green and white tablecloths cover the ten cast-iron tables which provide seating capacity for 34 people. Contrary to appearances, owner Mano is in fact Turkish and his restaurant boasts a truly international menu. A meal of whitebait, followed by duck pilaff plus pears in burgundy wine and coffee will cost around £5.

REMBRANDT RESTAURANT, Easton (Norwich 880241)
Open: Tue-Sat 12noon-2.15pm, 7-10.30pm, Sun 12noon-2.15pm

C ♫ P

Proprietors Bruno and Trudie Riccobena moved here from London five years ago and they have since introduced a wide range of menu styles to suit all tastes, including one for children. The restaurant also has facilities for invalids. Without careful selection, the à la carte can easily exceed our limited budget, but the special 'Business Lunch' and 'Holidaymaker's Lunch' at £3.25 or less are very good value. Main course might be gammon, calves' liver, plaice, omelette or salad, and two or three international dishes are available each day. Under the Rembrandt chef's 'Taste of England' series, steak and kidney pies, in particular, are selling like hot cakes!

SAVOY RESTAURANT ✕✕✕ 50 Prince of Wales Road (Norwich 20732)
Open: Mon-Sun 12noon-2.30pm, 6pm-1.30am

C ♫ P

The Athenian Room on the ground floor is elegantly green with chandeliers, Greek pictures and small booths. The windows overlook an enclosed patio with vines and plants galore. Downstairs is the Cellar Taverna, seating over 100 on two levels, complete with a small dance floor. Three-course table d'hôte lunch in the Athenian Room is about £3 on weekdays and £4 on Sundays. Main course choices are particularly good – roast beef or chicken, moussaka, kebabs, plaice or ham salad. The à la carte menu is very extensive, with Greek, English, Italian and French cuisine, but you will have to select a three-course meal carefully to stay around the £5 limit.

SMEDLEY'S ✕✕ Princes Street (Norwich 23193)
Open: Mon-Fri 12noon-3pm, 7-11pm, Sat 12noon-3pm, 7pm-12mdnt

[C] [S]

The ground floor lounge bar seats about forty around a brick-topped bar surface. Adjacent to this is a dining room where simple plated meals, roughly ranging from 80p-£2, are served. Items such as chicken casserole, whitebait and salad and dressed crab are available for both lunch and dinner. Upstairs is the main restaurant, pine-ceilinged with booths and hanging lights, where there is an extensive à la carte menu with a large price range and a three-course set menu. Try a starter such as rich game soup, followed by (amongst other choices) rump steak, and then a sweet from the trolley for around £5.

TATLERS, 21 Tombland (Norwich 21822)
Open: Mon-Sat 6-11.30pm, Sun 12.30-2.30pm, 7-11pm

[P] [S]

You'll find Tatlers amongst the beautiful buildings of Tombland. A group of young people have converted an old house into this attractive restaurant, with a bar upstairs, and have succeeded in creating an air of Victorian opulence by the use of floral wallpaper, red curtains, Victoriana lamps, and mirrors. High-backed settles arranged around plain wooden tables provide a degree of privacy and seclusion. All food is prepared on the premises, the accent being on traditional Norfolk dishes prepared from local produce. Starters include pâté or mussels in white wine (about £1.20) and main course dishes range in price from meat loaf at £2.50 to peppered fillet steak at £4.70. More unusual dishes include rabbit in mustard and rosemary (£2.80) or pigeon, duck and orange pie at about £2.60. Vegetables are likely to add about 50p-70p to these prices. Sweets (the list includes syllabub and chocolate fudge cake) cost an average of 80p.

Saffron Walden

EIGHT BELLS, Bridge Street (Saffron Walden 22790/22764)
Open: Restaurant: Tue-Sun 12noon-2pm, Mon-Thu 7-9.30pm, Fri-Sat 7-10pm and normal licensing hours

[C] [P]

Situated in a comfortable spot on the edge of town, like the noble old sentinel it is, this four hundred-year-old inn retains its original pub sign and a good deal of olde worlde charm. Both the budget lunches (with main courses such as roast ribs of beef carved from a silver trolley), and the more pricey à la carte selection are of extremely high standard (including such delights as saffron gilded chicken at around £5.45 with appetisers, dessert and coffee with chocolate mints). There's a cold buffet served in the bar at around £1.45-£2. Don't miss a delicious dessert.

Shoeburyness

SHORE HOUSE RESTAURANT
Ness Road (Shoeburyness 3408)
Open: Tue-Fri, Sun 12noon-2pm, Tue-Sat 7-12mdnt (2am Thu-Sat)

[C] [P]

If the fresh air gives you an appetite you'll find this sea-front eating place a very tempting proposition. However, the plush restaurant with its warm red décor is likely to just tip our limit. Three courses from the interesting à la carte menu can cost from £4-£6 although a set three-course lunch with excellent choice of dishes is £4.50 plus service. You'll have to stick to the bar buttery if you want a real budget-priced meal. For about £3.50 you can have a very good two-course lunch such as egg mayonnaise, roast turkey with stuffing, new potatoes and fresh vegetables.

Southend-on-Sea

CAPRICE CARVING ROOM
96 The Ridgeway, Westcliff (Southend-on-Sea 76417)
Open: Tue-Sat 12.30-2.30pm, 7-10.30pm, Sun 12.30-2.30pm

Two hundred yards from Chalkwell station on the north side of the railway, the Caprice enjoys quiet surroundings at the corner of a residential square. For around £4.10 the choice is yours from the hot or cold Carving Table, featuring such dishes as prime roast beef with fluffy Yorkshire pudding and roast leg of English pork with apple sauce. Vegetables and a choice from the sweet trolley, or cheese and biscuits, are included in the price, but even with extras such as home-made pâté, roll and butter and coffee the cost is only around £5. First-class service is a prime consideration here and you will probably want to linger over a speciality coffee, freshly brewed with a cream topping, chosen from the list of over a dozen. Children's portions are available at around £3.

CHINATOWN, 28 York Street
(Southend-on-Sea 64888)
Open: Mon-Thu 12noon-2.30pm, 5pm-12mdnt, Fri-Sat 12noon-2.30pm, 5pm-1am, Sun 12noon-12mdnt

[P] [S]

This cosy Chinese restaurant close to the town centre offers an enormous choice of traditional Chinese and English dishes at budget prices. Well-cooked and pleasantly served by Ken, the owner's son, Wan Tun soup is extremely tasty and roast duck Hong Kong style, decorated with Chinese mushrooms and peppers and costing about £2.50 is highly recommended. Chop suey and chow mein dishes are excellent value for money. A special set dinner for one person, which includes coffee, costs less than or around £2.50 and is excellent value for money when you consider the amount of time spent in preparing the dishes.

CHRYSANTHEMUM CHINESE RESTAURANT, 202 Eastern Esplanade
(Southend-on-Sea 582360)
Open: Mon-Sun 12noon-3pm, 6pm-12mdnt

[C] [♫] [P] [♿]

Southend's renowned Chinese restaurant is on the seafront road to Thorpe Bay. It enjoys great popularity built up over ten years, particularly for the Friday and Saturday night music and dancing sessions in the suitably-lit basement. Specialities such as roast Shanghai duck, Chrysanthemum fried chicken and barbecue spare ribs range in price from around £4 to £4.50 and are well worth trying, but the long menu gives tremendous choice. For the adventurous, the Chef recommends two set meals which include two appetisers such as crab claw and Chinese kebab, two meat dishes, two vegetable dishes, fried rice and coffee around £6.

COTGROVES RESTAURANT,
11 High Street
(Southend-on-Sea 338155)
Open: Mon-Thu 11.45am-9.15pm, Fri-Sat 11.45am-9.45pm, Sun 11.45am-9.15pm

[C] [♫] [P] [S] [♿]

David and John Cotgrove now run the successor to their grandfather Arthur's original High Street restaurant opened in 1896 – a modern, 185-seater imaginatively adapted from a former supermarket building. The décor carries forward a family tradition of 'fish and ships' including a colourful tiled entrance lobby – the work of a local sculptor – and several drawings and oil-paintings executed by John himself. Almost everything you could wish for is on the menu, from a T-bone steak or fresh crab salad down to steak, kidney and mushroom pie or a three-course 'special' at lunchtime for less than £2.50. A wide range of good quality fried or grilled fish is featured, and the sweets vary from a simple ice-cream to a 'banana special' replete with ice-cream, chocolate sauce and whipped cream (£1.20). The restaurant is licenced and a full range of draught and bottled beers, table wines and liqueurs are stocked. Cotgroves house-wine (red, sweet or dry white and rosé) is sold by the litre bottle (£4.90) or by the glass (65p).

THE PIPE OF PORT, 84 High Street
(Southend-on-Sea 614606)
Open: Mon-Thu 11am-2.30pm, 6-10.30pm, Fri-Sat 11am-2.30pm, 6-11pm, Sun 12noon-2pm

[C] [P] [S]

This wine bar is situated just off the High Street in a basement premises underneath Greenfields. There is a good, and recently-expanded menu with some interesting starters, such as the toasted fingers topped with anchovy, sardine or Stilton at around £1.10 for six. A three-course meal of soup, smoked mackerel (two fillets) with salad and fresh fruit salad can be had for around £4.25 – a very satisfying and nutritious repast.

SPENCER'S, 20 High Street, Hadleigh
(Southend-on-Sea 558166)
Open: Mon-Thu 10am-2.30pm, 6-10.30pm, Fri-Sat 10am-2.30pm, 6-11pm, Sun 10am-2.30pm, 6-10.30pm

[♫] [P] [S]

This wine bar is easily spotted by the attractive pavement patio. Comfortable banquette seating and French cane-back chairs enable you to take your ease while absorbing the interesting reading on the walls. Chalkboards display the menu, offering plenty of choice. Pâté is about 95p, lasagne around £1 and beef curry about £1.20. The poppy seed French bread is very good as is the help-yourself salad selection from around £1.50 and the chili con carne at about £1.20. Brian Spencer selects all his own wines and a glass of excellent French house wine costs around 65p in the restaurant.

There was a rocky valley between Buxton and Bakewell, . . . divine as the vale of Tempe; you might have seen the gods there morning and evening, – Apollo and the sweet Muses of the Light . . .

PRAETERITA, JOANNA'S CAVE

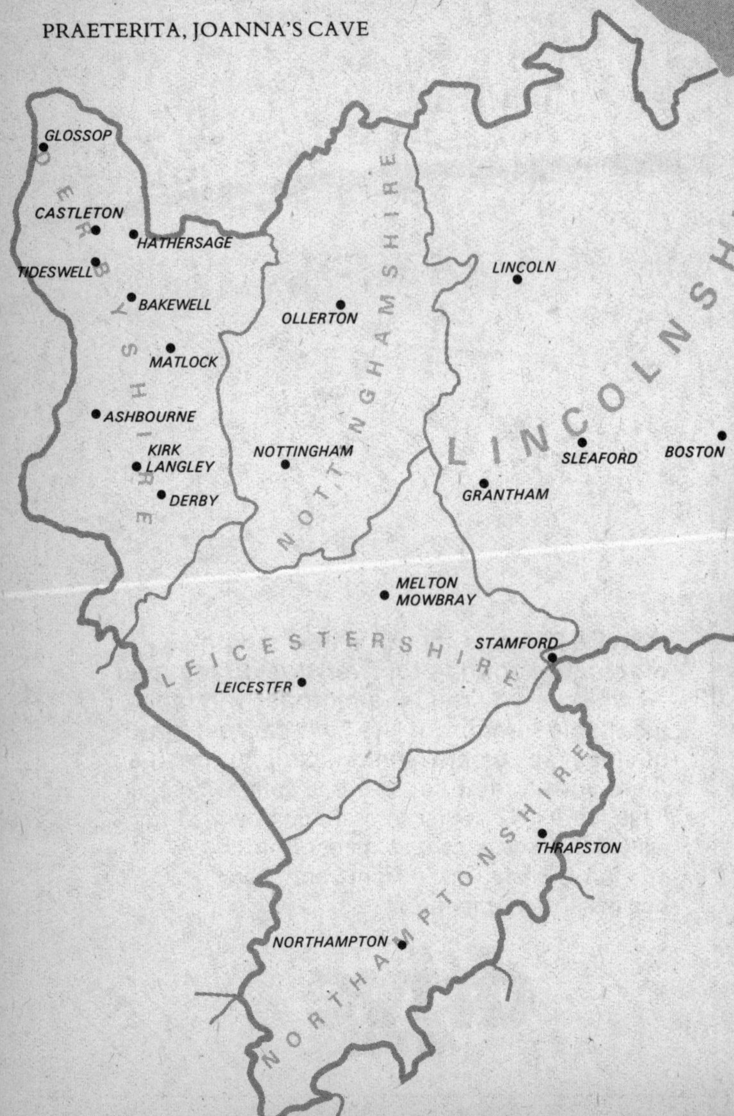

East Midlands and the Peak District

SUTTON-ON-SEA

SKEGNESS

7

Regional Dishes

Melton Hunt Cake
Mansfield gooseberry pie
Quorn bacon roll
Nottingham Bramley tart
Melton Mowbray pie
Stilton, Sage Derby and Red Leicester cheese
Hallaton hare pie

Ashbourne

THE ASHBURNIAN, Compton
(Ashbourne 42798)
Open: Mon-Sat 12noon-2pm, 6-10pm, Sun 12noon-6pm

C S

The restaurant with its white rough-plaster walls and dark beams with reproduction brass lanterns, has a pleasantly olde worlde atmosphere. A comfortable cocktail bar adjoining has hessian-clad walls and copper-topped tables. The menu is very reasonably priced, with starters ranging from around 40p-£1.10 – including prawn cocktail and a choice of seven main courses, all served with vegetables and including a sweet (such as apple tart with cream) in the listed price. Half a roast chicken is around £3.

CARY'S, Workhouse Yard, Dig Street
(Ashbourne 42811)
Open: Mon-Sat 10am-3pm, 7-11pm
Sun 12noon-2pm, 7-10.30pm

C

Named after John Cary, the famous 18th-century cartographer, Cary's is a pleasant, rather trendy place, situated near the centre of this old market town in premises that date back some 300 years. Recently opened as a wine bar, it is run by the Proprietor's daughter and some young female assistants in a friendly and informal manner. Décor is clean and fresh with exposed brickwork and ceiling beams and stripped pine furniture. Diners are entertained by piped pop music. A typical meal might include mushrooms Armenienne for starters at about 85p, a main dish of turkey stroganoff or pork barb-be-que with rice and side salad for around £3.25 and gâteau at 75p for dessert.

SPENCER'S COFFEE HOUSE RESTAURANT, 37-41 Market Place
(Ashbourne 3164)
Open: Mon-Sat 9am-5.45pm

P S

This attractive little restaurant is housed in Georgian premises overlooking the cobbled market square of this historic town. A daily-changing lunch menu offers a good selection of traditional dishes, an example of which would be cream of leek soup with roll and butter, home-made steak and kidney pie with new potatoes and green peas, and apple and blackcurrant tart – all for around £4.

Bakewell

FISCHER'S, Bath Street
(Bakewell 2687)
Open: Mon-Sun 10am-6pm, 7-10pm

P

This olde-worlde restaurant, originally a barn, features white painted stone walls and cottage furniture. Set lunches consist of traditional, home-cooked dishes, with choices such as home-made soup followed by steak and kidney pie or braised beef in brown ale followed by a good English pudding or ice cream at around £3.50. The evening meal is just beyond our limit.

MILFORD HOUSE ★ Mill Street
(Bakewell 2130)
Open: Mon-Sun 1-1.30pm, 7-7.30pm

P

Situated on the ground floor of the Milford House Hotel, this pleasant ten-table dining room offers quality meals at sensible prices. The whole operation has been personally run by the Hunt family for many years and service is their keynote. Set lunches are £4.60 and feature roast chicken and grilled plaice. Five course evening meals are only slightly dearer (£5.20), with roast stuffed loin topping the bill. After tasting dessert specialities such as strawberry pie with cream and orange trifle, you'll surely agree that Bakewell is an apt location for the restaurant. Coffee is included in the price. A word of warning – the short opening hours mean that advance booking is a must.

Boston

THE CARVING ROOM, NEW ENGLAND HOTEL ★★ Wide Bargate
(Boston 65255)
Open: Mon-Thu 12noon-2pm, 7-10pm, Fri-Sun 12noon-2pm, 7-10.30pm

C P

At the rear of the imposing New England Hotel is the elegant, Regency-style Carving Room, with white pillars, rich red-patterned carpet and green wallpaper, leather upholstery and tablecloths. Here you may eat a superb roast lunch or dinner. The carving table is bedecked with large roast joints, fresh vegetables and salads – you help yourself to as much as you want. This, together with the choice of a sweet from the trolley, will set you back £4.35. Appetisers are extra, but hardly necessary! Potted shrimps or avocado pear with prawns are the most expensive at around £1.50, but soup is only 60p. Children can help themselves and are charged the special reduced price of £2.50.

THE THREE TUNS, 43/44 Market Place (Boston 66600)
Open: Mon-Sun normal licensing hours

[♫] [P] [S] [♣]

Close by an Estate Agents and up seventeen steps is this first-floor wine bar decked out like a vineyard. A trellis supporting flowers and grapes is suspended from the ceiling and brown and beige is the theme of the décor. Lunch 'specials' at £1 include pizza, quiche and Boston burger, but for £1.75 you can have roast chicken or Lincolnshire sausage. Starters at 50p include pâté, soup or mackerel, and 55p will buy you a piece of gâteau or cheesecake. The à la carte menu is more expensive, but with rump steak, rainbow trout or duckling on offer, you could easily be tempted – and still stay within the budget.

Castleton

THE CASTLE HOTEL AND RESTAURANT (Hope Valley 20578)
Open: Mon-Thu, Sun 12noon-2pm, 7-10pm, Fri-Sat 12noon-2pm, 7-10.30pm

[C] [P]

Within the Peak District National Park and in the village centre, is this stone-built 17th-century coaching inn, its interior a wealth of exposed stonework and beams. Excellent table d'hôte menus operate for lunch and dinner – you are spoiled for choice. Lunch costs £4.45, with sixteen starters including avocado viniagrette, pâté-filled mushrooms in batter and smoked mackerel. Four roasts head the long list of main dishes. The roast beef with vegetables, ratatouille, horseradish sauce and Yorkshire pudding is particularly recommended. Fillet of pork à la crème, chicken chasseur and cider-baked ham with cinnamon peaches are other possibilities. A selection of sweets on the trolley are all served with fresh cream. Dinner is £4.95 and offers even more choices.

Derby

BEN BOWERS, 13-15 Chapel Street (Derby 367688/365988)
Open: Mon-Fri 12noon-2pm, 7-11pm, Sat 7-11pm, Sun 12noon-2pm

[C] [♫] [P] [S] [♣]

Located above the Blessington Carriage public house is this long, rectangular restaurant, with seating for about sixty at polished wooden tables. A three-course lunch of (for instance) home-made soup of the day, minute steak au poivre with salad and French fried potatoes and a sweet from the trolley costs about £3.95, with children's portions at around £2.25. The dinner menu features dishes from Russia, Mexico, Austria and the Caribbean and is on the pricey side. £5 would restrict your choice, but for £6 it's worth splashing out on one of the 'special' nights when a cabaret is provided. Downstairs in Betty's Buffet Bar, excellent pub lunches are served.

THE CATHEDRAL RESTAURANT LTD ✕✕ 22 Iron Gate (Derby 368732)
Open: Mon-Wed, Fri 12noon-2pm, 7-10pm, Thu 12noon-2pm

[C] [♫] [P] [S] [♣]

In the shadow of Derby Cathedral, this elegant little restaurant with its low ceiling, exposed central beam and sparkling table tops, glassware and cutlery, is housed in a building dating back to 1530. Then a nunnery, it has since been a Ladies' club and a chartered accountants' office. At lunchtime a four-course table d'hôte menu is available at £3.50. Choice is good and dishes include salads, omelettes, pizza, spaghetti bolognese and steak, kidney and mushroom pie while shish kebab, grilled trout, chicken cathedral, sirloin steak and jumbo scampi are examples of the more pricey fare. In the evening there is a similar, though slightly dearer table d'hôte dinner, and the à la carte menu, though tempting, is expensive.

THE FRENCH REVOLUTION, Friargate (Derby 40581)
Open: Mon-Sat 12noon-2pm, 7.30-10.30pm (Fri-Sat 11pm)

[C] [♫] [P]

A touch of France in the centre of Derby – this intimate little bistro with its French posters, prints, music and cuisine is deservedly popular. The table d'hôte lunch menu at about £5 offers soup, prawn cocktail or fruit juice with a choice of sirloin steak served plain or in a red wine sauce and a choice of desserts. In the evenings, typically French table d'hôte dinners are served: three courses cost around £4 and four courses about £5.

LETTUCE LEAF, 21 Friar Gate
(Derby 40307)
Open: Mon-Sat 10am-7.30pm

[P] [S]

Beyond the little craft shop selling handthrown pottery, woodcrafts and books on yoga and health food is this white-walled restaurant with its bright curtains, basket-work lamp shades, wooden tables and tasty vegetarian menu. Vegetable soup or fruit juice are inexpensive starters at around 35p. Omelettes, salads, savouries and snacks supplement a daily speciality such as marrow provençale, lasagne, gratin Dauphinois, pizza or celery hotpot. Most main dishes cost under or around £1.20, with sweets such as fresh fruit salad, yoghurt with honey or lettuce leaf muesli under 60p. Finish with a dandelion coffee – full of flavour.

Glossop

CROWTON'S, 14 High Street East
(Glossop 63409)
Open: Tue-Sat 12noon-2pm, 7-9pm

[P] [S] [🍷]

If Victoriana is your scene you'll love this restaurant. For behind its brown and cream exterior lies an eating place furnished in the style of great-grandmama's front room – complete with black lead grate! The food however is right up to date, with steaks, poached salmon and scampi featuring on the menu for around £4 to £5. There's the usual array of starters, and to finish with you might fancy a chocolate nut sundae or fresh pineapple with cream for less than £1. Coffee and mints are served for around 30p in an atmosphere of bygone days. It comes as quite a surprise to learn that Crowton's was established in 1979.

Grantham

CATLIN'S, 11 High Street
(Grantham 5428/9)
Open: Mon-Tue 9am-6pm,
Wed 9am-2pm, Thu-Sat 9am-6pm

[P] [S] [🍷]

Steeped in history, the olde worlde

grocery and confectionery shop of Catlin Bros Ltd, boasts a restaurant with wood-panelled walls, oak beams, pottery and bric-à-brac on the first floor. The property dates back to 1560 and its claims to fame include the 'discovery' of Grantham gingerbread and the ghost of one Captain Hamilton, a Royalist officer during the Civil War. Snacks are served throughout the day and a typical meal from the à la carte menu might be home-made soup (40p), pepper and salami pizza with salad (£1.50) and fresh fruit pancake with cream (95p). French house wine is very reasonable at 60p a glass. In fact for the buff there is an interesting range of wines from non-fashionable countries. Service is efficient and courteous.

Hathersage

BRADGATE BUTTERY, Main Road (Hope Valley 50665)
Open: Tue-Sun 11am-12mdnt

[P] [S]

English cuisine is the order of the day at this attractive Tudor-style restaurant with its Minstrel's Gallery where fifty evening diners can enjoy a meal with a view. Entrées include lamb chops with mint sauce, mixed grill and chicken and range in price from £2.30 to around £4. Together with farmhouse soup, roll and butter, home-made gâteau, coffee with cream the average meal costs £4.75.

Kirk Langley

MEYNELL ARMS HOTEL ★★
Ashbourne Road (Kirk Langley 515/6)
Open: Bar meals: Mon-Sat 12noon-2.30pm, 6.30-9.30pm (Sat 8.15pm), Sun 12noon-2pm, 7-8.30pm, Restaurant: Mon-Sat 6.30-8.30pm

[C] [P]

An excellent stopping place en route for the Peak District, the lounge bar serves a range of wholesome dishes at lunchtime and in the evening. Three courses can be easily enjoyed for less than £3 – soup of the day, followed by chicken and chips or home-made steak and kidney pie and a sweet from the trolley is a typical example. A three-course table d'hôte dinner offers a good choice for around £6. Main courses include roasts, lemon sole or gammon and pineapple.

Leicester

DU CANN'S WINE BAR, 29 Market Street (Leicester 556877)
Open: Mon-Fri 11.30am-2.30pm, Sat 11.30am-3pm, Wed-Sat 7-11pm

[S]

In one of the city's many little side streets is the popular split-level wine bar. The attractive ground-floor room offers self-service selection of a variety of cold carvery items (turkey, ham, beef etc and some speciality seafood dishes) against a background of plain green walls, livened up by old prints, shelves of crock casks and old wine bottles. A varied three-course meal can be had for about £4.50. Below it is the white-walled cellar with its glimpses of original brick, where a full waitress service operates. In the evenings succulent steaks – around £6, chops and grilled trout – both about £4, supplement the cold selection.

THE GOOD EARTH, 19 Free Lane (Leicester 26260)
Open: Mon-Thu 12noon-3pm, Fri 12noon-3pm, 7-11pm, Sat 12noon-6pm

[P] [S]

Tucked away in narrow Free Lane is this inviting first-floor wholefood restaurant. Inside all is natural wood, with displays of farming implements, hanging brass lanterns and a large farmhouse dresser with old plates and storage jars of preserved fruits, vegetables and grains. Help yourself to hot or cold dishes from the buffet display. A full meal will cost around £3, for which you choose from a selection of soups, hot savoury dishes or roasts, savoury rissoles, a variety of nourishing salads, home-made cakes, fresh fruit and natural goat's milk yoghurt. Parties of twenty or more can arrange to eat an evening meal on nights other than Friday.

THE HAYLOFT, HOLIDAY INN ☆☆☆☆
Nicholas Circle (Leicester 531161)
Open: Mon-Sun 11am-10.30pm

[C] [♫] [P] [ ]

In striking contrast to the modern hotel accommodation, the Hayloft restaurant has an old tithe barn atmosphere, with suitable décor of a hay cart, horse and oxen trappings, and enough room for 100 people. A satisfying three-course meal can be had here for around £5.40. Try the farmhouse soup (freshly made from the cauldron) followed by a 'good and wholesome salad' or baked mackerel with capers 'just like mother used to make', and parsley potatoes. To finish you may choose crème caramel or pie or gâteau from the pastry shop plus a cup of coffee (served from a bottomless pot for one charge). A special attraction on Sundays is the 'splosh and nosh' menu; for just over £5 (half-price for children) per person you can enjoy a swim in the hotel pool, followed by a three-course meal with coffee. If you find swimming a little too energetic, the regular weekend dinner dances might be just your thing.

THE POST HOUSE HOTEL ☆☆☆
Branstone Lane East (Leicester 896688)
Open: Barge Buttery: Mon-Sun 7am-10.30pm

[C] [P] [ ]

Longboat owners will feel very much at home in this bright and original buttery, where the ceiling is curved to resemble an abstract version of an upturned boat, and the walls sport a colourful mural of a bargee family and their craft. Red-and-blue paintwork and a scattering of water cans and kettles complete the canal-boat atmosphere. The imaginative menu gives excellent scope for a satisfying three-course meal for upwards of £4. Tasty starters and grills supplement the quick-and-easy hamburgers, salads and omelettes, most of which are around £2.75. A selection of 'filled fit to burst' sandwiches (toasted or otherwise) cost around £1.20. A children's menu is available on request.

A SPANISH PLACE, 38a Belvoir Street
(Leicester 542830)
Open: Mon-Sat 9am-6pm

[S]

An orange awning and pot plants gives this small modern restaurant a continental flavour. Inside, the emphasis is on home-made cuisine and a friendly, hospitable atmosphere, heightened by the fresh posy of flowers on each table. Snack foods and main meals are available throughout the day. Sandwiches and toasted snacks are made from freshly baked bread and cost between 60p to £1.20. A tasty three-course meal could include a Spanish omelette as an appetiser (around 50p), fried chicken, peas and jacket potato (about £2) and home-made fruit pie with fresh cream for around 50p. Business lunch boxes are made up by Susan and Josef Arroyo, the proprietors, to suit individual customer's requirements. Unfortunately, A Spanish Place is unlicensed.

SWISS COTTAGE RESTAURANT
52-54 Charles Street (Leicester 56577)
Open: Mon-Sat 9.30am-7pm

[P] [S]

Opened about 18 years ago, this smart restaurant with attractive exposed brickwork, dark wood-effect tables, copper light shades and waitresses dressed as Swiss maids, was the first of six similar eateries which have sprung up in Leicester. Each site has been chosen for its ease of access for shoppers and business people in the city centre. At lunchtime, chops, steaks, home-made steak and kidney pie, chicken and gammon steak are served at prices ranging from around £2-£3.25. Soup is around 40p and there is an excellent choice of home-made pies served with fresh cream for around 50p. Sister establishments are located in Churchgate, Lee Circle, Odeon Arcade and the Haymarket. The Swiss Cottage

Garden, one of two places at the Haymarket, is the only licensed premises.

TOWER RESTAURANT, Lewis's, Humberstone Gate (Leicester 23241)
Open: Mon-Sat 11.30am-3pm

C P S ♣

The sleek, 137-foot tower of Lewis's store, topped with coloured lighting was the talk of Leicester and district in 1936, when it was built. The fourth floor restaurant takes its name from this and its interior décor is based on one of the Queen's ships of the Thirties – all turquoise and gold with a rich, red patterned carpet. A special shopper's lunch costs just £2.50. The table d'hôte three-course lunch is also excellent value at just under £3.50. There is a choice for each course and a typical meal would be soup, followed by grilled ham and pineapple with sweet of the day to finish. The à la carte menu is extremely reasonable, with most main courses such as roasts around £4 and sweets from the trolley from 50p-70p. There is a special children's menu for under 11s. There is no service charge and VAT is included.

Lincoln

CRUSTS, 46 Broadgate (Lincoln 40322)
Open: Mon-Sat 11.30am-2.30pm, 7pm-12mdnt

C ♫ P ♣

Only the name 'Crusts', printed in bold lettering on the window distinguishes this restaurant from the quaint little shops on either side of it. The building occupies the site of the original Roman wall which surrounded the city and, inside, the walls are decorated with framed bills and receipts dating from 1837 when an inn stood on this site. A cosy atmosphere is created within by the use of country-style furniture, whitewashed walls and dark beams, and a rich red carpet. This is a comfortable place in which to enjoy the good food and hospitality of proprietors Clive and Rita Barkes. Business lunch is a must for the budget-conscious as you can have soup of the day; southern fried chicken, peas and French fries; roll and butter, and a choice of cheesecake or ice cream for only £2.25. Carte du jour offers a selection of entrées with prices from £3.16 for fried North Sea cod to £5.90 for an 8oz prime fillet steak – half price for children. Unbelievably, this price includes soup or fruit juice, a special Crust salad, French fries, garden peas, roll and butter followed by home-made ice cream or a selection from the cheeseboard.

THE DUKE WILLIAM, 44 Bailgate (Lincoln 21351 and 30257)
Open: Mon-Thu 11.30am-3pm, 6.45-10.30pm, Fri-Sat 11.30am-3pm, 6.45-11pm, Sun 12noon-2pm, 7-10.30pm

C P ♣

This charming 18th-century pub stands in the oldest part of the city, close to the famous cathedral. The simple décor of white-painted stone walls and beamed ceiling is complemented by tapestries and bric-à-brac which create an olde worlde atmosphere in keeping with the age and character of the building. Lunch here is a homely affair with dishes such as home-made steak and kidney pie, grilled plaice or ham salad, and the price of a three-course meal is around £3. For around £6, a fairly extensive dinner menu offers such dishes as fried whitebait, grilled trout with almonds or chicken à la crème. Coffee and wine are extra, so evenings can be rather expensive unless care is taken in selection.

HARVEY'S CATHEDRAL RESTAURANT, 1 Exchequer Gate, Castle Square (Lincoln 21886)
Open: Mon-Sat 12noon-2pm, 7pm-12mdnt, Sun 12noon-2pm

C P S ♣

In the shadows of Lincoln Cathedral and Lincoln Castle is Bob and Adrianne Harvey's bright, split-level restaurant, housed in a historic building once a pub (complete with drunken ghoul). Lunch here any day and you will receive excellent value for money and a good choice of well-prepared food. On weekdays all the starters are about 65p-95p and a selection of salads, including fresh trout range from around £2.25-£3.20. Daily special hot dishes are similarly priced and sweets cost about 95p. On Sundays the three-course lunch always includes massive ribs of roast beef and costs £4.95-£2 for children. A weekday lunch for Senior Citizens costs around £2.50. The five-course dinner is unfortunately a little beyond the scope of this guide.

ZORBA'S RESTAURANT, 292-3 High Street (Lincoln 29360)
Open: Mon-Fri 11.45am-2.30pm, 6.30-11.30pm, Sat 11.45am-11.30pm

[C] [P] [S] [🍷]

Modern décor with banquette seating and contemporary refectory tables recommends this city-centre first-floor restaurant where good wholesome English and Greek cuisine is served with speed and efficiency. A small adjoining bar with Mediterranean bric-à-brac completes the scene. You can enjoy a three-course special lunch from £3, with plenty of choice of English fare such as roast beef and Yorkshire, haddock and chips or farmhouse grill. The à la carte menu includes hors d'oeuvres from around 75p for spaghetti bolognese to about £1.25 for prawn cocktail. Roasts and grills vary from around £3 to £5. A dozen continental dishes are on offer as are some Greek specialities such as Cypriana meze – a selection of hot and cold Greek dishes for about £5.

Matlock

THE ELIZABETHAN RESTAURANT
Crown Square (Matlock 3533)
Open: Mon-Sun 12noon-6pm, Tue-Sat 7-10.20pm

[S] [🍷]

The Gilding family's pleasant dining-house stands near the town centre on the main A6 through-road. Two adjoining rooms are cleanly decorated with white-painted, half timbered walls and there are refectory-style tables with Windsor chairs in simple surroundings. Smart and friendly waitresses have been serving good, wholesome food here since 1978. Starters range from 35p-95p and examples are pâté de maison and egg mayonnaise. Main dishes are very good value (how about gammon at £2.35 or grilled rump steak at £3.50?) and include potatoes and vegetable of the day. All desserts are under £1, so why not go mad and finish with a knickerbocker glory?

Melton Mowbray

CERVINO RISTORANTE ITALIANO
1-3 Leicester Street
(Melton Mowbray 69828)
Open: Mon-Sat 12noon-2pm, 6.30-11pm (11.30pm Sat)

[C] [♣]

Unmistakably Italian, this pale pink restaurant is rich in memorabilia from the empty Chianti bottles that hang from the ceiling to the many picture postcards and posters of the home country which adorn the walls. The green gingham of the tablecloths provides a fresh contrast. An all-Italian menu offers such specialities as tonno e fagioli (tuna fish with bean salad) for £1.20 followed by pollo imperiale (chicken with cream, mushrooms and asparagus) at £3.40 including vegetables of the day and potatoes. Banana del Vesuvio is a mouth-watering Italian sweet of baked banana with cream, rum and sugar – a special treat at £1.15. Coffee in a glass with cream is 35p.

Northampton

THE VINEYARD ✕ 7 Derngate
(Northampton 33978)
Open: Mon-Fri 12noon-2pm, Tue-Fri 7.30-10.30pm, Sat 7-10.30pm

[C] [♫] [S]

A gaily striped canopy and half-curtained window give a continental-café look to this modern restaurant in Northampton's busy centre. Inside, the décor is simple and effective, one wall being clad in pine with illuminated niches displaying a variety of antiques and bric-à-brac. The short but imaginative menu is changed fortnightly and offers dishes of British, European and Middle Eastern origin. For a truly international meal you might choose Mrs Cromwell's Grand Sallet (a 17th-century English dish with chicken or prawns) as an appetiser followed by jambonneau aux lentilles, with dondurma kaymakli (and Egyptian ice-cream flavoured with mastic) for dessert.

Nottingham

BEN BOWERS, 128 Derby Road
(Nottingham 413388)
Open: Mon-Fri 12noon-2pm

[C]

A sister to its namesake in Derby, this restaurant offers a good value three-course meal (*eg*, soup of the day, poached fillet of sole with white wine, cream and mushroom sauce and lemon meringue pie), plus coffee, for under £4. Below in the basement, Betty's Buffet Bar has a wide range of snacks (40p-£1.45) and cold meat salads (around £1.50). In 1981, an extension was added to the bar to cater for another thirty-eight patrons, and service is now 'American fast food' style.

EVIVA TAVERNA AND KEBAB HOUSE, 25 Victoria Street
(Nottingham 50243)
Open: Taverna: Mon-Sat 7pm-2am
Kebab House: Mon-Sat 10.30am-7pm

[C] [♫] [P] [S]

If you want to let off steam you can buy plates for smashing here. First, though, enjoy your meal in this basement restaurant transformed by white walls, vines, bunches of grapes and olive branches to a little bit of Greece in the heart of England. There are a few grills and roasts on the menu, but the chef's specialities – stifado (a rather special beef stew), kleftiko (lamb cooked with herbs) and dolmas (stuffed vine leaves) are particularly good and won't break the bank. Starters are priced from around 40p and most of the sweets (including baklava) cost in the 80p range. For two people dining together a half bottle of wine is provided free of charge, or you may choose from the list and have £1 knocked off the wine bill, which really is a worthwhile concession. Having enjoyed all this, listened to Greek music and watched Greek dancers in an adjoining room, you may feel like showing your appreciation by a bit of plate-smashing. Above the taverna is a kebab house run by the same proprietor, Mr Kozakis. This is a pleasant place to stop for a snack or for lunch, and the doner kebab, served with pitta bread and salad, is specially recommended.

GRANGE FARM RESTAURANT
Toton (Long Eaton 69426)
Open: Mon-Sat 12noon-2pm, 7-9pm

[P]

A much extended brick-built farmhouse dating back to 1691 is quite a find just two miles off the M1 (exit 25), especially if it offers generous portions of wholesome English fare attractively presented, as this restaurant does. The dining room itself is in one of the oldest parts of the building, where oak beams and white brick abound, and there you can sample a quite superb table d'hôte lunch for around £4.75. A seemingly limitless choice of dishes is available – there are around nineteen starters including whitebait, lasagne, melon and pâté, twelve main dishes such as

rainbow trout, rabbit pie or supreme of chicken Marengo, all served with two vegetables and both creamed and roast potatoes, and almost twenty different sweets, some rather unusual, like green figs with cream, ice cream with blackberry brandy or meringue Chantilly.

LA GRENOUILLE RESTAURANT ✕
32 Lenton Boulevard
(Nottingham 411088)
Open: Mon-Fri 12.30-1.30pm, 7.30-9.30pm, Sat 7.30-9.30pm

[♫] [P] [⚘]

Imagine white-painted tables (only seven of them), white chairs with black cord upholstery, placed on black and white vinyl flooring against brick-red hessian walls highlighted with French posters; then add red tablecloths and matching table napkins. There you have La Grenouille – a little corner of France on the corner of a terrace of large Victorian houses. Young owner Yves Bouanchaud provides superb French food using mainly fresh products. Don't chance the à la carte menu if you're really hard up but it's worth going a bit over the £5 to enjoy a meal here if you can afford it. The table d'hôte menu offers a starter of home-made soup or terrine, a main dish as boeuf bourguignon with vegetables and salad (this changes daily) and a sweet such as fruit salad or chocolate gâteau with cheese as an alternative, at around £4.90. Coffee is extra.

THE KINGFISHER, 127 Mansfield Road
(Nottingham 45449)
Open: Tue-Sat 12noon-2pm, 7-11.30pm

[P] [S] [⚘]

Salmon steak, king prawns, lobster and haddock are amongst the twenty main dishes available in this licensed fish restaurant on a busy road from the town centre. The rear of the premises houses a functional dining room with plain wooden tables and curtain-divided booths in which to take your meal in comfort. Eight starters and sweets such as rum baba, gâteau and apple pie with cream are available, all at around 60p a fattening portion.

MOULIN ROUGE ✕ 5 Trinity Square
(Nottingham 42845)
Open: Mon-Sun 12noon-2pm, 6-10.30pm

[C] [P] [S]

Not strictly a French restaurant but very much a Continental haunt, the Moulin Rouge is close to the Victoria shopping centre and the Theatre Royal. The sparkling restaurant has predominantly red décor, with crisp white table linen and banquettes. The à la carte menu includes appetisers, soups, fish, omelettes, entrées, poultry, curries, grills, salads and desserts, with a wide range of prices. A daily main course 'Special' costs £1.95, but three courses must be selected with care if you are to avoid going too much over £5. If you cannot find the meal you crave 'the menu is only a suggestion, our chef is at your command'.

THE PARAQUITO RESTAURANT
473 Mansfield Road
(Nottingham 609447)
Open: Tue-Sat 12noon-1.45pm, 7-10pm

Since taking over the Paraquito in 1976, Jan and Sheila Laskowski have been trying to live down the 'egg and chip' image it had acquired before they bought it, by now offering fine service and a good quality menu. Their three-course lunch, costing under £3 (including VAT) embraces four choices of starter, one of four main dishes such as roast pork, chicken chasseur or braised lambs liver, plus vegetables of the day and a choice of sweet or cheese. Alternatively, try the steak platter, which includes prawn cocktail, sirloin steak, a side salad, chips and all the trimmings with a dessert or cheese for under £6. In the evening, a four-course dinner is available, under £6, with main dish choices of trout, chicken, lamb cutlets and many more. There's a 10% service charge in the evenings only, when the restaurant becomes crowded with the famished folk of Nottingham.

PASTRAMI'S, 6 Hurts Yard, Upper Parliament Street (Nottingham 46888)
Open: Mon-Sat 12noon-2.30pm

[C][♫][S][🍷]

Simple, good taste is the hallmark of this lunchtime diner, tucked away in a narrow alley dating back to Georgian times. Habitat furniture, posters, pictures and plants create a 'trendy' air. Food is cheap, home-made and varied. Starters include spare ribs in barbecue sauce (around £1), soup of the day and fresh melon chunks in blackcurrant syrup (90p). Pastrami's Specials such as chickebab (chicken pieces with herbs on a skewer served with French fries), gammon with peach and barbecue sauce, or Pastrami on rye (pure beef, marinated with herbs, served on hot rye bread with salad) – are all around £1.75. 'Kidstuff' – from 80p-£1.20 includes juniorburger or spaghetti. Salads and hamburgers are also available – try a Lo-Cal burger – absolutely *no* bun or French fries, but enough salad to stuff a large rabbit! Super desserts such as hot waffles or hot fudge sundae will ruin any diet.

THE SAVOY HOTEL ★★★ Mansfield Road (Nottingham 602621)
Open: Colonial Restaurant Mon-Sat 12noon-2.15pm, 7-9.30pm, Sun 12noon-2.15pm, Steak Bars: Mon-Thu 12noon-2.15pm, 6.30-11pm, Fri-Sat 12noon-2.15pm, 6.30-11.30pm, Sun 12noon-2.15pm, 7-10.30pm, Salad Bar: Mon-Fri 12noon-2pm

[P][🍷]

One of the most popular eating places in Nottingham, this large, luxurious hotel has a sumptuous restaurant and richly decorated steak bar on the ground floor. The lower ground floor houses a second steak bar with exposed stonework and a salad bar with exposed wall and ceiling timbers. Food is excellent value for money. The restaurant offers a three-course lunch with a vast choice for all three courses, from around £4.50. A five-course dinner with even more choice is about £5.80, some choices such as poached salmon steak with prawn sauce adding around 60p to the bill. The steak bars serve very good grills – T-bone steak with all the trimmings and a choice of dessert is only about £4.60. Children's portions at reduced prices are available on certain dishes. The Cromwell salad bar offers a selection of reasonably priced salads, filled rolls and gâteaux at less than 50p a portion.

SWISS COTTAGE, 18 Chapel Bar (Nottingham 411050)
Open: Mon-Sat 9.30am-7pm

[♫][P][S][🍷]

Peter and Bernard Morritt have made this modern, canopied premises in a cul-de-sac the seventh of their family chain of restaurants. Amidst the exposed brickwork and copper lighting it is possible to sample anything from the most simple sandwich (around 20p) to the tastiest rib steak (about £4.40, with all the trimmings, chips and vegetables) preceded by a choice of soups at around 35p. Finish with a delicious strawberry pancake topped with fresh whipped cream (at around 65p), home-made cherry pie or cheese and biscuits. The restaurant is unlicensed so you will have to forego a glass of house wine.

THE WATERFALL, 7-8 Hurt's Yard, Upper Parliament Street (Nottingham 42235)
Open: Mon-Fri 11.30am-2.30pm, 7-11pm,
Sat 10am-5pm, 7-11.30pm

[C][♫][S][🍷]

It's well worth the search for this interesting little restaurant nestling in the Georgian shopping centre, reached by means of a narrow flagstoned alleyway by the side of the Fox Inn. A wide bow window fronts the restaurant which seats about sixty within its three sections, each with a distinctive olde worlde atmosphere. The waterfall forms part of a cool and splashing grotto which provides an attractive focal point. The dark-wood tables take on a more sophisticated look in the evenings with the addition of Nottingham lace tablecloths and flickering candles. An interesting and reasonably-priced à la carte menu offers a traditional selection of dishes including minute steak at around £2.50. For the same price, a three course business lunch offers such dishes as home-made soup, roast lamb or pork cutlet chasseur, sweet plus coffee. If your taste is for the more exotic, you may choose veal cordon bleu or fillet of sole Monte Carlo from the speciality à la carte menu – but beware, prices are higher and you'll have to be selective to stay within our limit.

Ollerton

ROSE COTTAGE, Rufford
(Mansfield 822363)
Open: Mon-Sun 12noon-10pm,

[♫] [P] [☘]

Two miles south of Ollerton on the A614 and almost opposite the entrance to Rufford Abbey is this quaint brick cottage with small leaded windows, surrounded by an immaculate garden. Inside is all wood panels and beams, with three separate areas for dining. A wide range of fare is available from midday throughout the week. A three-course table d'hôte lunch for around £3.50 could include minestrone soup, braised lamb chops and vegetables and ice cream gâteau. Also available are snack items such as plaice, chips and peas for £2.25 or minute steak for £4.25. Desserts at 75p include chocolate fudge gâteau or mandarin sundae. A more sophisticated menu is used in the evening, when care will be needed to avoid exceeding the budget.

Skegness

THE COPPER KETTLE, Lumley Road
(Skegness 67298)
Open: summer: Mon-Sun 9.30am-10pm, winter: Mon-Wed, Fri-Sat 10am-5.30pm (closed Jan-Feb)

[♫] [P] [S] [☘]

Set amongst the shops in one of the town's busiest streets, you could easily dismiss this brown, bow-windowed restaurant as yet another gift shop. However, once inside, you can forget the hurly-burly world of amusement arcades and trumpery, and relax in the peaceful atmosphere created by rich green carpeting with subtly contrasting white plaster and plain brick walls. Modern lights, masquerading as old-style oil lamps, hang from the ceiling at strategic points between the pine tables. The fare is limited, but will prove very good value for money. Starters include melon and fried Camembert and cost between 65p-£1.50 with main courses such as chicken Kiev at £3.50. Home-made desserts are about 80p.

Sleaford

CARRE ARMS HOTEL ★
(Sleaford 303156)
Open: 12noon-2pm, 6.30-8pm

[C] [P] [S] [☘]

The red-brick public house built in 1906 is on the edge of the town centre near a level crossing. The bright, well-maintained dining room offers a good selection of mainly grill and roast dishes at reasonable prices. Even if you do splash out on a steak, surrounded by a simple starter and sweet, you are unlikely to go far beyond £5.

Stamford

THE BAY TREE COFFEE SHOP
10 St Pauls Street (Stamford 51219)
Open: summer: Tue-Sat 9am-5pm, Sun 1-6pm, winter: Tue-Sat 9am-5pm, Sun 2-5pm

[S] [☘]

This quaint, bow-windowed little coffee shop is located in one of Stamford's quieter streets, close to the main shopping area. Horse brasses displayed on dark beams and prints on the cream walls create a pleasant period atmosphere. Emphasis is on home-made fare and prices are astonishingly reasonable. Soup of the day plus roll and butter is 35p, main courses such as steak and kidney pie with two veg, lasagne or cheese and asparagus with side salad are around £1.50 and a delicious dessert such as a fresh fruit Pavlova is only 50p.

YE OLDE BARN RESTAURANT
St Mary's Street (Stamford 3194)
Open: Mon-Sun 12noon-2pm, 6-10pm (closed Sun in winter)

[P] [S]

Step into the alleyway at the rear of Ye Olde Barn coffee shop and you will find this two-storey restaurant, crowded with fine antiques and gleaming with well-polished copper and brass. The upper floor seats sixty below the rafters of the fine timbered roof, where a small cocktail lounge is also to be found. Downstairs is a slightly smaller restaurant boasting the same low prices and excellent value for money. Gammon steak, pork chop, steak and mixed grills are served with vegetables and cost anything from £1 upwards, with warming dishes such as home-made steak and kidney pie served with jacket *and* creamed potatoes and a selection of vegetables at around £2.15. Cold meat salads are under £2.50. A sweet such as profiteroles with chocolate sauce rounds things off nicely, and sets you back under £1.

Sutton-on-Sea

ANCHOR, 12 High Street (Sutton-on-Sea 41548)
Open: summer: Mon-Sun 10am-5.30pm, 7-10pm,
winter: Fri-Sat 10am-5.30pm, 7-10pm, Mon-Wed, Sun 10am-5.30pm

[C] [&]

A canopied doorway and bow windows pick out this country-style restaurant, converted from an old house reported to be a home of Alfred Lord Tennyson. Food to suit the pocket and palate of any poet is served here. For around £3.40 a three-course lunch including minute steak garni is yours, and for £4.95 a three-course dinner plus coffee could include melon, chicken escalope Holstein and a sweet from the trolley. The à la carte menu is also very reasonable, with a good choice of starters, roasts, fish dishes, salads, grills and desserts well within our budget. Half portions are available for children.

Thrapston

THE COURT HOUSE, Huntingdon Road (Thrapston 3618)
Open: Mon-Sun 12noon-2pm, 6.45-10pm (10.30pm Fri & Sat)

[&]

This restaurant is contained in the old Thrapston court and police station, but grim-faced magistrates handing out fines and sentences have been replaced by smiling waitresses with plates of food. Relics of the former function decorate the dining room, in the shape of police memorabilia, helmets, badges, truncheons and handcuffs. The old cells were demolished to make room for modern bedrooms, so even the worst-behaved guest need have no fear of being locked up for the night! A wide range of food is offered at The Court House; from sandwiches, ploughman's and beefburgers, through to more substantial dishes of steak, fish, gammon etc – all fitting easily into our budget. In the evening try the chef's special which could be carbonnade of beef, chicken supreme or even Bobby's Buster (no it's not a truncheon but a huge steak, kidney and mushroom pie).

Tideswell

MADEIRA HOUSE, 5 Commercial Road (Tideswell 871176)
Open: Tue-Sun 12noon-2pm

[S] [&]

Portuguese proprietor Mr Abreu is proud that his restaurant dates from before the discovery of the New World by his fellow countryman Christopher Columbus. So be prepared for the low ceilings, supported by sturdy oak beams. Although open in the evening when an international cuisine is served, it is for the more simply-priced and prepared lunch and bar meals that Madeira House is noted in this guide. A home-made soup of the day (60p), can be followed by a choice of main dishes (such as fish, pizza, or minute steak) all served with salad and chips, and none costing more than £2. Sweets – gâteau, trifle, or fresh fruit – are around the 75p mark.

Heart of England

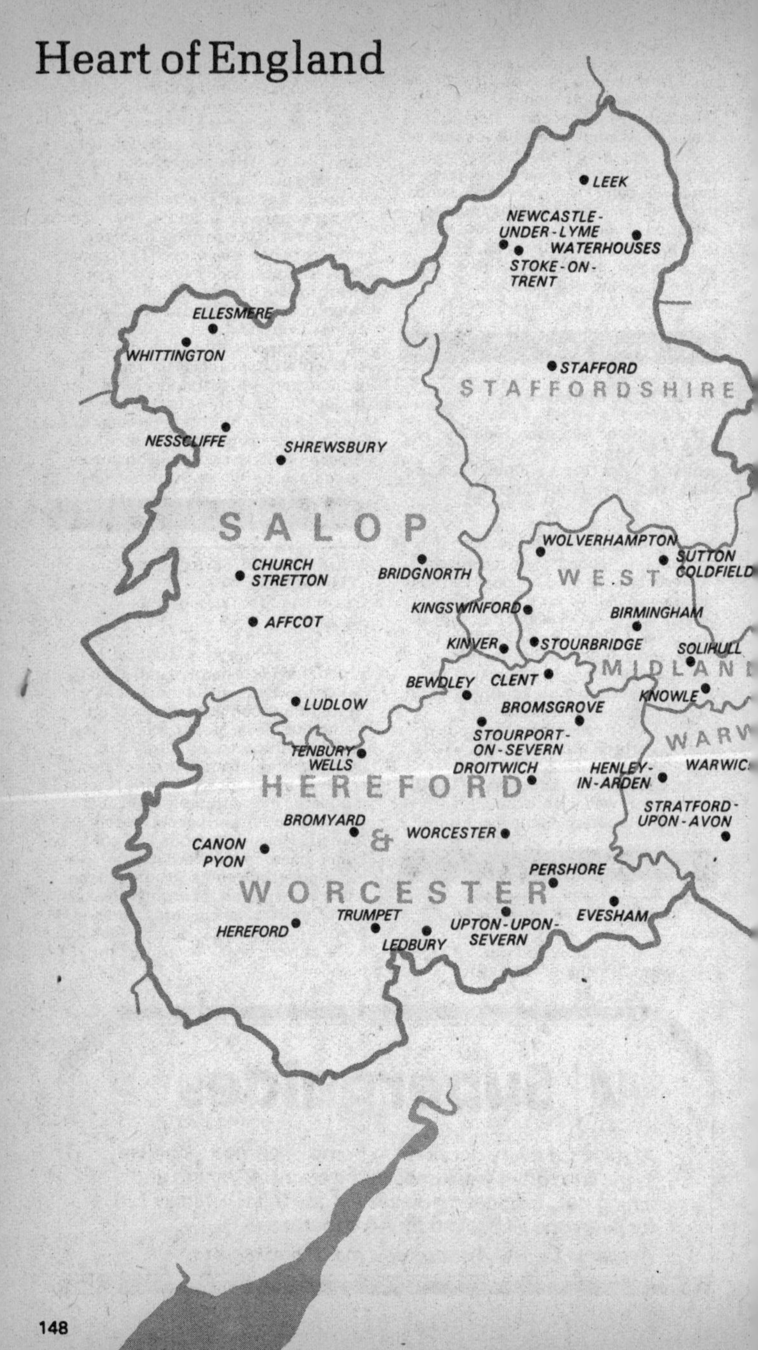
LEEK
NEWCASTLE-UNDER-LYME
WATERHOUSES
STOKE-ON-TRENT
ELLESMERE
WHITTINGTON
STAFFORD
STAFFORDSHIRE
NESSCLIFFE
SHREWSBURY
SALOP
WOLVERHAMPTON
SUTTON COLDFIELD
CHURCH STRETTON
BRIDGNORTH
WEST
KINGSWINFORD
BIRMINGHAM
AFFCOT
KINVER
STOURBRIDGE
SOLIHULL
MIDLAN
BEWDLEY
CLENT
KNOWLE
LUDLOW
BROMSGROVE
STOURPORT-ON-SEVERN
WARW
TENBURY WELLS
DROITWICH
HENLEY-IN-ARDEN
HEREFORD
STRATFORD-UPON-AVON
BROMYARD
WORCESTER
CANON PYON
&
PERSHORE
WORCESTER
EVESHAM
TRUMPET
UPTON-UPON-SEVERN
HEREFORD
LEDBURY

'St Clement! St Clement! A Cat by the ear!
A good red apple, a pint of beer,
Some of your mutton, some of your veal,
If it is good, give us a deal,
If it is naught, give us some salt.

Butler, butler, fill the bowl,
If you fill it of the best,
God will send your soul to rest,
But if you fill it of the small,
The Devil take butler, bowl and all!'

TRADITIONAL

8

Regional Dishes

Shrewsbury lamb cutlets in butter and aspic
Hereford roast beef
Warwick honey scones with butter
Hereford pigeon pie
Nutmeg curd cakes

Affcott

THE WHITE HOUSE, Church Stretton (Marshbrook 202)
Open: Wed-Sun 12.15-2pm, Tue-Sat 7-9.30pm

C P

Be sure to book in advance if you are planning an evening sortie to this tiny roadside restaurant, which once housed the village smithy. A typical country cottage, the décor is simple but effective, with white walls and black beams brightened by pot plants. The lunchtime menu often includes a tasty fresh mushroom soup or gazpacho, followed by roast loin of lamb, its stuffing rich with walnuts. Braised kidneys or fresh salmon are possible alternatives. A display of mouth-watering sweets could include delights such as grape and banana vacherin or hazelnut meringue. Sunday lunches are about £4, half price for children.

Bewdley

BACK OF BEYOND COFFEE SHOP
55 Load Street (Bewdley 403144)
Open: Mon-Sat 10am-4.45pm

S

You needn't go to the back of beyond to find a good meal or light snack – just visit this quaint historic town on the banks of the River Severn. Here, at the rear of a shop called 'Room Interiors' and across a covered courtyard, you will find the popular little restaurant run by Angela Collip. A variety of home-made goodies awaits your enjoyment, including the lunchtime special (at about £1.10) which changes daily and could be moussaka, cottage pie or beefburgers. Start with home-made soup with French bread and choose from a tempting array of cream cakes and gâteaux for dessert and you'll have a satisfying meal for around £2. For a more unusual accompaniment to the meal, try a pot of speciality tea (Lapsong Souchong, perhaps) for about 30p per person.

Birmingham

BLACK HORSE HOTEL, Northfield (021-475 1005)
Open: Mon-Fri 12noon-2pm, 7-10pm
Sat 7-10pm

C P S

The Barons' Bar Grill Room is upstairs in this impressive 'black and white' inn on the Bristol road. Overhead is the original raftered roof, but the barn-like aspect is counteracted by hessian-covered walls and the solidity of oak furniture. The menu is standard for Davenport inns, and the main dishes are those found in most grill rooms, the accent being on steaks for between £4-£5, with other dishes including plaice and gammon (both around £3), all prices including vegetables. Starters fall between 40p and £1, desserts from around 80p.

THE CAPTAIN'S TABLE, HOLIDAY INN ☆☆☆☆ Holiday Street (021-643 2766)
Open: Mon-Sun 7am-10.30pm

C P S

You could almost be at sea in this restaurant, with its rope ladders, and old sails draped from the ceiling. Meals 'from the tavern' are a little pricey, with 'tempters' such as corn-on-the-cob or Chef's own country style pâté about £2. Mixed meat salad as a main dish is a little over £2 and a variety of pies, sweets and gâteaux, served with cream is just over £1. You can therefore eat a pleasant three-course meal, but careful selection will be needed to keep within our £5-£6 limit. A novelty children's menu offers Batman's Supersonic

Dinner (beefburger and chips) for around 90p and a host of other popular junior dishes including Uncle Orinoco's 'Afters' – various ice creams at 50p or more.

THE FOUR SEASONS RESTAURANT
Lewis's, Bull Street (021-236 8251)
Open: Mon-Fri 11.45am-2.30pm, Sat 11.45am-2.30pm

C S

The decorative theme is, appropriately, the four seasons of the year depicted in relief in four attractive fibre-glass murals. The à la carte menu offers a traditional list of grills, omelettes, salads etc. at reasonable prices and the table d'hôte menu with two daily specialities provides very good value at around £2.75 for three courses. A children's menu, cleverly designed in the form of a 'Wanted' poster entitled 'Big shots for small fry' offers a main course, ice cream and cold drink at prices to please any parent. There is even a bowl of assorted vegetables, potato and gravy plus a dish of custard for baby at half the children's price.

LA GALLERIA, Paradise Place
(021-236 1006)
Open: Mon-Sat 11am-2.30pm, 5.30-10.30pm, Sun 7-10.30pm

C P S

This modern wine bar and restaurant has small, old fashioned pub-style tables and deep red mahogany woodwork. The display counter houses a range of cold meat salads and a blackboard menu above lists hot dishes. The emphasis is on Italian meals, with six varieties of pizzas from about £1.20-£1.80 and pasta dishes such as lasagne at around £1.80. Veal à la crème, chicken chasseur and various steaks come from £2.25 upwards. Starters include minestrone soup, mussels or home-made pâté and there is a choice of desserts for about 60p-80p.

GAYLORD ✕✕ 61 New Street
(021-632 4500)
Open: Mon-Sun 12noon-3pm, 6-11.30pm

C S

The mirror-lined hallway decorated with pot plants is a foretaste of the authentic Indian atmosphere in the spacious green restaurant above, where Tandoori cooking can be viewed through glass windows while you wait. The menu offers a wide range of dishes with a lunchtime 'eat as much as you like' menu for around £5. A special vegetarian meal is offered for around £4.50. Dishes on the à la carte menu are reasonably priced at lunchtime and chicken, lamb or fish delicacies flavoured with oriental spices abound within our price range.

GINO'S BELVEDERE RESTAURANT
East Mall Shopping Centre
(021-643 1957)
Open: Mon-Wed 12noon-11pm, Thu-Fri 12noon-11.15pm, Sat 12noon-11.30pm, Sun 12noon-10.30pm

C P S

Walls decorated with enlarged engravings of old Venice give an immediate Latin flavour to this popular, centrally-situated Italian restaurant. You can make do with just a pizza or omelette, or choose from the extensive à la carte menu at around £4 for three-courses and coffee. A special three-course lunch is available at an all-inclusive price of £2.50. There is a speciality menu offering a selection of more sophisticated items which are a little more expensive.

THE GRAPE VINE, Units 2 and 3, Edgbaston Shopping Centre, Hagley Road, Five Ways (021-454 0672)
Open: Mon-Sat 12noon-2.30pm, 5-9pm

C P S

Proprietor Peter Gully is a man with a mission. His aim is to lead people away from using processed foods – artificially flavoured, bleached or dyed, and preserved with chemicals; he is opposed to 'battery' farming too, and believes a sensible vegetarian diet can improve health as well as making inhumane production of animal proteins unnecessary. There are always home-made soups, hot flans and nut roasts, and main dishes use peas, beans, nuts, rice, free-range eggs and rennet-free cheeses to provide the necessary protein element. A representative three courses such as soup (75p), cashew nut roast (£1.95) and trifle (£1) gives some idea of what to expect.

THE GREAT AMERICAN DISASTER
40 Cannon Street (021-643 3650)
Open: Mon-Thu, Sun 12noon-12mdnt, Fri-Sat 12noon-1am

[S]

A quiet side street, close to one of the city's main shopping areas, is the setting for this American hamburger restaurant. A large sign outside and another across the window proclaim its name but it is a treat rather than a disaster that awaits within. The dark walls and ceiling are enhanced by subdued lighting and a series of prints with an American theme, pine tables and bentwood chairs provide a striking contrast. Food is cooked in the open kitchen area and consists mainly of charcoal-grilled hamburgers, with six different toppings, hot-dogs and grilled chicken or steak. With the addition of French fries, sesame seed bun and a selection of relishes, these constitute a filling meal at reasonable cost. With a starter of corn on the cob or spare ribs, plus home-made chocolate fudge cake with ice cream to finish, a three-course meal will cost around £3. At that price you can afford one of the exotic cocktails from the impressive list.

HAPPY GATHERING
54-56 Pershore Street
(021-622 2324/3092)
Open: Mon-Sun 12noon-12mdnt

[C] [♫] [P]

This successful Cantonese restaurant is situated on the outskirts of the main city centre. The interior is very clean and typically Chinese with red embossed wallpaper, wood panelling and brightly-painted oriental pictures. Food is authentic Cantonese and proprietor Mr Lai is particularly proud of the baked crab in black bean sauce and the duck in plum sauce. Businessperson's lunch costs around £1.50 and includes a choice of two starters, four main courses, boiled or fried rice and a pot of China tea. Because of the nature of Chinese eating, a choice from the à la carte menu can be as cheap or expensive as you like depending on the variety of dishes chosen. Chicken with lemon sauce is £2.60. There is a more formal set dinner at around the £4 mark.

HAWKINS CAFE-BAR, King Edward Buildings, 205-219 Corporation Street (021-236 2001)
Open: Mon-Fri 8.30am-11pm, Sat 10am-11pm, Sun 5-11pm

[C] [♫] [S]

Situated close to the law courts and Aston University is this new concept in food and drink. The strong art nouveau décor proves an interesting blackcloth to the half-hour lighting extravaganzas on Friday and Saturday and occasional appearances of guest artists such as George Melly or Georgie Fame. On to the food – prices range from about 75p for home-made soup to around £2.50 for roast rib of beef with fresh salad. A dish of the day, filled baked potatoes and pizzas are also available – all freshly-made on the premises.

HEAVEN BRIDGE ✕✕ 308 Bull Ring Centre, Smallbrook Ringway
(021-643 0033)
Open: Mon-Fri 12noon-11.30pm, Sat 12noon-12mdnt, Sun 12noon-11.30pm

[C] [♫] [P] [S]

The à la carte menu, in Cantonese and English, lists nearly 200 dishes. Hors d'oeuvres, from around 80p-£1 include rice rolls, dumplings, croquettes and water-chestnut pâté and in addition twenty-four choices of soup are offered. Main courses, varying in price from about £3-£5 include an exciting array of dishes – seafoods such as cuttle-fish, crab, oyster and lobster and meat and poultry in main guises. A large glass of che foo (Chinese sweet wine) costs around 55p.

HORTS WINE BAR AND BISTRO
Harborne Road, Edgbaston
(021-454 4672)
Open: Mon-Sat 12noon-2.30pm, 5.30-10.30pm, Sun 12noon-2pm, 7-10.30pm

[P] [S]

Easily recognised in fine weather by the 'overspill' of tables and chairs onto the wide pavement outside and the distinct French flavour in the simple brown-and-beige décor, this is a popular haunt of local business people. An assortment of nourishing English and Continental food is available, including a dish of the day such as risotto, pâté and various salads at around £1.65. Home-made soup is 50p, whilst desserts such as gâteau or American cheesecake are about 65p, leaving you plenty of change from £5. There's a small raised area at the rear, for the more intimate and quiet meal.

MAXWELL'S PLUM WINE BAR & BISTRO, 163 Broad Street, Fiveways (021-643 0274)
Open: Mon-Sat 12noon-2.30pm, Mon-Fri 5.30-10.30pm, Sat-Sun 7-10.30pm

[♫] [P] [S]

Plate glass windows and a gay striped awning distinguish this wine bar from its neighbours in the shopping area. A speciality worthy of note is the spicy Welsh sausage, served with fried potato, tomato and onions, but a good selection of quiches, flans and home-made sweets are available on the buffet. Daily hot dishes include prawn provençale, lamb curry, pork chop Milanese and cod Mornay. Tuesday and Sunday evenings are highlighted by the regular appearance of Continental or folk musicians.

MICHELLE ✕ 182-184 High Street, Harborne (021-426 4133)
Open: Mon-Sat 12noon-2pm, 7-10pm (Closed Aug)

[S] [♣]

Step into Michelle's French restaurant and you move back in time – to the heyday of the small-time grocer's shop. Dark mahogany shelving, a tiled bacon area and large mirrors belonging to the original Co-op grocers shop it once was, form the basis of a most unusual décor. Of the typically French cuisine, the coq au vin and boeuf bourguignon are among the best French dishes to be had this side of the Channel. Even the à la carte dinner menu allows you to eat well for under £7 but, the one-choice-only table d'hôte at lunchtime is excellent value at only £2.65.

NEW HAPPY GATHERING ✕✕
43-45 Station Street (021-643 5247)
Open: Mon-Sun 12noon-12mdnt

[C]

Mr Heny Wong offers traditional Cantonese cuisine at this gracious and comfortable restaurant. A staggering menu boasts more than 100 dishes, the majority in the £2-£3 range. Portions are generous and you can choose from a variety of not-so-familiar dishes such as a steamed duck with plum sauce, water-chestnut pudding or braised duck's web in oyster sauce. Sweets include various fritters in syrup for around 70p and Chinese pastries cost about 35p. Set meals offer a good variety of savoury dishes from around £4.

PINOCCHIO'S ✕ Chad Square, Hawthorne Road, Harborne (021-454 8672)
Open: Mon-Sat 12.15-2pm, 6.30-10.30pm

[P] [S] [♧]

Tucked between a hairdresser's shop and a newsagent, in a tiny, modern shopping centre, close to the village of Harborne, this converted shop also acts as a sort of unofficial art gallery, for the restaurant exhibits and sells pictures by local artists. The menu is wide-ranging and tempts extravagance, but if you stick to the three-course table d'hôte lunch menu you'll be surprised at the amount of change you'll get from £5 a head.

PLAKA TAVERNA, 63 New Street (021-643 6694)
Open: Mon-Fri 12noon-2.30pm, 5.30-11.30pm, Sat-Sun 12noon-11.30pm

[C] [♫] [S] [♧]

Of the many Greek specialities served here, Kleftiko – lamb cooked in the oven, served with a Greek salad and pitta – is worth a special mention as it is very tasty, filling, and good value at around £3.95. With main courses like this you don't really need a starter but one of the 'dips' at about 85p may tempt you, or there are stuffed vine leaves costing a little more. If you've fallen for an hors d'oeuvre you'll need to look for a less-filling (and less-expensive) main course. There are a number to choose from with prices under £4 – kebab lamb or pork, two different sausage dishes, and fillet of sole served with chips and salad, are examples. A dessert will not add much more than 70p. Step out of busy New Street into the discreetly-illuminated interior of this restaurant and you can imagine yourself in Greece. Paintings from the Mediterranean create an exotic atmosphere. It comes as a surprise when the oracle speaks with a Midlands accent.

RAJDOOT ✕✕ 12-22 Albert Road (021-643 8805)
Open: Mon-Sat 12noon-2.30pm, 6.30pm-12mdnt, Sun 6.30pm-12mdnt

[C] [♫] [P] [S]

Ornate brass, red silk and hessian walls and burning joss sticks complete the transition from West to East, in this authentic Indian restaurant offering Punjab and Tandoori cuisine. Excellent set lunches are available from Monday to Saturday at around £3.50. Dinners are à la carte, with an average meal coming just outside our budget. Tandoori specialities (charcoal clay oven barbecues) include delicious rashmi kebab – chicken minced with onion, chillies, fresh mint, coriander and herbs and spices.

ROCK CANDY MOUNTAIN
High Street, Harborne (021-427 2481)
Open: Mon-Sat 12noon-2.30pm, 5.30-10.30pm, Sun 12noon-2pm, 7-10.30pm

[C] [♫] [S] [♧]

Bright, gaudy, garish but immaculate is the only way to describe this 'latest concept in wine bars – music – restaurants – meeting places and astral food'. Set in the centre of Harborne, it hums with activity and welcomes everyone. 'Kiddies' have their own special spaghetti-hamburger-ice-cream menu. The comic-strip menu offers pizzas, salads, hamburgers, BBQ ribs, chicken Kiev, chili con carne and steaks. Prices start at £2. Kick off with corn on the cob (95p) and finish with chocolate fudge cake with ice cream (85p) – one of a selection of way-out desserts.

SANDONIA, 509 Hagley Road, Bearwood (021-429 2622)
Open: Tue-Sat 11.45am-3pm, 6-11.30pm

[C] [S] [♧]

Owner Mr Constantinou (known to his regulars as Mr Conn) comes from Cyprus and opened this restaurant over seventeen years ago. 'Regulars' include a couple who have dined at the same table every Thursday night for fifteen years – there's faithfulness for you! The table d'hôte lunch at around £1.60 consists of soup or fruit juice, a choice of items such as a roast or braised steak with vegetables, and ice cream or fruit pie with custard. A three-course lunch à la carte is likely to cost about £4: for this one might have soup; a main course of a roast or a 'fry-up' such as egg, sausages, chips and peas, an omelette or a fish dish. A sweet chosen from a long list is likely to cost around 45p. The dinner menu is more expensive but one could still make a choice within the £5. Grilled halibut or curried prawns, roast Norfolk turkey, a number of grills and kebab or chicken pilaf all under £3 are examples, these prices including potatoes and two green vegetables. There is a good selection of starters at about 80p and sweets are priced from around 65p.

VALENTINO'S ✕ High Street, Harborne (021-427 2560)
Open: Mon-Sat 12.30-2pm, 7-10.30pm, Sun 12.30-2pm

[C] [♫] [P] [S] [ⓒ]

A smart little Italian eaterie, converted from one of the main street shops in which decoration is kept simple enough to have a relaxing effect. A table d'hôte lunch of egg mayonnaise, grilled sirloin steak and a piece of gâteau costs about £3.50 with coffee and wine extra, though the à la carte menu could tempt you over the limit if you have extravagant tastes. Coffee and cream is around 45p.

WHITE SWAN, Harborne Road, Edgbaston (021-454 2359)
Open: Mon-Fri 12.30-2.30pm, Tue-Sat 7.15-10pm

[C] [P]

When Ron and Norma Phillips took over this old established inn they were told that a ghost prowled around the upstairs area; so far they have no trace of the uninvited guest, but keep your eyes open just in case! Ghost or no ghost, the White Swan is a popular eating place, so booking is advisable. Steaks and grills are served in the restaurant at prices from around £3-£5. Appetisers range from about 50p-£1, sweets from 60p-80p. At lunchtime a cold buffet is available in the skittle alley.

Bridgnorth

BAILEYS WINE BAR AND BISTRO
78 High Street (Bridgnorth 3445)
Open: Mon-Sat 11am-2.30pm, 6-10.30pm (11pm Fri-Sat), Sun 12noon-2pm, 7-10.30pm

[S]

John Porter opened Baileys in September 1980, after he and his wife had completely gutted the original premises and removed a remarkable 300 tons of rubble. The exposed beams, stained wood floors and occasional rugs create a pleasing atmosphere, and diners should scan the walls for details of special offers of the day. Popular dishes such as beef provençale (£1.25), Bailey's potato and meat pie (60p), and turkey vol au vent take a lot of beating, but salads and open sandwiches are warm-weather winners. Sweets and starters are excellent value for under £1.

Bromsgrove

ANDRÉS, 7 High Street (Bromsgrove 73163)
Open: Mon, Thu 11am-3pm, Wed 11am-7pm, Tue, Fri 9.30am-7pm, Sat 8.30am-6.30pm

[♫] [ⓒ]

Gay brown and gold awnings tell you that you've arrived at Andrés, a modern restaurant, tastefully decorated in pine with pottery lampshades and tiled floors. A daytime menu provides quick grills, salads and omelettes for shoppers and business people at less than £3 for three courses. There is an extensive selection of traditional English fare such as sirloin steak with trimmings at £3.25 and scampi at £2.30. A starter of soup or fruit juice at 25p and dessert of sweet pancake at around 55p is within our budget.

Bromyard

THE OLD PENNY, 48 High Street (Bromyard 3227)
Open: Mon, Wed-Sat 12.15-1.30pm, 7-9pm, Sun 12.15-2pm

[C] [S] [ⓒ]

This simple, 17th-century restaurant

has exposed beams and white walls. The dining room is divided by an attractive archway. Proprietors Norman and June Williams are known locally for using only best-quality meat and fresh vegetables in their wholesome English meals. Speciality of the house is roast duckling with orange sauce. The budget conscious are advised to stick to the table d'hôte lunch at £3.50 and dinner at £5.95. A typical meal from these low price menus would consist of mushrooms in garlic butter followed by sirloin of beef and Yorkshire pudding and chocolate nut sundae with fresh whipped cream.

Canon Pyon

THE BARN RESTAURANT, Bush Bank (Canon Pyon 435)
Open: Tue-Sat 7-9.30pm, Sun 12noon-2pm

♫ P

In the heart of the Hereford countryside, just over a mile north east of Canon Pyon is this picturesque half-timbered converted barn. Once a drover's stopover between Wales and Hereford the minstrel gallery and exposed beams are probably little different since those bygone days. Everything is cooked on the premises and the dinner menu is varied and wholesome. Some items are beyond the scope of this guide, but interesting starters such as tuna-stuffed tomatoes, grilled grapefruit with rum and borsch (beetroot) soup are all around 95p. A main dish such as chicken Alexander (in cream and white wine sauce with asparagus) costs about £4.50. A selection of home-made sweets such as poached peaches cost 90p. Sunday lunch at £4.25 offers a good choice for all four courses. Try ham and chicken pancake, followed by moussaka and a home-made dessert if you want to treat the family to something different this Sunday. Coffee is extra at about 40p.

Church Stretton

THE STUDIO, 59 High Street (Church Stretton 722672)
Open: summer: Mon-Sat 12noon-2pm, 7.30-10pm, winter: Mon 7.30-10pm, Tue-Sat 12noon-2pm, 7.30-10pm

C ♫ P S

After housing a potter's studio earlier this century, part of this row of 300-year-old white-painted cottages has reverted to its former business of hospitality. For in the days when there were reputedly more pubs than houses in Church Stretton, the 'studio' was an inn. Inside is a small, cosy bar and a dining room with an atmosphere of clean simplicity. The standard lunch menu can easily keep within £3 for three courses, and features home-made steak and kidney pie. The more exciting dinner à la carte has tempting specialities together with more conventional dishes, but is likely to break the budget.

Clent

FOUR STONES, Adams Hill (Hagley 883260)
Open: Tue-Sat 12.30-2.30pm, 7-11.30pm, Sun 12.30-2.30pm

♫ P

In the heart of the scenic Clent Hills, just south of the A456 'twixt Kidderminster and Halesowen, is this quaint little bow-window fronted cottage which has been converted into a country-style restaurant. Dark wooden beams, posts and horsebrasses complete the rural atmosphere. Here you may enjoy a set three-course lunch which could include soup of the day, a choice of roasts and a home-made dessert for less than £3. The à la carte menu is much more extensive, and provided you avoid the Chef's Specials, you should be able to have a feast within our budget. Appetisers range from 45p for soup to £1.50 for smoked trout, with prawn cocktail at less than £1. Two pork chops or half a chicken with vegetables and side salad are about £3.25. Desserts from the trolley are around 60p and are tempting examples of the home cooking here.

Coventry

CORKS WINE BAR, Whitefriars Street
(Coventry 23628)
Open: Mon-Fri 11am-2.30pm, 6-10.30pm, Sat 6-11pm, Sun 7-10.30pm

♫ P

Dark green walls, a raftered ceiling, tiled floor and old tulip-shaped wall lights create a yester-year effect enhanced by cast-iron and refectory tables, old French street name plates, prints and mirrors. Two plat du jour blackboards list the range of cold and hot dishes available, these changing every day. Prices range from around 50p-£3. Soup of the day is about 40p, gâteaux 65p, pizzas about 90p, meals of the day such as spaghetti or boeuf bourguignon just over £1, meat salads £1.75 and steak at around £3.45. If you're feeling adventurous, escargots at £1.80 are an interesting alternative.

NELLO PIZZERIA, 8 City Arcade
(Coventry 23551)
Open: Mon-Thu 9.30am-11.30pm, Fri-Sat 9.30am-1am

C P S

An informal atmosphere and freshly-baked food have established the Nello as a popular eating place – ideal for weary shoppers and tourists alike. Pastas are listed as starters on the menu, though a plate of home-made lasagne or cannelloni is a tasty meal in itself. Pizzas include the Special Pizza Nello – a banquet of cheese, tomato, tuna, prawns, mushrooms, anchovies, egg, ham and olives – all this for around £2.25. Grills and roasts are also available, ranging in price from about £1.50 for sausages and chips to £4.50 for steak.

Droitwich

THE SPINNING WHEEL RESTAURANT
13 St Andrews Street
(Droitwich 770031)
Open: Mon-Sat 10am-5.30pm, 7.30-10pm, Sun 12noon-2.30pm

♫ P S

Popular with shoppers, tourists and local businesspeople, the Spinning Wheel enjoys a prime position in Droitwich's new shopping centre. Access to this attractive cottage-style restaurant is across a paved patio area complete with fish pond and garden furniture. Friendly waitresses will serve you from a comprehensive menu ranging from light snacks to more substantial grills, omelettes etc. A table d'hôte three-course meal consisting of soup of the day, roast pork and apple sauce with vegetables, plus sweet costs £2.25. Main dishes from the à la carte are also reasonably priced with pizza or steak and kidney pie at around £1.65 to grilled gammon with pineapple at £3.45. With starter, a fresh cream sherry trifle at 60p and coffee, the whole need cost no more than £3.

Ellesmere

THE BLACK LION, Scotland Street
(Ellesmere 2418)
Open: Restaurant: Mon-Fri 6.30-9.30pm, Bar: Mon-Sat 11.30am-2pm, 6.30-9.30pm, Sun 12noon-1.30pm, 6.30-9.30pm

C P S

This early 16th-century inn stands in the centre of Ellesmere. In the dining room, with its exposed beams and simple décor, steak, chicken and scampi are supplemented by sole in prawn and mushroom sauce (one of the most expensive dishes at £4 plus), and lasagne (about £3.30). There's a wide range of standard bar meals. The special Black Lion Ploughman's for around £1.20 is guaranteed to satisfy the most ravenous ploughman, with its red and white Cheshire and Stilton cheeses, bread and salad.

Evesham

SMALL TALK, 58 Bridge Street
Open: Mon-Sat 9.30am-5.30pm

[S] [wine]

White walls and exposed dark-wood beams are offset by a charming small floral print used for tablecloths and curtains in this convivial snack bar with a bird's eye view of the town. Appetisers include grapefruit segments or soup of the day for around 35p. Venison and beef pie costs around 80p and quiche Lorraine is even cheaper. Chicken and ham pie with salad is around £2. Desserts such as blackcurrant and apple pie with cream, lemon meringue pie or various fresh cream gâteaux are in the 55p-60p range. You will have to wash your meal down with a cup of excellent tea or coffee because Small Talk is unlicensed.

Henley-in-Arden

THE LITTLE FRENCH CAFE
28 High Street (Henley-in-Arden 4322)
Open: Mon-Sat 10am-6.30pm,
Sun 2.30-6.30pm

[wine]

Stop at this pretty creeper-clad cottage with its heart-shaped sign in picturesque Henley-in-Arden for a snack or a well-prepared, home-cooked light lunch. Mike and Linda Parker have recently re-opened the café which is now convincingly Olde Worlde in style – whitewashed walls, exposed beams, stone-flagged floor, chintzy curtains and all. Start with home-made pâté, then decide between a selection of cold savoury flans with salad at around £1.80 or Hot Dish of the Day – such as kedgeree served with a selection of side salads at around £2. A delicious home-made dessert costs about 50p. An assortment of drinks is available – none of which is alcoholic as the café is unlicensed.

Hereford

CATHEDRAL RESTAURANT
Church Street (Hereford 65233)
Open: summer: Mon-Sat
9.30am-7.30pm, winter: Mon-Wed
9.30am-4pm, Fri-Sat 9.30am-4.30pm,
7-10.30pm. Closed: Thu-Sun

[C] [music] [wine]

As its name would suggest, this small restaurant is set close to the cathedral in a quiet street. The black beams and white walls typify the tourist's idea of Hereford. John Browne, who for eight years worked in Florida and Bermuda, recently bought this restaurant and opened a cellar extension. Special meals of the day are listed on a blackboard, and usually include fresh local produce. A four-course dinner including pâté, coq au vin, fruit pie, coffee and wine can be had for the all-inclusive price of £4.

THE CITY WALLS, 67 St Owen Street
(Hereford 67720/69134)
Open: Wed-Fri 12noon-2pm,
Tue-Sun 7-11pm

[music] [P] [S] [wine]

This restaurant is built on part of the original city wall – at a point where taxes were collected in bygone days. Included in the price of the main dish (half roast duckling or chicken, for instance) is the vegetable of the day, French fries, home-made apple pie with cream or ice cream. With a starter and coffee the £5 budget may just be exceeded.

THE OVEN DOOR COFFEE HOUSE
St Peter's Close, Commercial Street
(Hereford 2557)
Open: Mon-Sat 9am-5pm

[S] [wine]

This unusual restaurant nestles coyly in the shadow of St Peter's church. There's a paved patio area around the entrance where meals may be taken in summer, while the inside resembles a pine-built chalet. Hot lunch dishes include lasagne at about £2, and hot sausage roll platter or 'grilled cheesy' at around £1. Cold dishes include a ploughman's at about £1.10, pâtés and flans.

TUDOR RESTAURANT
48 Broad Street (Hereford 58374)
Open: Mon-Sat 9.30am-5.30pm
Sun (Jun-Oct) 10.30am-5pm

[S] [wine]

This 17th-century building in one of the busiest streets of Hereford is situated near the cathedral. Proprietor Mrs Joan Edwards is an avid weight-watcher and, keen to dispel the myth of salad being an inferior substitute for a meal, she spends most of her time in the kitchen preparing nutritious creations such as continental salad with salami and olives, the Tudor Danwich (brown bread with lettuce, cheese, egg and tomato) and many others, plus the usual list of grills and pies. Children are given a particularly warm welcome in this homely restaurant.

Kenilworth

ANA'S BISTRO, 121 Warwick Road (Kenilworth 53763)
Open: Mon-Sat 12noon-2pm, 6.30-10.30pm.

[P] [🍷]

This cosy cellar bistro is part of Diments restaurant in the small town of Kenilworth. The bill of fayre is recorded each day on a blackboard and includes a choice of four or five hot dishes of the day with such exotic items as chicken in courgette and mint sauce or dressed crab. Soups are home-made and the average three-course meal costs around £5. Although the main menu in the upstairs restaurant is above our limit there is a good table d'hôte lunch on offer for around £3.95. With a stock of over eighty wines you'll be spoilt for choice for an accompaniment to your meal.

Kingswinford

BICKLEY'S BISTRO, 11 Townsend Place (Kingswinford 287148)
Open: Mon-Fri 12noon-2.30pm, Mon-Sat 7-10pm

[C] [S] [🍷]

Tucked away in a small shopping area off the busy A491 is this charming little bistro. Originally the local post office, it has been transformed into a cosy eating place of mainly black-and-white brickwork decorated with antique cooking utensils and pot plants. The tempting menu offers excellent variety, but care is needed to stay within our £5 budget. A typical meal could comprise a tomato/herb salad starter at around 55p, brown trout in rosemary with seasonal vegetables at around £3.45, and a lemon water ice dessert at 75p; with fresh coffee and cream for about 35p, you have a meal to remember. A plat du jour lunch changes daily and is good value at around £1.50, and for a really special finale how about café calvados: a fine Viennese coffee, blended with calvados brandy and topped with whipped cream and cinammon for less than 90p? Booking is advisable.

Kinver

MAGPIE RESTAURANT, 116 High Street (Kinver 2621)
Open Wed-Mon 12noon-2pm, 7-10pm (Closed Tue, Sun eve)

[P] [🍷]

Known locally as a beauty spot for its sandstone caves and breathtaking views, the village of Kinver now boasts a stylish new main street restaurant. Parts of the black-and-white beamed premises date from the 13th century, and the several small dining rooms ooze olde-worlde charm. Home-made soup steak and kidney pie and lamb cutlets often feature on the menu, and three courses should cost from £4 to £5.

Knowle

YE OLDE BAKEHOUSE, Warwick Road, Chadwick End (Lapworth 2928)
On the main A41 Birmingham/Warwick road
Open: Tue-Sun 12.30-1.30pm, Mon-Sat 7.30-9.45pm

[C] [P] [🍷]

Inside this black-and-white shuttered cottage with its bright flower tubs, diners receive a warm welcome from mother-and-son team Nick and Iris Worrall. Bits and bobs of bric-à-brac and open fires add to the homely atmosphere. A table d'hôte lunch, with the choice of four starters and five main courses, comprises fresh vegetables such as new potatoes, French beans, peas, broad beans, carrots and stuffed marrow at exactly £5, including home-made sweet and coffee. In the evening the à la carte menu lists specialities such as Bakehouse breast of chicken at £3.65.

Leamington Spa

NELLO PIZZA AND SPAGHETTI HOUSE, 86 Regent Street (Leamington Spa 22070)
Open: Mon-Sat 10am-11pm, Sun 12noon-10pm

[♫] [P] [S] [🍷]

Exciting décor is the hallmark of this split level pizzeria where one of the white walls has a tiled, roof-like projection creating the illusion of courtyard eating. The average cost of a three course meal including coffee is around £4.50 though a home-made pizza alone will satisfy most people. Starters include pastas, soup of the day and prawn cocktail. The choice of eight main course pizzas includes the special pizza Nello with cheese, tomato, tuna, prawns, mushrooms, anchovies, egg, ham and olives – all for about £1.80!

PARKES, 19 Park Street
(Leamington Spa 23741)
Open: Mon-Sat 12noon-2pm, 7-11pm

[C] [♫] [P]

A décor of green and cream with mirrors and plants sets the scene. The menu is quoted as 'merely a guideline' which can be altered on request. Exciting starters include Parkes' special mushrooms, a bowl of chili topped with cream and chopped onions or crudités with assorted home-made dips (around £1.30). To follow are enormous main courses, with specialities such as chicken breasts in vermouth at around £3, or salads, lasagne and pizzas – all about £2.20 – and the inelegantly named 'gut expander' (a giant hamburger served on a bun with the largest portion of French fries served in the Midlands) costing around £2. A special children's portion of hamburger and chips is around £1.30 and there is a list of 'Ice Cream Orgies' – 'for adults only when containing liquor'! There is a disco with dancing every night.

THE REGENT HOTEL ★★★ Regent Street (Leamington Spa 27231)
Open: The Vaults Restaurant: Mon-Sat 12.30-2pm, 7.30-11pm. Chandos Restaurant: Mon-Sat 12.30-2pm, 6.45-8.45pm, Sun 12.30-2pm, 7-8.30pm, Fast Food Bar: normal licensing hours

[C] [♫] [P]

The imposing Regent Hotel in the centre of this famous spa was the largest hotel in Europe when it was built in 1819 and renowned for its VIP visitors, including Queen Victoria and Napoleon. Today it boasts three excellent eating places. The Vaults, a transformed basement wine cellar serves an excellent table d'hôte lunch. A choice of seven starters, four main courses including sweetbread à la crème and coffee costs just under £6. The elegant Chandos Restaurant offers a table d'hôte lunch with far greater choice but is likely to go beyond our budget. Fish salad, roast beef and Yorkshire pudding and a sweet from the trolley makes a satisfying meal. If you only want a quick snack, try the Cork and Fork Bar, where you can choose one of twelve very reasonably priced hot dishes and get a starter and sweet thrown in for as little as £2.

Ledbury

APPLEJACK, 44 The Homend
(Ledbury 4181)
Open: Tue-Sat 12.30-2.30pm, 7.30-10.30pm

[S]

The cosy 'old world inn' atmosphere is retained here at Applejack where owners Anna and Bob Evans have converted this 17th-century inn into a snug two-storey bistro and antique shop. A racing driver, Bob started the bistro as a hobby while his wife Anna concentrates on the antique business. At lunchtime the menu is chalked on a large blackboard where a limited selection of interesting dishes is offered. A sample meal could be home-made pea soup, guinea fowl casserole with trimmings and a generous helping of rhubarb crumble followed by as much freshly ground coffee as you can drink – all for under £5. The printed dinner menu is more extensive with dishes such as Hoi-sin pork (charcoal-grilled chops with barbecue sauce) at £2.95 or asparagus chicken (marinated in cider with fresh asparagus and cream) at £2.95 to tempt your palate. Vegetables are 50p extra in the evening but with reasonable care the bill need not exceed £5.50. Situated in the main shopping street of Ledbury, this black and white inn is convenient for shoppers and businesspeople.

Leek

THE JESTER AT LEEK, 81 Mill Street
(Leek 383997)
Open: Mon-Sun 12noon-2pm, 7-8pm

[P]

This beige, pebble-dash restaurant has an inviting, cottagey interior. A good variety of wholesome basic English fare

is available and a three-course Sunday lunch with a choice of seven starters, eight main courses and sweets from the trolley comes at around £4. The à la carte menu, with starters, grills and roasts at reasonable prices, includes a lot of fish and seafood. Try fresh salmon at around £3.75, or golden seafood platter at about £3.50. Budget meals at lunchtime cost about £1.75 and include home-made steak and kidney pie, breaded plaice and a dish of the day.

Ludlow

EAGLE HOUSE, Corve Street
(Ludlow 2325)
Open: Oak Room: Mon-Sun 12noon-2.30pm, 7-10pm,
Pine Room: 9am-7pm

P S

Known as 'The Eagle and Child' when it was first built in the 17th century as a coaching inn, this half-timbered building still retains evidence of a cobblestoned blacksmith's yard. In the entrance, traces of wattle and daub plastering have been exposed to show the original construction. Extremely fine oak panelling in the Oak Room restaurant came from nearby Acton Scott Hall and Bitterley Court and is an outstanding feature. The three-course lunch is remarkable value at under £3.50 – you could start with grapefruit and orange cocktail, then savour roast lamb and finish with Queen of Puddings – though there are several other choices for each course. Table d'hôte dinner costs £5.25 and offers a wide selection including roast duckling and chicken al' spagnolé. With careful choice, the à la carte menu could be within our budget. If you are after a quick snack, then climb the stairs to the Pine Room, where anything from a pot of tea to steak and chips is available.

PENNY ANTHONY ✕ 5 Church Street
(Ludlow 3282)
Open: Mon-Sat 10.30am-2pm, 7-10pm

C P S

Close to the castle entrance, a charming Georgian-style building houses this popular little restaurant. Three courses can cost from around £3-£6 depending on your choice. Delicious cold dishes include terrine of duck and salads (about £2) or pâté maison and garlic bread (around £1.40). Snails in garlic, onions and parsley, hazelnut roast and salad, seafood pancakes or lasagne are hot dishes costing about £2.50. Steak is around £5. A more sophisticated and expensive evening menu includes specialities such as pork fillet with sage (marinated in dry white wine) and chicken with pernod, at around £5.50 including vegetables.

Nesscliffe

THE OLD THREE PIGEONS
(Nesscliffe 279)
Open: Tue-Sun 12.30-2.30pm, 7-10.30pm (closed Sun eve)

P

You'll find more than just good food and ale at the Harrison's 15th-century roadside inn. For pre-dinner entertainment you can enjoy tales of philanthropic highwayman Humphrey Kynnaston who supped many a jar at The Old Three Pigeons, his favourite retreat. The country-style décor is given a homely touch with a grandfather clock and large Welsh Dresser. Home cooking is the order of the day too, with roast 'beer fed' pork a popular main course choice at around £3. With a range of starters averaging about 85p, and sweets likewise, the cost of a three-course dinner is quite within our reach. The table d'hôte lunch is also reasonably-priced at £4 or so for three courses such as a sardine salad starter followed by chicken chasseur with a choice of sweet to follow. Bar snacks such as home-made pigeon pie are available for around £1.60.

Newcastle-under-Lyme

POSTILLION RESTAURANT, COFFEE SHOP AND AUTHOR'S BAR, THE POST HOUSE ☆☆☆Clayton Road (Newcastle-under-Lyme 625151)
Open: Postillion Restaurant: Mon-Sun 12.30-2.15pm, 7-10.15pm,
The Buttery: Mon-Sun 7.30am-10.30pm,
Author's Bar: Mon-Sun 12noon-2pm

C P

Stick with the three-course table d'hôte lunch and dinner menus here, if you want to stay around the £5 limit. Next door is the Coffee Shop which offers a wide range of food from snacks to full meals for all occasions. Ideal for all the family, it has children's favourites such as hamburgers, pork sausages and omelettes plus tempting goodies such as fruit pie and chocolate banana nut sundae. Choose from a selection of cold meats, pâtés and as much salad as you want for less than £2.50.

Pershore

SUGAR AND SPICE, High Street (Pershore 3654)
Open: Mon-Sat 9.30am-5.30pm, Sun 10.30am-5.30pm

Painted pink, this eaterie stands out from its more sober-fronted high street neighbours. In true tea shop tradition, you'll find the cheerful restaurant by walking through a patisserie and extensive gift shop. At the rear there is an attractive patio setting for when the weather's fine. Soup here costs 40p and pizza 70p, whilst cottage pie with potatoes and peas (£1.85) and ploughman's lunch (£1.20) are examples of the no-nonsense main dishes available. For dessert, there's a large counter of mouth-watering confectionery to delight the most discerning gâteau gourmet. Whatever your choice, the meal (including coffee) will cost much less than £5 per head.

Shrewsbury

BRISTOL FRIGATE, Frankwell Quay (Shrewsbury 4225)
Open: Mon-Sat 7pm-12mdnt, Sun 12noon-2pm

C

It's the fact that it floats that will probably attract you to the Bristol Frigate initially. The bright blue and white painted 'vessel' stands out against the duller colours of the River Severn near the Welsh Bridge. Though purpose-built as a restaurant, brave attempts have been made to create a nostalgically salty atmosphere, the focal point being the original wheel from an old clipper, together with admirals' swords, bells and ropes. The soft lighting and carpeting are definitely geared to modern comfort – and you certainly won't get scurvy! The main course choice is steak (8oz sirloin £3.30) or pizza (from £1.15) with salad (60p). Desserts are of the calorie-oozing variety like dairy cream gâteau (75p) or chocolate fudge sundae (£1.25).

CAVALIER RESTAURANT, PRINCE RUPERT HOTEL, Butcher Row (Shrewsbury 52461)
Open: Mon-Sun 12noon-2.45pm, 7-10.15pm

C P S

The restaurant has an air of opulence with its oak beams and pillars, rich red carpet, velvet curtains and cartwheel-converted chandeliers. Oil paintings adorn the white walls, which contrast the dark wood setting. At lunchtime here a table d'hôte menu offers a choice of seven starters and main dishes (eg ravioli au gratin, followed by roast leg of pork with apple sauce), plus a sweet from the trolley, all for £5. A more adventurous three-course evening meal, with several more options, costs around £6.

CORNHOUSE RESTAURANT AND WINE BAR, 59A Wyle Cop (Shrewsbury 241991)
Open: Mon-Sat 11.30am-2.30pm, Sun 12noon-2pm, Mon-Thu 6.30-10.30pm, Fri-Sat 6.30-11pm, Sun 7-10.30pm

C

This restaurant occupies the ground and first floors of a warehouse built in the mid 1800s, a few minutes walk from the town centre. The present proprietor has carried out considerable improvements to the premises, including the installation of a beautiful wrought-iron spiral staircase. Stripped pine furniture, exposed brickwork and beams, polished floorboards, potted plants and spotlights complete the pleasing effect. Customers may choose to eat a light meal or snack in the ground floor wine bar, or go upstairs to the restaurant for a more substantial meal.

DELANY'S, St Julians Craft Centre for Shropshire, off Fish Street (Shrewsbury 60602)
Open: Tue-Wed 11am-5pm, Thu-Sat 11am-9pm

[♫] [S] [⚘]

A more unlikely place for a restaurant than the vestry of a church is hard to imagine, but Delany's – a vegetarian's delight – looks quite at home among the original wood panels and highly-polished boards and beams. Soups instead of sermons are the order of the day now the old church has become a restaurant and craft centre. Tasty and original dishes such as cauliflower, mushroom and cheese bake and aubergine nut crumble (under £2) are served on the cheerful green-and-white-clothed tables, each equipped with flowers, a pot of fresh ground rock salt, dishes of soft brown sugar and unsalted butter. The menu is not extensive but all the dishes are inexpensive.

THE DICKENS RESTAURANT, LION HOTEL ★★★ Wyle Cop (Shrewsbury 53107)
Open: Mon-Sat 12.30-2pm, 7-10pm, Sun 12.30-2pm, 7-9pm

[C] [P] [S] [⚘]

The popular, elegant 18th-century Lion Hotel stands in the centre of Shrewsbury. Distinguished visitors have included Disraeli, Paganini and, of course, Dickens. A three-course lunch is offered for around £4.95 and might consist of devilled whitebait, roast beef and gâteau, and a similar table d'hôte dinner costs £5.95 for four courses.

DUN COW, Abbey Foregate (Shrewsbury 56408)
Open: Mon-Sun 12noon-2pm, 6.30pm-10.30pm

[C] [P] [⚘]

You're not likely to find a more historic eating house than the Dun Cow, reputed to be one of the oldest pubs in England, dating from circa 1085. Thanks to the research efforts of the owners, you can read about its amazing history including the sightings of a ghost in the dress of a Dutch cavalry officer, from the special leaflet they have produced. The dining room is more modern than the rest of the premises but an effort has been made to capture the 'olde worlde' atmosphere with exposed beams, rough plaster walls and some exposed stonework. Dishes on the interesting à la carte need careful selection as some prices will exceed our limit. Trout Sabrina – two trout dressed with almonds and lemon, and lamb Shrewsbury – cutlets of lamb with port wine and honey, are two of the more unusual and less expensive main courses.

JUST WILLIAMS, 62-63 Mardol (Shrewsbury 57061)
Open: Mon-Sat 11am-11pm, Sun 7-11pm

[C] [♫] [P] [S] [⚘]

Not far from Shrewsbury's main street is this pretty little wine bar, where a small bow window gives glimpses of a black and white, flower-decked interior. Renoirs and other French prints adorn the walls and an old converted gas lamp adds atmosphere. The food includes home-made soup (around 50p), meat salads (ranging from about £1.95 to £2.95) and the evening hot dishes such as pork-filled vol-au-vents (at around £2.50) are advertised on a blackboard. With desserts at around 75p, the average cost of a three-course meal and coffee is still under £4.

THE OLDE TUDOR STEAK HOUSE Butcher Row (Shrewsbury 53117)
Open: Tue-Sun 12noon-2.15pm, Tue-Fri 7-10.30pm, Sat 7-11.30pm

[C] [P] [S] [⚘]

The Steak House restaurant occupies the second floor of fine 16th-century black and white timbered premises. Refectory tables, paintings and bric-à-brac help to create a Tudor atmosphere. Table d'hôte lunch is very good value at around £2.50 on weekdays, £3.20 on Sundays. Three courses include soup of the day, a choice of seven main courses such as chicken in red wine and a sweet of the day which could be a delicious chocolate mousse. The à la carte menu is predominantly grills and though more expensive, with care three courses can be enjoyed for around £5.

ROYALIST PIZZA BAR, Church Street (Shrewsbury 52461)
Open: Mon-Sat 12noon-2.15pm, 6-10.15pm

[P]

A side shoot of the Prince Rupert Hotel, this little pizza bar boasts an unusual 'olde worlde' setting with dark oak beams and white-painted reproduction furniture, chandeliers, leaded windows with coats of arms and white embossed walls. As the name suggests, the most popular main course is pizza. There are four varieties to choose from, all freshly prepared, even the base, while you wait. Soup of the day, Siciliana (a tasty concoction of tomatoes, anchovies, Mozzarella cheese, mushrooms and black olives, ice cream and coffee will cost around £2.50.

STEAK AND PIZZA BAR
50 Mardol (Shrewsbury 4834)
Open: Mon-Sat 11.30am-2.30pm, Mon-Sun 6-11pm

[C] [🍷]

A large bay window and a vivid sign announce these charming little premises, ideally situated for cinema-goers, shoppers and riverbank walkers. The walls are dotted with posters of Italian landmarks and bright red and white gingham cloths cover the tables. All beefburgers and pizzas are freshly made on the premises, and represent excellent value for money.

THE STEAK BAR, Fish Street (Shrewsbury 52463)
Open: Mon-Sat 12noon-2pm, 6-10.45pm

[C] [P]

Shrewsbury's original steak bar is situated in a quiet side street opposite the Prince Rupert Hotel. On entering the small cocktail bar that leads to the restaurant, a mouth-watering aroma wafts temptingly towards you from the open servery. Inside, the majority of tables are arranged to create intimate dining alcoves, whilst the oak-beamed ceiling and leaded windows add a certain Tudor aura. So, what catches your eye on the menu? Maybe French onion soup (35p), followed by a 6oz rump steak with all the trimmings (only around £3) and a fruit salad (60p) to finish. Coffee will round off an inexpensive meal.

Solihull

BOBBY BROWN'S, 183 High Street (021-704 9136)
Open: Mon-Sat 12noon-2.30pm, 7-11pm

[S]

Chris, Caroline and Annie are three young friends who met while working in someone else's wine bar. They decided to stay together as a team and open their own restaurant. The result of their labours is this cosy, informal place with a courtyard where spontaneous barbecues are often held. A blackboard lists specialities of the day such as cold celery and apple soup (55p), spicy chicken with rice (£2.75) and many more. Choices from the cold table include cheddar cheese and pineapple, home-made chicken liver pâté and honey baked ham served with three kinds of salad. Sweets cost around £1.

WHITE CAT RESTAURANT
165 High Street
(021-705 1657)
Open: Tue-Sun 12noon-2.15pm, 7-9.45pm
(closed Tue & Sun eves)

[C] [🍷]

This attractive restaurant consists of three black-and-white cottages which were originally converted into a 'tea shoppe' by a lady who kept white cats – hence the name. The cottage style has been retained by Allan Jones and his family, although it is now a more formal restaurant. Mrs Jones or her daughter is in the foyer to greet you as you enter and direct you to your table in the dining room where the warm, homely atmosphere is enhanced by friendly waitresses. There is a three-course weekday lunch for around £3, and on Sundays a special roast lunch costs about £4.15 adults, £2.60 children. The evening à la carte requires careful selection but a three-course meal of grapefruit cocktail followed by breast of fresh farm chicken served with fresh cream sauce on a bed of rice, fruit Melba and coffee with cream costs around £5 in this restaurant.

Stafford

ANEMOS, 22 Crabbery Street (Stafford 48940)
Open: Mon-Wed 9am-5pm, Thu-Sat 9am-5pm, 7.30-11pm

[S] [🍷]

The small upstairs dining room of this shop-fronted Greek restaurant serves a cosmopolitan range of light lunches – omelettes, salads, pizzas, pasta dishes and moussaka are all between £1-£2. A more substantial lunch can be enjoyed from a choice of fourteen starters – including soup of the day at 40p or dolmades at £1.15. Main course could be sofrito (a Corfu speciality of beef in wine sauce served with a side salad – costing about £2.95), beef Stroganoff (£3) or prawn kebab with salad and rice at £4.50. Desserts include gâteaux at about 55p. The evening menu is basically Greek and more expensive, but three courses could be savoured for around £5.

HAND AND CLEAVER INN, Ranton (Stafford 822367)
Open: Mon-Thu 12noon-2pm, 7-10pm, Fri-Sat 12noon-2pm, 7-10.30pm, Sun 12noon-1.30pm, 7-10pm

[C] [♫] [P] [🍷]

The restaurant of this beautiful inn, built as a farmhouse in 1733, was once the cowshed. The original stalls have been kept and tables installed, but the names of their previous occupants remain: Snowdrop, Poppy, Rosebud, Daisy and Violet among them. Above this area is the old hay loft, and diners can gaze down into the main restaurant. Lunches here are well within the limit – a three-course Sunday lunch at £4 could include Florida cocktail, roast beef and a sweet from the trolley. The same meal for a child is £2. Snacks such as scampi and chips (£1.70), rump steak, chips and peas (£3.65) or beef salad (£1.75) are available in the bar. The sophisticated evening à la carte menu is a little beyond our limit for most selections, but you could *just* manage three courses.

Stoke-on-Trent

CAPRI RISTORANTE ITALIANO
13 Glebe Street (Stoke-on-Trent 411889)
Open: Mon-Sat 12noon-2.15pm, 6-11pm

C P

Entering the rear of this little Italian restaurant from the car park has been compared with walking into the famous Blue Grotto of Capri. Blue and green lighting creates the illusion, which is enhanced by scenes of Italy painted on the white stucco walls by proprietor Vittorio Cirillo. Good, home-cooked Italian fare is highly recommended, with minestrone or salami to start at around £1, lasagne, spaghetti, penne alla arrabiata or penne al ragu as the main course, all about £1.70 and delicious desserts such as profiteroles (95p) or orange slices with liqueur (80p). You will be left with plenty of change from £5 for a cup of frothy espresso or cappucino coffee.

THE POACHERS COTTAGE ✕✕
Stone Road, Trentham
(Stoke-on-Trent 657115)
Open: Mon-Sun 12noon-2pm, Tue-Sat 7-9.30pm

P ₰

This black and white cottage is easily located on the A34, close to Trentham Gardens. The cottage atmosphere has been retained inside, with black beams, natural stone and tapestry upholstered chairs. White linen tablecloths and colourful carpets add a touch of luxury. The lunchtime menu has excellent value roasts and grills. Rollmop herring hors d'oeuvres, roast chicken with trimmings, a sweet and coffee will just top £5.

RIB OF BEEF, GRAND HOTEL ★★★
66 Trinity Street, Hanley
(Stoke-on-Trent 22361)
Open: Mon-Sun 12.30-2.30pm, 7-10pm

C P S ₰

Situated on the lower ground floor of the impressive Stakis-run hotel close to Hanley city centre, the Rib of Beef restaurant boasts some tasty local favourites. Try the excellent table d'hôte menu. For only about £4.50 at lunchtime you can choose home-made broth – one of three starters – then take your choice of roast ribs of beef, fish, grilled lamb chops – it's different every day! Try the delicious vegetables and sauces and, if you have room for it, the sweet trolley offers a host of gooey goodies. Dinner is a little beyond the limit of this guide.

ROOSEVELT'S RESTAURANT
24 Snow Hill (Stoke-on-Trent 269544)
Open: Mon-Sun 12noon-12mdnt

C ♫ ₰

As the name implies, an American-style fast service operates here, the result of owner Philip Crowe's long observations in the States. Judging by the hordes of people that frequent the restaurant, the system is a great success. Brown hessian walls, a quarry-tiled floor and Liberty-print tablecloths create a warm, welcoming effect and the many photographs and posters continue the Americana theme. Having started with, perhaps, corn on the cob (60p), you can choose from several hamburger specials, all with French fries and trimmings, costing around £1.70 or £2.50, depending on burger size. At these prices you can afford to splash out on a knickerbocker glory, enjoy a cup of coffee and still get change from a fiver.

SHOULDER OF MUTTON, Meadow Lane, Fulford (Blyth Bridge 7375)
Open: Thu-Sat 7-10.30pm, Sun 12noon-2pm, 7-10.30pm

C P ₰

A village-centre pub which has been modernised and extended to incorporate a grill room with olde worldo appeal. A T-bone steak, plus French fries, garden peas and salad is only about £5. Appealing dishes at budget prices are available on the à la carte menu – steak chasseur (£4.25) and golden-fried scampi (£3.30) are examples. All starters are less than £1, whilst desserts cost around 65p.

SPOT GATE, Hilderstone Road, Spot Acre (Hilderstone 277)
Open: Mon-Fri 12noon-2pm, 7.30-9.30pm, Sat 7.30-10.15pm,

Sun 12noon-2pm, 7.30-9pm

[C] [♫] [P] [🍷]

Lunch or dinner aboard this Cavalier Steak Bar is certain to be a gastronomic journey you'll never forget, as diners sit in two beautifully restored dining cars from the famous old Bournemouth Belle. Ursula is the name of the first class compartment seating sixteen in luxurious armchair-style seats plus the two small private dining compartments with intimate seating for four. The other, christened Maggie, seats almost fifty in surroundings of beautiful veneer panelling, brass-framed windows, heavy brass hat and luggage racks and comfortable seating with antimacassars from the days of slicked back hair. Meals are more varied than usual in a steak bar with a range of fish, poultry or meat dishes from around £3.50-£6. Half a chicken with sweet and sour is particularly popular at £3.85.

Stourbridge

BELL HOTEL ★★ Market Street (Stourbridge 5641)
Open: Tue-Sat 12.30-2.15pm, 6.30-8.30pm, Sun 12.30-2.15pm

[C] [P] [S] [🍷]

As one might expect from an area famous for its glass, this seems to be the theme in this restaurant, with large mirrors, glass skylights, glass doors, old leaded windows and glass partitions. Gold-coloured flock wallpaper blends effectively with the red patterned carpet, which together with the neatly-laid tables, old chairs and uniformed waitresses creates a rather timeless atmosphere. Special three-course lunches of soup, grilled lamb garni with vegetables followed by fruit Melba can be had for around £3.50, coffee included.

THE GALLERY RESTAURANT ✕
121 Bridgnorth Road, Wollaston (Stourbridge 2788)
Open: Tue-Sat 7.30-9.30pm

[C] [S]

Just mention the 'restaurant above the butcher's' to anyone in this area and you will be directed to Bill and Janet Harris's popular 'Gallery'. Bill runs the butcher's shop on this main shopping street and Janet is in charge of the successful little eating house above. Lamb chops, sole and scampi feature on the à la carte menu, all at around £4. With soup at 65p and trolley desserts around £1 you may have to break the bank to sample coffee.

THE OLD WHITE HORSE INN
South Road (Stourbridge 4258)
Open: Mon-Sat 11am-2.30pm, 6-11pm, Sun 12noon-2.30pm

[♫] [P] [🍷]

This imposing public house stands close to the entrance of Mary Steven's Park. The table d'hôte lunch menu, for around £3.50 gives a good selection of three courses – try sardine salad, braised ham with Madeira sauce and a delicious sweet from the trolley. The à la carte menu is extensive, and a little beyond our budget, but appetising meals are served at lunchtime in the main lounge.

TALBOT HOTEL ★★ High Street (Stourbridge 4350)
Open: Mon-Sat 12noon-2pm, 7-9.30pm, Sun 12noon-2pm

[C] [♫] [P] [S] [🍷]

This town centre hotel has been popular for many years. The ground floor dining room seats about seventy in comfortable alcoves screened by velvet half-curtains hung from brass rails, and it is here that lunch on weekdays and Saturdays is chosen from a buffet with mainly cold dishes; though a Chef's Special is always provided. The Sunday lunch menu offers traditional roasts of chicken, lamb, beef or pork with all the trimmings, and a starter and sweet for about £4. Evening meals consist mainly of grills such as rainbow trout or lamb cutlets. Prices are very reasonable for both table d'hôte and à la carte.

Stourport-on-Severn

LOCK, STOCK AND BARREL
2a High Street
(Stourport-on-Severn 6014)
Open: Mon 10am-2.30pm,
Tue-Sat 10am-2.30pm
(5.30pm May-Sep)
7pm-10pm

This attractive canalside bistro has a recently-opened buffet bar, which enables a greater range of home-made specialities, including quiches, pâtés and salads, to be offered at lunchtime and for suppers. A three-course lunch including hot dish of the day will cost around £3.50. In the evening an economy 'Special' (in honour of this guide) enables you to enjoy three courses of home-cooked fare with coffee and wine for £5.95. A regularly changing menu is offered in the downstairs candlelit bistro and after sampling an unusual cocktail or aperitif, careful choosing will allow you to dine on Shropshire fidget pie, jugged beefsteak or mead syllabub, amongst many more intriguing dishes.

Stratford-upon-Avon

THE DIRTY DUCK, Waterside
(Stratford-upon-Avon 297312)
Open: Mon-Sat 12noon-3pm, 6-12mdnt

[C] [S] [&]

This typically English pub-restaurant is a favourite haunt of the theatre world, due to its olde worlde charm, and its nearness to the Shakespeare theatre. Apart from serving meals before and after performances, they also offer a good lunch here. Main dishes range in price from £3-£5 with plaice fillet and braised kidneys as representative examples. There are ten or so starters with prices up to £1 and a sweet or cheese costs about 60p.

GROSVENOR HOUSE HOTEL ★★★
Warwick Road
(Stratford-upon-Avon 69213)
Open: Mon-Sun 12noon-1.45pm,
6-8.45pm

[C] [P] [&]

Just five minutes' walk from the Royal Shakespeare Theatre is this elegant, family-run hotel. You can enjoy a three-course steak-based lunch in the luxurious restaurant for around £4. The menu offers a choice of prime fillet or succulent sirloin steak with a freshly made starter and gooey sweet such as chocolate profiteroles with fresh cream. Dinner is a little beyond our budget at £6.50 but worth that bit extra as the three-course meal always includes the option of home-made soup with home-made bread rolls, and main courses served with crisp, fresh vegetables.

HATHAWAY TEA ROOMS AND BAKERY, 19 High Street
(Stratford-upon-Avon 292404)
Open: Mon-Sat 9am-5.30pm,
Sun 11.45am-5.30pm

[S]

Although the name suggests otherwise, this impressive building, with its olde worlde atmosphere goes a good deal further back than Shakespeare's era – the original site dates back to 1315. The tea rooms are reached by passing through the shop up the Jacobean staircase to the tiny landing, which houses a superb grandfather clock. Once inside, you will find everything you expected – dark oak beams, white walls, an open fireplace and antique dressers and tables. A good old-fashioned lunch menu offers traditional dishes such as roast beef and Yorkshire pudding or steak and kidney pie, each for about £2, spotted Dick, apple and raspberry tart and banana split at around 55p.

HORSESHOE BUTTERY AND RESTAURANT, 33-34 Greenhill Street (Stratford-upon-Avon 292246)
Open: Mon-Sun 9am-10pm

[P]

Handy for pre-film and theatre snacks, this bay-windowed, period-style restaurant with its charming mock-Tudor façade lies opposite the cinema and just fifty yards from the famous clock tower. An exceptionally good value table d'hôte lunch still costs less than £2.50 for three courses (eg, soup, steak and kidney pie, home-made fruit pie), and coffee. A special two-course meal costs under £2. Both are served in a warm, friendly atmosphere.

THE OPPOSITION RESTAURANT
13 Sheep Street
(Stratford-upon-Avon 69980)
Open: Tue-Sat 12noon-2.30pm, Mon-Sat 6-11.30pm

[S]

No need to feel bloodthirsty to enjoy the steakburger – Macbeth style. It's innocent enough to look at with its topping of melted cheese. Other varieties (including Texan and American styles) are well worth trying, as they are made to the proprietor's own recipe by a local butcher. Pizzas (all around £2), spaghetti and pastas are also available, and there's a small list of 'specials' including sirloin, fillet or rump steak, veal and chicken tagliatelle with prawn and wine sauce.

THE THATCH RESTAURANT
Cottage Lane, Shottery
(Stratford-upon-Avon 293122)
Open: Mon-Sun 9am-6pm

[P]

Next to the famous Anne Hathaway's Cottage you will find this delightful thatched restaurant with its olde worlde dining room and rustic canopied terrace. Here you can enjoy a fine traditional English lunch with three courses, including roast beef and Yorkshire pudding followed by a slice of home-made apple or lemon meringue pie for about £5. Cream teas are good value at £1.

Sutton Coldfield

PIMPERNELL, 59/61 Birmingham Road
(021-354 9808)
Open: Tue-Sat 12noon-2.30pm, 6-10.30pm

[C]

Just the place to eat before or after a film at the nearby cinema. Green and red tasteful décor complements the excellent and inexpensive cuisine. The à la carte menu offers dishes from many countries and is well within our budget. Particularly good value fare may be sampled from the Daily Special lunchtime menu. Soup – such as asparagus – is only 25p and main courses at £1.65 could be roast beef, chicken casserole or grilled plaice. Desserts at 30p include apple and raspberry pie. It would be very difficult to exceed the budget here!

RISTORANTE STEFANO
358 Birmingham Road
(021-373 8576)
Open: Tue-Sat 12noon-2.30pm, 7-10.30pm, Sun 12noon-2.30pm

C S ♨

Black beams and pillars contrast strikingly with the white embossed ceiling and walls of this little Italian restaurant created out of a former shop. Value for money is the keynote of the daily menu, which offers such starters as soup of the day at 35p, assorted salamis at 75p or smoked mackerel salad at 90p. Main course dishes include rigatone and napolitaine (£1.25), halibut steak Mornay, chicken chasseur or roast of the day – all at £1.85. Home-made desserts such as fruit crumble (35p) or lemon meringue pie (55p) complete a satisfying meal.

Tenbury Wells

THE PEACOCK INN, Worcester Road
(Tenbury Wells 81-0506)
1 mile east of Tenbury Wells on the A456
Open: Mon-Sat 10.30am-2.30pm 6-10.30pm, (11pm Fri-Sat) Sun 12noon-2pm, 7-10.30pm

P ♨

Amid the famous hop fields and orchards of the beautiful Teme Valley is this half-timbered, 14th-century inn, run by partners Alastair Hendry and Bernard Bond, who returned to England two years ago after spending almost thirty years in Malaysia. It follows that one of the house specialities should be Malaysian curry (£2.50), but where they learned to make such marvellous lasagne (£2.10) is quite a mystery. A starter such as smoked salmon mousse will cost around £1 and a sweet (could be rum and walnut gâteau) only 75p.

Trumpet

THE BISTRO, The Verzons Hotel
(Trumpet 381)
Open: Mon-Sat 10.30am-2pm, 6.30-10pm

C P ♨

Nestling in the peace of the Herefordshire countryside is the busy and popular Verzons Hotel. Originally a Georgian farmhouse, it stands in a lush four acres. In winter bistro diners can wallow in the warmth of an open log fire while supping a plateful of home-made Stilton soup followed by a generous portion of lasagne verdi, all for approximately £2. Summer sees guests outside in the wooded beer garden enjoying views of the recently-excavated Victorian sunken garden while their meal is served. A speciality of the bistro is the home-made desserts which include the mouth-watering mallow nut fluff laced with Grand Marnier. A fine range of traditional ales and real local cider adds to the convivial atmosphere created here by owners John and Angela Rose.

Upton-upon-Severn

CROMWELLS, 16/18 Church Street (Upton-upon-Severn 2447)
Open: Mon 9.30am-2.15pm,
Tue-Sat 9.30am-2.15pm, 7.15-10pm

Oliver Cromwell is reputed to have waved to a pretty lady at an upstairs window of this charming black-and-white half-timbered cottage. With a craft shop at the side, the rear houses a bistro with exposed brick walls and beams, leading on to a walled garden where children may let off steam. Upstairs is 'Oliver's Bar' where diners may sip an aperitif and study the blackboard menu. A typical lunch menu could be home-made vegetable soup at around £1, prawn and cheese vol-au-vents with a tossed salad (totalling £2.60) and lemon syllabub at around £1. The dinner menu offers more choice – seven possibles for each course including frog's legs as a starter! Stilton and onion soup costs 95p, scrumpy chicken £3.95 and Cromwell gâteau or lemon syllabub around £1.

Warwick

CINDY'S, 48 Brook Street
(Warwick 493504)
Open: Mon-Sat 9.30am-5pm

[C] [S]

Only about twenty people can be seated in this country kitchen style restaurant found above a tempting delicatessen, so booking in advance is advised. Dominated by pine furniture, Lowrie prints and paintings for sale by a local artist, it offers freshly prepared dishes attractively displayed on the large pine dresser. During summer, a hot dish of the day, home-made quiches and pies accompanied by a selection of salads and gâteaux are the bill of fare. In the winter months, delicious soup and hot main dishes are available.

NICOLINI'S BISTRO, 18 Jury Street
(Warwick 459817)
Open: Tue-Sun 9.30am-10.30pm

[C] [P] [S]

Located on one of the main thoroughfares of the city is this delightful little restaurant with its stripped pine chairs, potted plants and effective spot lighting. A well-stocked glass counter displaying fresh salads and tempting sweets immediately attracts the eye, and other dishes are available, such as tasty home-made pizzas. A three-course meal will, on average, be from £3-£4.

Waterhouses

THE OLDE BEAMS (Waterhouses 254)
Open: Tue-Sat 12noon-2pm,
6.30-10pm, Sun 12noon-2pm

[P]

In the centre of the village is this charming white stone and brick-built house with shuttered windows. Originally an inn, it was built in 1746, and the restaurant has exposed ceiling beams, refectory tables and Windsor chairs. Table d'hôte menus for lunch and dinner offer three courses, with good choices, for £4.50 (£5.25 for Sunday lunch). All the food is home-made, including a selection of delicious sweets on the trolley, the soup of the

day, and delicious bread rolls. The à la carte menu offers imaginative fare, much of which is within our budget.

Whittington

WHITTINGTON INN WINE BAR
(Kinver 2110)
Open: Mon-Sat 12noon-2.30pm, 6.30-10.30pm, Sun 12noon-2pm, 7-10.30pm
On the A449

[P] [⊘]

If you want to know the real story of Dick Whittington the legendary Lord Mayor, you could do no better than to eat a meal in the attractive attic wine bar in his ancestral home. A potted history of the Whittington family dating from 1307, is available for any interested diner to read. The interior of the wine bar is mainly white-painted brick, effectively decorated with old prints and posters, antique bed warmers and armoury and with the original black oak beams and rafters a prominent feature. A selection of food is made either from the mouthwatering array of salads, pies, sweets and cheeses displayed behind a glass counter, or from a blackboard which lists hot or cold specialities such as lasagne or chili con carne at around £1.80.

Wolverhampton

LE BISTRO STEAKHOUSE
6 School Street (Wolverhampton 24638)
Open: Mon-Sat 12noon-2.30pm, 6-11.30pm

[♫] [S] [⊘]

A variety of bottles hanging against white walls, black wrought-iron partitions, and red-patterned carpet create a welcoming atmosphere in this first-floor restaurant. The kitchen is supervised by owner 'Steve' Kyriakou who makes sure that Greek specialities such as moussaka (about £2) and afelia (around £2.50) are cooked to perfection. Lunchtime table d'hôte menus offer a choice of Greek or English food for around £2 with a sweet about 35p extra.

PEPITO'S, 5 School Street
(Wolverhampton 23403)
Open: Mon-Sat 12noon-2.30pm, 6-11pm, closed 3 weeks in Aug

[♫] [P] [S] [⊘]

For those who like Italian food, Pepito's offers the real thing in a pleasant modern restaurant with glass partitioning providing a degree of privacy. Owner Mr Catellani supervises the cooking while his wife, helped by two young ladies, looks after the customers. The two-course table d'hôte lunch is good value at around £1.50, with a choice of four starters and a main course pasta dish or, perhaps, goulash or a roast – there are seven or eight items to choose from.

Worcester

NATURAL BREAK, 17 Mealcheapen Street (Worcester 29979)
Open: Mon-Sat 10am-5pm

[S] [⊘]

Brown-tiled tables and natural pine create an informal, cottagey atmosphere in this popular rendezvous, where newly-wed proprietors Sandra and Nigel Wolfenden pin notices of local societies' meetings on the wall alongside paintings by local artists which are offered for sale. The board menu lists a choice of eight interesting salads at around 25p – potato, carrot, mushroom, apple, celery and walnut – ideal to accompany the home-made savoury flans and quiches which only cost about 60p. Desserts include home-baked apple pie, meringues and pastries – freshly prepared every day.

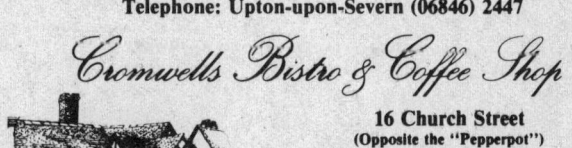

The North West

BOLTON-LE-SANDS
MORECAMBE
LANCASTER
LANCASHIRE
GISBURN
CLEVELEYS
ST MICHAELS-ON-WYRE
CLITHEROE
BLACKPOOL
BROUGHTON
BURNLEY
KIRKHAM
SAMLESBURY
FRECKLETON
PRESTON
BLACKBURN
SOUTHPORT
PARBOLD
ROCHDALE
ORMSKIRK
BOLTON
WIGAN
OLDHAM
GREATER MANCHESTER
MERSEYSIDE
MANCHESTER
ASHTON-UNDER-LYNE
STOCKPORT
LIVERPOOL
WEST KIRBY
MARPLE
HAZEL GROVE
ALTRINCHAM
HALE
DISLEY
WILMSLOW
KNUTSFORD
ALDERLEY EDGE
PRESTBURY
MACCLESFIELD
CHESHIRE
CHESTER
CONGLETON

'O tell her, Swallow, thou that knowest each,
That bright and fierce and fickle is the South,
And dark and true and tender is the North.'

ALFRED TENNYSON

9

Regional Dishes

Bury simnel cake
Black pudding
Cheshire cheese and onion pie
Haverbread
Parkin (ginger and oatmeal cake)
Eccles cakes
Lancashire hotpot
Fleetwood hake
Morecambe Bay cockles

Alderley Edge

NO. 15 WINE BAR, 15 London Road (Alderley Edge 585548)
Open: Mon-Sat 12noon-2pm, 7-10.30pm (Fri-Sat 7-11pm)

[♫] [P] [S]

The blackboard menu offers starters including pâté at about £1 and prawn cocktail at around £1.20 and hot main dishes such as moussaka, lasagne, chili con carne and tagliatelli, all for around £2.25. Prawn or trout salads are about £2. Desserts at around 85p include Jamaican fudge cake. A good selection of wines is available by the glass at about 65p. In summer you can eat in the walled and well-tended garden.

Altrincham

THE CRESTA COURT HOTEL ☆☆☆
Church Street (061-928 8017)
Open: Lodge: Mon-Sat 12noon-2pm, 6-10pm, Sun 12noon-2pm
Quarterdeck: Mon-Sun 12noon-2pm, 6.30-11pm (Sun 6.30-10pm)

[C] [♫] [P]

This bright, new hotel has two steak bar restaurants. The Tavern Lodge offers the usual combination of steak, chicken, scampi and fish costing from £2 to about £3.95 all served with vegetables. The Quarterdeck is a little more sophisticated, with main dishes from over £2 to £4.50 and a good selection of vegetables in addition to those included in the price of the meal.

GANDERS, 2 Goose Green (061-941 3954)
Open: Mon-Thu 12noon-3pm, 7-10.30pm, Fri 12noon-3pm, 7-11pm, Sat 12noon-4pm, Sat-Sun 7-11pm

[C] [S]

Surprisingly, goose is not on the very varied menu of this pleasant wine bar and bistro, housed in a 300-year-old cottage in a quiet alley close to the town centre. A dozen appetisers range in price from 45p for home-made soup to £1.45 for avocado with crab. Tuna fish pâté, ham and prawn cornets, rollmop herring or 'Cranks' vegetarian salad are other tasty choices. Lancashire hot pot is a good, traditional main course for £1.75, but why not go overboard and try fondue bourguignon – a bargain at around £3 per person? You will need to have three other people with you to sample this delicacy. Desserts are in the 60p-70p bracket and include such delights as passioncake, fresh strawberries and cream and 'real' sherry trifle.

THE OLD HALL, Stockport Road (061-928 2965)
Open: Mon-Sun 12noon-2pm, 7-10pm (Sat 7-10pm only)

[C] [♫] [P]

Value-for-money food consists mainly of unpretentious grills such as gammon with two eggs, or fresh trout with chips, roll and butter for about £2.40. Starters include rollmop herring at around 75p and home-made soup at 60p or so, and a sweet from the trolley costs about 75p.

Ashton-under-Lyne

CORNICHE GRILL, Oldham Road (061-339 5469)
Open: Mon-Sun 12noon-2.30pm, 6-10.30pm (Sun 7-10.30pm)

[C] [P] [S]

Car dealers, Wm Monk claim that this gallery restaurant overlooking the car showroom is a new idea 'direct from Paris', and the first of its kind in this country. Grills are the main feature on the menu with rump steak for £4.50 or so, and all dishes include French fries or jacket potato and a roll and butter. Sweets and cheese and biscuits are also included in the price of the main course.

For about 80p you can choose a connoisseur coffee such as a Monte Carlo (with Cointreau) or a Brands Hatch (with whisky), or have a 'customised' coffee to suit your taste.

Blackburn

KENYON'S STUDIO BUTTERY
31 Penny Street (Blackburn 60347)
Open: Mon-Wed 9am-5pm, Thu 10am-1.30pm, Fri 9am-5pm, Sat 9am-4.30pm

[P] [S]

This sparkling, modern coffee shop in the centre of town is a self-service style operation offering good food at remarkably low prices. A three-course meal starting with soup of the day at about 25p, followed by lasagne or steak and kidney (both less than £1 but the most expensive savoury dishes on the menu) and completed with Black Forest gâteau at around 45p is excellent value.

Blackpool

THE DANISH KITCHEN
Vernon Humpage, Church Street (Blackpool 24291)
Open: Mon-Sat 9am-5.30pm

[S]

Pine tables and pine beams with mock oil lamps adorn this bright, clean, split-level serve-yourself operation in the centre of town. Freshly made soup is about 30p and there is a tempting array of Danish open sandwiches (crab, prawn, beef, smoked salmon etc) from around 60p, salads from 65p, omelettes from 70p and pizzas from £1. The Danish pastries from 30p, are excellent.

Bolton

THE DROP INN and BUMBLES BEE-STRO, THE LAST DROP ★★★
Bromley Cross (Bolton 591131)
Open: Inn: Mon-Sun 12noon-2pm, Bee-stro: Mon-Thu 7-10.30pm, Fri Sat 7-11pm, Sun 3.30-9.30pm

[C] [♫] [P] [S]

A collection of derelict 18th-century farm buildings has been imaginatively converted to create a modern hotel complex with traditional village atmosphere. The Drop Inn pub even sports a honky-tonk piano to accompany evening sing-songs, as well as oak beams and a blazing log fire. Bar snacks are served in the evening, but it's at lunchtime that the food scene is best, with an excellent, self-service lunch for around £3. The stone-floored Bee-stro, with its low-arched ceiling, wood and brick surfaces and candlelight, offers main course, salad selection, starter and sweet (try Jamaican bananas), for about £3.50. The menu is changed monthly and includes fish, salad, burger and one or two more unusual dishes.

THE LAMPLIGHTER
26 Knowsley Street (Bolton 35175)
Open: Mon-Fri 12noon-2pm, 5.45-10.30pm, Fri 12noon-2pm, 5.45-11pm, Sat 12noon-11pm, Sun 3-6pm

Pictures, prints and posters of the Victorian era cover the walls, and gas lamps and stuffed animals' heads add to the overwhelming 19th-century atmosphere. Every dish is given the name of a Victorian cigarette card character; the Pawnbroker's Treat, for instance, is hot poached salmon dripping in best butter, and the Knocker's-Up Nosh – a juicy rump steak with garden peas and a garnish of cress, tomato and potatoes. Fresh fruit, ice cream or cheese is included in the main course price, so nothing tops our limit.

Bolton-le-Sands

WILLOW TREE, By Pass Road (Hest Bank 823316)
Open: Tue-Fri 9.30am-1.45pm 4.30-8.30pm, Sat 4.30-9pm Sun 11.30am-9pm

[P] [🍷]

This single-storey building with its neatly tiled roof and white stucco walls is just the place to feed the family. Service is prompt and efficient in the two well-appointed, wood-panelled dining rooms, where a lunch of soup or fruit juice, minute steak, lamb chops or grilled plaice, served with potatoes or chips and peas, a sweet and coffee, is likely to cost around £3.50. Light lunches run from 85p-£1.75. The reasonably-priced evening menu offers more choice.

Broughton

THE ORCHARD, Whittingham Lane (Broughton 862208)
Open: Tue-Sat 12noon-2pm, 7.30-9.30pm, Sun 12noon-2pm

[C] [♫] [P] [🍷]

The cluster of buildings which forms 'The Orchard' includes a barn now used for functions. Natural stone walls and beams are a foil for brass, copper, china

and pictures, the general effect being neat, bright and cheerful. The set lunches are excellent value, three courses costing from £3 on weekdays and from about £3.15 on Sunday, the main course giving several choices including traditional roasts. The à la carte menu offers a wide range of speciality dishes and costs from £5.50 upwards.

Burnley

SMACKWATER JACKS, Ormerod Street (Burnley 21290)
Open: Mon-Sun 11.30am-3pm, 7-11pm

[♫] [P] [S] [&]

A town centre steak and hamburger joint set in a stone and brick-built cellar. The lighthearted menu is written in brash Americanese – start with fruit juice ('we got orange an' we got tomato') and move on to stuffed baked potatoes or a 'hillbilly chili' – ('the way Pa likes it') – at about £1.45. For dessert there's cheesecake 'frigate', fruit salad and various sundaes, all under or around £1.

Chester

BOLLANDS BUTTERY, St Werburgh Street (Chester 43264)
Open: Mon-Sat 10am-10.30pm, Sun 12noon-10.30pm

[C] [♫] [P] [&]

The interior of this modern restaurant is decorated in restful colours with Romanesque motifs. A fairly extensive menu offers dishes to suit all tastes from the 'Continental quickies' through wood pigeon or rabbit pie to the 'Great British specialities' such as roast beef and Yorkshire pudding or jugged hare. Prices are reasonable and although some steaks may exceed our limit, a substantial three-course meal would cost around £5 with coffee.

CLAVERTON'S WINE BAR, Lower Bridge Street (Chester 319760)
Open: Mon-Sat 12noon-2.30pm, 5.30-12mdnt, Sun 12noon-1.45pm, 7-12mdnt

[&]

Come early to this popular basement wine bar, as it's sure to be busy, especially in the evenings. The white rough-cast walls, stone floors and polished tables with red and white cloths give a bright, clean appearance, enhanced by the tempting array of food. A selection from the cold table costs around £2, and for a little less you might choose avocado poisson or pâté with bread. Home-made soup costs around 50p, as does the cheesecake or gâteaux for dessert. On a fine day you can sip your wine on the patio and watch the world go by.

THE COURTYARD ✕✕
13 St Werburgh Street (Chester 21447)
Open: Mon-Sat 10.30am-2.30pm, 6-10pm

[C] [♫] [&]

This popular gourmet restaurant is set around a pretty courtyard, within the city walls and the sound of the Cathedral bells. Upstairs at lunchtime a 'help yourself' smørgasbrød operates. Á la carte lunch includes sirloin steak at around £4.50, lamb cutlets at about £3.80 and a selection of starters and sweets. Dinner is more adventurous with such delights as lambs' sweetbreads braised in Madeira, but it is more expensive. There is also an evening bistro offering a very reasonable fixed price buffet.

DEERINGS CARRIAGE RESTAURANT
Mercia Square, Frodsham Street (Chester 23469)
Open: Mon-Sat 12noon-2.30pm, 5.30-10.30pm, Sat 5-11pm, Sun 5-9pm (summer only)

[P] [S] [&]

This modern glass-fronted restaurant, with its separate wine bar, is to be found in a shopping precinct close to the city walls. The interior is of unusual design with iron and wood arches forming banquettes at one end of the room and an open-plan area with mock-Gothic ceiling at the other. An extensive menu offers a three-course meal, with coffee for around £5. To be on the safe side however, choose from the excellent selection on the more modestly priced set menu: there are only four starters but chicken provençale, Cumberland grill and deep-fried fillet of plaice served with lemon wedge, home-made tartare sauce and fried croquette potatoes are among the main dishes. Puddings such as the giant éclair filled with ice cream and topped with chocolate sauce and the chocolate mousse are all freshly made on the premises. Coffee may be taken in place of dessert at no extra charge; otherwise coffee is additional, but still within our budget.

THE FARMHOUSE, 9-13 Northgate Street (Chester 311332)
Open: Mon-Sat 9am-6pm

P

This friendly mid-city eaterie, situated above Millett's camping stores, has a pine-equipped interior interspersed with oodles of pot plants. The daily-changing choice of dishes is chalked up on a blackboard, but there's always a very good salad selection and, with prices ranging from £1.50-£2, you should find this farmhouse-style kitchen an economical haven.

THE GALLERY, 24 Paddock Row (Chester 47202)
Open: Mon-Sat 12noon-2.30pm, Tue-Sat 6.30-9.30pm

P S

Owner Edward Jones has created a refreshingly-different eating place along the lines of a conservatory with earthy brown carpets and tree-green walls. A beautiful array of pot plants add to the atmosphere. Meals too are a little out of the ordinary. Soup of the day is laced with sherry and cream and main dishes include asparagus and cheese-filled crêpes and rainbow trout – pan fried with almonds and cream. Situated at one end of one of Chester's Rows in the centre of town it is also the ideal rendezvous for shoppers. Price is right here too – three-course lunch with coffee and wine will cost around £4.

PIERRE GRIFFE WINE BAR
4/6 Mercia Square (Chester 312635)
Open: Mon-Fri 11.30am-3pm, 5.30-11pm, Sat 11am-3pm, 5.30-11pm, Sun 12noon-2pm, 7-11pm
(Sun in summer only)

P S

Close to the Cathedral, this very popular wine bar has brown walls and carpeting which give emphasis to the attractive pine furniture. A long bar counter has a good display of salads and meats. The menu is displayed on a blackboard and three courses can easily be savoured for around £3. Start with French onion soup at 65p, then try pork goulash with rice, Malayan chicken salad or minced beef curry – all at around £1.60. Cheescake costs 55p, gâteaux 60p.

SIR EDWARD'S WINE BAR
30 Bridge Street (Chester 24921)
Open: Mon-Sat 12noon-2.30pm, 6.30-10.30pm (11pm Fri and Sat)

C P S

This cosy little wine bar enjoys an attractive situation on street level beneath one of Chester's famous 'Rows'. Inside, walls of open brick-work, 200-year-old wood panelling and dark paintwork are adorned with old books, posters and pots. Green gingham tablecloths and flickering candles contribute to the intimate atmosphere and enhance the simple décor. A good selection of starters include avocado, pâté and home-made soup (with fresh ingredients). If you choose the top-priced main course of prime beef steak at about £3.50 with French fried potatoes and a side salad (priced separately) the total, with dessert and freshly percolated coffee (with cream) would well exceed the £5 budget. However a meal of corn-on-the-cob (hors d'oeuvres), gammon steak with peaches and side salad, gâteau and coffee would total only around £4. Service is at the customer's discretion. As one would expect from a wine bar, there is a comprehensive range of wines available with red, white or rosé house wine.

Cleveleys

SAVOY GRILL, 6 Bispham Road (Cleveleys 85 3864)
Open: summer: Sun-Mon 11.30am-7pm, Tue 11.30am-8.30pm, Wed-Sat 11.30am-10pm, winter: Tue-Fri 11.30am-7pm, Sat-Sun 11.30am-9pm

P S

A popular, corner-house restaurant near the seafront, the Savoy Grill is well-known for its friendly atmosphere and unpretentious food. Soups and pies are all home-made by proprietor Mrs Dorothy Richardson, and a set three-course meal including soup, steak and mushroom pie and ice cream can be had for the extremely modest price of £1.70. A special children's menu lists old favourites such as fish fingers, beefburgers or roast beef and ranges in price from 75p-£1, though apart from these budget meals, a full à la carte also operates.

Clitheroe

CASTLE RESTAURANT, Parson Lane (Clitheroe 24587/24442)
Open: Mon-Sun 12noon-2pm (1.30pm

Sat) 7.30-9.30pm (10pm Fri-Sat)

C S

Situated in this small market town, and standing, as its name suggests, in the shadow of Clitheroe Castle, this is a restaurant to suit all tastes. If yours is the burger and pizza-style appetite you can choose from a variety including the Hawaiian burger topped with cheese and pineapple for around £1.60. Or there's the local cuisine including Bury Black Pudding served hot or cold for less than £1. A more substantial meal can be had of fresh Ribble trout or griddle-cooked, local-cured ham with pineapple for around £2. A selection from the more ambitious table d'hôte menu could include smoked mackerel fillet with horseradish sauce, followed by supreme of chicken Castle (breast of chicken filled with crabmeat and cooked in white wine) served with vegetables, mixed salad and a roll and butter. The meal is rounded off with a choice from the sweet trolley, cheese with biscuits, celery and crispy apple and a pot of coffee with cream and chocolate mints – all for just over £5.

Congleton

THE GINGERBREAD COFFEE SHOP
3 Duke Street (Congleton 71627)
Open: Mon-Tue 9.30am-4.30pm,
Wed 9.30am-1.30pm,
Thu-Sat 9.30am-4.30pm

P S

This is a quaint cream-and-brown painted restaurant where many of the dishes, such as chicken casserole, savoury flan, pizza and pâté are available for just over £1 and all are served with vegetables or salad. Starters, at around 40p include grapefruit segments and soup of the day. A sweet such as home-made fruit pie with fresh cream or meringue glacé costs about 50p.

Disley

THE GINNEL, 3 Buxton Old Road
(Disley 4494)
Open: Tue-Sun 12.30-2.15pm,
Tue-Fri 7.30-10.15pm, Sat 7.15-10.30pm

C

Entry to this cosy wine bar is by means of a narrow passageway, hence the name Ginnel – a local word for passage. Old silk embroideries and open brickwork add character to the delightfully furnished interior, where a tempting menu awaits your attention. Beef cooked in ale, peppers stuffed with savoury mince and trout with oatmeal and parsley butter are just a few of the more exotic main courses, ranging in price from around £2.15 to £3.25. With a starter such as home-made pâté and a strawberry meringue nest for dessert, you can be sure of a memorable meal for under £5. Traditional Sunday lunch is also reasonably-priced at around £3.75, with children's portions for just £2.

Freckleton

THE SHIP INN (Freckleton 632393)
Open: Quarter Deck Restaurant:
Mon-Sun 12noon-2.30pm, 7-9.45pm,
The Galley: Mon-Sun 12noon-2.30pm,
Sat 7.30-10.15pm

C P S

The Ship was built about ten years ago on the site of a hostelry of the same name which dated back to 1630. The interior is designed along the lines of a ship, with a 'Sharp End' bar and another called the Galley. In the latter you can get a help-yourself repast called 'Scandhovee' for about £3.25 at lunchtime (£2.85 evenings), which is very popular locally. You can take an à la carte meal in the Quarter Deck Restaurant but it would be all too easy to top the £5 mark. The speciality is fish

with even the salads weighted on the side of seafoods. The table d'hôte lunch is well within limits, three courses costing around £3.50 – melon, grilled pork chop and apple sauce with vegetables, followed by sherry trifle, is an example of what to expect.

Gisburn

COTTAGE RESTAURANT, Main Street (Gisburn 441)
Open: Mon 12noon-2pm, Tue-Sun 11.30am-6pm (closed Wed)

[♫] [P] [garden]

With its low-beamed ceilings and warmth of welcome from proprietors Mr and Mrs Farnworth, the Cottage Café lives up to the traditional charm suggested by its name. Home cooking – the steak and kidney pie and home-cooked ham are particularly good – is accompanied by chips and peas, salad or jacket potato. A meal will cost under £5 for three courses.

Hale

HALE WINE BAR
106-108 Ashley Road (061-928 2343)
Open: Mon-Thu 12noon-2pm, 7-10pm, Fri-Sat 12noon-2pm, 7-11pm

[P] [S]

Two dress shops were transformed into this fashionable wine bar by enterprising owners, Nick Elliot and Tim Eaton. Victoriana is the theme of the two rooms which are on different levels. An excellent menu offers starters such as cheese and tuna pâté or quiche Lorraine for around £1, main courses for about £2.25 include lasagne, moussaka, tagliatelli and prawn salad. Puddings cost around 85p and Jamaican fudge cake, lemon soufflé cake or chocolate mousse are some of the choices. Lunch here is a treat for the weary shopper or jaded office worker.

Hazel Grove

THE GEORGIAN HOUSE, 399-401 London Road, (061-483 5517)
Open: Mon-Sat 12noon-2.30pm, 6-11pm (Sun 5-11pm)

[P] [garden]

You'll recognise the Georgian House by its attractive bow-windowed frontage and, as the name might suggest, here is a place where you can enjoy fine English cuisine. Go there for lunch and you'll find a special value treat awaits you in the form of a 6oz rump steak served with vegetables, tomato, cress and French fried or baked potato, roll and butter and choice of sweet for the amazing all-inclusive price of £2.50. Cheaper combinations include salmon with salad or French fries and half a roast chicken with vegetables and potatoes. Certain dishes are available at half price for children. The evening menu offers a more extensive range of steaks, roasts and fish dishes as part of three courses in which coffee is included.

Kirkham

THE GEORGIAN RESTAURANT
Blackpool Road, Newton-with-Scales (Kirkham 685896)
Open: Tue-Fri 12noon-2.30pm, 7-10pm, Sat 12noon-10.30pm (closed between 2.30pm and 5pm in winter), Sun 12noon-7pm

[♫] [P] [garden]

Situated on the Preston-Blackpool road, this modernised yet unpretentious restaurant has a friendly, welcoming atmosphere. The menu for weekday lunches and all day Sunday is very reasonably priced and includes roast chicken with all the trimmings at around £2.25 and freshly-made prawn salad at about £2.50. Sweets from the trolley, such as banana boats or peach melba cost around 80p. The à la carte menu for lunch or dinner includes some quite expensive items.

Knutsford

SIR FREDERICK'S WINE BAR
44 King Street (Knutsford 53209)
Open: Tue-Sat 12noon-2.30pm, 6.30-10.30pm

[C] [♫] [P] [S]

You'll enjoy the relaxed and friendly atmosphere at this pleasant town centre wine bar. Décor is simple with rough cast walls and arches decorated with posters and block board prints. A limited à la carte menu is accompanied by an ample wine list. A three-course meal here will cost around £4.50 with a choice of cold table and Continental salads. Hot dishes such as gammon steak with peaches cost around £2.50.

Lancaster

OLD BRUSSELS, 53 Market Street (Lancaster 69177)
Open: Mon-Sat 8am-6pm

[C] [♫] [P] [S] [garden]

Old Brussels is a family-owned and run restaurant serving good food, reasonably priced and nicely presented. Soup or fresh orange juice costs around 30p, and can be followed by one of a dozen main courses, such as home-baked meat and potato pie or farmhouse grill at around £1.75. Home-made lemon meringue pie, flans or ice cream concoctions follow at only 45p.

SQUIRRELS, 92 Penny Street (Lancaster 62307)
Open: Mon-Sat 12noon-2pm, 6-10pm, Sun 7-10pm

[C] [♫] [P] [S]

The smart brown-and-cream exterior of this city-centre wine bar attracts hungry shoppers and wine buffs alike. Inside, the cavernous, cellar-like atmosphere has a pleasing effect and complements the good range of food. Main courses include beef steak and oyster pie at £3.50, with filled baked potatoes, pâté and salads as possible (and cheaper) alternatives. With home-made soup as your starter, and a slice of full-cream gâteau for sweet, you have a tasty and wholesome three course meal at under or around £5.

Liverpool

CASA ITALIA, Temple Court, 40 Stanley Street (051-227 5774)
Open: Mon-Sat 12noon-10pm

[♫] [P] [S]

This bright, bustling pizzeria, surrounded by more sombre city buildings, instantly commands attention. The menu lists a dazzling selection of pizzas and pastas, averaging around £1.95. If the Italian hors d'oeuvres are sampled (around £2.25), plus one of the delicious sweets from the trolley and espresso coffee, the meal will still cost less than £5.

D'ANNA, Armour House, Lord Street (051-709 1177)
Open: Mon-Sat 11.30am-10.30pm, Sun 12noon-2.30pm

[C] [♫] [P] [S]

In the heart of 'Scouseland', close to the Mersey, you will find this small, unpretentious restaurant decorated in restful green with alcoves and dark oak tables. The bill of fare covers a broad spectrum, from omelettes and veal dishes at around £2 to fish dishes ranging from £2 for plaice to around £4.50 for Dover sole. Grills are similarly priced and cold buffets, including prawn salad, are around £2.50. Children can order beefburgers and chips at a mere 95p.

EVERYMAN BISTRO, Hope Street (051-708 9545)
Open: Mon-Fri 12noon-2pm, 6-11.30pm, Sat 6-11.30pm

[S]

This interesting bistro is situated in the basement of the Everyman Theatre in the centre of town. Blackboards display a menu based on fresh produce and it is easy to eat three courses here for around £2.50. Home-made soup or quiche Lorraine are two of the starters with dishes such as spicy Caribbean pork, broccoli cheese, salads and casserole as main courses. There is a selection of home-made sweets, various cheeses and live yoghurts to finish with.

LA GRANDE BOUFFE, 48a Castle Street (051-236 3375)
Open: Mon 10am-3pm, Tue-Fri 10am-11pm, Sat 11am-3pm, 7-11pm

[♫] [P] [S]

La Grande Bouffe is a typical French-style basement café. French pictures adorn the walls. The menu is on a blackboard and dishes include home-made soup such as potato and watercress at about 50p, quiches for around 60p, beef sausage-meat and spinach pie for around £1 and Armenian lamb or rare roast beef for about £2. Cold dishes include fresh mackerel with salad at about £1.50. Desserts (60p-80p) are also home-made. It is a self-service operation – ideal for a quick, tasty meal. The à la carte evening meal is likely to be beyond our limit.

ST GEORGE'S HOTEL ★★★★ St John's Precinct, Lime Street (051-709 7090)
Open: Buttery: Mon-Sat 10am-10pm

[C] [P] [S]

The stylish modern buttery of this sumptuous hotel serves a comprehensive range of food. For a quick snack, toasted sandwiches, hamburgers of all varieties, authentic curried chicken and egg dishes are on the huge menu for around £1.50 to £3.50. There is also plenty of scope for a three-course meal within our budget. A choice of eight starters includes minestrone with Parmesan at about 60p. A good selection of fish and grills from about £2.25-£5 make a substantial main course. Sweets range in price from around 55p-80p.

ZODIAC COFFEE HOUSE, ADELPHI HOTEL ★★★★ Ranelagh Place (051-709 7200)

Open: Mon-Sun 8am-10pm

[C] [♫] [P] [🍷]

No fortunes told here, but your luck's in as far as having a good meal at a reasonable price is concerned. Set lunch costs from £2.75, with a choice of soup or fruit juice followed by anything you fancy from the sumptuous cold buffet or a hot dish of the day. A sweet from the trolley is extra at £1. The à la carte menu offers a standard range of dishes at slightly higher prices, but still within the limit.

Macclesfield

DA TOPO GIGIO, 15 Church Street (Macclesfield 22231)
Open: Tue-Sat 12noon-2pm, 7-10.30pm

[P] [S] [🍷]

Half-way down the quaint, cobbled street of this old silk-manufacturing town is this informal restaurant, named after the famous Italian mouse. Fresh produce is put to good use in the thick minestrone soup – only 60p but almost a meal in itself – chicken carbonara or salmon cooked to choice, both under £3. Home-made sweets start at 50p, so a three-course lunch can cost as little as £4.25 here.

Manchester

THE CAFE, 3-5 Princess Street, Albert Square (061-834 2076)
Open: Mon-Sun 12noon-4am

[♫] [P] [S]

Just the place for the late-nighter, this modern-fronted steak and burger restaurant is in the city centre. As well as the char-grilled steaks and pure beefburgers there is a good selection of 'Café Extras' such as poussin Continental – a baby chicken cooked in a rich wine sauce with a hint of garlic for around £3. For the vegetarian there is the veg-burger and the Café-casserole, both under £2. Sweets, including fresh cream Black Forest gâteau, rum baba, sorbets and cheesecakes range from 75p-85p.

DANISH FOOD CENTRE, Royal Exchange Buildings, Cross Street (061-832 9924)
Open: Copenhagen Restaurant: Mon-Sat 12noon-3pm, 6-12mdnt, Danmark Inn: Mon-Sat 9am-7pm

[S]

This popular Danish eaterie is situated in the city centre, within the Royal Exchange Buildings. A beautifully-decorated three-tier cold table provides the centrepiece of the main restaurant, though a help-yourself choice to as much as you like from the appetizing array of dishes offered here will pass the £5 mark a little. Of course, you can always plump for the nourishing open sandwich known as smørbrød. Snaps and a good wine list are available, although the Danish lagers are enthusiastically recommended!

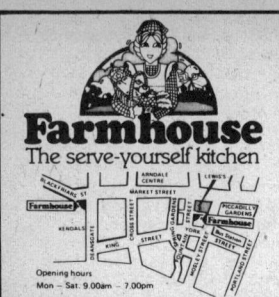

FARMHOUSE KITCHEN, Fountain Street (behind Lewis's) (061-236 5532)
Open: Mon-Sat 9am-7pm

A sister to the restaurant of the same name across the city, but somewhat smaller. Pine tables and partitioning make for a fresh, bright atmosphere. Food is listed on a daily-changing blackboard list. There's always a big variety of goodies and you'll have a job to spend more than £3 per head.

FARMHOUSE KITCHEN
42 Blackfriars Street (near Deansgate) (061-832 7001)
Open: Mon-Sat 9am-7pm (8pm Thu)

P S

This Farmhouse serve-yourself Kitchen attracts shoppers and business people to its convenient location in the city centre. Hot and cold dishes are available at very reasonable prices and the excellent salad selection has proved particularly popular. Of the hot meals, the chicken in wine sauce at £1.75 is worth trying as are the fried haddock and cheese and potato savoury or quiche, all around £1.25. An extremely nourishing three-course meal can be had for around £3.

KWOK MAN ✕✕ 28-32 Princess Street (061-228 2620)
Open: Mon-Sat 12noon-5am

S

Just the place for anyone suffering from night starvation! There are around one hundred authentic Cantonese dishes to choose from, some quite exotic such as shark's fin and chicken soup, Chung Yaù chicken with spring onion brandy sauce and fried crab claw, but if you're with a group, the set menus are recommended. With different selections for two to five people, they offer a good introduction to Chinese-style eating at a cost of £4-£5 per person. Table d'hôte lunch is also reasonably priced, three courses with coffee can be had for around £2.

THE LANCASHIRE FOLD, Kirkway, Alkrington, Middleton (061-643 4198)
At the junction of Mount Road and Kirkway and near M62 junction 20
Open: during normal licensing hours
Restaurant: Tue-Fri, Sun 12noon-2pm, 7-10pm, Sat 7-10pm

C P S

For those who prefer to get away from the city centre, The Lancashire Fold may provide the answer. This modern extension to a pub has a brick-and-timber décor and comfortable furnishings. Although the à la carte menu is not cheap, it is possible to choose a three-course meal within the £5 limit. Choose chilled melon at around £1, suprême de poulet Maryland with additional vegetables at around £3.45, a sweet from the trolley or cheese at around 80p and you are left with just enough for a glass of wine. At lunchtime you can get a good table d'hôte meal for about £3.

MARKET RESTAURANT
30 Edge Street (061-834 3743)
Open: Tue-Sat 6.30-10.30pm

Energetic owners Su-Su Edgecombe and Elizabeth Price have breathed new life into an almost-dead part of the city with their delightful new restaurant. Pale primrose walls offset with dark green woodwork and simple stone flooring create a plain but pleasing effect, with a smattering of pictures, prints and bric-à-brac to add interest. Candles on the tables and lace curtains are the finishing touches. A starter such as chilled Lebanese cucumber soup made with yoghurt, cream and fresh mint costs around 90p, and could be followed by spinach and mushroom pancakes au gratin (£1.95). Finish with a sweet such as French gooseberry tart at around 95p and you are well within the budget.

OSCARS, 11 Cooper Street
(061-236 6752)
Open: Mon-Sun 11.30am-3pm (closed Sat), 5.30-10.30pm

[C]

This city-centre, self-service restaurant has a popular pub-type atmosphere, particularly at lunchtime. Mock beams and rough-cast walls give a friendly 'local' feel – as does the regular clientele. At lunchtime choose from a blackboard menu such dishes as traditional roast for just under £2, kidney turbigo at around £1.65 or chicken and mushroom pie for about £1.55. There is a self-serve salad selection for around £2 and a choice of sweets at around 70p. In the evening you can have a sirloin steak chasseur for £3.65 or, further down the scale there's Spanish omelette for around £1.30. Coffee with cream is about 30p.

PIZZERIA BELLA NAPOLI
1 Kennedy Street (061-236 1537)
Open: Mon-Sat 12noon-11.30pm, Sun 6.30-11.30pm

[P] [S]

This friendly basement eating house has typical Italian-style décor, stuccoed walls and tiled floors. Being much smaller than the Pizzeria Italia, its sister restaurant across the city, tables can be hard to come by at peak periods. The slick young staff serve a variety of pastas and pizzas, such as cannelloni ripieni (pancakes filled with beef, eggs and spinach – about £2) or pizza marinara (mozzarella cheese, anchovy, olives, tuna and prawns in tomato sauce – £2). Sweets run from 80p-£1.

PIZZERIA CAPRI, 34 Deansgate
(061-834 4423)
Open: Mon-Thu 12noon-12mdnt, Fri-Sat 12noon-2am, Sun 6pm-12mdnt

[C] [P] [S] [ ]

This small, attractive restaurant in the centre of Manchester is run by partners Mano from Brazil and Mario from Italy. The décor is reminiscent of South America, with its tiled floor, rough-cast walls and cane ceiling. There's plenty on the interesting menu that will break the bank, but a selection such as prawn cocktail, fresh trout Brazilia and hot cherries and ice cream will keep you well within the budget.

PIZZERIA ITALIA, 40-42 Deansgate
(061-834 1541)
Open: Mon-Sat 12noon-11.30pm, Sun 6.30-11.30pm

[P] [S]

A corner-sited pizza house on two floor-levels, Pizzeria Italia is decorated in the true Italian style with tiled floors and lusty pot plants. Low-priced dishes including soups, fish and chicken supplement the enormous and varied plate-sized pizzas, excellent value at under £2. Service is snappy, operated by well turned-out and efficient all-Italian staff.

RAJDOOT RESTAURANT ××
St James House, South King Street
(061-834 2176/7092)
Open: Mon-Sat 12noon-2.30pm, 6.30-12mdnt, Sun 6.30-12mdnt

[C] [ ] [S] [ ]

One step inside the door of the Rajdoot Indian restaurant is a step into a different world. Waiters in their national costumes wait to greet you – the atmosphere is sultry and authentic. An extremely wide and varied menu is available and the specialities of the house are the Tandoori murghi (£3.80), Tandoori fish and Makhan chicken at around £2.60 or lamb pasanda at a little less. A set meal of Tandoori murghi, shish kebab, nan, rogan josh, prawn masalla, rice, dessert and coffee is excellent value at around £6, though 3 courses need cost no more than £4.

SAM'S CHOP HOUSE ×
Back Pool Fold, Chapel Walks
(061-834 8717)
Open: Mon-Fri 12noon-3pm

[ ]

If you enjoy a lunch in a place which oozes in friendly charm, Sam's Chop House is a must for you. Set in a back alley, below street level, the décor is plain and simple. Stone walls are adorned by large prints and hanging mock oil lamps enhance the cosy atmosphere. Friendly waitresses serve you with good standard English fare: various steaks from between £4-£5, lamb cutlets and roast chicken garni at around £3-£4 are examples. Extra large portions of scampi or plaice are served for gluttons.

Marple

WOODHEYS FARM, Glossop Road (Glossop 2704)
Open: Tue-Sat 11.45am-2pm, 7-10pm, Sun 11.45am-2.30pm
On A26 between Glossop and Marple

[C] [P] [&]

The impressive stone-built Woodheys Farm occupies an idyllic setting overlooking the beautiful Etherow Valley, and once you've feasted on the views outside, an equally impressive culinary triumph awaits you indoors. Unfortunately, a set dinner price of over £8 – although excellent in its class, precludes the evening meal from our readers, but a similar repast can be sampled at lunchtime for a set price of around £3.75. Appetites large and small are catered for here as all food is displayed in a central cabinet where diners can help themselves to as much or as little as they want (second helpings are not frowned upon!). Appetisers include shell fish, melon and pâté on the cold table, or there's farmhouse soup, whitebait or deep-fried mushrooms served hot. The Carvery offers an unrestricted choice of traditional English roast joints, braised game, casseroles and pies with vegetables, potatoes and salad. Remember to leave room for one of the scrumptious desserts such as fresh cream gâteaux, fresh fruits in season or the speciality – brown bread and brandy ice cream. Coffee is served with mints and home-made sweetmeats.

Morecambe

COFFEE SHOPPE, 35 Princes' Crescent, Bare (no telephone)
Open: summer: Mon-Sat 9.30am-5.30pm, Sun 10.30am-5.30pm, winter: Mon-Sat 9.30am-4.45pm

[P] [&]

This typical, pleasant little tea shop is set in a row of shops, just off the sea front. Salads, home-cooked meat pies, cakes, pastries and sandwiches are available and very reasonable and tasty three-course meals can be had for around £2. Try home-made soup, followed by cottage cheese and peach salad then finish with one of Heather Millen's luscious creamy cakes.

Oldham

MOTHER HUBBARD'S
270 Manchester Street
(061-652 0873)
Open: Mon-Sun 11.30am-11.30pm

[C] [P] [&]

The cupboard is far from bare at this modern, detached fish restaurant. A variety of fresh fish, delivered daily from Grimsby, ensures that you're in for a piscine treat. A smart interior features spindled wooden divisions (to allow that little bit of privacy at tables) and a Georgian-style bar. The friendly waitresses serve a simple starter, plus main fish dish (scampi, halibut, haddock or plaice with all the trimmings, and a coffee) with ice-cream to finish at a cost of £2-£3.50 depending on your fish choice.

Ormskirk

TOWER AND STEEPLE
15 Church Street (Ormskirk 72017)
Open: Tue, Wed, Fri 10am-2.30pm, 7-10.30pm, Thu 10am-4pm, 7-10.30pm, Sat 10am-4pm, 7-11pm, Sun 12noon-2.30pm

[P] [S] [&]

Lunches are particularly tempting here, with ham and pineapple, grilled plaice and dish of the day all around £2. A three-course Sunday lunch offering a variety of roasts and desserts from the trolley can be had for just over £3.50. The dinner menu includes a host of seafood starters and a variety of steaks and grills. Special 'family' dinners are available at around £3.50.

Parbold

THE WIGGIN TREE, Parbold Hill (Parbold 2318/2593)
1 mile east of Parbold, 2 miles from junction 27 of the M6
Open: Mon-Sun 12noon-2.15pm, Mon-Fri 7-10pm, Sat 7-11pm, Sun 4.30-9pm

[C] [P] [♧]

Versatility is the keynote of this 18th-century, stone-built cottage restaurant. While retaining its olde-worlde charm, with oak-beamed ceilings, stone fireplace and treadle sewing machine tables, it is nonetheless able to cope with a steady flow of hungry customers. Waitresses dressed as serving wenches will bring you the interesting menu, from which it is possible to choose a three-course meal for as little as £2.85. Try a starter of black pudding followed by fried whiting with a choice of vegetables or salad and potatoes and finish off with a home-made dessert or ice cream. À la carte eating is also possible if care is taken to keep within the budget and, at the other end of the scale, good bar meals are always available.

Prestbury

PRESTBURY PLACE, New Road (Prestbury 828423)
Open: Tue-Sat 7.30-10pm

[P]

Built at the end of a row of 17th-century cottages, this 'home from home' is friendly, relaxed and informal with a simple green décor. The menu, chalked up on a blackboard, includes smoked trout and salad at £2.75, game pie, salad and jacket potato at £2.55, Alabama chili or chicken on rice all around £2.65 and an excellent cheesecake at about 75p.

Preston

ALEXANDERS, Winckley Street (Preston 54302)
Open: Mon-Fri 12noon-2.30pm, 7-10pm

[C] [♫] [P] [S] [♧]

Originally a 19th-century coach house and stable, this elegant building is set in a courtyard in the centre of town. A sumptuous atmosphere is created inside with fawn and burgundy suede-look wall covering, dark-wood panels and 'picture' mirrors, and the whole effect is enhanced by subtle lighting from mock-Victorian wall lamps. A very good table d'hôte menu is available at prices around £3.50. Changed twice weekly, it offers superior main courses such as chicken Americaine and grilled gammon with mushrooms. An ambitious selection of dishes appear on the à la carte menu which is rather more expensive – but very tempting, the fillet of plaice at £3.50 being particularly good.

LA BODEGA, 21 Cannon Street (Preston 52159)
Open: Wine Bar: Mon-Thu 11am-3pm, 7-10.30pm, Fri-Sat 11am-3pm, 7-11pm, Sun 7-10.30pm, Bistro: Mon 11.30-2pm, Tue-Sat 11.30-2pm, 8-11pm, Sun 8-10.30pm

[P] [S]

Upturned barrels as tables, wine posters and gingham tablecloths exude a Continental air echoed in the names of dishes such as paella and chicken Basque style. Steak forms the basis of most dishes on the menu, try the Drunken Bull – sozzled in red wine and brandy for under £4. Lunchtimes are self-service.

THE DANISH KITCHEN, 10 Lune Street (Preston 22086)
Open: Mon-Sat 9.15am-5.15pm
Steak Kitchen: Mon-Sat 12noon-3pm, 6-11pm

[P] [S]

Bright and refreshing, this town centre Danish Kitchen is gaining in popularity with businesspeople and shoppers, with its choice of eating styles. Upstairs is the budget self-service operation where Danish open sandwiches, salads, omelettes and pizzas are available, together with delicious pastries and gâteaux. Downstairs is the new Steak Kitchen, where you choose your own steak from a refrigerated display, then see it cooked over charcoal while waitresses serve you with a starter. Pine tables and beams accentuate the fresh, Continental atmosphere.

FRENCH BISTRO ✕ Miller Arcade, Church Street (Preston 53882)
Open: Mon-Sun 12noon-2.15pm, 7pm-12.15am

[C] [♫] [P] [S]

Colourful posters and French wall

prints adorn the walls of this small, friendly bistro with its informal atmosphere. At lunchtime, dishes such as pâté and salad, chili con carne and boeuf bordelaise cost from £1-£2. In the evening the menu offers 36 starters and 30 main courses, including pepper pot and South American king prawns.

THE PATIO, TRAFALGAR HOTEL ☆☆☆
Preston New Road, Samlesbury
(Samlesbury 351)
On A59 east of Preston at junction with Blackburn road
Open: Mon-Sun 7am-11.30pm

[C] [P]

The nostalgic French design of the menu, the costumed waitresses, and the opportunity to eat all day long sets the scene. Tiled floors and glass-topped tables, potted plants and a fountain make a refreshing environment. Variety is the order of the day: the French connection is continued with a small selection of sweet and savoury pancakes (for around £2), over the borders to Italy for a choice of pizzas, and further afield for chicken Kashmir shish kebab or American burgers. The home front is not forgotten, with Lancashire hot pot or fisherman's pie (at about £2.50) and grills. An added bonus is the invitation to help yourself to the free salad while you wait. At lunchtime the carvery choice features a roast, salads and Danish-style open sandwiches.

THE TICKLED TROUT ☆☆☆
(Samlesbury 671)
Open: Kingfisher Restaurant: Mon-Sun 12noon-2.15pm, 7-10.15pm

[C] [P]

The oak-beamed Kingfisher Restaurant with its alcoves, antiques and views of the River Ribble offers a table d'hôte, three-course lunch for around £4.50, consisting of (for example) salad niçoise followed by grilled gammon and peach with a selection of vegetables and potatoes, and a slice of fresh cream gâteau. A price reduction is made for children under ten years. The à la carte menu is beyond our means.

WELCOME INN, Hennel Lane, Lostock Hall (Preston 38569)
2½ miles from junction 29 on the M6
Open: Sun-Fri 12noon-1.45pm, 7-9.45pm, Sat 7-10pm

[P]

Situated on the fringe of Preston, this modern public house boasts an attractive bistro where service is attentive and friendly. Here you will find a choice of bar snacks or steak or fish dishes in the restaurant, with a four-course traditional roast meal offered on Sundays for £4. Numerous different liqueur coffees offered make a satisfying end to your meal.

Rochdale

ALPINE GASTHOF PUB AND RESTAURANT
Whitworth Road (Rochdale 40953)
Open: Mon-Thu 12noon-2pm, 7-10pm, Fri 12noon-2pm, 7-10pm, Sat 7-10pm, Sun 12noon-2pm

[C] [♫] [P] [🍷]

A taste of Bavaria in the heart of Rochdale – that's the Gasthof. Even the outside of the restaurant has been modelled on its popular namesake at the foot of the Bavarian Alps. Inside, the warm glow of pine weaves a subtle spell, conducive to good eating. The à la carte menu can be pricey, but you'll be well within the budget if you stick to one of the specialities such as hanchen Ayingerbrau – chicken breast stuffed with butter and German mustard at around £3.40 – and choose the accompanying courses with care. Home-made sweets from the trolley are specially recommended. For lunch, hot or cold buffet is good value at about £3.50.

MARIO'S PIZZERIA
115 Yorkshire Street (Rochdale 46286)
Open: Mon-Sat 12noon-2.30pm, 6-11.30pm

Mario Andreotti and his English wife make their cellar pizzeria a warm, welcoming haven for the hungry. Gingham tablecloths, padded benches and plain white rough-cast walls help to give the place a simple charm which compensates for the fairly predictable menu of pizzas and pastas. Even the most expensive dish – a sirloin steak cooked in Chianti – is still likely to be around £4. A whole three-course meal will cost little more if you stick to the modest Italian fare.

THE SIR WINSTON CHURCHILL
Bury Old Road (Heywood 60530)
Open: Mon-Sun 12.30-2.30pm, 7-10pm

[♫] [P] [S] [🍷]

The grill room of this modern public house is attractively furnished and an array of pot plants adds an agreeable freshness to the décor. There are a few items on the menu which exceed the budget, but you could get, say, soup, pork chop or grilled trout with potatoes and another vegetable, sweet, and coffee for around £5.

YEW TREE INN, Thornham
(Rochdale 49742)
Open: Mon-Fri 12noon-2pm, Sun-Thu 7-10pm, Fri-Sat 7-11pm

[C] [P]

Although you may never have been near Rochdale in your life it is quite possible you've dined in the restaurant of the Yew Tree before. The Pullman coach which adjoins the inn travelled 1 250 000 miles between 1951 and 1968 and at various times was in service on 'Tyne Tees Pullman', 'Master Cutler', 'Queen of Scots', and 'Bournemouth Belle', and has the great honour of having been pulled by that famous locomotive 'Mallard'. Now restored to its former glory, the Pullman Diner can be entered directly from the bar of this typical black-and-white Lancashire Inn. A steak bar menu operates with starters such as pâté or mackerel costing from 20p-90p, and main courses (gammon, fish, steaks, chicken) from £2.15-£5.70 including vegetables. Various ices and blackberry and apple pie are typical sweets.

St Michaels-on-Wyre

THE CHERRY TREE GRILL
Garstang Road (St Michaels 661)
Open: Mon-Thu, Fri 6-9pm, Sat 10.30-11.45am, 12noon-2pm, 5-9pm, Sun 12noon-2pm, 3-7pm

This stone-built end-of-terrace house was once the village smithy and is now a small but pleasant grill restaurant. The three-course lunch is all-inclusive for the price of the main course varying between £3.50-£5. A more extensive à la carte menu is available for high tea with sirloin steak or scampi at around £5.75. To finish there is a tempting array of desserts – how about raspberry Pavlova or orange chocolate sundae?

Southport

PIZZERIA-RISTORANTE PARADISO
120 Lord Street (Southport 40259)
Open: Mon-Sat 12noon-3pm, 5.30-11pm, Sun 12noon-2pm, 5.30-11pm

[S]

With main courses ranging from pizza margherita at about £1.45 and spaghetti bolognese at around £1.75 to beef Stroganoff at around £4.50 you can be sure of a good meal within our price range either in the restaurant, or in the newly-opened Mateus Wine Bar on the first floor, where a cold buffet costs £1.50. There are twelve starters priced between 55p and £1.35 and a sweet from the trolley costs about 60p. The décor is pleasantly simple with gold wallpaper.

VESUVIO, 329 Lord Street (Southport 42275)
Open: Tue-Sun 12noon-3pm, 6.30-11pm

[C] [P] [S]

Set in a small alleyway leading off Lord Street, this diminutive, attractive restaurant offers a whole range of dishes, from pizzas and pastas to scampi provençale. Venetian pictures and bric-à-brac are complemented by cream and brown walls and Chianti bottles. Particularly tempting is a three-course menu, available at lunchtime and in the evening, for only £2.90. A choice of six starters includes pâté maison and minestrone soup. Main dishes offer a choice of English or Italian – plaice or chicken for patriots or lasagne, spaghetti bolognese or cannelloni for those with a more exotic palate. Desserts are apple pie, crème caramel or ice cream.

Stockport

GEORGIAN HOUSE
59-61 Buxton Road (061-480 5982)
Open: Mon-Sat 12noon-2.30pm, 6-11pm, Sun 5-11pm

[P]

The bow-windowed Georgian House restaurant on the A6 doesn't go in for frills but you can get good, reasonably-priced meals there, with half-price portions of certain dishes for children. The special two-course lunch is particularly good value. A half roast chicken, garnished, served with vegetables, roll and butter and a choice of sweet costs about £2; replace the chicken by a 5oz rump steak and the price goes up to a moderate £2.30. The à la carte menu, too is modestly priced, starters costing between 35p for soup and £1.40 for smoked trout. The price quoted for main course includes vegetables, roll and butter and a sweet or cheese and biscuits. Only lobster salad at aroud £6 is beyond reach and the Georgian specialities are all near the £5 mark.

THE WISHING WELL, 26a Bramhall Lane South, Bramhall (061-440 8970)
Open: Tue-Thu 12noon-2pm, 6.30-10pm, Fri-Sun 12noon-2pm, 7-10.45pm

[C] [P] [S]

This rather special Yugoslavian restaurant is in an unlikely location above a greengrocery in one of Manchester's desirable residential suburbs. Vlado Barulovic, the proprietor, features some of his country's mouth-watering dishes in the superb value set lunch which will only set you back around £3 – and coffee's included. Try a Podverak ad Curetine (sauerkraut and onions with roast turkey) or Bosanki Lonac (beef and pork with vegetables in wine). The evening à la carte will call upon a strong will if you are going to spend under £6, and has more emphasis on international meat and fish dishes. Mr Barulovic, will, however, prepare a Yugoslavian speciality to order.

West Kirby

WHAT'S COOKING?
34 Banks Road (051-625 7579)

Open: Mon-Sat 12noon-11.30pm, Sun 1-11.30pm

[C] [♫] [S]

The bright cream and green exterior of this first-floor restaurant is just as inviting as its name. Ideal for shoppers and families, What's Cooking? is located close to the town centre and specialises in American and Continental-style cuisine. Menu selections include beefburgers with a choice of toppings plus home-made dressing, pizzas, steaks and chicken or 'mouth-watering, mammoth salads'. Chili con carne (just under £2.50) or spare ribs (around £2.00) are interesting alternatives. A full three-course meal will cost about £5 if you want a full-scale blow-out.

Wigan

ROBERTO'S, Rowbottom Square (Wigan 42385)
Open: Restaurant: Mon-Sat 11.30am-2pm, 7-10pm.
Pizza Bar: Mon-Sat 11.30am-2pm

[C] [♫] [&]

Nestling in what were once the cellars of the local newspaper, this pine-tabled restaurant, with its pot plants and pictures, offers pastas, pizzas and inexpensive 'English' meals of the chicken or plaice and chips variety in a pizza bar next door, and an excellent table d'hôte menu in the restaurant. A three-course lunch, which could consist of egg mayonnaise, cannelloni and sherry trifle works out at only £2.30 per head.

Wilmslow

GREYHOUND STEAKHOUSE
Wilmslow Road, Handforth (Wilmslow 23193)
Open: Mon-Sat 12noon-2.30pm, 6-11.30pm, Sun 12noon-2.30pm, 7-11pm

[C] [♫] [P] [S] [&]

This Schooner Inn steakhouse, about ten miles south of Manchester, features natural stone combined with timbers from Fleetwood pier. For starter you can have soup (about 50p) or prawn cocktail (around £1). Main courses (the price includes an ice cream sweet or cheese) vary from fillet of plaice with lemon, tartare sauce, peas and jacket potato or chips at the £3 mark to a mixed grill (steak, gammon, lamb, sausage and kidney with tomato, peas, jacket potato or chips) at about £5. Lunchtime snacks such as shepherd's pie or filled rolls are available at the bar.

'Whear 'as tha' been sin'
ah saw thee?
On Il-kla Moor baht 'at
Whear 'as tha' been sin'
ah saw thee?
Whear 'as tha' been sin'
ah saw thee?
On Il-kla Moor baht 'at
On Il-kla Moor baht 'at.'

TRADITIONAL

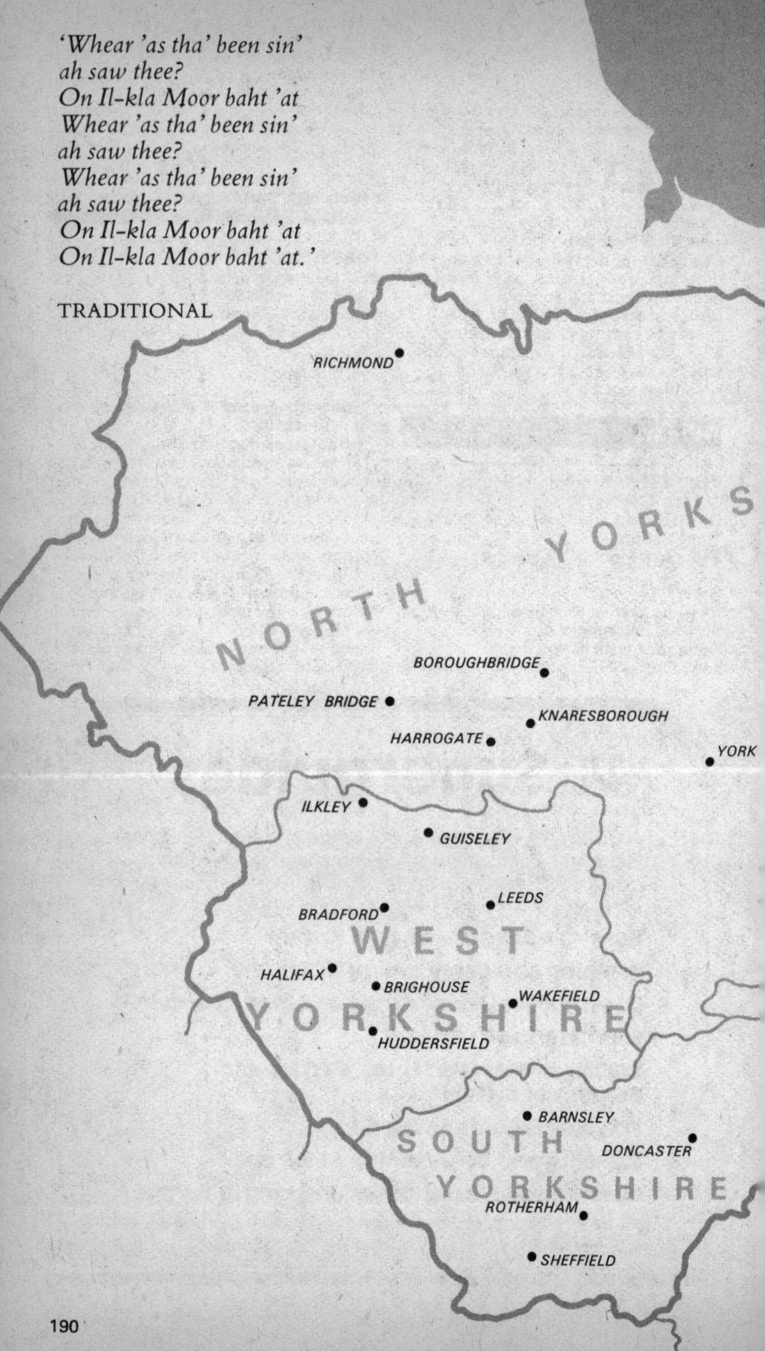

Yorkshire and Humberside

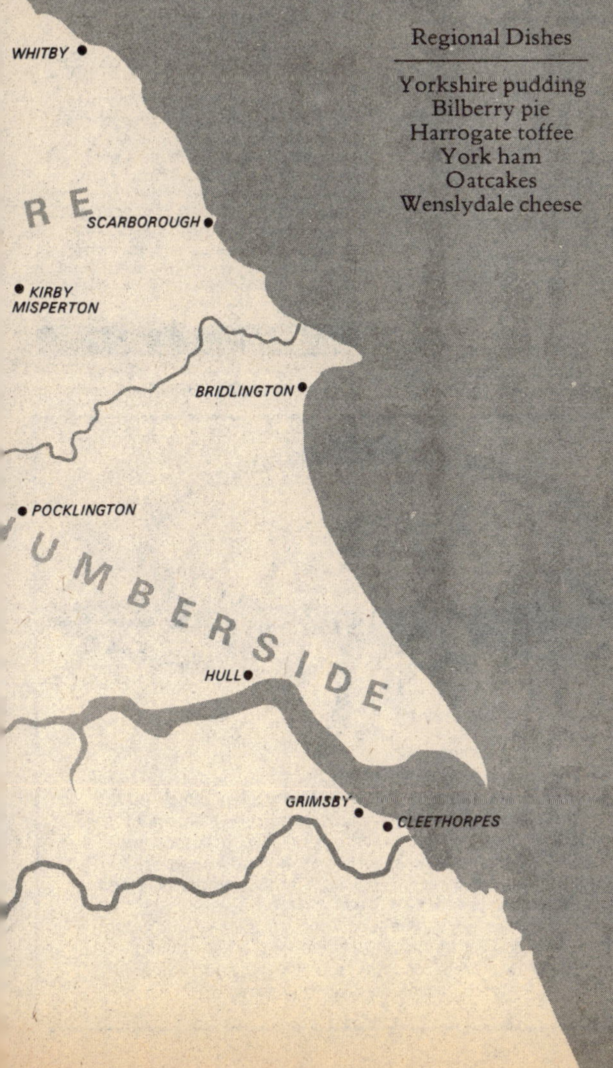

Regional Dishes

Yorkshire pudding
Bilberry pie
Harrogate toffee
York ham
Oatcakes
Wenslydale cheese

10

Barnsley

BROOKLANDS RESTAURANT
Barnsley Road, Dodworth
(Barnsley 84238/6364)
Open: Mon-Sun 12noon-2.30pm, 6.30-9.30pm

[C] [P]

Within 500 yards of the M1 is this single storey building housing three dining rooms, each featuring splendid displays of fresh fruit and wines. Meals are exceptionally good value, a three-course lunch costing about £4. The choice is excellent and imaginative (try chicken poche á la crème – chopped, poached chicken with mushrooms in a cream sauce). Chef's special dishes are also included, such as moussaka or roast pork. You are also invited to ask for more – 'and it shall be freely given'!

QUEEN'S HOTEL ★★ Regent Street
(Barnsley 84192)
Open: Mon-Sat 12noon-2.15pm, 6.30-10pm; Sun 12noon-2pm, 7-9pm

[C] [S]

An imposing Victorian three-storey building, conveniently close to the railway station and town centre, houses this cheerful split-level restaurant where décor is in the best tradition of Victorian design. Main courses in the Carvery and Buffet are around £2.20 and £1.60 respectively. Starters are from 50p upwards and desserts cost about 70p. There is also a selection of snacks, 'quickies' and 'fillers' – sandwiches, salads and savoury pancakes.

Boroughbridge

THREE ARROWS ★★★ Horsefair
(Boroughbridge 2245)
Open: Mon-Sun 12.30-2pm, 7.30-9.30pm

[C] [♫] [P]

This restaurant has a long, tree-lined entrance through lawns and gardens. Elegant though it is, the place is not ruinously expensive. Table d'hôte lunch and dinner for around £4 and around £5 respectively, offer three courses of honest-to-goodness English fare, with a selection of vegetables, though the à la carte can work out too dear unless you drop one course. Beef Strogonoff and duckling with cherry sauce are cheap choices.

Bradford

THE LAST PIZZA SHOW, 50 Great

Horton Road (Bradford 28173)
Open: Mon-Sat 12noon-2pm
6-11.30pm (12mdnt Fri & Sat)
Sun 6-11.30pm

[C]

A very Italian pizza-restaurant this – complete with marble-topped cast-iron tables, hanging baskets and helpful Italian waiters. If you stray away from the pizza and pasta main courses you could find the steak takes you above our limit, but with a choice of twelve pizzas, including the chef's special at under £2, there should be no need. With corn on the cob as a starter, and a sweet of home-made ice cream, the bill with coffee will total less than £4.50. A set meal with a choice of three starters, main courses such as pork escalope charcutiere or chicken chasseur followed by dessert, is offered at around £2.30.

THE VINTAGE, 18-22 Hall Ings
(Bradford 27463)
Open: Mon-Sun 11.30am-2.30pm,
5.30-11.30pm

[C] [♫] [P] [S]

This steak house in the city centre, with its warm and pleasing décor in red and gold, is designed in Victorian style. There are two rooms, each with arched 'cellar' ceilings and a smart bar with comfortable seating and 18th-century pictures. Mainly grills, steak, chops and chicken dishes are served with salad and vegetables and it is not difficult to stay within £5, particularly with the special lunch menu which is likely to cost less than £4 with VAT included.

Bridlington

BARN RESTAURANT, Prince Street
(Bridlington 75661)
Open: summer Mon-Sun
12noon-11.30pm, winter: Mon-Wed
12noon-3pm, Fri-Sat 12noon-11.30pm,
Sun 12noon-6pm

[P]

This bright and attractive restaurant, with a décor predominantly red, prides itself on being able to suit all tastes by serving salads and burgers plus a variety of snack-type 'specials' alongside a more formal à la carte selection. Traditional dishes such as home-made steak and kidney pie are on hand for the less adventurous, children are catered for with sausages, beefburgers or fish-fingers and chips, while other dishes are aimed modestly at the 'gourmet' (try the chef's own charcoal grilled steaks or chili con carne). A delicious selection of home-made sweets and ices are available, with liqueur coffee to follow.

THE OLD FORGE, Main Street,
Sewerby (Bridlington 74535)
Open: Mon-Sat 10.30am-5pm,
7.30-10pm (Fri-Jul & Aug only),
Sun 10.30am-5pm (evening by appointment)

[♫] [P]

One of a double row of stone-built fishermen's cottages of some age and interest, modernised and converted from its more recent use as a blacksmith's forge, the Old Forge is a convenient eating place for visitors to Sewerby Hall with its gardens, museum and zoo. With children's portions at about half the price of the regular meal, this is a particularly attractive restaurant for the whole family. Service is efficient and a good selection of English fare is offered, locally-caught fish being a speciality with fried haddock around £2.

Brighouse

BLACK BULL HOTEL, Thornton Square
(Brighouse 714816)
Open: Mon-Sat 12noon-2pm

[P] [S]

The homely restaurant of the Black Bull Hotel with its rose-patterned wallpaper is an ideal place for shoppers and motorists who enjoy a traditional English lunch. With a choice of starters and good basic sweets, a 'roast beef and Yorkshire' meal complete with coffee will cost about £3.50. Grills are more expensive, but fillet steak garni, accompanied by a starter and a sweet will still be within budget. Established in 1740, this hotel is the oldest in Brighouse and a faithful band of locals make up the best part of its clientele, although dinner is served to residents only.

Cleethorpes

CAVALIER STEAK BAR,
THE LIFEBOAT HOTEL ★★
Promenade Kingsway
(Cleethorpes 67272)
Open: Mon-Fri 12noon-2pm,
6.30-10.15pm, Sat-Sun 6.30-10.15pm

[C] [P] [S]

The Lifeboat Hotel overlooks the North Sea, so the lounge bar, where you can sip an aperitif, has a nautical theme. The restaurant, with contrasting white chipboard décor and dark wooden cubicles under a beamed ceiling, also has nautical pictures and fittings. A special lunch menu operates from Mondays to Fridays – you can enjoy soup, steak and kidney or roast chicken, apple pie, coffee and a glass of wine for just over £5. Typical choices on the à la carte menu are pâté (80p), lemon sole (£3.65) and gâteau (80p).

Doncaster

BACCHUS, 44 Hallgate
(Doncaster 20232)
Open: Mon-Sat 12noon-3pm, 6pm-12mdnt, Sun 7.30-12mdnt

C ♫ S ☙

It's tempting to believe that Bacchus, the god of wine, also knew a thing or two about the importance of good quality food – his disciples certainly believed they inherited the powers inherent in what they ate. If you're feeling adventurous you might like to try some stuffed shrimps for a starter and spicy kebabs with pitta bread, yoghurt and fresh green salad sounds like a mouth-watering main course. Evenings are table service only, when the bill can nudge the £5 limit if you're not careful, but you queue at a self-service counter for lunch, choosing from a menu chalked on a blackboard offering a stew of the day for about £1.95, and other English dishes ranging from £1.85 to £2.25. The wine list is extensive and reasonably priced – and there's even live music for good measure. From Monday to Saturday, drinks are cheaper during 'Happy Hour' – 6-7pm.

THE EQUESTRIAN WINE BAR
High Street, Bawtry (Doncaster 711057)
Open: Mon-Sat 11am-3pm, 6-11.30pm, Sun 6-11.30pm

C ♫ P S ☙

No, you can't take your horse inside this two-storey wine bar overlooking the old market place, but there are murals of racing and showjumping scenes to justify the name. On the ground floor the main room serves bar meals for lunchtime and evening. Home-made minestrone soup is hot favourite here and, along with lasagne, spaghetti or quiche at around £2.20 per portion, appears chalked on a blackboard menu behind the bar. The first-floor restaurant is open evenings only with waitress service, offering a more varied menu, also with an Italian bias. A typical meal might be melon (£1), spaghetti bolognese (£2.20) and a scrumptious gâteau from the trolley. House wine is Italian too, and costs 50p per glass.

FERRARI'S RESTAURANT
36-38 East Laithgate
(Doncaster 63712/63801)
Open: Mon-Sat 11.30am-2.15pm, 6-11.30pm, Sun 7-11.15pm

C ♫ P S ☙

If you're doing a day's shopping in the town, where better to break for lunch than this centrally situated (near the famous market) Italian restaurant. You'll recognise it by the prancing horse emblem and the glimmering Ferrari sign. Chrome and black wood furniture and colour pictures of gleaming sports cars form the basis of the interior decoration. Specialities of the day can include trout meunière (around £3.95) and a 308GT pizza at around £2.25. The menu lists several pasta dishes – lasagne, cannelloni and spaghetti. Sweets are priced from about 55p-£1.25 and include a 'dusky maiden' made from soft Italian ice cream, chocolate sauce, fresh cream and a chocolate flake.

REGENT HOTEL RESTAURANT ★★
Regent Square (Doncaster 64336)
Open: Mon-Sat 12noon-2pm, 6-10pm, Sun 12noon-2.30pm, 7-9.30pm

P S ☙

At the edge of Doncaster's main shopping area, this restaurant serves, in the words of our inspector, 'good substantial, no-nonsense' meals matched by low prices. Sunday lunch (roasts or trout) table d'hôte is about £4, the weekday three-course business lunch (various home-made pies, chicken or plaice), about £2. In the evenings, an à la carte menu only is available, with three courses priced by the main dish. Apart from fillet steak, all these are within our budget – from plaice and tartare sauce at £3 to sirloin steak at £5. Starters include home-made pâté or ravioli and a choice of various ice creams or Chef's Special sweet of the day concludes the meal which will not burn a hole in anybody's pocket.

RISTORANTE IL FIORE IN LEGARDS
50-51 High Street (Doncaster 23287)
Open: Mon-Sat 9.30am-5pm

C S

Situated above a smart ladies' boutique, this elaborately-named ristorante has a fresh green décor and overlooks the busy shopping street below from original Georgian bow windows. The menu offers a wide selection of sandwiches, gâteaux and toasted snacks, served all day. At lunchtime, for around £3 for three courses, you can choose from five starters, a main course such as pizza, canelloni or home-baked roast ham salad and a dessert of hot apple strudel or pineapple sundae with fresh cream.

VINTAGE STEAK BAR
Cleveland Street (Doncaster 64786)
Open: Mon-Sun 11.30am-2.30pm, 5.30-11.30pm

[C] [♫] [P] [S] [&]

A Victorian flavour here, with red furnishings and mellow wooden chairs and tables. The varied menu offers fourteen starters from about 50p, including smoked trout, iced melon and fried scampi, with a selection of fish, omelettes, grills and salads to follow. Each main course dish, such as steak, duck, chicken, lamb and pork, is served with French fried potatoes, tomato and garden peas and costs from £3.50 for lamb to £5 for steak. A sweet or cheese and biscuits may be chased down by a potent liqueur coffee in the restaurant or bar-lounge, and there's a separate room available for private parties and receptions. The central position of the Vintage Steak Bar is another plus.

Grimsby

THE LANTERN BISTRO
Freeman Street (Grimsby 56480)
Open: Mon-Sat 11.30am-2pm, Tue-Sat 7.30-10.30pm

[C] [♫] [P] [S] [&]

Discreet background music greets visitors to this rustic bistro, which has captured the flavour of France in its décor of plain wooden tables and colourful posters, adverts and pictures of Paris. It's a great find on one of Grimsby's busiest shopping streets, close to the indoor market. Lunchtime dishes, chalked up on two blackboards, include starters such as salami and prawn salad at 50p and main courses such as roast pork and apple sauce or moussaka, both around £1.50 and served with vegetables and croquette or new potatoes. Fresh cream desserts add the finishing touch.

Guiseley

HARRY RAMSDEN'S, White Cross (Guiseley 74641)
Open: Mon-Sun 11.30am-11.30pm

[P] [&]

Claiming to be 'the most famous fish and chip restaurant in the world', this biggish restaurant has changed hands many times since one Harry Ramsden first opened up over sixty years ago. Outside the mainly brick building, several benches are interspersed along a verandah for 'eating out'. Inside, the smartly-dressed waitresses scurry between the many pot plants with high efficiency. After a soup or fruit juice starter, you can choose from any one of the nine main fish dishes, all at under £3 and including chips, bread and butter and a drink (children's portions are about £1). If you're not already full up, a strawberry sundae or choc'n'nut dessert will soon put that right!

Halifax

DA CAMILLO, Southgate (Halifax 54573)
Open: Mon-Sat 12noon-2pm, 7-11pm
Sun 11.30am-3pm

[S]

Conveniently sited over a central pedestrian precinct in a busy shopping area is this second-floor pizzeria. The simple décor is predominantly deep brown with cork and plaster walls. Red linen tablecloths add a splash of colour. Business lunch and the fixed evening menu consist of tasty Italian dishes – cannelloni, lasagne, spaghetti bolognese, plus a selection of salads all in the £2 range – including a starter. Coffee is extra and a sweet can be had for around 30p, bringing the total to around £3. Sirloin and fillet steak served with mushrooms, peas and jacket potato or salad are also available but will add another £2 on to your bill.

Harrogate

APOLLO RESTAURANT, 34 Oxford Street (Harrogate 504475)
Open: Tue-Sat 12noon-2.30pm, 6-11pm

[♫] [P] [S]

Apollo is a first-floor city centre restaurant, situated close to the multi-storey car park. The classical décor of Ionic pillars is reminiscent of the Parthenon and the atmosphere is enhanced by the Greek music in the background. Dishes offered are international, with a Greek bias, but most of those appearing on the à la carte menu are too expensive for a meal around £5. However, a three-course lunch with home-made soup of the day, a main course of fish, grill, chicken, a Greek special or salad, and home-made fruit pie or Greek sweet, coffee and wine can be had for around £4. Seating is mostly in curtained cubicles just right for an intimate dinner.

BETTY'S, 1 Parliament Street
(Harrogate 64659)
Open: Restaurant: Mon-Sat
11.45am-2pm
Tea-room: Mon-Sat 9.30am-5.30pm
[P] [S] [⚭]

There are two eating places in Betty's – a tea-room where tea and cakes or more substantial grills and salads can be had throughout the day, and a lunchtime restaurant offering an excellent three-course lunch such as selected hors d'oeuvres, roast chicken, savoury stuffing and vegetables and Yorkshire curd tart with double cream for around £3.70. Tasty home-made cakes and pastries are also sold in the confectionery department at the entrance. Betty's enjoys a fine view across the Montpelier Gardens.

THE EMPRESS, Church Square
(Harrogate 67629)
Open: Mon-Fri 12noon-2.30pm,
7-10.30pm, Sat 7-10.30pm
Sun 12noon-1.30pm
[⚭]

In a stone building on the edge of town, with rich gold, turquoise and purple Regency décor and tasteful fittings, the restaurant is on the first floor, above the ground-floor lounge bar. A three-course businessperson's lunch including a choice of varying hot dishes or cold meat salad, served with potatoes and two veg is particularly good value at around £3 and even an extensive à la carte comes easily within our limit except in the case of a few speciality dishes. An extensive buffet table laden with flans, cold meats and salads is available at lunchtime. Children are also well catered for with a specially-designed menu complete with children's puzzles which they can take away as a souvenir.

OPEN ARMS, 3 Royal Parade
(Harrogate 503034)
Open: Tue-Sun 12noon-2pm,
Tue-Fri 6pm-10pm, Sat 5.30-10pm
[C] [S] [⚭]

True to its name, this town-centre restaurant offers a warm welcome with a glowing red décor, oak-clad walls and a menu designed to tempt the family. Meals are reasonably priced with emphasis on traditional English fare – omelettes, roasts, grilled meat and fish dishes. A children's lunch consisting of a couple of roasts or haddock – costs around £1.30, and the house specialities including beef steak pie, made with golden short-crust pastry and served with vegetables of the day are good value at around £2.

PINOCCHIO'S, Cheltenham Parade
(Harrogate 60611)
Open: Mon-Sat 11.30am-2.30pm,
5.30-12mdnt, Sun 5.30-11.30pm
[C] [♬] [⚭]

Immediately you walk inside this pizzeria, with its gay posters and pictures of the Italian homeland, unashamedly deep pink and brown walls plus foot-tapping Latin music, you could easily imagine yourself on an Adriatic holiday. Once seated at one of the marble-topped tables, you'll find that the menu continues the dominant theme with a mouth-watering variety of pastas and pizzas ranging from £1.30-£1.80. Calamari Fritti (deep-fried squid with oodles of lemon) is specially recommended. Apart from Italian dishes there's chicken Kiev (£3.50), chili con carne (£1.90) or barbecue spare ribs (£2.90). Soup costs 65p and desserts (including Black Forest gâteau and profiteroles) run from 60p-90p.

TUDOR RESTAURANT, 3 Ripon Road
(Harrogate 68701)
Open: Mon-Sat 12noon-2pm,
6.30-11pm
[C] [♬] [P] [⚭]

This old, gracious, stone-built Victorian house boasts a comfortable oak-panelled bar and restaurant. Close to the exhibition and conference centre, it is ideal for business lunches, which for around £4, consist of three-courses with an excellent choice of main dishes: home-made steak and kidney pie, chicken à la king, prawn or crab salad, braised oxtail and deep fried chicken with pineapple. Apart from ice cream or cheese and biscuits there is a tempting choice of sweets from the trolley. The à la carte menu prices dinner out of this guide.

VANI'S, 15 Parliament Street
(Harrogate 501313)
Open: Mon-Sat 12noon-2pm,
6-11.30pm, Sun 6-11.30pm
[C] [S]

This Italian restaurant has a casual, easy atmosphere guaranteed to soothe the most jaded shopper. The décor is imaginative, with cast-iron tables with round Italian marble tops, wicker-seated bentwood chairs and a basically red background. Starters include home-made soup and pâté and various seafood appetisers, most of which cost around £1.20. The list of pastas and pizzas is impressive and they mainly cost around £1.50. There is a good selection of home-made sweets from the trolley. Three courses will cost you about £4 in this restaurant.

Huddersfield

PIZZERIA SOLE MIO, Units 3 and 4, Imperial Arcade, Market Street (Huddersfield 42828)
Open: Tue-Fri 12noon-2.30pm, 5-11.30pm, Sat 12noon-11.30pm, Sun 5.30-11pm

[S]

Here you will discover Italy in the heart of Huddersfield, in a shopping arcade. Outside it has a terrazza and canopy blinds, inside roughcast walls, open brickwork, ceramic tile-topped tables and high-backed ladder chairs emphasise the Italian atmosphere. There is an extensive menu of home-made pastas including lasagne and cannelloni at around £1.70. The formidable list of pizzas range in price from under £1.25 to £1.75. Imaginative starters, including snails, are available.

Hull

PECAN PIZZERIA, 32 Silver Street (Hull 20835)
Open: Mon-Thu 12noon-2.30pm, 6-11pm, Fri-Sat 12noon-2.30pm, 6-11.30pm, Sun 6-11pm

As part of an imposing stone Victorian building in the heart of Hull's commercial district, the Pecan could be taken for another finance house. Even inside, there are strong overtones of the Stock Exchange, with lofty ceilings, classical pillars and arches and Victorian décor. But enthusiastic Italian waiters in red-check shirts, contemporary music and an extensive, mainly Italian menu dispel any stodgy banking atmosphere. The menu is almost a meal in itself with its mouth-watering descriptions, but tread carefully as far as the specialities are concerned. If you stick to the interesting starters, pizza or pasta dish and a sweet you should spend around £5.

Ilkley

BETTY'S, 32-34 The Grove (Ilkley 608029)
Open: Mon-Sat 9.30am-5.15pm

[S] [🍰]

In Ilkley's main shopping street, Betty's modern restaurant serves snacks all day with a limited selection of hot dishes and a mouth-watering variety of cakes, sandwiches and savouries. A satisfying meal could consist of home-made soup, Welsh rarebit (made with farmhouse cheddar and Yorkshire ale) served with apple or tomato chutney or ham and pineapple salad, followed by whole lemon or orange sorbet and coffee – for less than £5. A wide selection of speciality coffees and teas can be chosen from separate descriptive menus.

CAFE KONDITOREI, Spa Flats, The Grove (Ilkley 601578)
Open: Mon-Sat 10am-5.30pm, Sun 12noon-5.30pm

[P] [S] [🍰]

Converted from one of the old spa hotels, all the produce served in this café is home-made. Lunches start at noon and high teas after 4pm, when children's portions are available. Cork walls and classical pillars create an elegant, restful atmosphere. Soups are home-made and are delicious eaten with hot herb or garlic bread (about 60p for the two). Special dishes of the day include seafood vol-au-vents with chips and salad for around £2. Danish open sandwiches – try chicken with peach and Waldorf salad at £1.55, omelettes and salads are also served. Desserts range from 40p-80p and examples are lemon or fruit-filled pancake, sherry trifle and a variety of continental gâteaux and torten.

Kirby Misperton

BEAN SHEAF RESTAURANT ××
(Kirby Misperton 614)
Open: Tue-Sun 12noon-2pm

[♫] [P] [🍰]

This single-storey wayside cottage, converted and extended, offers a comfortable respite to the motorist, and to visitors to Flamingo Land Zoo. On entry, a comfortable lounge bar decorated in quiet fawns and browns leads through to a large, colourful dining room divided in two by an arch with classical pillars. Evening meals are rather above our limit but three-course lunches, weekdays and Sundays are very good value at around £3.50. All dishes are prepared personally by the proprietor and include such main meals as sweetbread villeroy (sliced, fried and served with the chef's special sauce), escalopes of pork Milanaise and chicken fried American style. An extensive wine list offers a choice of over 100 reasonably-priced wines.

Knaresborough

HIGH BRIDGE RESTAURANT
Harrogate Road (Harrogate 862521)

Open: summer: Mon-Sat 10.30am-7pm, Sun 12noon-3pm, winter: Thu-Sat 7-10pm

[icon]

This pleasant licensed restaurant is delightfully situated on the main A59 overlooking the River Nidd, beside the famous Dropping Well. Nearby there are amusements, boating and the small Knaresborough Zoo. Inside, two separate rooms are carpeted in blue and there's plain chipboard on the walls interspersed with pictures. A choice of five standard starters range from 35p-90p. Main courses are very reasonably priced – roast chicken with stuffing, chips and vegetables cost £2.30 (and just £1.55 for children). The dearest sweet is fresh cream gâteau at 65p, so you'll be well within the budget. In addition, late afternoon salads are popular here and a traditional Sunday lunch won't be over £4 all in – a real bargain.

Leeds

THE ALLERTON, Nursery Lane, Alwoodley (Leeds 686249)
Open: Mon-Fri 12noon-2pm, 7.15-11pm, Sat 7.15-11pm

C P

The tasteful restaurant is dominated by the ceiling, which is buttressed by low, shallow arches. The table d'hôte lunch is excellent value at around £3 and includes a choice of four starters, seven main courses and sweets from the trolley. There is a set three-course special dinner which includes steak or scampi at about £5 and there is also an extensive à la carte menu from which it is possible to keep within the limit of the guide by choosing dishes carefully. Diners seated before 7.45pm receive 20% discount.

KEN MARLOW'S FISH RESTAURANT, 62 Street Lane (Leeds 666353)
Open: Tue-Fri 12noon-2pm, 6-10pm, Sun 4.30-10pm

S

Fish is the order of the day at this restaurant set in a modern development close to the northern ring road. A small bar with a few seats leads into an open-plan restaurant with bold green décor. All main courses feature fish – fried, except when in salad form, and chipped potatoes are included. No fancy fare is offered, but a wholesome three-course meal can be had at around £3.60 per person with coffee extra.

NEW INN, Wetherby Road, Scarcroft (Leeds 892029)
Open: Mon, Wed-Sat 12noon-2.30pm, 7-10.30pm, Sun 12noon-2pm, 7-10pm

C ♬ P [icon]

This modern pub and restaurant stands by the roadside and has extensive lawns. The fawns and browns of the pleasant décor blend well with the exposed brickwork and coloured spotlights. Pictures of Falstaffian scenes decorate the walls. Only the set lunch menu at £3.50 qualifies for the limited budget meal as the à la carte menu would need very careful choice to keep to a bill of around £5. For lunch, starters include ravioli au gratin and Florida cocktail, with roast pork or lambs liver with onions for main course.

NEW MILANO ✕✕ 621 Roundhay Road (Leeds 659752)
Open: Mon-Fri 12noon-2.30pm, Sat 7-11.30pm

C P S [icon]

On the main road into the town stands this smart, ground floor restaurant; an oasis in the desert of shops around it. Food is English and Italian – expensive in the evening but well within our means for lunch. A table d'hôte menu offers a choice of eight starters and eight main-course dishes served with vegetables of the day. A sweet from the trolley or cheese completes a very substantial meal for around £3.20.

THE TRAVELLER'S REST
Harewood Road, East Keswick (Collingham Bridge 72766)
Open: Mon-Sat 12noon-2pm, 7-10pm, (Sat 10.30pm)
Sun 12noon-1.30pm, 7.10.30pm

C ♬ P [icon]

This first-floor restaurant enjoys a prime location overlooking the beautiful Wharfe Valley. The small Tudor-style room with its dark wood beams and furniture, partitioned cubicles and rich red carpeting provides a cosy, restful eating place for about fifty people. Main courses comprise grills and fries, with a choice of steaks at the top end of the price scale. It is possible to overdo the limit here, but it is also quite easy to stay within £5 with a meal such as smoked mackerel, followed by deep-fried breast of chicken with sweetcorn and pineapple plus a choice from the sweet trolley and coffee.

THE VINTAGE STEAK BAR
Merrion Street (Leeds 454312)
Open: Mon-Sun 11.30am-2.30pm, 5.30-11.30pm

[C] [♫] [P] [S]

Soft lighting, a red and brown colour scheme, cubicles with red velvet dividing screens and walls adorned with Edwardian motoring and cycling prints create comfortable surroundings in the steak bar with adjoining large bar. The à la carte menu includes fourteen starters with soup of the day at about 50p. Main dishes range from lamb cutlets at around £3 to pepper steaks or tournedos Rossini at about £5. A special menu which changes daily offers less expensive meals – for example soup or grapefruit cocktail for around 50p, roast pork or braised steak for around £1.25, minute steak for about £2.50 (all served with potatoes and two veg) and plaice and chips for about £1.75. Sweets are in the 70p-95p range and coffee is very reasonable at about 30p.

Pateley Bridge

BRIDGEWAY RESTAURANT
1 High Street (Harrogate 711640)
Open: Tue-Fri, Sun 12noon-5pm

[P]

This first-floor restaurant overlooks the valley of the River Nidd in upper Nidderdale where the road bridge spans the river. Dark oak tables, wheelback chairs, light oak-clad walls and a beamed ceiling complete the rustic feeling. Home-made country fare is a special feature, from lentil soup at 70p to English kidneys braised in red wine sauce (£2.50), home-made beef steak, kidney and mushroom pie, roast topside and Yorkshire pud and roast Nidderdale turkey – both around £2.75. Home-made fruit pies with fresh cream cost 75p.

Pocklington

BAYERNSTUBL, 4-6 Market Place (Pocklington 2643)
Open: Tue-Sun 12noon-10.15pm (10.45pm Sat)

[P] [S]

This converted pantiled cottage in the centre of town is furnished in natural wood to emphasise the Bavarian atmosphere. The popular lunchtime menu is basically English fare with sandwiches, home-made fruit pies and gâteaux at extremely reasonable prices, enabling one to eat a three-course meal for about £1.80. A meal from the main 'Speisekarte', written in German with English subtitles, will probably cost you around £5.50. Start with krabben salat (prawn cocktail), then sample a rich, spicy German dish such as paprika huhn (paprika roasted chicken) and round it off with apfel strüdel and cream.

Richmond

THE BLACK LION HOTEL
Finkle Street (Richmond 3121)
Open: Mon-Sun 12noon-2pm, 7-9.30pm

[P]

Once a coaching inn, this quaint 17th-century building has a restaurant on the first floor with a low, beamed ceiling, white décor, wheelback chairs and 19th-century prints. Meals are honest-to-goodness English fare, well-prepared, pleasantly served and excellent value, with a table d'hôte three-course lunch at around £4 and a three-course dinner at about £6. Main dishes include roasts, hot pot, curry, steak and kidney pie and pork chops in cider. Home-made desserts include fresh gâteaux.

Rotherham

THE DUNGEON, Wortley Road, Kimberworth (Rotherham 557701)
Open: Mon-Fri 12noon-2.30pm, Wed-Sun 8-10.30pm

[P] [S]

Below The Drawbridge pub you will find the Dungeon. Simulated rock and cave décor, solely illuminated by coloured lighting from electric storm lanterns, sets the scene. Lunches are excellent value and the menu offers a wide choice of starters, main courses and sweets. The most expensive choice costs around £6.50, the least expensive, close to £3.50. Seafood platter, sirloin steak garni, gammon steak and omelettes are usually available; or you may select from the Drawbridge cold buffet table where cold meats, continental sausage, fish and mixed salads are all individually priced and an average plateful will cost around £2.

Scarborough

MEDI'S, Crown Crescent (Scarborough 61938)
Open: Mon-Sun 5.30-11.30pm

Italian and Greek background music imparts a cheerful foot-tapping atmosphere in this recently opened pizza parlour on the South Cliff side of town. A bright décor in white and pink with mirrors and arched pillars is complemented by the use of spotlights and soft inset ceiling lights. Potted palms and other plants add the final touch. The huge pink and white menu offers pasta and pizza dishes at around £2 (many under), burgers – home-made and served on a bun with salad and French fries – at around the same price and charcoal-grilled kebabs are £4. Finish with a glorious Italian sweet.

Sheffield

ASHOKA, 307 Ecclesall Road (Sheffield 686177)
Open: Mon-Thu 12noon-2pm, 6-12mdnt, Fri-Sat 12noon-2pm, 6pm-1am, Sun 12noon-2pm, 7-12mdnt

What the Ashoka lacks in ethnic décor and atmosphere it more than compensates for by the range and quality of its Indian cuisine. Main courses, all eastern variations on a theme of chicken, fish or meat, are reasonably priced at around £2.65. Two or more people could dine in style very easily for around £4.50 per head by sharing a selection of dishes. For that special celebration, a party of six can order a lamb masallam – a leg of lamb marinated in a rich sauce with herbs and spices, roasted and then carved at your table. It is served with ghee rice and costs around £30. But you'll have to warn the chef you are coming – he requires two days' notice if he is to prepare this masterpiece to your satisfaction. Authentic starters and sweets can be had for around £1.15.

DAM HOUSE RESTAURANT, Crookes Valley Park (Sheffield 661344)
Open: Mon-Fri 12noon-2.30pm, Tue-Thu 7-11pm, Fri-Sat 7pm-2am

C P S

A more peaceful setting in which to enjoy a meal would be hard to find, particularly so close to the heart of a city. The 18th-century Dam House is set in a lush green valley with a terraced patio/garden overlooking a boating lake which was once a small reservoir (hence the name). Food is predominantly English, with the traditional Yorkshire pudding with onions and gravy featuring as a starter. Main dishes on the three-course lunch menu, which costs around £4 include the tried-and-true favourites, beef and kidney hotpot and home-made steak and kidney pie. A glass of house wine, cheese and biscuits and coffee with cream will add another £1.30 or so to your bill. Beware of dinner prices; the extensive à la carte menu in the evening is likely to be rather more than £5. For the energetic, there's disco dancing until the small hours each weekend, at no extra charge.

NAMELESS, 16-18 Cambridge Street (Sheffield 29751)
Open: Mon-Sat 11am-11.30pm, Sun 12noon-11.30pm

[symbol]

This pizza-biased restaurant is located in the city centre and boasts an authentic Victorian atmosphere. Walls are adorned with 19th-century pictures, whilst intricate ceiling lights and hanging aspidistra-like plants hover above the cast-iron dining tables. The whole of this long bar is itself overlooked by the Minstrel Gallery where you'll find a pleasant wine bar. Although the surroundings are decidedly Victorian, the food is bang up-to-date with a wide variety of burgers, pizzas and other Italian dishes ranging from £1.50-£2.50. Leaving aside sirloin and T-bone steak, you'll soon see that it's difficult to reach the £5 limit – even if you sample a delicious Tia Crêpe dessert (ice cream plus Tia Maria folded into a crêpe, topped off with whipped cream). A special kiddies' meal costs just over £1 for a mini pizza, ice cream and a fizzy drink.

RAFFLES, Charles Street (Sheffield 24921)
Open: Mon-Sat 12noon-2.30pm

[♬] [S] [symbol]

A small entrance between shops in busy, down-town Sheffield leads to this first-floor restaurant. A grotto-like staircase takes you, via goldfish tanks, to a pleasant green-ceilinged room with mood-setting floodlights. Glass-topped bamboo tables are interspersed across a green-striped carpet. Random fishing nets and glass floats set the scene for a predominantly seafood menu. Prawns, oysters, mackerel and crab are all available with side-salad from £1.60-£3. Cold meat salads and curries are alternatives for non-fish lovers. If you choose cheesecake, for example, at 50p and round things off with a coffee (30p), you'll see a fair bit of change from a fiver. In the evenings there's a disco here, but the menu soars out of our range.

WAGGON AND HORSES, Abbeydale Road, Millhouses (Sheffield 361451)
Open: Mon-Sun 12noon-2.45pm, 7-11.30pm (Sun 10.30pm)

[C] [P] [symbol]

Part of the Falstaff taverns group, this two-storey, stone-built inn overlooks a pleasant recreation area. A three-course lunch is served here daily, when for about £4 you can sample a plain but wholesome range of dishes against a charming background of exposed stone walls, oak beams and wrought-iron screens. Typical choices from the menu would be soup, grapefruit cocktail or juices followed by mixed grill, steak and kidney pie or fried plaice, plus a sweet such as mandarin cheesecake. Specialities and à la carte dishes are reasonably-priced, although you may have to forgo sweet or starter if you plump for something like beef Stroganoff or fillet steak. The Sunday lunch menu, offering two roast dishes and other choices is inexpensive.

Wakefield

STONELEIGH HOTEL AND RESTAURANT ★★★ Doncaster Road (Wakefield 69461)
Open: Mon-Sun 12noon-2pm, 7-10pm

[C] [P] [symbol]

Once a row of elegant Victorian terraced houses, this smart hotel is located close to the Trinity rugby league club. 'Quality' is the key word in the sophisticated dining room where full silver service is employed to complement high class international cuisine. Dinner (as may be expected), outsteps the budget, but a good table d'hôte lunch is within our means at around £4.95. There is a choice of eight starters followed by nine main-course alternatives such as lemon sole mornay, grilled lamb chop with mint sauce or sauté of beef with tomato. Finish with the pick of the sweet trolley, fresh fruit or cheese.

THE VENUS RESTAURANT
51 Westgate (Wakefield 75378)
Open: Mon-Sat 12noon-2.30pm, 6.30-11.30pm, Sun 7-11pm

[C] [♬] [P] [symbol]

Those who venture beyond the somewhat unimpressive side-street entrance of the Venus Restaurant will be pleasantly surprised by the warm, sumptuous interior, with oak panelling and gold dralon furnishings. The menu is rich in English and Greek cuisine with some Greek speciality dishes such as kebabs and afelia (pork fillet cooked in wine sauce with coriander and cream) – both around £4.50 including rice or Greek salad, but the à la carte menu will require careful selection to keep the costs around £5. The three-course table d'hôte lunch is ideal, offering traditional dishes such as fish, roasts or salads, with one Greek special for around £3.50. Though part of the Black Bull Tavern, children are catered for with half portions of selected dishes – at half price.

Whitby

THE GEORGIAN, 25 St Hilda's Terrace (Whitby 3345)
Open: summer: Mon-Sun 11.45am-2pm, 7-9pm (closed Fri and Sun eve)
winter: Mon-Sat 12noon-2pm

Did you know that many of the horrible deeds of Bram Stoker's Count Dracula actually took place in Whitby? Well, you may rest assured that such fiendish goings on will not trouble you in The Georgian restaurant – it used to be the vicarage. Attractively situated, with fine lawns and rose beds, the restaurant is conveniently placed for access to the town centre. Prices are reasonable and a meal of soup, chicken Georgian (chunky chicken in a sauce of onions, tomatoes and pimentoes) served with a selection of fresh vegetables, meringue glacé and a pot of tea, can be had for under £3. If you're less hungry, perhaps a cream tea for around 75p, served in the garden, would suffice.

KHYBER PASS RESTAURANT AND GRILL (Whitby 603500)
Open: summer: Mon-Sun 11am-5.30pm,
winter: Sat-Sun 11.45am-5.30pm

The wandering road from the harbour up on to the West Cliff is called the Khyber Pass – the name has been adopted by this single storey café which overlooks the beach and harbour entrance. At lunchtime three courses are priced by the main dish – from sausage at £2 to roast beef and Yorkshire pudding at around £3.65. Whitby crab salad is offered at £3.45. Starters include soup of the day and a selection of six desserts offer home-made fruit tart and custard and crème caramel. Junior Choice at £1 is served all day – choose from fish fingers, fish, sausage, beans, eggs – any of these with chips, ice cream and a glass of squash. The evening menu is more sophisticated – curries, kebabs, fish and grills all cost over £3, so three-courses can only be enjoyed with the cheaper main dishes.

MAGPIE CAFE, 14 Pier Road (Whitby 602058)
Open: Mon-Thu, Sat-Sun 11.30am-2.30pm, 3.30-6.30pm

At the quayside you will find this converted merchant's house with its distinctive bow windows and black-and-white exterior. Beside the fish-landing harbour, it is well placed to specialise in fresh Whitby seafood from the dockside. Proprietors Sheila and Ian McKenzie claim that their menus provide a meal to suit *all* tastes though a special effort is made to cater for families, with cradles and high chairs provided. A Magpie Special Lunch for about £2.80 offers home-made soup of the day as one starter, home-made steak pie, chips and peas and a choice which includes fresh cream sherry trifle or strawberry flan, Black Forest gâteau or apple pie. The Magpie Special Fish Lunch at £3.40 offers a choice of Whitby crab, prawn cocktail or potted shrimps as appetisers, cod or haddock with chips and a selection of about ten sweets. With both lunches a pot of tea is included, since The Magpie is

unlicensed, but since there is a choice of four liqueur mousses in each case, you won't be totally on the wagon! A special children's meal for around £1.20 offers sausage, beans and chips, jelly and ice cream and a glass of orange. Paintings by local artists adorn the white walls of the dining room.

York

BESS'S COFFEE HOUSE, Royal Station Hotel, Station Road (York 53681)
Open: Mon-Sat 9.30am-2.30pm, 3-9pm, Sun 9.30am-2pm

[C] [P] [S]

The theme of Bess's Coffee House is that of the legendary ride from London to York of Dick Turpin, on his mount Black Bess. Tables are set between stage coach doors; a highwayman's pistol and a mural, depicting Turpin's ride and ultimate capture, line the walls. The menu offers a good range of well-priced dishes and a typical meal might include Yorkshire broth (made from an ancient local recipe) at around 55p, savoury chicken and mushroom pancake with salad for £2.25 and cheesecake with whipped cream for about 85p. The set lunch is a satisfying meal for less than £3 for dishes such as leek and potato soup, followed by casserole of chicken with green peas and new potatoes, cheese and biscuits and coffee. Children can have a main meal of chicken leg and chips or fish fingers and chips for £1 or under.

BETTY'S OAKROOM RESTAURANT AND TEA ROOM, St Helen's Square (York 22323)
Open: Mon-Sat 12noon-2pm, 5.15-9pm (closed Mon-Wed evenings in winter)

[P] [S]

This three-storeyed corner-house complex was the haunt of the boys of No. 6 Bomber Squadron during World War II, but today's fare won't cost you a bomb! The main restaurant is in the basement and takes its name from the all-oak furnishings. A three-course meal here such as Chef's special cauliflower soup, fried fillet of plaice with full garnish and Swiss sherry trifle to finish, is around £4.50. Above, in the cafeteria you can dine on fruit juice, roast beef and Yorkshire pud, plus a gâteau for less than £3.50.

BIBIS, 115-119 Micklegate (York 34765)
Open: Mon-Fri 6-11.30pm, Sat 12noon-2.15pm, 6-11.30pm, Sun 12.15-2.15pm, 6-11pm

[P] [S]

Very Italian, this ballroom-sized ground-floor restaurant with its granite-topped tables, black salt and pepper mills, deep green ceiling and tiled floor. Very Italian the food, with a wide selection of pastas and pizzas as well as blackboard-listed specials such as chicken, fish, or steak dishes. Starters include fresh Whitby crab when in season, buttered corn-on-the-cob, and honeydew melon, and there is a selection of home-made desserts and flambé ice creams. A three-course meal is likely to cost around £4 with coffee. Full-bodied Italian wines are sold by the bottle or the carafe.

CHARLIE'S BISTRO, County Hotel, Tanner Row (York 25120)
Open: Mon-Thu 12noon-2pm, 6-11pm (closed Mon evenings),
Fri-Sat 12noon-2pm, 6-12mdnt

[♫] [P] [S] [♧]

This little bistro on the ground floor of the County Hotel is decorated in 1920s style, with pictures of Charlie Chaplin around the walls. The choice of dishes à la carte includes peppered fillet steak with baked potato and salad at about £3 and York gammon with egg and chips at about £2.50, and there are a number of delicious sweets around 50p as well as mouth-watering sweet crêpes (a little more expensive). For a really cheap meal you'd find it hard to beat the two-course lunch costing about £1.50. This consists of soup followed by a choice from items such as home-made steak and kidney pie, seafood salad and lasagne.

DREAMVILLE, King's Square (York 36592)
Open: Mon-Sun 10am-11pm

[S] [♧]

Dreamville is exactly what it sounds – an American-style food-fantasy, with a colourful gangster theme. The entrance is reminiscent of an ice cream parlour of the 1920s and opens up on to a more tasteful dining area. The menu lists all kinds of burgers named after shady characters such as Al Capone, Frankie Yale and Lucky Luciano, and they range in price from £1.70 to around £3.50 depending on size and content. Other dishes include fish'n'fries, lasagne and barbecued spare ribs all at the £2 mark. Finish with a luxurious ice cream extravaganza (thirty-six varieties available) and perhaps an American style milk-shake or ice-cream soda.

PUNCH BOWL HOTEL, Micklegate Bar

(York 22619)
Open: Mon-Sat 12noon-2.30pm, 7-10.30pm, Sun 12noon-2pm, 7-10pm

[C] [♫] [P]

You can imagine yourself in an old coaching inn when you take a meal at the 18th-century Punch Bowl. In fact this is what it once was, but later it became first an almshouse and then a dwelling house. Now refurbished as a hotel and steak house, the Punch Bowl offers a very reasonable table d'hôte lunch of starter, main dish and dessert. An example is grapefruit cocktail, Sam's original recipe game pie with vegetables and potato, and apple pie and cream at around £3.15. Coffee with mints add the finishing touch. Choosing a £5 meal from the à la carte menu is easily done – the price includes vegetables and a sweet or cheese.

RAFFLES TEA ROOMS, 41 Stonegate (York 29812)
Open: Mon-Sat 12noon-5pm

[C] [S]

Historic Stonegate, with its overhanging windows so typical of the Middle Ages, was the main route to the Minster in times past and is now open only to pedestrians, five million of whom are said to pass through each year. Situated above a fashionable boutique, the tearoom is designed as a replica of the Buttery of its namesake – an internationally-renowned hotel in Singapore. Apart from the mouthwatering selection of sandwiches, cakes and cream teas which are served all day, the lunch menu includes pâté de campagne as a starter for around £1, pizza Marina (seafood special) at £1.60 for main course and dessert such as pear belle Helene for about 80p. £5 goes a long way here!

RISTORANTE BARI, 15 The Shambles (York 33807)
Open: Mon-Sun 11.30am-2.30pm, 6-11pm

[C] [♫] [P] [S]

Do you fancy Sophia Loren? A 'scalloppe' of that name, made of fillet of pork with cheese, brandy, and tomato sauce, costs about £4.20 (including vegetables) in this Italian pizzeria. The range of *paste* and *pizze* includes lasagne or cannelloni at around £1.90, spaghetti bolognese at around £1.80, and the Chef's special pizza at about £2. Coffee costs 45p or thereabouts for espresso or cappuccino.

TIGGA, 45 Goodramgate (York 33787)
Open: Mon-Sat 9.30am-9pm, Sun 10.30am-8pm

[C] [♫] [P] [S]

'Tigga', housed in a renovated Tudor merchant's home, combines a gift shop with an enterprising restaurant operation. Proprietors Rodger and Rosalie Kilvington are now specialising in 'Taste of England' dishes. Many combinations of three courses come within the region of £5 here. Those who would like to sample the traditional meal of Yorkshire pudding served as a starter, roast English beef with appropriate vegetables, apple pie served with cheese, and coffee must order a couple of hours in advance and be prepared to exceed our limit. But if you're looking for a cheaper evening meal thare are a number of supper dishes, and at any time of day Tigga Burgers may be your choice. The most expensive is a Tigga Burger Henry VIII (with brandy) and the others decrease in price through his six wives, the cheapest being a 'weight watcher' named after Anne of Cleves. Anne Boleyn is awarded a cream sauce with onions, mushrooms and brandy – such a pity 'er 'ead's tucked underneath 'er arm. There is a quick lunch at about £1.85 which is particularly good value and a children's version at around £1.

'A North Country maid up to
London had strayed,
Although with her nature
it did not agree,
Which made her repent,
and so bitterly lament
"Oh I wish once again
for the North Country.
Oh the oak and the ash
and the bonnie ivy tree,
They flourish at home
in my own country!"'

TRADITIONAL

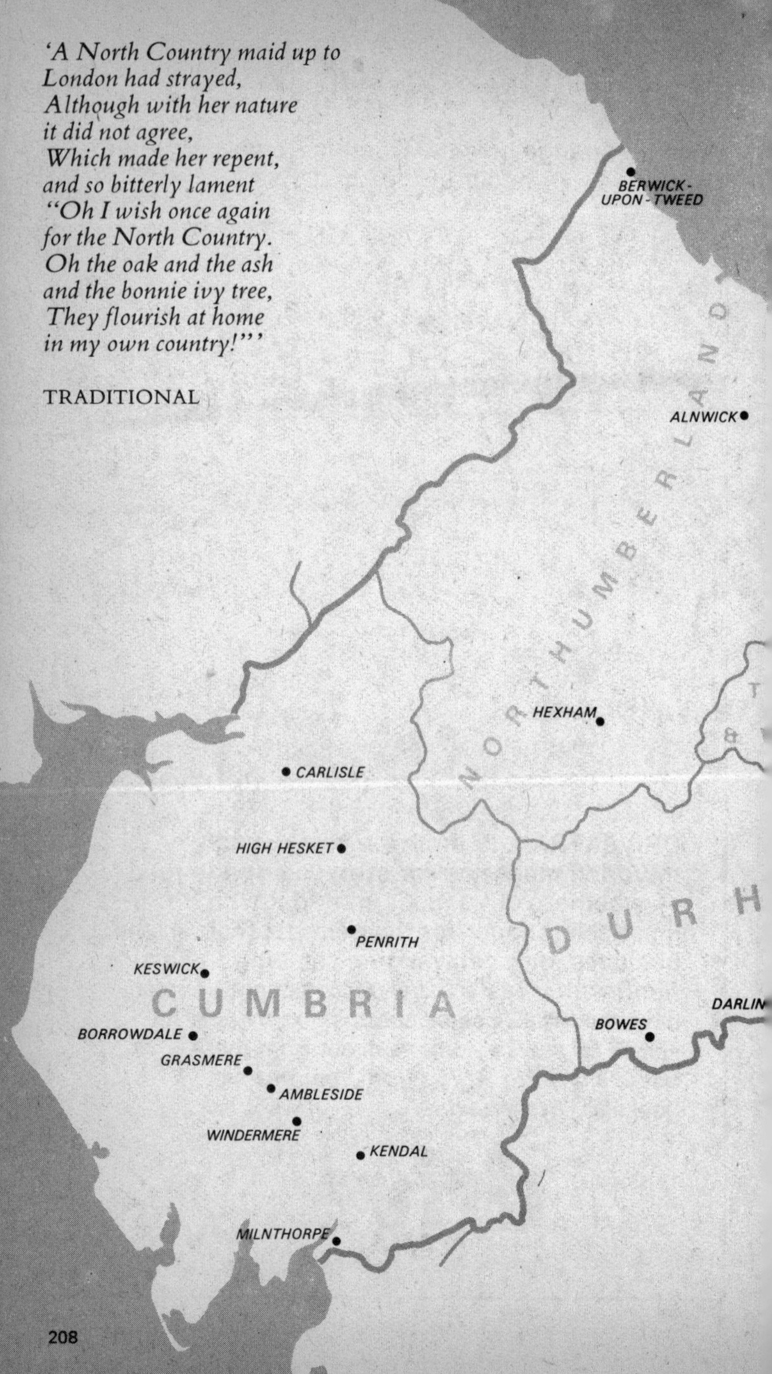

The North and the Lakes

Regional Dishes

Kendal mint cake
Grasmere gingerbread
Cumberland sausage
Herdwick lamb tatie pot
Cumberland sweet pie
Oak-smoked Craster kippers
Pease pudding with boiled ham

Alnwick

HOTSPUR HOTEL ★★
(Alnwick 602924)
Open: Billy Bones Buttery: Mon-Sun 12noon-2pm, summer: 7-9.30pm, winter: 6-9pm
Percy Restaurant: summer: Mon-Sun 7-9pm, winter: Mon-Sun 7-8pm

[♫] [P] [S] [🍷]

Billy Bones was piper to the Duchess of Northumberland in 1815, when the Duke leased Hotspur House to him. There he established a hostelry. In 1971, a local businessman turned it into a hotel again and converted the stable into the Billy Bones Buttery, where horse brasses on the walls proclaim the building's former use. Here you can get a super lunch for about £3.50 – soup or fruit juice, a choice of four main dishes likely to include a roast, fish, and cold meat with salad, and an 'English' sweet – perhaps fruit crumble with custard or a sponge pudding. The à la carte menu is also within our budget, with basket meals including pork sausage, tomato, onion and chips at around £1.50 and – at the other end of the scale – deep-fried seafood selection with chips at over £3. Steak is the most expensive bar meal, costing £4.95. Starters include soup and fruit juice and sweets are ice cream-based, costing up to 90p. The Percy Restaurant (Percy is the family name of the Dukes of Northumberland) does a table d'hôte dinner at around £6.

Ambleside

GEMINI RESTAURANT, Lake Road
(Ambleside 2528)
Open: Feb-Nov: Mon-Sat 10am-7pm

[P] [S] [🍷]

A friendly, informal family-run roadside restaurant with large rear car park. Three small open-plan areas create a comfortable atmosphere and a good selection of wholesome hot dishes are provided. Starters include grapefruit and mandarin cocktail at around 55p and main courses, predominantly grills, range in price from around £1.65-£4 with specialities such as duckling à l'orange or sole in prawn and mushroom sauce – both about £5. There is an excellent choice of desserts from around 50p-70p. Special children's dishes are around £1.10. Try grape or apple juice which costs about 35p a glass – no fermented grapes here as the restaurant is unlicensed.

THE JACARANDA RESTAURANT
Compston Road (Ambleside 2430)
Open: Mon-Fri 12noon-8.30pm, Sat 5-8pm, Sun 12noon-8pm

[P] [🍷]

There's a touch of nostalgia in the name of this neat little restaurant. The jacaranda is a beautiful flowering tree found in the tropics, notably the Caribbean island of St Lucia where proprietors Keith and Jean Stead gained much of their catering experience. Malawi and Nairobi were also bases for the Stead's work abroad and prints and pictures of these places lining the wall are a colourful feature of the restaurant's interior. However, this taste for the foreign is not extended to the menu which offers mainly grills, fish and salads. Almost any combination will come within our limit; a sample meal would include home-made chicken liver pâté with hot buttered toast at 80p, rainbow trout meunière with vegetables and potatoes or full salad for £2.95 (a more expensive choice), fresh cream dessert chosen from display (60p) and coffee and wine for less than £1.

Berwick-upon-Tweed

KING'S ARMS HOTEL ★★ Hide Hill
(Berwick-upon-Tweed 7454)

Open: summer: Mon-Sun 8-9.30am, 12noon-10pm, winter: Mon-Sun 12noon-2pm, 6.30-9pm

[C] [P] [S]

The King's Arms was once a coaching inn, a regular stop for the London to Edinburgh Highflyer – 18th-century equivalent of the Flying Scotsman. Today a Highflyer menu ranging in price from £3.50-£4.95 is served in its oak-panelled dining room at lunchtimes or evenings. The adjoining Brambles Bistro, open all day in summer provides a quick-service meal from £2. You may buy a three-course table d'hôte Sunday lunch for about £4.50. The Hunting Lodge bar does lunches, including farmhouse soup for around 40p and hot pies and chips for around £1.

POPINJAYS, 30 Hide Hill
(Berwick-upon-Tweed 7237)
Open: Mon-Sat 9.30am-5pm

[P] [S]

Georgina Home-Robertson is the enthusiastic owner of this farmhouse-style coffee shop which boasts a walled patio at the rear with ruined stables providing a dramatic backcloth. Coffee shop Popinjays may be, but down market it definitely is not. Food here is simple but nicely prepared with salads at around £1 and various hot dishes including basic grills and omelettes at about 75p. All ingredients for a good three-course meal are here except for a glass of wine – Popinjays is unlicensed.

QUEEN'S HEAD HOTEL ★ Sandgate
(Berwick-upon-Tweed 7852)
Open: Mon-Sun 7.30-9.30am, 12noon-2pm, 7-9.30pm

[P] [S]

One of two Berwick hotels owned and run by Mr Geoffrey Young and his family, the Queen's Head lies at the bottom of Hide Hill, near the river. The pleasant restaurant with its dark oak furniture and flock wallpaper offers three-course table d'hôte lunch at around £3.75 with coffee extra. There is also an à la carte menu with fish, entrées and roasts at prices ranging from £2.50 to £3, the total cost working out between £4.50-£5 for three courses.

RAVENSHOLME HOTEL ★★
Ravensdowne
(Berwick-upon-Tweed 7170)
Open: Mon-Sun 7.30-10am, 12noon-2pm, 6.30-9.30pm

[C] [P] [S]

Geoffrey Young owns this hotel and he and his family run it personally. The Ravensholme has two restaurants, a downstairs Wallace Room with Wallace tartan carpet, and an upstairs Gold Room. The Wallace Room offers a good range of dishes including fried fillet of Eyemouth haddock or two lamb chops and various steaks on the à la carte menu, and three courses can cost around £5-£6. An excellent table d'hôte lunch offers three courses for under or around £4. The Gold Room serves bar lunches and suppers in summer. The historic building, formerly a private house adjoins the town's interesting Elizabethan fortifications.

THE RUM PUNCHEON RESTAURANT, Golden Square
(Berwick-upon-Tweed 7431)
Open: Mon-Sat 9.30am-9.30pm

[C] [P] [S]

You can't linger late over dinner here, but this oak-clad 18th-century restaurant is certainly worth a visit. The Stoddart family has been in business selling groceries, wines and spirits there since 1834. In the restaurant you can buy a three-course lunch for something around £3 or the main course only for about £2, as well as separate à la carte dishes such as scampi, steak or salmon, all at between £2-£3.50. Substantial bar lunches are also served, with main courses for just over £1 to about £3 and sweets from 45p upwards.

Borrowdale

THE YEW TREE, Seatoller
(Borrowdale 634)
Open: Tue-Fri, Sun 12noon-8pm, Sat 6-9.30pm

[P]

Nestling at the foot of the spectacular Honiston Pass, this whitewashed restaurant was originally built as two cottages in 1628. Massive oak beams and a slate floor emphasise the antiquity of the dining room, with its wheelback chairs and wooden tables. Food is simple and wholesome. Try home-made soup with a roll as a starter for 60p. Smoked salmon at £1.50 is one of the more expensive appetisers. Main courses offered are grills, omelettes and salads. Speciality of the house is Borrowdale trout with almonds (£3) and ham and egg (£2.90). Cumberland sausage with salad and mushrooms is £2.20. A very tempting selection of sweets include pot of chocolate (55p), brandy meringue (60p) or bilberries and cream (75p). Starred items on the menu are available in smaller portions for children at two-thirds of the full price.

Bowes

ANCIENT UNICORN HOTEL ★★
(Teesdale 28321)
Open: Mon-Sun 11.30am-2.30pm, 6-9.30pm

C P ♨

This attractive coaching inn, built around a cobbled courtyard, has been offering accommodation and refreshment to weary travellers since the 16th century. Prices in the restaurant of this two-star hotel are somewhat beyond our limit so we are concentrating on the very reasonable and extensive bar snack menu. A sample of dishes available are sardine and tomato salad for starter at £1, chicken curry with rice and peas at about £2.60 and, to finish with, a sweet chosen from a selection at 90p.

Carlisle

THE CENTRAL HOTEL ★★ Victoria Viaduct (Carlisle 20256)
Open: Mon-Sun 12noon-2pm, 7-9pm

C ♫ P S ♨

A comfortable and popular Greenall Whitley hotel managed with great style by Stanley Cohen. Bar lunch here is excellent with a good ploughman's at about £1, a wide range of cold and hot dishes for around £1.30 and specials including scampi at about £2. Outstandingly good value, too, is the Central's table d'hôte dinner at about £5.25.

THE CITADEL RESTAURANT
77-79 English Street (Carlisle 21298)
Open: Mon-Sat 11.30am-10.30pm, Sun: normal licensing hours

C ♫ P S ♨

Is this the ideal haunt? Certainly the friendly ghosts keep coming back for more. So, it seems, do the patrons who claim to have seen several unearthly apparitions in this 100-year-old citadel, including a wizened old lady and a chap in 18th-century garb. The restaurant is situated above a tangle of ancient passageways which once led to the cathedral and old jail. Now it's handy for the station and shops. Warm and bright, it serves straightforward no-nonsense meals at fairly reasonable prices. Particularly good value are a three-course shopper's lunch at about £2.25 and the à la carte seafood dishes, none of which will set you back more than £3.

THE CROWN AND MITRE ★★★
English Street (Carlisle 25491/33354)
Open: Scott's Restaurant: Mon-Fri 12.30-2.30pm, 6.30-10pm, Sat-Sun 6.30-10pm, Coffee House: Mon-Sat 9am-10.30pm, Sun 10am-10pm

C ♫ P S ♨

Scott's Restaurant, within the Crown and Mitre Hotel, offers a fully inclusive three-course meal from £3-£5, with starters such as prawn cocktail followed by delicious meat dishes featuring steaks, lamb cutlets, pork chops or Cumberland sausage. A typical sweet would be gâteau or ice cream. In the Peace and Plenty Bar substantial snacks start at £1.20.

CUMBRIAN HOTEL ★★★ Court Square (Carlisle 31951)
Open: during normal licensing hours, Victoria's Restaurant: 12noon-2pm, 7-9.30pm, Cumbrian Kitchen: summer: 9.30am-9.30pm, winter: 10am-8pm

C P S ♨

As its name implies, the Cumbrian's well-appointed main restaurant has a Victorian décor. The à la carte menu is very English, but rather expensive, although the express lunch at about £2.75 and dinner at around £6.50 are both excellent buys. The Cumbrian Kitchen is a different matter altogether. You can have a snack and a cup of coffee here, with change from £1.50, or a substantial meal for less than £4. Bar snacks, available at lunchtime, include chicken salad at about £1.50, and an Albert's Special (half a French loaf buttered and filled with just about everything) at about £1.20.

THE MALT SHOVEL, Rickergate (Carlisle 34095)
Open: during normal licensing hours, Brew House Restaurant: Mon-Sat 12noon-2pm, 7.30-9.30pm

C ♫ P S ♨

The Brew House Restaurant has a most appropriate décor of malt sacks and malt shovels and is very bright and clean, with comfortable chairs and a relaxed, intimate atmosphere. The lunch menu prices start at around 95p for a ploughman's. A T-bone steak garni at about £4.75 apart, none of the main dishes costs much more than £2.50. But the Malt Shovel is at its best in the evening, with nineteen starters at prices ranging from around 40p-£1.50, and a superb selection of fish dishes, poultry, roasts, grills and entrées at prices that average out around £4. Incidentally, Scottish bard Robert Burns slept at the Malt Shovel, we are told. It's a pity he missed the food.

Darlington

TAJ MAHAL TANDOORI
192 Northgate (Darlington 68920)
Open: Mon-Sun 12noon-2.30pm, 7pm-12mdnt

[C] [♫] [P]

A small, intimate restaurant situated very close to the town centre, the Taj Mahal offers unbelievable value with its three-course lunch for only £1.60. The lunch menu includes twelve Indian dishes such as chicken and prawn curry and four English dishes including rump or sirloin steak with soup or fruit juice to start and a sweet to follow. A prominent feature of the dining area is a large Eastern-style mural covering one wall, the other three walls are hung with soft drapes, and the Indian atmosphere is enhanced by traditional background music. The à la carte menu offers a large variety of dishes with many tandoori specialities for around £2-£3.

Durham

THE BROTHERS RESTAURANT AND WINE BAR KITCHENER
4 Framwellgate Bridge, Milburngate Centre (Durham 46777)
Open: Mon-Sat 12noon-3pm, 7-10.30pm

[C] [P] [S]

Situated in the shadow of the Gothic cathedral and castle is this olde worlde eating place. The fact that it is run by two brothers (and their wives and mother) accounts for the name, but they have developed this to incorporate a monastic theme in style and décor – though the food is anything but frugal! Eight-ounce jacket potatoes with a choice of fillings, a dozen assorted salads and at least two lunchtime hot dishes a day give plenty of scope for inexpensive eating. For those who have made no vow to poverty, there is a comprehensive (and more pricey!) à la carte menu. An evening meal in the wine bar will cost about £2.95.

RISTORANTE LA CANTINA
North Road (Durham 46050)
Open: Tue-Sat 11.30am-2.30pm, Mon-Sat 6.30-10.30pm

[C] [♫]

Once inside this second-floor restaurant, one could almost be in an eating place in Rome or Florence. Inside, there are no windows and lighting is by coach lamps. Italian music strums gently in the background and Italian posters and Chianti bottles decorate the brick and rough-cast walls. A gallery dining area completes the scene with large wagon wheels and halved barrels set into the walls. An excellent selection of pasta and pizza dishes are offered, all for around £1.90, so that a three-course meal could easily be had for around £4.

ROYAL COUNTY HOTEL ★★★★ COFFEE HOUSE, Old Elvet
(Durham 66821)
Open: Mon-Sat 10am-8pm, Sun 10am-5pm

[C] [♫] [P] [S]

Youngsters enjoy their meals in this attractive buttery as there is a menu of children's favourites such as bangers and mash at about 75p and sweets (including 'Thunder and Lightning' – ice cream, golden syrup and whipped cream!) at around 45p. À la carte dishes are reasonably priced and you can choose an appetising meal such as soup with roll and butter, fried breast of chicken with banana fritter, chips and peas, a slice of chocolate gâteau and coffee for around £5.60.

THE SQUIRE TRELAWNY, 80 Front Street, Sherburn (Durham 720613)
Open: Tue-Sat 7.30-12mdnt

[C] [P]

Away from the city centre, this tiny, low-ceilinged bar and restaurant has a wealth of heavy old beams, horse brasses, harnesses and stirrups, set off by heavy rough-cast walls. Subtle lighting is by coach lamps. The à la carte menu is pricey, but an excellent-value 'snack' menu is served from Tuesday to Thursday inclusive. A choice of minute steak, scampi, roast chicken or gammon and apricot – all served with chips and peas – costs £2.30. Soup of the day at 75p and a sweet from the trolley at around the same price, complete a satisfying and inexpensive three-course meal.

Grasmere

THE SHEPHERD'S CROOK, Stock Lane (Grasmere 342)
Open: Mon-Sun 12noon-3pm, 6-8.30pm

[P] [♣]

An old-English atmosphere is created inside this quaint roadside restaurant by the small-paned leaded windows, soft low lighting and walls lined with willow-patterned crockery. Separate menus are offered for lunch and dinner, priced at an average of £3.50 and £5 respectively, for three courses. The emphasis is on good, homely cooking and warm friendly service. Try the rainbow trout with almonds served with two vegetables and a choice of four types of potato or salad for around £3, followed by a helping of home-made fruit pie and cream (just over 70p). In the evening prawns au gratin or the farmhouse grill (lamb chop, sausage, bacon, egg, mushroom and tomato) may take your fancy.

THE SINGING BIRDS RESTAURANT
Town End (Grasmere 268)
Open: Mar-Nov: Mon-Sun 10.30am-3pm, 3.30-6pm, 7-9.30pm

[C] [P]

Close to Dove Cottage and the Wordsworth Museum is a quaint white cottage housing an antique shop and restaurant. Inside, rough-cast walls, dark beams and brass and copper bric-à-brac emphasise the rustic atmosphere. All the lunch menus include a host of home-made dishes. 'Light' lunches include soup of the day with granary bread for around 75p, savoury flan or quiche served with an interesting salad for about £2.75 and open sandwiches such as 'shrimps in a crowd' for around £1.75. Three-course à la carte lunches vary in price from £4 upwards and include pâté maison, home-made chicken and mushroom pie or spaghetti bolognese. A three-course Sunday table d'hôte lunch for about £5.50 offers excellent choices – try egg and prawn surprise followed by chicken chasseur or lamb's kidneys turbigo.

Hexham

HADRIAN'S WALL (Hexham 81232)
Open: Mon-Sun 12noon-2pm, 7-9pm

[P]

Overshadowed by the Roman wall, this smart ivy-clad inn dating back over 250 years enjoys a well-deserved local reputation for its good and efficient service. A four-course lunch of home-made soup, a fish dish, a main course of steak and kidney pudding, lemon sole, curry or trout plus a sweet and coffee with cream will come to around £5.

High Hesket

THE ASTRA (Southwaite 541)
Open: Mon-Sun 11am-10pm

C P ♨

If you want a meal on your journey, without the time-consuming business of finding your way round a strange town, you could do much worse than stop at the Astra. This modern brick-built complex stands on the A6 half way between Carlisle and Penrith. Uniformed waitresses give efficient, speedy service in the restaurants, where you can have a good three-course lunch and coffee for around £4 (less than £2 for children under ten, no charge for those under three). For this you may choose as a starter fruit juice, soup, or a relish. Main dishes include home-made beefsteak pie and roast chicken with stuffing, and there is a choice of four sweets such as sherry trifle or apple pie and custard. A snack menu includes a two-course lunch for around £3 and ploughman's at about £1.30. A minimum of 50p per head is charged in the restaurants.

Kendal

CHERRY TREE RESTAURANT
24 Finkle Street (Kendal 20547)
Open: Mon-Sun 10am-9.30pm, (closed early Thu in winter)

S

The entrance to the Cherry Tree lies up an alleyway. The main first-floor restaurant is very bright and clean, with good dark oak furniture and excellent quality crockery. The décor has white rough-cast walls and beams. You can buy hot and cold snacks here and Danish open sandwiches, as well as a four-course lunch for about £3. Dinner costs very little more and offers an excellent choice with salmon, veal, chicken and turkey well within the budget.

THE MASH TUN, The Brewery Arts Centre (Kendal 25133)
Open: Mon-Sat 10am-2pm

♫ P S

The Mash Tun is housed in a converted stone-built brewery. The food is under the personal supervision of Annette Tarver. Popular with local business folk and farmers, The Mash Tun offers a choice of pies and flans, roast chicken leg, silverside of beef and fresh trout all at around £1.50, and all with chips or salad, as well as a great variety of similarly-priced fish or cold meat salads. There is a choice of three sweets for about 50p.

THE WOOLPACK HOTEL ★★★
Stricklandgate (Kendal 23852)
Open: normal licensing hours, Ca Steean Restaurant: Mon-Sat 12.30-2pm, 7-10pm, Shepherd's Pie Buttery, summer: Mon-Sat 10am-9.30pm, winter: Mon-Sat 10am-6.30pm

C ♫ P S ♨

The Ca Steean Restaurant offers fine food in elegant surroundings. A three-course meal can be had from the à la carte menu for around £6, if you stick to the lower price range, or there is the table d'hôte at around £3.50 for lunch and around £6.50 for dinner with hot grill-style main courses or cold buffet. The Shepherd's Pie Buttery is a more casual eating place with pine-clad walls and lantern-style lighting where a three-course meal costs around £3. Bar snacks include a hamburger bap with onions at about 50p and a good ploughman's lunch at around 75p.

Keswick

BAY TREE, 1 Wordsworth Street (Keswick 73313)
Open: Mon-Sun 10am-4.30pm, 7-9pm, winter: evenings only

P S ♨

This attractive terrace restaurant and guesthouse is easy to spot by its brown canopy and corner position. Victoriana is the style for interior décor, with old prints, china, porcelain and highly-polished tables and chairs. The three-course dinner menu (changing daily) is just in our range at £5.95-£6.95.

DERWENTWATER HOTEL ★★★
Portinscale (Keswick 72538)
Open: Mon-Sun 8.30-9.30am, 12noon-2pm, 3.30-5.30pm, 7.30-9pm

C P ♨

A friendly, informal hotel this, in a superb position close to the shores of Derwentwater. An excellent bar lunch will set you back a little over £3. Cold platters include, incidentally, a 'rock dub' of smoked salmon, prawns, sardines, tuna, pilchards and herrings with salad at just under £3 and a vegetarian dish of cheese, pineapple, carrot and salad for around £2. Every item on the special children's menu costs in the region of 95p. The dinner menu is priced a little over the odds for this book and is aimed more for the hotel guests than casual trade.

THE DOG AND GUN, 2 Lake Road (Keswick 73463)
Open: Mon-Sun, during normal licensing hours

P S

This is a genuine old coaching inn, and one of the oldest pubs in Keswick. The intimacy of its low, beamed ceiling and, in winter time, the welcoming open fire, make the Dog and Gun popular with locals and visitors alike. Food is prepared by the proprietress and is available during opening hours. Last orders are at 2.30pm (1.30pm Sundays) and 10pm. The menu is changed twice a year. In the winter hot meals such as home-cooked ham with jacket potato and fresh vegetables cost around £3. In summer rare roast beef and salad costs about £3.50. Specialities of the house such as Hungarian goulash (£3) and Cumberland sausage with mushy peas are available all year. Sweets include chocolate orange pot served under a float of orange curaçao.

YAN TYAN TETHERA, 70 Main Street (Keswick 72033)
Open: summer: Mon-Sun 12noon-3pm, Tue-Sun 6.30-10pm, winter: Mon-Sun 12noon-2.30pm, Thu, Fri, Sat evenings by appointment only

♫ P S ♧

No Chinese chippy this, as you might think, for 'yan, tyan, tethera, etc' is how they count sheep in Borrowdale. The day menu includes starters from around 50p to £1.30, hot dishes, including Cumberland sausage, from about 70p to £2.50, and fish from about 80p to £2.50. In the evening, owner Judith Szucs' specialities have a bias towards seafood, but they are popular, so do book. 'No service charge or gratuities please' the menu says. 'Just come back again!' English wines are a speciality here.

Milnthorpe

CROOKLANDS HOTEL BUTTERY AND COFFEE SHOP (Crooklands 432)
Two minutes from the M6 (No. 36 interchange) on the A65 going towards Kendal town centre.
Open: Mon-Sun 7.30am-2.30pm, 6.30-10.30pm. Closed winter evenings

C P ♧

The buttery of the Crooklands Hotel is a small, bright and cheerful restaurant, well worth knowing about. You can get a good lunch here, including home-made soup with roll (about 55p) and the 'pie of the day' (around £2 with vegetables). A three course meal with coffee is an unbeatable £3.50 and includes some traditional choices such as hot pot and liver and onions. On summer evenings you can have a fresh salad.

Newcastle upon Tyne

BLACKGATE RESTAURANT
Milburngate House, The Side (Newcastle-upon-Tyne 26661)
Open: Tue-Fri 12noon-2.30pm, 7-10.30pm, Sat 7-10.30pm

C ♫ ♧

This is a place for home-made food. All bread rolls, ice creams, desserts, petit fours and pâtés are freshly prepared on the premises. The table d'hôte lunch menu lists combinations of dishes in the region of £4-£6. Choose an unusual starter such as cheese and avocado mousse followed by roast leg of lamb with rosemary, a sweet (what better than pistachio ice cream?) and coffee. Prices are rather higher for dinner.

CAVALIER STEAK BAR DENTON HOTEL, West Road (Newcastle-upon-Tyne 742390)
Open: Mon-Sun 12noon-2pm, 7-10.30pm

C ♫ P S ♧

The impressive Denton Hotel's steak bar has a bright cocktail bar and an intimate, beamed restaurant with subdued lighting. Soup is around 40p and there is a fine choice of steaks, fish and poultry. Gammon steak is about £3 and Cavalier mixed grill is excellent value at around £3.60 – both are served with potatoes, peas and salad garnish. A sweet from the trolley is about 75p and a glass of house wine costs around 50p. A 'Junior Cavalier Menu' is available for children.

CLEEVES RESTAURANT
21 Kingston Park Centre
(Newcastle-upon-Tyne 868024)
Open: Mon-Sun 12.30-2pm (closed Sat), 7-10.30pm (closed Sun)

[C][S][⚘]

This modern, tastefully-decorated restaurant is part of the King's Court public house. Although the à la carte menus for lunch and dinner rather exceed our budget, it is possible to eat well here on the table d'hôte lunch or bar meals. A lunch of home-made vegetable soup, King John's steak and kidney pie served with potatoes and fresh vegetables of the day, ice cream and coffee can be yours for around £2.75. On Sunday, a more elaborate lunch including traditional roast joints of beef, lamb or pork, and coffee and mints served by the fireside costs a little less than £5. Bar food is a good choice for the budget-conscious with vegetable soup at 30p, moussaka for around £1.25 and a choice of sweets for only 35p.

COFFEE HOUSE, NORTHUMBRIA HOTEL ★★★ Osborne Road
(Newcastle-upon-Tyne 814961)
Open: Mon-Sun 10am-11.30pm

[C][P][S]

The Scandinavian pine décor of this attractive buttery is complemented by a cocktail bar where the works of local artists are displayed. The Coffee House serves Danish pastries, lunchtime snacks such as seafood pancake at about £1.85 and full three-course meals. Home-made soup of the day, a main dish such as asparagus and cheese pancake or fillet of plaice and a generous slice of fresh cream gâteau will leave you plenty of change from £5 to sample a cup of coffee.

THE FALCON, Prudhoe
(Prudhoe 32324)
Open: Mon-Sat 12noon-2pm, 6.30-10pm, Sun 12noon-1.45pm, 7-10pm

[C][P][⚘]

The grill room of this modern pub has picture windows the full length of one wall, giving a view of the surrounding countryside. Clean lines and simple furnishings, with an open grill bar give a feeling of uncluttered elegance. The menu is unpretentious and you can get a good three-course meal very reasonably. Starters, which include smoked mackerel at around 75p, range in price from 50p to £1.50. Main dishes include pork chop at £2, fillet of plaice at around £2.40 and mixed grill in the region of £3.50, all served with chipped or croquette potatoes, and there are various salads, all priced at £1.80. Desserts range from about 30p for ice cream-based sweets to 65p if you select from the trolley. For children there is a special 'Mr Menu' which includes a main meal, an orange, ice cream (and the colourful menu itself!), all for 85p or thereabouts.

THE GOLDEN BENGAL RESTAURANT, 39 Groat Market
(Newcastle-upon-Tyne 320471)
Open: Mon-Sat 12noon-2.30pm, 6-11.30pm, Sun 7-11pm

[C][♫][P][S]

Soft Indian background music and a décor of Indian murals capture an Oriental atmosphere in this city centre restaurant. Soup or fruit juice are followed by chicken curry, keema pillau with vegetable curry or roast chicken and vegetables, with a sweet or fruit to complete the meal. The à la carte menu contains a wealth of Indian specialities – curries mild and hot, medium hot or very hot – at around £2.35. Biriani dishes served with vegetable curry are in the £2.70-£3.80 range and Tandoori clay oven-cooked chicken or king prawns are around £2.80-£3.80. Fruit such as guava or mango served with fresh cream is about 65-75p.

RISTORANTE ROMA ✕
22 Collingwood Street
(Newcastle-upon-Tyne 320612)
Open: Mon-Sat 12noon-2.30pm, 7-11.30pm, Sun 7-11.30pm

[C][♫][P][S][⚘]

A Spanish guitarist entertains guests every night in this charming restaurant. As a gesture to Italian culture the menu has everything from chariot races to Chianti bottles and offers Sophia Loren (a juicy steak dish) and Gina Lollobrigida – the Chef's secret on a plate in the à la carte menu. Who could ask for more? Further temptations are artichoke hearts in a cream sauce and lobster mornay, plus a star-studded list of sweets headed by crêpes suzette and banana, peach or pineapple flambés. Midday budget items include lasagne or cannelloni for around £1.80, sole or chicken for around £2.50 with vegetables and sirloin steak for around £2.65 with vegetables!

Penrith

OLD VICTORIA HOTEL ★
46 Castlegate (Penrith 62467)
Open: Mon-Sun 12noon-2pm, 7-9.30pm

[♫] [P] [ ]

The two bar lounges of this quaint, roadside hotel are all aglow with crackling fires and old oak beams dripping pewter and brass. Meals such as prawn cocktail with brandy and cream, followed by steak, fish, gammon and other hot dishes, a ploughman's, various cold meat and smoked fish salads or sandwiches (ranging from approximately 50p-£5.50) may be taken here. At dinner time the same menu applies, but there's also a more expensive à la carte menu.

WAVERLEY HOTEL, Crown Square (Penrith 63962)
Open: summer: Mon 10am-2pm, 6.30-8.30pm, Tue-Sat 10am-8.30pm, Sun 12noon-2pm
winter: Mon-Sat 12noon-2pm, 7-8.30pm. Coffee Shop: summer only

[C] [P] [S]

On the fringe of the town centre is this very popular hotel dining room with a small, intimate cocktail bar. The attraction is very reasonably-priced home-made food and fresh vegetables. The main menu includes barbecued spare ribs, steak and kidney pie and beef curry, all for around £2 and a selection of pizzas for around £1.50. Various dishes of the day cost from £1, and there is a newly-opened cold buffet table from £1.25. A choice of home-made sweets cost about 75p.

Sunderland

THE MELTING POT, 9 Maritime Terrace (Sunderland 76909)
Open: Mon-Sat 12noon-2.30pm, 6pm-12mdnt

[C] [P] [S]

Peacock blue drapes covering three walls create a comfortable atmosphere in this intimate Indian restaurant situated in Sunderland's pedestrian precinct. The 'lunchtime special' menu, offering a choice of soup or fruit juice, ten traditional Indian dishes such as chicken or prawn curry, five English dishes including rump steak, plus sweet, is superb value at £1.50. The extensive à la carte is also well within our budget. Wine is not sold by the glass, but in a minimum of half-bottles at around £2.75 a time, so you would be wise to take a friend or two along.

Windermere

LODGE RESTAURANT, Ellerthwaite Lodge, New Road (Windermere 5115)
Open: Mon, Wed-Sun 10am-2pm, 3-10pm

[P] [ ]

The Lodge Restaurant makes an elegant addition to Mr and Mrs Hudson's Cumbrian hotel. Plain white walls are tastefully complemented by a wealth of warm reds – carpet, drapes, seating and tablecloths. The focal point of this restaurant, though, is a charcoal grill set into a plinth made of local stone and slate. At dinner the chef is at work on grills and flambé before your very eyes. Actually, during the evenings you have to choose carefully to keep within the budget, but soup, scampi, sweet and coffee make a very pleasant meal for around £4.50. At lunchtime it is a different story. Beef pie, moussaka and Cumberland sausage are just some of the excellent home-made main courses for only £1.50. Add soup at 45p and dessert (again all home-made) at around 60p and there will still be more than enough left in the kitty for 60p-worth of French house wine.

SCOTLAND

The fountain . Glasgow

Glencoe Hotel, Carnoustie

The Mill Hotel, Tynet

Soroba House Hotel, Oban

The Green Park Hotel, Pitlochry

'Away across the border in old Edinboro toon
A Scottish laddie said adieu to his wee Jessie Doon.
He wore a bunch of heather which she'd pluck'd for him that day,
And she said "Twill bring fond memories when you are far away,"
The laddie said, "My bonnie lass, aboot me dinna fret,
For you and dear 'Auld Reekie' well, I never can forget!"'

J F LAMBE

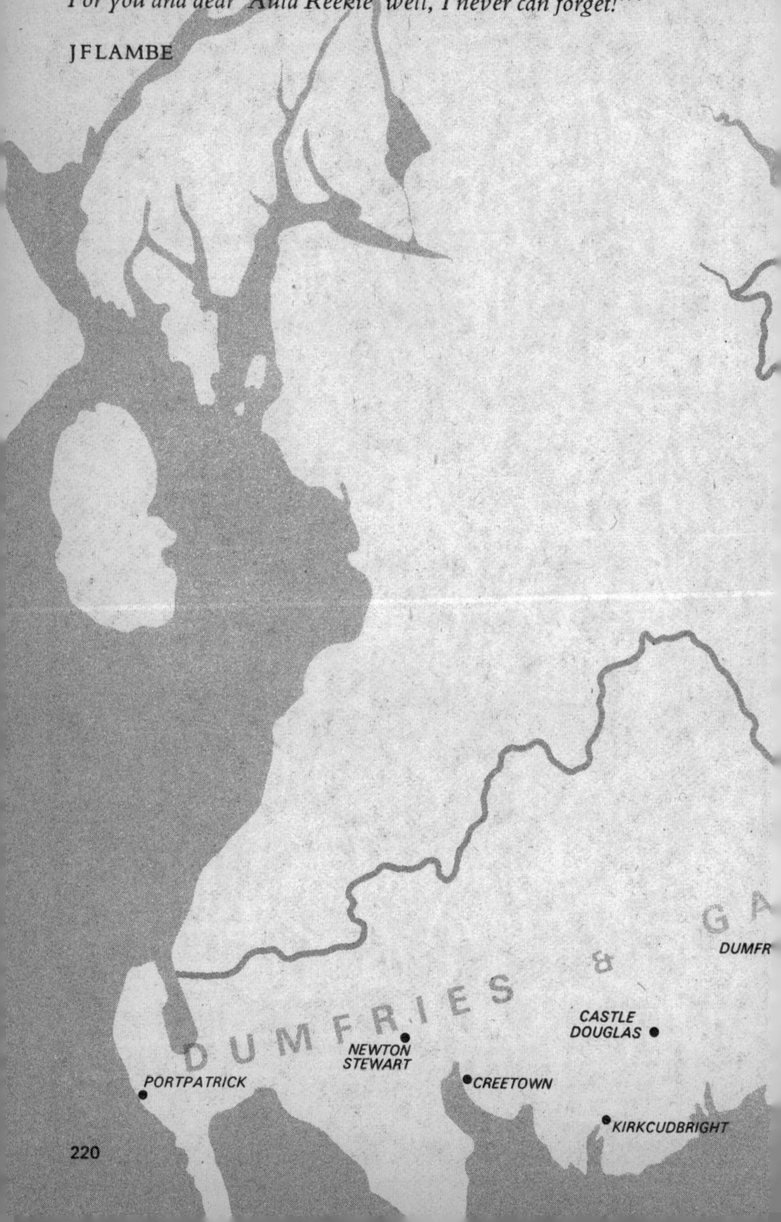

DUMFRIES &

CASTLE DOUGLAS

NEWTON STEWART

PORTPATRICK

CREETOWN

KIRKCUDBRIGHT

Edinburgh and the Border Regions

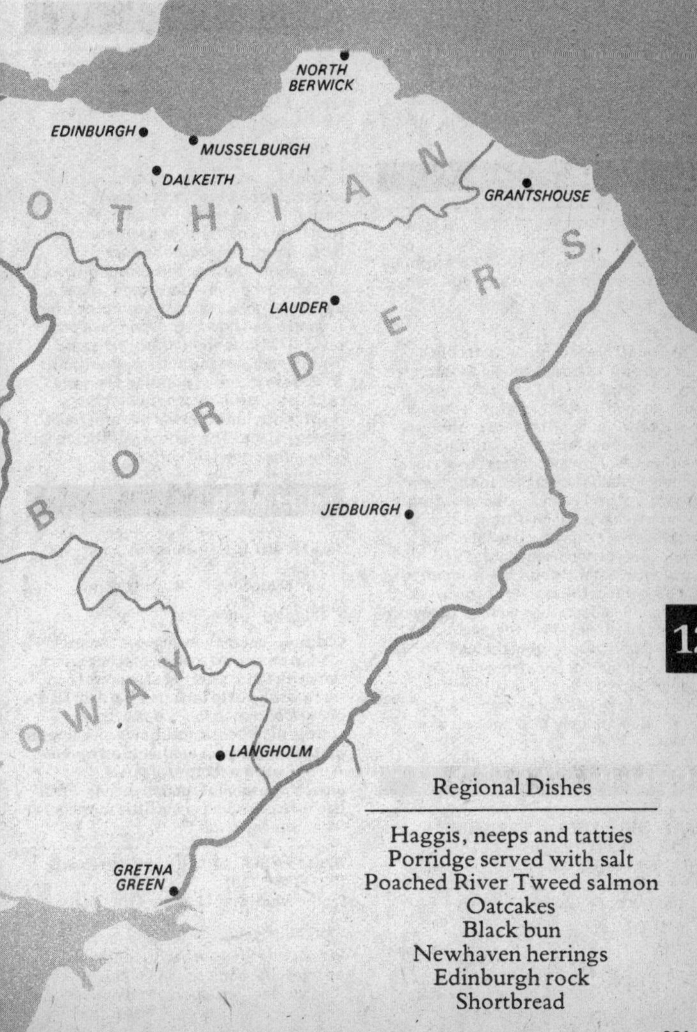

12

Regional Dishes

Haggis, neeps and tatties
Porridge served with salt
Poached River Tweed salmon
Oatcakes
Black bun
Newhaven herrings
Edinburgh rock
Shortbread

Castle Douglas

ROSE COTTAGE, Gelston (Castle Douglas 2513)
Open: Mon-Sun 9am-5pm

[P] [&]

This cottage restaurant, with its lovely gardens, in the rural village of Gelston, two miles south of Castle Douglas, is a veritable haven from the ravages of inflation. Where else could you enjoy soup, followed by gammon steak with chips and vegetables, plus home-made gâteau to finish, for about £3.50? Amazingly, children's portions bring this price down even lower. As well as a choice of nine main dishes, friendly owners Mr and Mrs Donaldson offer generous Devonshire teas for about £1. Coffee is about 25p a cup.

Creetown

CREETOWN ARMS HOTEL, St John Street (Creetown 282)
Open: summer: Mon-Sun 12.30-2pm, 7-9pm, winter: Mon-Sun 12.30-2pm, 7-8pm

[P] [&]

This small granite inn with its blue shutters dates from 1780 and is situated on the main road (A75), in this attractive village overlooking Wigtown Bay. A good range of Scottish fare is offered here with specialities including venison, Galloway beef and fresh local salmon. Meals are served in the bar or restaurant and prices vary accordingly. A typical bar meal costing around £2.85 might be egg mayonnaise followed by braised steak with vegetables and croquette potatoes and fresh cream trifle for dessert. In the restaurant you could have pâté maison followed by gammon steak and pineapple with meringue glacé and coffee for less than £5. For 50p extra you may choose from a more adventurous à la carte with such main courses as fillet of pork marsala and braised venison in port and red wine sauce.

Dalkeith

GIORGIO PIZZA & SPAGHETTI HOUSE, 128 High Street (031-663 4492)
Open: Mon-Sun 12noon-2.30pm, 5pm-1am

[C] [♫] [P] [S] [&]

Grapes, hanging bottles, wrought-ironwork and lighting by lanterns convey the atmosphere of an Italian bistro, and indeed owner Giorgio Crolla does come from a village near Rome. Pasta dishes are prevalent as may be expected, and £1.70 or so will buy a substantial main course such as lasagne al forno or spaghetti marenara. A three-course business lunch for around £1.85 offers exceptionally good value, and high teas are served from 5pm to 7pm. If you want a special meal, you may prefer to choose escalope Garibaldi or bistecca pizziola, either of which costs about £3.50.

Dumfries

OPUS, 95 Queensberry Street (Dumfries 5752)
Open: Mon-Wed, Fri-Sat 9am-5pm, Thu 9am-1pm

[P] [S] [&]

A bright, cosy restaurant decked out with red tables and much wood panelling, but tricky to locate. You'll find it up two flights of stairs above a fabric shop. Snacks are served throughout the day, but at lunchtimes a blackboard menu offers a bewildering variety of goodies. Take your pick from several salad bowls and cold meats for just £1. Or how about the hot dishes? Spicy vegetable pie and lasagne (both £1.25) are the most popular. Desserts, calculated to test a weightwatcher's resolve, include cheesecake and fresh cream gâteau. The eaterie is unlicensed, but try the excellent coffee.

Edinburgh

AEROGRILL, Edinburgh Airport (031-344 3272)
Open: Mon-Sun 11.30am-9.15pm

[C] [P] [S] [&]

Children, more than anyone, regard a visit to an airport as a special occasion, though a family outing of this sort can often work out to be rather hard on Dad's pocket. Not so if you lunch at the Aerogrill, where a children's menu with matching prices is available on request. Apart from a selection of grills, omelettes, salads and fish dishes, a full three-course meal costs little more than £4 in this restaurant.

BAR ITALIA, 100-104 Lothian Road (031-228 6379)
Open: Mon-Sun 12noon-4am

[♫] [P] [S] [&]

Pizza delle Stagioni, with tomatoes, mozzarella, ham, salami, clams, mushrooms, artichokes and green peppers, costs around £2.65 and you have a choice of twelve other varieties, the cheapest being a pizza margherita for about £1.55. In the same price range you can choose from fifteen pasta dishes, and there are also a number of more straightforward dishes such as roast chicken with chips (£3) or grilled sirloin with chips at around £4. A starter and sweet could add two or three pounds to the bill, but if you're watching the pennies you could choose soup and ice cream (the cheapest choices).

BAR ROMA, 39a Queensferry Street (031-226 2977)
Open: Mon-Sat 12noon-3am, Sun 5pm-3am

S ♧

This bright, spacious restaurant-cum-pizzeria is a sister to the Bar Italia in another part of the city. A very good selection of Italian dishes appear on the menu at fairly keen prices. Risotto con funghi (rice with mushrooms) at £2.10 and penne piccanti (hot chili and tomato sauce) at £1.85 are examples of the pasta range. There are over a dozen different pizzas, varying in price from £1.75-£3. Desserts start at 65p, rising past assorted gâteaux at £1.20 to affocato al cognac at £1.50. If you indulge in some of these fancier desserts (and why not?) you'll probably need to forgo the antipasto (starter). Flavoursome expresso coffee is 40p but for the liqueur variety add £1.

CAFÉ CAPPUCCINO, 15 Salisbury Place (031-667 4265)
Open: Mon-Sat 9am-8.30pm

P S ♧

The menu includes a wide variety of omelettes, salads, toasted sandwiches and filled rolls, all very reasonably priced, and if you are looking for a real meal there is an equally wide choice of fish or meat dishes which, with vegetables, mostly cost between £1 and £2.50. There is a good selection of ice-cream confections with prices around 50p. The Café Cappuccino is not licensed but you can take your pick from a range of twenty non-alcoholic beverages of which frothy cappuccino coffee is one choice.

LE CHÂTEAU, Castle Terrace (031-229 1181)
Open: Mon-Sat 12noon-2.30pm, 6-11pm

C ♫ ♧

From its impressive frontage you might expect Le Château prices to be well above our limit, but Bill and Bridget Morgan's restaurant is recommended for good food at reasonable prices, for its bright and comfortable interior, and friendly atmosphere. Starters include a house pâté, prawn cocktail for around £1.10 and piping-hot soup at 50p or so. There is a choice of four or five dishes and of the usual grills at around £4. Among the house specialities are lasagne and chicken.

CRAWFORD'S, 31 Frederick Street (031-225 4579)
Open: summer: Mon-Sat 8am-11pm (7pm winter)

S ♧

This is one of the very handy Crawford's chain of restaurants, catering for families and shoppers. The ground-floor restaurant's décor has a country theme with pine wood and terra-cotta ceramic tiles. As with most Crawford's you can get a quick and reasonably-priced meal from the attractively laid out cold counter, or if you prefer, there is a tempting range of flans, pies and casseroles. To finish with, the range of gâteaux befits one of Scotland's best known bakeries.

DANISH KITCHEN, 124 Princes Street (031-226 6669)
Open: Mon-Sat 9.30am-4.50pm

S ♧

On the mezzanine floor of Austin Reed at the west end of Princes Street, the self-service Danish Kitchen provides very good food at a reasonable price, in most pleasant and comfortable surroundings. You can choose from freshly-made soup, Danish open sandwiches, salads, toasted sandwiches and omelettes. There is a tempting selection of sweets and freshly-baked pastries, and beverages include tea, coffee, fruit drinks, and milk shakes. Indeed a satisfying meal here need cost no more than £2.50 including wine.

DENZLER'S ✕✕ 80 Queen Street (031-226 5467/5227)
Open: Mon-Sat 12noon-2pm, 6.30-9.50pm

S

The Swiss origins of the Denzler husband-and-wife team are revealed in both wine list and menu. Lunchtime starters at around 40p include unusual fruit juices such as blackcurrant or apricot, main courses such as escalope de porc Cordon Bleu and êntrecote chasseur cost from around £2.50 including potatoes or rice. Exciting sweets such as banana à la Grùyere, wild strawberry sorbet or blueberry cheesecake cost around £1. Dinner menu is even more adventurous and more expensive – you'll find it difficult to keep within our limit.

THE DORIC TAVERN ✕ 15-16 Market Street (031-225 1084)
Open: Mon-Sat 12noon-2.30pm, 6-9.30pm

[S]

If local lawyers and journalists gather in a restaurant, it's a sure sign that you'll get value for money. With a set three-course lunch for under £3 and four-course dinner for under £4, prices are hard to beat. Filling British dishes such as boiled silverside and dumplings or haggis and turnips are featured. The extensive à la carte, which includes an excellent mixed grill for about £2.50, is also very good value. Mr McGuffie, proprietor for the last quarter-century, believes in traditional service.

FORTROSE GRILL, 71 Rose Street (031-225 8012)
Open: summer: Mon-Sat 11am-10pm, Sun 12.30-10pm, winter: closed Sun

[S] [⚲]

Rose Street, with its boutiques and up-market restaurants is the 'in' shopping and eating area of Edinburgh. The Fortrose Grill is small and simple, the welcome and service friendly and informal. There is a good-value business lunch at about £2 and the à la carte menu is quite reasonable, with soup and 'fruity' starters up to 50p. Salads, pastas, and omelettes are in the £2-£3 range and a mixed grill of steak, sausage, bacon, tomato, mushroom and chips is one of the most expensive meals at around £4.40. Sweets are variations on the theme of ice cream, coffee is around 30p. The menu finishes with the words 'Servis non compris' which doesn't mean 'I don't understand how the washing machine works' but suggests discretion when tipping.

MADOGS, 38 George Street (031-225 3408)
Open: Mon-Sat 12noon-3pm, 6pm-1am

[C] [♫] [S]

This is very much a Latin-American restaurant, a visit to which is like an express trip to the USA. There is an interesting menu which includes dishes made from materials specially imported from the States by the young American owners. The staff are American and Mexican, friendly, and efficient. The lunch menu includes beefy American burgers at £2.60, and at dinner time a portion of paella will cost around £4. Exotic cocktails complete the transatlantic experience.

THE PANCAKE PLACE, 130 High Street (031-225 1972)
Open: Mon-Sat 10am-6pm, (9pm summer) Sun 11am-9pm

[♫] [S] [🍷]

Occupying a prime position in the city's historic Royal Mile, this restaurant, as its name suggests, specialises in pancakes large and small, sweet or savoury. The limited range of starters offers soup of the day or fruit juice at prices around 35p. You then launch into the mind-blowing array of savoury pancakes; hot ones with such fillings as haddock Mornay, bacon and maple syrup (an American favourite), and chicken curry, all under £2, and a selection of 'cool crisp salads', cheeses, ham, chicken or egg, served with two thin pancakes, mayonnaise or pickle on a bed of lettuce, tomato or cucumber for around the same price. If you have enough room to spare (the menu does warn that all sweet pancakes can ruin your diet) try an 'American' – three sweet pancakes layered with butter and served with a jug of maple syrup for about £1.50. A couple of 'spoon size' pancakes topped with sliced banana and cream cost 80p.

POST HOUSE HOTEL ☆☆☆
Corstorphine Road (031-334 8221)
Open: Coffee Shop: Mon-Sun 12.30-10pm

[C] [P] [S] [🍷]

Very handy for the zoo, this bright and modern coffee shop serves anything from large and colourful double-decker sandwiches to a three-course meal. Try soup at 65p, followed by an omelette, burger or salad at around £2, and finish with cheesecake or sherry trifle at 75p. Babies are well-catered for here with 'strained dinner' or boiled egg and buttered fingers – and everything consumed within earshot of the animals!

THE QUERNSTONE, 4-8 Lochrin Buildings (031-229 5319)
Open: Restaurant: Mon-Sat 12noon-2.30pm, 5-10pm. Ice-cream Parlour: Mon-Sat 10.30am-10pm, Sun 1-9pm

[C] [♫] [P] [S] [🍷]

Juicy steaks and American burgers feature at The Quernstone, a restaurant and ice cream parlour famous hereabouts for its ice cream and extremely popular – particularly with King's Theatre folk, both audiences and performers – for its good, but inexpensive, home-cooked food. Italian dishes include various spaghettis at around £2.75 and pizziola steak at around £4. Boniburgers and Quernstoneburger Specials are around the £2 mark.

THE STABLE BAR, Mortonhall Park, 30 Frogston Road East
(031-664 0773)
Open: normal licensing hours
Restaurant: Mon-Sat 12noon-2pm

[♫] [P] [🍷]

Adjacent to the Mortonhall Caravan Park but occupying an 18th-century coach house, this bar/restaurant is situated in an extremely pleasant environment.Open for lunches only, the daily changing menu offers a limited choice but good value for money. A typical lunch gives the choice of two starters, three main courses and two sweets, the most expensive combination being pâté, braised ham with vegetables and gâteau which would cost around £3.40. With the addition of coffee this meal will still be around £4.

TATTOO GRILL, ROYAL SCOT HOTEL ☆☆☆☆ 111 Glasgow Road
(031-334 9191)
Open: Mon-Sun 12noon-2.30pm, 6-9.30pm

[C] [♫] [P] [🍷]

Pick your dishes from an interesting menu garnished with Scottish dialect. A simple Angus steak rejoices in the name of the Aberdonian, whereas scampi in batter is known as the Oban Bay Trawl. Other choices are the 'wee tasties' (sandwiches), 'cauld cuts' (a selection of cold meats and salad) and various sweets such as vanilla ice cream with whisky flavoured butterscotch and shortbread. A posh terrace restaurant in the same hotel offers a weekday-only set lunch at around £5.50.

TWO INNS, 26 Frederick Street
(031-225 2103)
Open: Mon-Sat 12noon-2.30pm, 5-10.30pm (11pm Fri), Sun 12.30-2pm, 6-10pm

[C] [🍷]

This is one of the Stakis Organisation steakhouses, and typical of its kind, offering a starter of soup, pâté or prawn cocktail, and sweets of peach melba, gâteau or apple pie inclusive in the cost of the main course. Haddock, gammon, chicken, or beefburger are under £4, steaks £5-£6, and all are served with jacket or chipped potatoes and peas. Lunchtime prices are £2-£4. Two Inns is in the heart of Edinburgh, just off Princes Street. It is spacious, and ideal for the family, with a three-course children's menu for £1.45.

Grantshouse

CEDAR CAFETERIA
(Grantshouse 270)
Open: Mon-Fri 7am-7pm,
Sat-Sun 9am-6pm
¼ mile south off A1

[P] [🍷]

A small, family-run roadside café which impressed our inspector with its spotlessness, and the fact that all food is freshly prepared on the premises. Main courses always available are roast beef, mixed grill, gammon steak and sirloin steak from £1.50-£2.50. The hot and cold sweets are well above the usual cafeteria standard, with fresh strawberries and ice cream or banana split firm favourites with the many regular customers.

Gretna Green

THE AULD SMIDDY RESTAURANT
Headless Cross (Gretna 365)
Open: summer only: 8am-7pm

[P] [S] [🍷]

Although you can no longer elope here with your sweetheart, you can enjoy a pleasant snack or full meal at very reasonable prices. Tucked just behind the world-famous blacksmith's shop, this low-ceilinged restaurant is festooned with brass bric-à-brac. A three-course lunch (which might consist of soup, roast beef with horseradish sauce, followed by apple tart) is still under £3, so even with coffee (25p) and a glass of wine (55p) you are well within the budget. In the early evening a high tea menu offers a variety of grills and cold meats from £2.30-£4.

Jedburgh

THE CARTER'S REST ✕ Abbey Place
(Jedburgh 3414)
Open: Mon-Sun 12noon-2pm, 6-9pm
(closed Sun in winter)

[♫] [P] [🍷]

This restaurant is built of stone plundered from the nearby Abbey, whose ruins dominate the outlook, and was the local 'Penny' School for a hundred years or so from 1779, then a real Carter's Rest for patrons of Jedburgh's horse fair. Today it offers excellent grills, bar lunches and dinners, as well as a popular Sunday cold buffet or traditional Scottish high tea. You can eat à la carte very well for around £5 here, stick to table d'hôte (at lunchtime three courses will cost £4, two courses £3.50) or make do with bar snacks. Hot buffet lunch specials include beef olives with trimmings at about £2.40, a £1.20 ham omelette, American-style burgers made with Scotch beef or a fresh Eyemouth haddock fish platter.

Kirkcudbright

THE COFFEE POT, 5 Castle Street
(Kirkcudbright 30569)
Open: summer only: Mon-Sat
10am-5pm, 6.45-8.30pm

[C] [S] [🍷]

The Coffee Pot with its bow-windowed frontage is a snug little restaurant just across from the old castle in the centre of historic Kirkcudbright. George and Rona Bower have devised an interesting à la carte menu to tempt the tourist and shopper alike at prices of around £5. Starters include mushrooms provençale and seven main courses include fried local trout, seafood crêpes and chicken Kiev. Raspberries St Moritz and crêpes Suzette are desserts.

Langholm

TH' AULD ACQUAINTANCE, 88 High Street (Langholm 80573)
Open: Wed-Sat 10.30am-8pm
Sun 10.30am-7pm

[P] [S] [wine]

Wood panelling, Regency wall-lamps and oak beams add a definite character to this homely, L-shaped restaurant. You can choose from four starters (from 55p-£1.25), and follow with any one of a dozen fish and meat grills, which range from £1.95 to £4 (except sirloin steak at just over £5). Trolley-borne sweets are around 75p, whilst half bottles of wine from the list start at £1.50. For those just feeling peckish, a snack menu offers sandwiches and rolls at modest prices.

Lauder

THE BLACK BULL HOTEL
(Lauder 208)
Open: Mon-Sun 8am-9.30pm
and normal licensing hours

[music] [P] [wine]

The jangle of harness and sound of posthorns no longer announces the arrival of travellers in need of rest and refreshment, yet The Black Bull retains the atmosphere of a coaching inn. Built in the 18th century, it survived the coming of the railways and has been revived and modernised to cope with the swing back to road transport. In the elegant dining room you can enjoy lunch and dinner at around £4.50 with five or six main dishes including roasts. For a cold meal or snack, try the Harness Room Grill, where you can feast your eyes on relics of coaching days whilst enjoying your choice from the bar menu. This includes a three-course lunch at around £2.55 and ploughman's at about £1.

Musselburgh

CAPRICE, 198 High Street
(031-665 2991)
Open: summer: Mon-Sat 12noon-12mdnt, Sun 4pm-12mdnt, winter: Mon-Sat 12noon-2.30pm, 5.30-12mdnt, Sun 4pm-12mdnt

[music] [P] [S] [wine]

'Our succulent pizzas are cooked in the traditional manner in a wood-fired oven to give them that extra taste of quality. Even the wood used, Scottish pine, is chosen because it adds the required flavour. . . .' That's how Cavalier Victor

Alongi introduces his customers to his pizzeria cum Italian restaurant. The sixteen different home-made pizza specialities have deservedly gained Victor and his son Alfredo a renowned reputation. A medium-sized pizza (12in diameter) provides a very generous meal for the average eater, but for those with voracious appetites the large pizza (15in) will prove a challenge. A choice from the extensive à la carte menu costs around £5 but two table d'hôte lunch menus offer good value at around £1.50 for three courses.

Newton Stewart

THE SALAD BOWL, 8 Albert Street
(Newton Stewart 3026)
Open: Mon-Sat 10am-6.30pm, 8-10.45pm (10pm Etr-Oct)

[S]

You're assured of a warm welcome at this pleasant little restaurant, which is ideally placed to catch all the town's passing trade. Inside, the rough-cast walls are ornamented by hanging plants, display cabinets and an antique clock. Tables are of wood with laminated tops. The lunch menu consists of soup, followed by a hot dish such as omelette and chips for a mere £1.25 including coffee. Fish predominates on the high tea menu, with a deep-fried haddock, for instance, costing £2.30 (again including a hot drink). In the evening a more adventurous, up-market menu offers a wide choice of starters and main dishes, but still within the budget if you choose carefully (eg stuffed tomato, trout meunière and apple tart is around £4.50).

North Berwick

LA BONBONNIERE, 1 Station Hill
(North Berwick 3622)
Open: Mon-Wed 10am-6pm, Thu-Sat 10am-10pm, Sun 11am-6pm

[P]

Tapestries by owner Mrs Moss lend a personal touch to the stone-walled, homely interior of this small, street-level coffee shop. This is a family concern, with true home cooking and friendly atmosphere. Good, basic meals such as liver and onions, casserole, or mince, are suitably priced; three courses will cost around £3. La Bonbonnière is newly licensed and has a small selection of good wine.

Portpatrick

THE OLD MILL HOUSE
(Portpatrick 358)
Open: Apr-Oct: Mon-Sun 10.30am-10pm

[P] [ ]

This picturesque, whitewashed old mill house, set amid beautiful gardens complete with trout stream and heated outdoor pool, ground its last barley in 1929 and the miller is said to haunt the premises still. Food includes a table d'hôte lunch menu of good British fare costing something over £3. A luscious Galloway steak can be sampled from the à la carte menu for about £4.50 and fresh Solway salmon is another tempting local dish. An interesting bar menu offers a wide selection of less pricey dishes including special children's meals for around 70p for such favourites as bangers, fish or pizza fingers with salad or chips. A three-course children's menu for younger hungers costs around £1.60. High teas range from around £2.70 to £4.70 according to the main dish chosen, with cheese and egg salad at the lower end and grilled sirloin steak at the top. This price is inclusive of hot home-baked scones with butter and jam, home-baked cakes and tea. All melons, cucumbers and tomatoes are grown on the premises for restaurant use.

Glasgow and the West

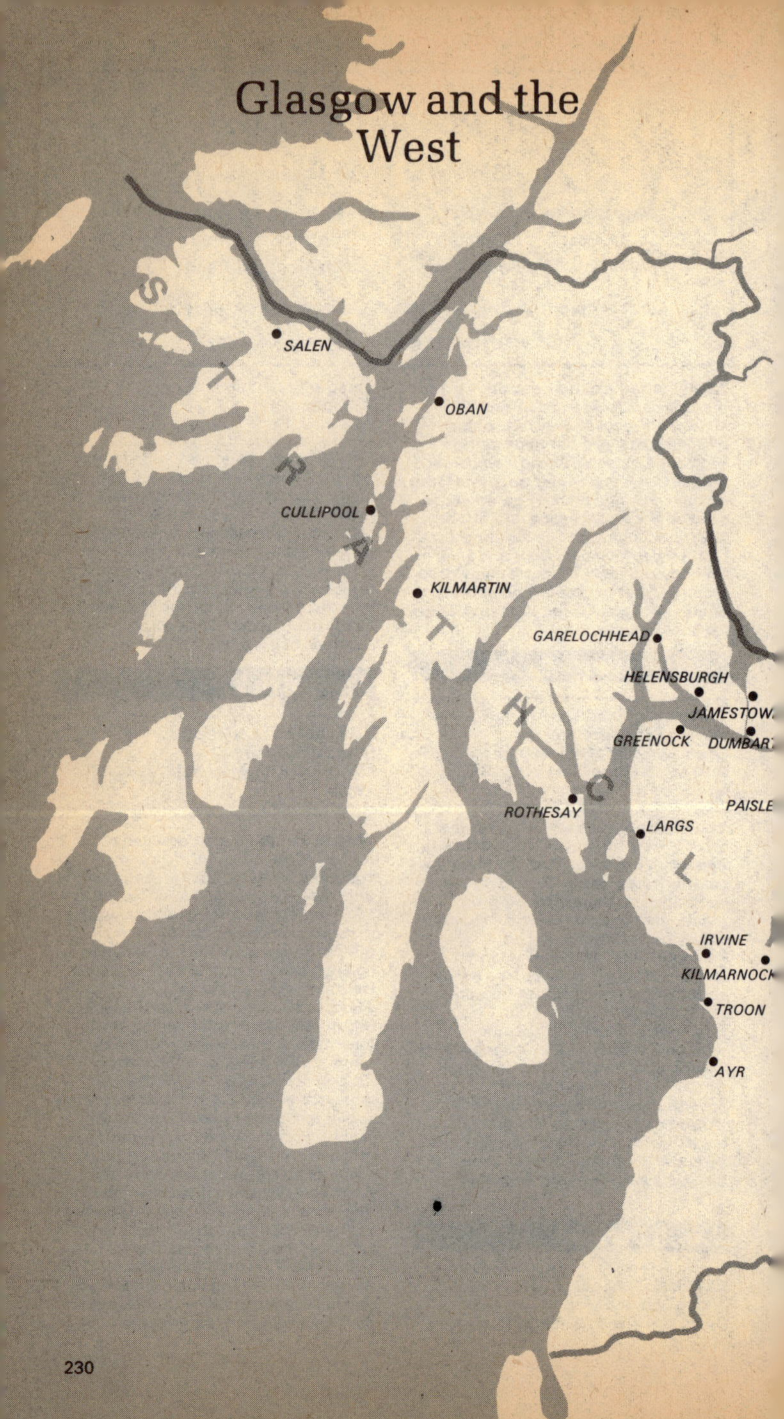

'Oh, ye'll tak' the high road, and I'll tak' the low road,
And I'll be in Scotland afore ye,
But me and my true love will never meet again,
On the bonny, bonny banks o' Loch Lomond.'

TRADITIONAL

Regional Dishes

Cock-a-leekie soup
Howtowdie (casseroled chicken)
Ayrshire roll
Cloutie dumpling (sweet boiled pudding)
Loch Fyne kippers
Rumbledethumps (Scottish bubble and squeak)

Ayr

THE BEEFHOUSE, Station Hotel ★★★
Burns Statue Square
(Ayr 263268)
Open: Mon-Thu 7-10pm,
Fri-Sat 7-11pm, Sun 12.30-2.30pm

[C] [♫] [P] [S]

One of a chain of Reo Stakis eating houses, this spacious restaurant has over sixty pine tables, individually lit to create a very attractive setting. Overhead, two large arches give the low ceiling a pleasing vault-like effect. With main courses being chiefly beefsteak, there's need to select carefully if you're not to exceed the budget. However, farmhouse-style Scotch broth (60p), cold roast beef and a crisp salad (£3.95) and a fresh fruit salad (95p) will just leave you enough for a coffee with cream.

THE COFFEE CLUB, 37 Beresford Terrace (Ayr 63239)
Open: Mon-Sat 10am-10pm

[♫] [P] [S]

This small and friendly establishment is situated near to Burns' Statue Square in the centre of Ayr. The clubby atmosphere extends to comfortable seating and low-level tables, making this a place to relax while you take your meal. An interesting variety of snacks, salads and light meals are served with a creative flair. Snacks range from pizza to substantial open sandwiches and there are a number of filling dishes such as ravioli, risotto, or chili con carne at around £1.70, and for the same price you can have a portion of savoury flan with salad. Sweets include pastries, fruit flan, and waffles, at around 50p.

THE COPPERFIELD
242 Prestwick Road (Ayr 267905)
Open: summer: Mon-Sat 10am-8pm
winter: Mon-Sat 10am-5pm

[C] [P] [S]

David himself would have felt quite at home amid the dark wooden beams of this pseudo-Dickensian eating house. Doubtless; he would have tucked into home-baked goodies (proprietor Mrs Holland's forté) with relish. Menu prices, although alas a long way from Mr Micawber's ideas on costs, are very low indeed. A full three-course meal is still only around £2 – remarkable considering all prices include VAT. Meals are traditional – roast beef, potatoes and veg, haddock, chips and veg or ham and peach salad – the kind of choice to suit a whole family's tastes. Even sirlion steak with all the trimmings comes to under £5 with soup to start with and strawberry flan and cream to finish.

OLDE WORLDE INN
48 Newmarket Street (Ayr 62392)
Open: Mon-Sat 12noon-2.30pm,
5-11pm, Sun 5-10pm

[C] [♫] [P] [S]

Whether Robbie Burns, whose statue stands some 100 yards away, would have felt at home in this 'olde worlde inn' is debatable, but he would have been assured of a good basic meal at a fair price. This member of the Reo Stakis chain has panelled walls and beams, with a rough stone archway creating a break in the interior. Main course prices include a starter, but sweets are extra. However, haddock, chicken, gammon or beefsteak burger, all for around £3 should fill you up and keep you within the budget. The special lunchtime menu is particularly good value, at around £2, and includes in the main course choice lasagne and spaghetti bolognese.

PLOUGH INN, 231 High Street
(Ayr 62578)
Open: Mon-Sun 11am-2.30pm, 5-11pm

[C] [S]

This Reo Stakis 'Olde Worlde' Inn is typical of the chain, with almost a North American flavour in its mellow lighting and unostentatious but comfortable furnishings. In the restaurant, a waitress-served meal of Scotch broth, prawn cocktail, pâté or fruit juice, followed by a main course such as steak, chicken or haddock costs around £4 (including appropriate vegetables, potatoes and a roll or chunky bread and butter). Apple pie and cream or Black Forest gâteau cost around 75p. There is a three-course children's menu too, for little more than £1, making this a good place to take the family. House wines are available by the carafe or glass.

THE TUDOR RESTAURANT
6-8 Beresford Terrace (Ayr 61404)
Open: Mon-Sat 9am-9pm

[P] [S]

The Tudor Restaurant may not be authentic 16th century, but for the family it offers a good wholesome meal at very reasonable prices. A table d'hôte lunch is still around £2 and includes soup or fruit juice, a main course such as beefsteak pie, cold meat with salad, or haddock and chips, and a sweet or cheese. There is a special children's menu at around £1.25. High tea, which comes with a pot of tea, bread, scone, jam and a cake (all home-baked), gives a considerable choice, from eggs on toast at around £1.80 to entrecôte steak at around £3.50, and again there is a children's version for considerably less. The restaurant is not licensed.

Cullipool

LONGHOUSE BUTTERY, Isle of Luing (Luing 209)
Open: Mon-Sun 11am-5pm, Thu-Sat 7.30-11pm

[P]

It's well worth the journey from the Scottish mainland across the Island of Seil and then the 90-second car ferry to this beautiful little island of Luing. The high spot of a visit must be this converted, whitewashed croft which incorporates a white and pine-clad restaurant with dispense bar and small gallery where partner Edna Whyte displays and sells gifts bearing her 'Old Rectory' designs. The other half of the partnership, Audrey Stone, is to be seen serving the delicious meals including such delicacies as buttery venison pâté, and fresh Luing prawns, served on wholemeal bread with crispy salad. Home-made sweets include the mouthwatering triple meringue with cream for 95p. A three-course lunch with coffee and wine costs in the region of £4.20. Unfortunately, the special dinner, including fresh lobster or salmon, would over-stretch our pocket.

Cumbernauld

OLD WORLD INN, Allanfauld Road (Seafar 27509)
Open: Mon-Sat 12noon-2.30pm, 5-11pm, Sun 12noon-2.30pm, 6.30-11pm

[C] [P] [&]

Situated on the west side of Cumbernauld, on a hill overlooking the main Glasgow/Stirling road, this restaurant is typical of the Stakis Steakhouse chain to which it belongs. Decorated in mock-Tudor style with beams and dark-wood furnishings, the room exudes a restful, relaxing atmosphere. Each main course on the menu incorporates in its price a choice of starters (farmhouse broth, country pâté, prawn cocktail or orange juice). Haddock, gammon steak and roast half chicken, all with suitable accompaniments, cost around £3.50, and for just below £5, you could enjoy a ½lb prime Angus steak. To finish with there is a choice of dessert or the cheeseboard for about 75p, or a speciality ice cream such as Bavarian black cherry for around 65p. Children get a good deal here with three courses, plus roll and butter and a choice of cola or orange drink, for less than £1.50.

Cumnock

THE ROYAL HOTEL ★★
1 Glaisnock Street (Cumnock 20822)
Open: Mon-Sat 12noon-2pm, 5-6.30pm, 7-9pm, Sun 12.30-2.30pm, 5-6.30pm, 7-9pm

[P] [S] [&]

It is a well-deserved compliment to this traditional and comfortable hotel that local businesspeople are regular customers. In the attractively lit dining room, a conventional choice of dishes is very well presented, and very well priced. Three lunch courses focusing on roast sirloin (with perhaps banana fritters or green figs with cream to follow) will not cost much over £3, and even if you go for the fresh salmon, you'll still be spending well under £5. The very substantial high tea might cost £4.50 for a mixed grill, tea, scones, and cakes. Dinner will be around the £5 mark.

Dumbarton

STAKIS STEAKHOUSE, New Shopping Centre (Dumbarton 64855)
Open: Mon-Sat 11am-2.30pm, 5-11pm

[C] [S] [&]

This restaurant is typical of the Stakis Steakhouse chain with its rustic, old-world décor. Situated in a spacious modern building, it overlooks the shopping centre's main square with its decorative pond and restored industrial engine. The food, as in all Stakis restaurants, is consistent in quantity and quality. Here, two people can have lunch of Scotch broth, fried fillet of haddock, French fries, peas and tomato, roll and butter, and coffee and the bill would just top the £5. A dessert of hot apple pie with cream or peach melba would bring the cost of each person's meal nearer to the £3 mark. All main course prices include starter and chunky bread or roll and butter, and in the evening a prime Angus steak with all the trimmings would cost about £4.95 – coffee and dessert extra. A children's choice menu includes soup, main course such as beefsteak burger or roast quarter chicken, ice cream with strawberry sauce and a choice of orange or cola drinks all for under £1.50.

East Kilbride

HONG KONG, 46-48 Kirkton Park (East Kilbride 20112)
Open: Mon-Sat 12noon-12mdnt, Sun 2pm-12mdnt

[C] [♫] [P]

A patio garden allows al fresco eating in summer, a touch which gives this Chinese restaurant a certain individuality. Inside, décor is unmistakably oriental with golden dragons set against black walls, and the à la carte is extensive and fairly typical, but it's the speciality teas, desserts and wine list which makes this restaurant stand out from the rest. Excellent value is the three-course business lunch at only £1.75, or the tasty salads and ploughman's at 60p-£1. You'll have to choose carefully if you're to keep within the limit on the à la carte menu but the set dinners, comprising six courses, coffee with cream and mint chocolate, offer excellent value at around £5. If you forgo the starter on the à la carte menu you might just afford a special sweet such as the Hong Kong Special – a delicate concoction of peaches, sparkling wine, soda water and angostura bitters costing £2.70 for two persons. Otherwise save your pennies for one of the sixteen unusual teas such as 'gunpowder green tea' described as an 'attractive clear fragrant liquor' at £1 per pot for two, and a cocktail from the imaginative list of twenty nine.

STAKIS STEAKHOUSE, Princes Square (East Kilbride 23222)
Open: Mon-Sat 12noon-2.30pm, 5-11pm

[C] [P] [S] [🍷]

Stakis are renowned for providing good, fast food, freshly cooked and not overpriced. Sirloin steak at around £5 includes peas, chips or baked potato and a starter. Alternatives are haddock, chicken or gammon. Sweets or cheese are around 75p. Situated in the middle of a modern shopping centre in Scotland's oldest 'new' town, this steakhouse is convenient and well-used by families and businesspeople.

Garelochhead

RISTORANTE AUGUSTO, Main Street (Garelochhead 810570)
Open: summer: Tue-Sun 12noon-3pm, 6.30-9.30pm, winter: Tue-Sat 7-9.30pm

[C] [♫] [P] [S]

An unassuming little Italian restaurant on the main road, distinguished by the charm and enterprise of proprietor Augusto Vitrano. He provides a novel contrast to an otherwise traditional Italian atmosphere as at weekends he sings, dances and generally entertains his customers, dressed in his kilt! The limited menu is pasta and pizza-based and a three course meal of minestrone soup, spaghetti vongole (with clams, onion and tomato) and zabaglione (traditional sweet made with egg yolks, sugar and Marsala), including a cup of espresso coffee, is just within our budget.

Glasgow

AD-LIB (MID ATLANTIC)
111 Hope Street (041-248 7102)
Open: Mon-Sat 12noon-2am, Sun 6pm-1am

[C] [♫] [S] [🍷]

With stainless steel floor (yes floor) and furniture, painted brick and hessian-hung walls covered with original movie posters of yesteryear, checked tablecloths and excellent service from friendly staff, this American diner, opposite Glasgow Central Station, is a good place for a quick lunch or a leisurely evening meal. A selection of American hamburgers, served with chips, salad and a choice of pickles, is available. Hamburgers are available at prices from around £2.50. Main courses include kebabs, vegetarian pancakes, and Texas-style chili and prices range from £2 to around £6 – the latter for a T-bone steak with accompanying vegetables. Sweets include pancakes with hot fudge and cream, and American cheesecake with fruit and cream, which explains perhaps, the diner's popularity with children. A business lunch of ¼lb hamburger with potatoes and salad, pancake, and coffee is available at the £2 mark – excellent value.

LA BUCA, 191 Hope Street (041-332 7120)
Open: Mon-Sat 12noon-11pm

[🍷]

There is a definite Italian air to this pleasant pizzeria in the heart of Glasgow, accentuated by the Italian background music and the red-shirted Italian waiters. Pizzas are freshly prepared and range in price from around £1.10 for pizza Napolitana to £1.40 for pizza Quattro Stajioni, a delicious concoction of ham, olives, anchovies and mozzarella cheese. With a starter of insalata di mare (seafood

Savour Eastern Flavour

Savour delights suited to the taste of a mandarin in the Hong Kong restaurant. Although a little off the main thoroughfare, the Hong Kong is heading in the direction for the connoisseur. It is a Chinese restaurant that is aiming for individuality.

The Hong Kong have concocted a menu that is easily on par with others and includes a few dishes special to themselves for European and Chinese tastes. What really distinguishes the Hong Kong from others is its astounding wine list, and inventive cocktails. You could be about to spoil yourself if you dine at the Hong Kong.

HONG KONG RESTAURANT

46-48 KIRKTON PARK,
EAST KILBRIDE

TELEPHONE 20112

salad) at about £1.50 and figs with fresh cream for dessert for around 65p, a satisfying three-course meal here need cost no more than £2.50. If you don't like pizza there are many other grills or pasta dishes to choose from such as sirloin steak with salad (more expensive at £3.80 or so) or lasagne all forno at £1.50.

THE CARVERY, EXCELSIOR HOTEL
★★★★ Glasgow Airport (041-887 1212)
Open: Mon-Fri 12noon-2.30pm, 6.30-10pm, Sat-Sun 12.30-2.30pm, 6.30-10pm

[C] [P] [S] [🍷]

If you are flying out, or meeting new arrivals to Glasgow, what better place to while away the time than in this modern carvery, situated just a hundred yards from the main terminal building. Suitably soundproofed to exclude all aircraft noise, the restaurant is a spacious room with comfortable seating and modern décor. A standard carvery menu is offered for lunch and dinner with an additional charge of about 50p in the evening. The chef will carve from a choice of beef, lamb or pork and there are the traditional accompaniments: roast potatoes and a selection of vegetables. Starter, sweet and coffee are included in the set prices of £6.25 and £6.55 for lunch and dinner respectively.

COPRA, 336 Argyle Street
(041-221 2460)
Open: Mon-Sat 9am-7pm

[C] [S]

Mr Joe Guidi has acquired a loyal and regular clientele since his family took over the Copra almost twenty years ago. Regular favourites such as lamb chops (two) and spaghetti bolognese appear on the otherwise varied menu each day, but there is also an extensive selection of entrées that changes daily offering such dishes as curried chicken, grilled rainbow trout with lemon or roast lamb. With both starters and sweets at around 50p it is not impossible to have a very satisfying meal here for around £2.50. Whilst this restaurant closes early, Mr Guidi also operates, and welcomes you to the Alhambra Restaurant, 350 Argyle Street, which stays open until 10.30pm and offers a similar menu.

DELTA RESTAURANT
283 Sauchiehall Street (041-332 3661)
Open: Mon-Sat 10am-7.30pm

[♫] [S] [🍷]

Situated at the western end of Sauchiehall Street, this tartan-floored basement restaurant with pine-clad walls welcomes you with soft music for a three-course meal which includes such wholesome dishes as Loch Fyne herrings in oatmeal or sizzling roast pork with apple sauce at around £3. Smart waitresses serve morning coffee, lunch and, after three o'clock, high tea consists of a main dish such as fried fillet of haddock with French fried potatoes plus a pot of tea and buttered toast for about £2.40.

HANSOM BAR, THE FOUNTAIN RESTAURANT
2 Woodside Crescent (041-332 6396)
Open: Mon-Fri 12noon-2.15pm, 6.15-10.15pm; Sat 6.15-10.15pm

[C] [♫] [S]

Not so much a bar, more a sort of bistro is the Hansom, downstairs in the elegant Georgian building which houses the upmarket Fountain Restaurant. There is always a good choice of cooked dishes available, such as mussel and onion stew at around £2.50 and Hansom Pie at about £2.65, for example. The Hansom is very popular and inclined to be crowded at lunchtime, but the atmosphere is friendly and relaxed nevertheless.

MASSIMO'S, 465 Clarkston Road, Muirend
(041-637 8568)
Open: Mon-Sat 10am-8pm

[🍷]

This simple eating house on the south side of the city puts the emphasis on quality and value for money. All food is freshly prepared daily and this is a place where the proprietor always finds time to chat with his guests and thank them for their custom. The almost obligatory chianti-bottle lights stand on clean pine tables with benches which seat around thirty people. Minestrone soup is a 30p starter and carbonnade of beef (£2.20) and roast beef salad (£1.45) are examples of the amazingly inexpensive main courses. As there's no sweet above 50p you'll have a job to spend even £4 per head.

MOUSSAKA HOUSE
36 Kelvingrove Street (041-332 2510)
Open: Mon-Sat 12noon-2.30pm, 6-12mdnt, Sun 6.30-11pm

[C] [♫] [P] [🍷]

'The best value in town' is the claim made for this restaurant's lunchtime menu at about £2 – and they could be right. As the name suggests, a variety of moussaka dishes are the main feature, but kebab, stuffed pepper, or plainer dishes are also available. Soup and sweet are kept simple. It should be easy

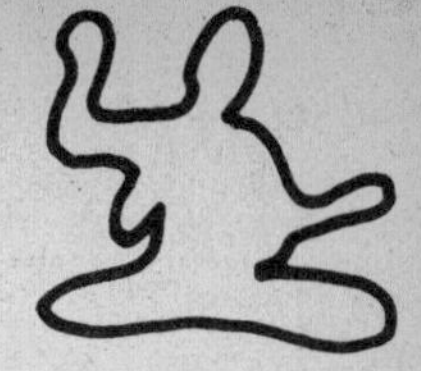

to choose an appetising meal of Greek specialities for about £5 from the à la carte. Try houmous (chick pea 'pâté') at about 75p, moussaka special (mince, aubergines, courgettes, potatoes, cheese and tomatoes) for about £2.75 and a sweet from the trolley for about 75p. A red and brown colour scheme, a plastic vine draped over a wooden archway and Greek music contribute to the Mediterranean atmosphere.

RAMANA, 427 Sauchiehall Street
(041-332 2528/2590)
Open: Mon-Sun 12noon-12mdnt

Never tried Indian food? Try Ramana then, for the well-designed menu explains what each dish contains and how it is cooked. The lounge bar, too, is well-designed with lush Kashmir furniture. Tandoori dishes (cooked in a charcoal-fired clay oven) are the house speciality – there's chicken tandoori with salad at around £2.90 or sheesh kebab Turkish (made with fillet steak) served with rice, salad and sauce at £4.25. And especially recommended for the 'beginner' are birianies and pillaus, priced between about £1.70 (for vegetable pillau) and £3.20 (for scampi biriani). If you're still not convinced that Indian food is for you, there's a list of Western dishes too, so you can choose fish and chips or grilled steak if you must. The businessperson's lunch at around £1.45 is very popular – doubtless for the oriental atmosphere which wafts the diner away from Glasgow for a little while, as well as for the good, low-priced food.

THE SPAGHETTI FACTORY
30 Gibson Street (041-334 2385)
Open: Mon-Sun 12noon-12mdnt

An extremely popular basement restaurant located in the student quarter, where an extravaganza of 'endless amusement combined with science' awaits you. The odd menu (in both size and content) lists a host of original dishes peppered with several outrageous tips on Italian eating – 'place fork in centre of pasta – twirl until fork is full. Try not to fall over' – plus other bits of whimsical information on the dishes. Typical main courses include spaghetti bolognese and pizza, both under £2 and hamburgers from around £2.65-£2.80. There is an attractive selection of sweets, and as the place is unlicensed, you are invited to bring your own favourite tipple. Highly recommended for anyone young at heart who enjoys good food and marvellous atmosphere.

Greenock

BANGALORE INDIAN RESTAURANT, 119 West Blackhall Street (Greenock 84355/6)
Open: Mon-Wed 12noon-12mdnt, Thu-Sat 12noon-12.30am, Sun 5-12mdnt

C ♫ P S

Just off the main Glasgow-Gourock road is this modern Indian restaurant. Decorated in traditional style, the interior is dimly lit and the walls have dark flock wallpaper decorated with Asian paintings. There is seating for about 100 at white-clothed tables; some in cosy alcoves offer a more intimate dining place. An extensive menu of Indian dishes is offered with prices around £1.70 onwards per main dish; beef roghan josh, a spicy dish in tomato and onion sauce, is recommended. Tandoori specialities such as shaslik or tandoori chicken are about £3.50. Chicken jal frazy or chicken begum behar are only around £2.50. The businessperson's lunch is excellent value at around £2 for three courses.

Helensburgh

SANGAM INDIAN RESTAURANT
45 Sinclair Street (Helensburgh 4817)
Open: Mon-Sat 12noon-12mdnt, Sun 5-12mdnt

C P S

You'll find this spacious, well-appointed restaurant on the first floor of a corner site in Helensburgh's main shopping area. Maroon wallpaper and curtaining, plus imitation oil lamps, create a cosy, intimate atmosphere. A variety of typical Asian food (for instance, beef byriani or shami kebab with salad – both around £2.50) is augmented by 'western dishes' such as steak and chips (£4) or prawn omelette (£2.30). A midday feature is the special three-course lunch, which is very good value at £1.50.

Irvine

THE COFFEE CLUB, 142 High Street
Open: Mon-Sat 10am-10pm

S

As in the other Ayrshire Coffee Clubs, this neat, modern restaurant with friendly waitress service offers an exciting selection of snacks, light meals and desserts at prices well within our budget. Fish and grills served with vegetables and chips are all under £2 and an assortment of flans and pies are served with a choice of salad and coleslaw, crunchy fried potatoes, or hot Vienna herb bread, for around £1.50 or so. Salads, omelettes, pizza or 'foreign foods' such as chili con carne with rice or moussaka and salad, are all under £2. For a meal on bread try one of the fourteen 'Danwiches' – open sandwiches with a mouthwatering variety of toppings starting from around 95p. In the 'children's corner' there is Paddington's Plateful (gammon, pineapple and chips) or Snoopy's Surprise (hamburger, beans and chips) for about 90p.

Jamestown

WHITELAW'S AMERICAN DINER
207 Main Street (Alexandria 54864)
Open: Mon-Fri, Sun 12.30-2.30pm, 7-11.45pm, Sat 12.30-2.30pm, 7-11.45pm

P S

If you like a friendly atmosphere in bright surroundings, this American diner is the answer. Portions are generous and the food is good. Starters such as soup of the day, stuffed peppers and a half portion of chili con carne are almost a meal in themselves. Prices range from 35p to just over £1. As well as the inevitable range of excellent budget burgers found in this style of operation, main dishes include gammon steak with pineapple rings and brown sugar (about £2.70), chicken served with honey (around £3.50) and scampi (less than £3). A selection of desserts include burnt almond parfait at 80p. A glass of wine costs 50p.

Kilmarnock

THE COFFEE CLUB ✕ 30 Bank Street (Kilmarnock 22048)
Open: Mon-Sat 9.30am-10pm

♫ P S

Friendly, speedy service and a pleasant décor, with roughcast walls, alcoves and tiffany lamps make this a popular meeting and eating place. Snacks are served upstairs, while full meals may be enjoyed in the basement. Assorted starters are from 50p – for a choice of soup and fruit juices. Ravioli, corn-on-the-cob, pâté and pickled herrings are among more expensive items. A galaxy of grills from £1.60-£4.95 offers a Scotsman's grill (haggis, peas, carrots and chips) or Italian grill (meat balls, onion, tomato sauce and spaghetti) to name a few. Fish dishes and 'a few foreign foods' are also available. Ravioli, lasagne, chili con carne and spaghetti bolognese cost between £1.50-£1.70. A three-course shopper's lunch costs around £1.75. A delicious selection of desserts is certain to tempt you – lemon meringue pie for only 50p is hard to resist.

Kilmartin

KILMARTIN HOTEL
(Kilmartin 244/250)
Open: Mon-Sat 11.30am-2pm, 6-9pm, Sun 12.30-2pm, 6.30-9pm

[P] [symbol]

Situated some thirty miles south of Oban on the A816, this traditional roadside inn has built up a local reputation for its good food and friendly atmosphere. All items from the extensive light meal menu are served in a simple six-tabled dining area, after you've ordered at the lounge bar. A starter such as home-made soup is 40p, whilst fried, breaded scampi (£1.90) and sirloin steak with onion rings (£3.75) are two of the more popular main dishes. Strawberry gâteau is a recommended dessert at 70p. If you book in advance, a more formal meal can be had in an intimate, candlelit dining room, but at £6.60 it's stretching our budget.

Lanark

SILVER BELL, 26 Bannatyne Street (Lanark 3129)
Open: Mon-Sat 11am-9pm, Sun 12.30-2.30pm, 4.30-6.30pm

[C] [P] [symbol]

Situated in the centre of a town that boasts its own racecourse, the Silver Bell takes this as its theme with prints of racehorses decorating the walls. High-backed chairs and dark beamwork add character, and the warm, relaxed atmosphere is enhanced by the friendly local waitresses. A table d'hôte lunch menu is offered at around £3.25 for three-courses such as home-made soup, beef steak pie, followed by pear belle Hélène. Tea or coffee is included in the price. The à la carte dinner menu is more extensive with sirloin steak (£5.40) and rainbow trout (£3.70) featuring on the menu, but be prepared to pay at least £2 more than lunch for your three courses. You may prefer high tea (around £2.50) which includes a main course such as farmhouse grill or French-fried chicken and bacon, tea, scones, cakes and bread.

THE TAVERN, Riverside Road Kirkfieldbank (Lanark 3163/2537)
Open: Mon-Sat 12noon-3pm, 6.30-9pm

[C] [♫] [P]

Ideal for the motorist, this white-painted tavern has a very popular lounge bar with a small wood-panelled restaurant adjoining. The à la carte lunch and supper menus are very reasonably priced, with the emphasis on grills. French fries, garden peas and carrots are included in the price of all main courses. A plateful of mouth-watering beef steak pie comes at around £2.80. A really satisfying three-course meal can also be enjoyed at somewhere between £2.40 and £3. Basket meals are very popular at around £1.80.

Largs

GREEN SHUTTER TEAROOM
28 Bath Street (Largs 672252)
Open: Mon-Sun 10am-6pm
Closed: Oct-Mar

[P] [symbol]

Just across the promenade from the sea, this restaurant commands a unique view of the beautiful Isle of Cumbrae. A three-course meal is excellent value – home-made soup of the day is about 35p and a wide selection of grills includes haddock with peas and chips (around £1.75) or gammon steak with pineapple (about £2.35). Sweets include home-made apple tart with cream, meringue nest with fruit and cream and brandy snaps with cream and ice cream – all less than 65p. A special 'Kiddies Corner' menu (for kids of ten and under) offers beefburgers, sausages, or fish-fingers with peas and chips and ice cream novelties all for about £1.

NARDINI'S, Esplanade (Largs 674555)
Open: Mon-Sun 12noon-3pm, 3.30-8pm

[♫] [P] [symbol]

A popular seaside establishment catering mainly for holidaymakers in the season; but the enterprising proprietor of Nardini's keeps his winter trade going by offering a three-course meal at around £2. Just what you get for this money depends upon the day of the week – fish and chips on Monday, steak and kidney pie on Wednesday, lasagne on Thursday, for instance, but there is a selection of grills, omelettes, etc, if you do not fancy the 'dish of the day'. In the summer you can have a substantial lunch or high tea for well under £5. A variety of salads are on offer at £1.25 and the special children's menu offers smaller portions at smaller prices – for example tomato soup, sausage and beans, and knickerbocker glory (and what meal would please most children more?) would set you back about £1.50. Grown-ups in knickerbockers have to pay over £1 for their glory, but there are a number of other tempting sweets for about half that price. You can get dinner here too, served from 8pm to 10pm, but the bill would almost certainly exceed five pounds.

Mauchline

LA CANDELA, 5 Kilmarnock Road (Mauchline 51015)
On the A76 to Dumfries
Open: Mon-Sun 12noon-2pm, 6.30-10pm

[♫] [P] [&]

Despite the evident Italian influence, the extensive menu is quite cosmopolitan, with the French and English getting a decent look in. The décor is continental and romantic, with alcoves to ensure privacy. The lunchtime choice is adequate but fairly basic, its great advantage being cost at around £3. The dinner menu caters for both the wealthy and the more penny-conscious, with Italian dishes taking the lead in the low-cost league. Pasta dishes range from £1.50-£2. Sweets cost under £1; starters range from 60p to £2 in the restaurant.

Motherwell

LAKESIDE RESTAURANT
Strathclyde Country Park
(Motherwell 54280)
Open: Mon-Sat 12noon-3pm, 7-11pm, Sun 12noon-7pm

[C] [P] [&]

Enjoying a magnificent setting amid this rambling country park, the Lakeside Restaurant, as its name suggests, overlooks a picturesque man-made lake which dominates the park. While watching the antics of yachtsmen and wind surfers from their cosy retreat, diners may choose a lunch from the table d'hôte menu for around £3 (£3.50 on Sunday). Simple, wholesome fare is the order of the day with main courses such as fried haddock, gammon steak and chef's roast of the day served with vegetables, boiled potatoes or French fries. In the evening the high tea menu offers simple dishes and misses out on starter at an inclusive price of £3 for adults and £2 for children. An extensive à la carte is available but prices are beyond our budget.

Newton Mearns

THE COFFEE CLUB, 114 Ayr Road (041-639 6888)
Open: Mon-Sat 10am-10.30pm

[C] [♫] [P] [S]

You'll have to come early for lunch or dinner to this popular, cosy little coffee shop, as demand far outweighs the seating availability. Situated in a block of ten shops on the main A77 road to Ayr, the soft brown interior with cork tiles and lots of pot plants offers shoppers and travellers alike a peaceful haven in which to relax and enjoy a meal such as soup of the day, egg, cheese, bacon and sweetcorn flan served hot with salad and coleslaw, cheesecake and Viennese coffee for around £3. The Coffee Club is unlicensed but coffee is, of course, a speciality of the house.

Oban

THE BOX TREE, 108 St George Street (Oban 64641)
Open: Apr-Nov: Mon-Sat 9am-10pm, Sun 6-10pm

[S]

Simplicity is the attraction of this unlicensed restaurant. Uniformed staff give friendly, attentive service in a floral wall-papered environment. Sit in your individual dining booth and choose from the short, simple menu. Lunch has an emphasis on salads (about £2), although fried Hebridean haddock (about £2.80) is also available. Dinner includes more expensive scampi and grilled gammon or steak, but will still cost around £4 for the three courses. Pâté with oakcakes for a starter sounds a pleasant departure from the norm. Burger snacks and sandwiches are also served if you want to keep the total bill beneath a staggering £2.

CORRAN HALLS RESTAURANT
Esplanade (Oban 64566)
Open: May-Oct: Mon-Sun 10am-8pm

[C] [P] [S] [&]

Mrs Violet Lockhart and her daughter Barbara aim to provide a service to Oban's many summer visitors and particularly to hungry children. The restaurant is handily placed for theatre-goers and boasts a pretty garden for 'eating out'. The à la carte menu provides a choice of three-course meals from a list of five starters, a dozen main dishes served with potatoes and vegetables and a selection of sweets, for around £4. The most expensive main dish is entrecôte steak garni at about £5, the least expensive is Scotch pie and beans at around £1.50. A choice of salads is also offered.

THE GALLERY RESTAURANT
Gibraltar Street (Oban 64647)
Open: Apr-Oct: Mon-Sun 9.30am-10pm

P S

Iain Reid is justly proud of his smart little restaurant situated in the busy town centre. Open all day, the Gallery offers hot or cold snacks and full three-course meals. In the evening the atmosphere is transformed as lights sparkle on the attractive watercolours adorning the cream walls. The special three-course 'farmhouse' dinner may cost about £4.95, with choices such as scampi or roast chicken. At lunchtime meals cost from £2 upwards. A selection of tempting cheesecakes and gâteaux are available for dessert.

McTAVISH'S KITCHEN, George Street (Oban 63064)
Open: Restaurant: summer: Mon-Sun 12noon-2.30pm, 6-10.30pm, Self-service: summer: Mon-Sun 9am-10pm, winter: 9am-6pm

S

Oban lives for and by its visitors and no-one does more to provide good wholesome food and entertainment in comfortable and congenial surroundings than James and Jeremy Inglis at McTavish's Kitchen. Their large, modern, purpose-built premises overlooking the sea, houses a downstairs self-service food bar seating 150 and a clean and bright upstairs restaurant with room for 270, as well as the Laird's Bar and the predatorily named Mantrap Bar. Food in both restaurant and self-service is very good of its kind and not expensive. As you might expect, this is the place for Scottish specialities and you can have a three-course meal including 'haggis and neeps' for around £4.60. A 'budget special' evening menu enables you to select three-courses and coffee for under £4. An added attraction during the summer are the Scottish Evenings featuring piping and highland dance. The unlicensed self-service restaurant offers no-nonsense eating-house fare at very reasonable prices. Helpings are generous and the dishes such as roast chicken (£3.55) or haddock and chips (£1.55) are well-cooked and presented with flair.

SOROBA HOUSE HOTEL
(Oban 62628)
Open: Mon-Sun 7.45-9.30am, 12noon-2.30pm, 7-10pm from May 1982 onwards

P

Take the A816 Lochgilphead Road out of Oban, for approximately one mile to David and Edyth Hutchinson's Soroba House Hotel standing in nine acres of its own grounds with commanding views over Oban to Mull. A very comfortable and pleasant hotel it is too, drawing something like 70% of its restaurant and bar trade from Oban folk. Although dinner is out of our league you can enjoy a four-course lunch here for around £4, comprising starter such as grapefruit and mandarin cup followed by soup of the day, then a main dish of roast half chicken with French fries and salad garnish or fried golden queen of scallops with vegetables. Sweets, including ice cream and various gâteaux, are chosen from the well-laden trolley and coffee is offered at 35p.

THE THISTLE HOTEL RESTAURANT
Breadalbane Place (Oban 63132)
Open: Apr-Sep: Mon-Sun 12noon-2.30pm, 5-9.30pm

[P] [&]

Whatever you do, don't come to Oban without trying the excellent locally-landed seafood. And Robert Silverman's Thistle Restaurant is the place for it. The décor is old-fashioned, but the white tablecloths are clean, the service prompt and efficient. Starters include rollmop herring and salad at around £1 and sweet pickled herring and salad at about the same price. There is a wide choice of fish dishes including Dover sole, fried scampi and grilled locally farmed trout at prices from around £2.50-£5, but lobster Thermidor, alas, breaks the budget. There is also a good choice of roasts and grills at prices ranging from about £2.75-£4. The table d'hôte menus are excellent value, the three-course lunch menu offering good choices at around £2.50 (plus VAT) and the three-course dinner menu including such dishes as egg mayonnaise, potage du jour, roast Angus beef and horseradish with vegetables, and Scotch cream trifle, is less than £5.

Paisley

CARDOSI'S, 46 Causeyside Street (041-889 5339)
Open: Mon-Sun 11am-11pm

[♫] [P] [S] [&]

After about twenty years of running the same restaurant in the same town, the Cardosi family has had plenty of time to get to know its clientele and how to please them. They cater for all tastes by operating a café and take-away counter as well as the first-floor restaurant and dispense bar, where it's possible to get a good three-course business lunch for around £1.85. A typical choice of dishes from this menu would include cream of asparagus soup, 'haggis, neeps and tatties' and banana crumble and custard. A reasonably-priced à la carte menu is always available, along with its list of chef's specialities – Mexico steak, chicken Kiev or Napoli steak with all the trimmings – and yes, you will still get change from £5.

MILLER'S TABLE AND STEAKHOUSE RESTAURANT, Watermill Hotel, Lomend (041-889 3201)
Open: Mon-Sun 12noon-2.30pm, 5-10pm

[C] [P] [S] [&]

This Stakis Steakhouse occupies a converted watermill, the wheels, old timbers and brickwork of which are still on display. Unbeatable value main courses of half a roast chicken, sirloin steak, gammon or fish come served with jacket potato or chips, tomato, peas and a roll and butter, and run from about £3.20 to £4.95. A starter such as farmhouse broth or prawn cocktail is included in the main course price. Children do very well with a three-course meal (including ice cream with strawberry sauce and a fizzy drink) for only £1.50.

Renfrew

THE ARMOURY RESTAURANT
Inchinnan Road (041-886 4100)
Open: Jul-Aug: 10am-3pm, 5-10.30pm, Sep-Jun: 10am-10.30pm

[C] [P] [&]

Another of the Stakis steakhouses, but there's not the olde worlde décor here that you'd expect. This is very much an up-to-date restaurant, featuring a circular wood ceiling with ultra-modern lighting. Still, as a contrast, the armoury itself has several medieval wall-hangings and drawings. Starter choices here are country pâté, prawn cocktail, farmhouse broth or fruit juice, and are included in the price of the main course. Most of the favourites are on the menu, such as gammon steak (£3.50), half-chicken (£3.45) and fillet of haddock (£3.20). There's a very good deal for children, too. Soup, a choice of three main courses with ice-cream and strawberry sauce to follow, plus a fizzy drink costs just £1.45. Whichever dessert the adults decide on it will cost 75p, and a 30p cup of coffee should round things off satisfactorily and keep things within budget.

Rothesay

LA COLOQUINTE, 63 Victoria Street (Rothesay 2324)
Open: summer: Mon-Sat 12noon-2.30pm, 7-11pm, Sun 7-11pm
winter: weekends, or check by phone for midweek opening

[C] [&]

The time to sample the French cuisine of this small, but popular restaurant is when the seersucker cloths cover the tables at lunchtime. Stroll first along the pier, or in the public gardens opposite to whet your appetite. There's a choice of four or five starters, including home-made soup; main courses may be spaghetti or fish orientated (such as turbot with cheesy sauce), or pork with 'fines herbes', and a choice of three sweets. When the dinner-time linen cloths replace the seersucker, prices rise, and only careful and disciplined selection from the enticing à la carte will keep you within budget.

Salen, Isle of Mull

THE PUFFER AGROUND ✕ Aros (Aros 389)
Open: Easter-mid Oct: Mon-Sun 12.30-2.30pm, 6.30-9pm, mid Nov-mid Jan: Fri-Sat (reservations only)

[P] [✿]

No need to find your sea-legs on this ship, though you may have doubts, as the restaurant's design is strikingly based on that of a Clyde 'Puffer', and maritime paintings line the walls. No less striking is the selection of American candies that greet your entrance. The restaurant shares its home in a row of converted roadside cottages with a craft shop. For about £4.50 you may sample a three-course meal (which could include local trout) and coffee. Excellent use is made of fresh local produce and as far as possible, each meal is individually prepared. Fisherman's pancake or shellfish soup with brandy and cream live side by side with more conventional, and cheaper starters. A main course salad or casserole will cost about £3.50, though you can spend more, and sweets such as baked sponge or fresh peach and cream roll, about 60p. Service is simple but very friendly.

Troon

CAMPBELL'S KITCHEN, 3 South Beach (Troon 314421)
Open: Thu-Sat 12noon-2pm, Tue-Sat 7-9.30pm

[P] [S] [✿]

Opened during 1979, Campbell's Kitchen already has a homely atmosphere. Red and white floral décor and red-stained pinewood chairs give a pleasant ambience, but the main attraction is the delicious smell of home-baking. Home-made meringues, gâteaux, and scones are all around 50p per portion. A 'special meal', including a fruit juice or soup, and a hot dish of the day, is available at about £1.50. Alternatively there is a choice of salads or various omelettes at about £1.50. Campbell's Kitchen welcomes disabled diners.

THE COPPER KETTLE, 18 West Portland Street (Troon 311394)
Open: Mon-Sat 10am-10pm

[♫] [P] [S] [✿]

In this friendly, relaxed restaurant there is a good selection of appetising snacks and savoury dishes from which to choose. Imaginative, and presented with flair, the food available is excellent value for money – an omelette, breaded haddock or scampi and chips will not burn a hole in your pocket.

Wishaw

ANVIL STEAKHOUSE, 254 Main Street (Wishaw 75546)
Open: Mon-Sat 12noon-2.30pm, 5-10pm, Sun 6.30-10pm

[C] [♫] [S] [✿]

In Wishaw's main street, this member of the Stakis Steakhouse chain is a popular lunchtime venue for local business people. The emphasis is on convenience, with good value, standard menus of the chicken, gammon and steak variety. Accompaniments are chips or baked potato and peas, with a salad garnish. A three-course meal will cost £3.20-£5.95.

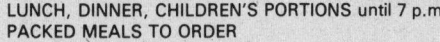

'O my love is like a red, red rose,
That's newly sprung in June,
O my love is like a melody,
That's sweetly played in tune.
As fair art thou my bonnie lass,
So deep in love am I,
And I will love thee still my lass,
Till a' the seas gang dry.'

ROBERT BURNS

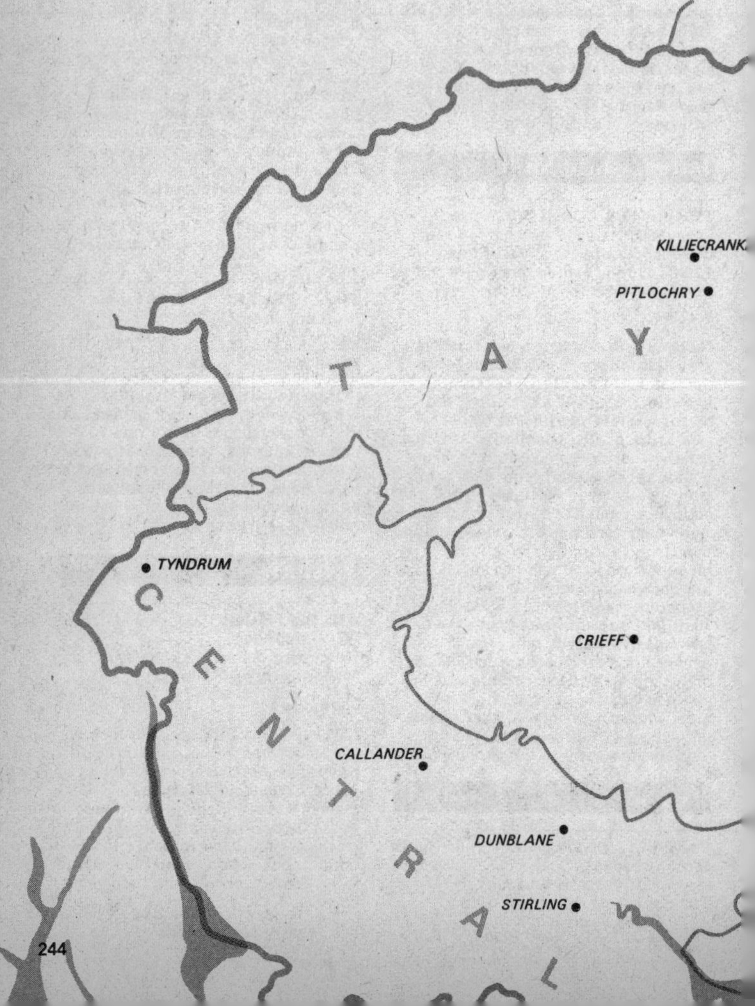

Central, Tayside and Fife

Regional Dishes

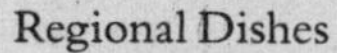

Dundee cake
Dundee orange marmalade
Arbroath smokie
Scots broth
Poached River Tay salmon

BRECHIN
MONTROSE
FORFAR
BLAIRGOWRIE
ARBROATH
CARNOUSTIE
DUNDEE
PERTH
ST ANDREWS
KIRKCALDY
FIFE

14

Arbroath

HOTEL SEAFORTH★★ Dundee Road
(Arbroath 72232)
Open: Mon-Sun 12.30-2pm
7-9pm (Sat 9.30pm)

[C] [P] [&]

This attractive hotel-restaurant boasts an array of tempting dishes for the hungry holidaymaker. Representative of the items on the lunch menu are melon cocktail, grilled pork chops with vegetables and sherry trifle, plus coffee, for the modest price of £3.50. The four-course set dinner (only available until 8pm) costs around £5 and includes the old favourite – roast beef and Yorkshire pudding. Later in the evening an extensive à la carte menu operates, but here the budget-conscious will have to choose very carefully. High teas (served between 5-6pm) vary in price from £3 to £5 and amongst the popular grills are Arbroath smokies and gammon with pineapple. Wholesome light lunches are always available in the bar.

Blairgowrie

THE HUB, 23 High Street
(Blairgowrie 2038)
Open: May-Oct Mon-Sat 10am-9pm, Sun 3pm-9pm Nov-Apr Mon-Sat 10am-5pm

[P] [S] [&]

Well named, 'The Hub' is a town-centre restaurant with unusual circular windows, split-level dining area and modern décor. The emphasis is on the popular grills, roasts, salads and fish dishes, all reasonably priced. In fact you could have entrecôte steak with all the trimmings plus soup, a sweet such as sherry trifle, coffee and wine for an inclusive price of around £4. For the busy shopper an afternoon tea including a pot of tea, toast, scone and butter, cake and biscuit costs only £1.25.

Brechin

NORTHERN HOTEL★★ 2 Clerk Street
(Brechin 2156)
Open: Mon-Sun 12.30-2pm, 5-6.30pm, 7-8.30pm

[C] [P] [&]

For those who relish a proper 'sit down' meal within the realms of a tight budget, this hotel is the ideal place. A three-course lunch or dinner such as salami salad, farmhouse grill and vegetables of the day, followed by Drambuie pancake costs around £5. Snacks in the bar and satisfying high teas are also available, and cost, for the most part, under £2.

Callander

PIPS, 23 Ancaster Square
(Callander 30470)
Open: summer: Mon-Sat 10am-6pm, Sun 11am-6pm, winter: Mon-Tue 10am-5pm, Thu-Sun 10am-5pm

[P] [&]

This eye-catching little restaurant snuggles in a corner of the Square. From the outside, attractive laboured brasswork, tinted windows and a sophisticated striped canopy invite further inspection. The interior is equally striking with white laminated tables and chairs and a bold décor with pictures mounted on hessian walls. Salads and home-baking are the specialities of the house, and desserts are served with lashings of cream. Great value at around £2.50 per head.

Carnoustie

GLENCOE HOTEL ★★ Links Parade
(Carnoustie 53273)
Open: Mon-Sun 1-2pm, 7.30-9pm

[C] [P]

The name Carnoustie is synonymous with golf, and this neat, family hotel has the distinction of overlooking the famous championship golf-course. Table lamps and soft music create a soothing atmosphere in the dining room, and the patio extension provides an ideal eating place with views of the golf-course. Lunch and dinner are both table d'hôte, dinner being five courses, with coffee. There is an excellent choice of tempting main course dishes such as grilled fillet of lemon sole Sorrento, cold baked gammon salad or beef and pheasant pie.

Crieff

THE HIGHLANDMAN, East High Street
(Crieff 4265)
Open: Mon-Sat 10am-7pm, Sun 12noon-7pm

[&]

The premises of The Highlandman, once a garage showroom and filling station, have been converted into a pleasant restaurant-cum-tearoom, where one can get anything from a cup of tea and a piece of home-made shortbread to a full three-course meal, anytime from morning to evening. Main dishes include sirloin steak or scampi at around £3, gammon steak at about £2.25, or various grills from around £1.25. Toasted sandwiches, hamburgers and salads exist for those who like a light lunch, and children's meals run from 40p for sausage and chips to £1.10 for fisherman's platter and chips. Incidentally, disabled persons will find access easy.

STAR HOTEL ★ East High Street (Crieff 2632)
Open Mon-Sun 12noon-2pm, 4.30-6pm (High Tea), 7-9pm

[C] [P] [S] [🍷]

The pleasant surroundings of the panelled dining room which overlooks the main street of this attractive Perthshire town provides an ideal venue for shoppers and tourists alike. Lunchtime specials such as fried fillet of haddock with lemon, grilled liver and onions or pizza – all served with French fried potatoes and two vegetables of the day – cost only £1.30. Starter, a sweet and coffee would add less than £1 extra to the bill. The à la carte menu is more extensive but still reasonable offering grilled Tay salmon, chicken Suedoise (sautéed in a delicious sauce of mushrooms, cream and white wine) or Wiener schnitzel for around £3.50. A high tea menu served from 4.30-6pm offers a selection of grills or cold meat salad with French fries and vegetables, tea, bread and butter, scones and cakes in a price range of £2.30 to £4.50.

Dunblane

FOURWAYS RESTAURANT
Main North Road (Dunblane 822098)
Open: Mon-Sat 9.15am-6pm, Sun 10am-6pm

[P] [🍷]

This small restaurant and gift shop enjoys a prime position within walking distance of the magnificent 15th-century cathedral and the Bishop's Palace and is consequently very popular with tourists. A friendly and caring staff serve mainly grills and home-made soups or pies. Top lunch price (inclusive of VAT) is around £4.95 but one can eat well for a lot less (for example, soup plus home-made steak and kidney pie with apple tart to follow is under £3). Unlicensed.

Dundee

GUNGA DIN, 99c-101 Perth Road (not on telephone)
Open: Mon-Sat 12noon-2.15pm, 6-11.30pm

[C]

For the lover of classical Indian dishes Gunga Din is the place to eat. Situated on the main road west of the city centre this attractive little Indian restaurant sits in the heart of the University area. All dishes are freshly-prepared and only the finest basmati rice, best cuts of meat, proper herbs and spices for each dish, and fresh seasonal vegetables are used. Patrons are asked to appreciate the time involved in preparing and cooking dishes, which are made as closely as possible to the original recipes, and not to expect the chef to sacrifice quality for speed. Mullagatawny soup provides a suitable starter for around 70p and main dishes should be mixed and blended in the Indian tradition (ideally friends should order dishes and share). Kofta (meatballs in curry sauce) or chicken curry costs around £2.50 as does sag gosh (meat with spinach) and a seafood muchi curry cost about £2.70. For £3.10 or so there is a speciality chicken tandoori masala or thali (a tray consisting of several Indian vegetarian dishes). Friendly staff will assist in the choosing and blending of dishes with their correct accompaniments. For dessert you should try kulfi, an Indian ice cream at about 75p.

OLDE WORLDE INN, 124 Seagate (Dundee 21179)
Open: Mon-Sat 12noon-2.30pm, 5-10.30pm, Sun 6.30-10pm

[C] [♫] [S] [🍷]

Handy for the new Wellgate shopping centre and opposite the main bus station, this is a typical Reo Stakis steakhouse, serving items from the organisation's standard menu. Main course items range from about £3.20 for a fillet of haddock to £5.35 for prime Angus steak and include a choice of starters. Biscuits and cheese or apple pie with cream cost about 75p. Special lunches at £1.50 offer a choice of meat salads or hot dishes daily. The children's special three-course meal with a soft drink is very good value at around £1.45.

PIZZA GALLERY, 3-7 Peter Street (Dundee 21422)
Open: Mon-Sat 10am-10.30pm

[S] [🍷]

A bright and modern eaterie situated in a quiet lane off a pedestrianised precinct in the city centre. The Gallery is on two levels and its walls are adorned by the works of local artists, some of whose paintings are for sale. Starters (they call them primers) are soup (40p), spaghetti (65p) and fruit juice (30p). The main-course pizzas are named after famous artists (the Van Gogh is flavoured with anchovies, green pepper and olives) and range from £1.15-£1.60. Even if you finish off with apple pie and fresh cream, all washed down with coffee, you've probably only spent £3 altogether. So perhaps you could have afforded that half-litre carafe of house wine at £2.10.

Falkirk

HATHERLEY HOTEL ✕✕ Arnot Hill Lane (Falkirk 25328)
Open: Mon-Tue, Thu-Sat 12noon-2pm, 7-9.30pm, Wed 7-9.30pm

[C] [S]

Although hidden behind a modern, purpose-built hotel, the Hatherley itself is a listed building dating from 1904, in the art nouveau style, and pleasantly secluded. It's a small hotel, specialising in Danish hospitality and smørgasbrød from proprietors Mr and Mrs Werner Gauster. The range of delicacies is wide. If you start with the home-made soup, two selections from the smørgasbrød and a sweet should satisfy your appetite and be no strain on the purse strings. It's a delight just to explore the menu with it's unfamiliar combinations, such as garlic sausage with asparagus, smoked eel fillets with lemon and lettuce, or hard-boiled egg with caviar (all around £1 or under). The house speciality, seafood salad is just over £4. Coffee is served with the added bonus of home-made peppermints.

Forfar

AUGUST MOON, 114 Castle Street (Forfar 64105)
Open: Mon-Sat 11.30am-2pm, 5-11.30pm, Sun 4-11.30pm

For those who think that all Chinese restaurants have a stereotyped appearance with very little individuality, a visit to August Moon will prove a pleasant experience. No embossed wallpaper or Chinese lanterns here. This little eating place has a charm and character all of its own, with white rough-cast walls and cosy Tudor-style banquettes. A comprehensive à la carte menu offers the usual complement of Oriental dishes plus a selection of European ones. The price of all main courses includes boiled rice, and a heated stand is laid on your table to keep the whole thing hot. Most dishes are around the £2-£3 mark and, a set meal for two of fried spring roll, sweet and sour pork, chicken with cashew nuts and vegetables, mixed vegetables, egg fried rice plus coffee or tea offers excellent value at just over £6.

Killiecrankie

KILLIECRANKIE HOTEL
On the A9, 2m NW of Pitlochry (Killiecrankie 220)
Open: mid-Apr-mid-Oct 12.30-2pm, 7-10pm

[P] [garden]

This white-painted building with its well-tended gardens is set in woodland close to a National Trust beauty spot. Bar lunches are very popular here and there's a good range of food for you to sample. After soup with roll and butter at 45p, two of the options on offer are fried haddock with chips and peas (£1.80) and tongue salad (£1.75). A similar bar supper service operates during the evenings. The table d'hôte is a little expensive for us, but if you stick to, say, game soup, then Tayside trout with ice-cream to finish, you should see some change from £5.

Kirkcaldy

GREEN COCKATOO RESTAURANT
275-277 High Street (Kirkcaldy 3310)
Open: Mon-Sat 9am-5pm (closed Wed)

[C] [P] [S] [garden]

At the north end of the High Street, you'll find a bakery and confectioner's shop. Go through the shop and up some stairs and on the first floor you will find the Green Cockatoo, a traditional Scottish tearoom with polished wood panelling, fresh white linen on the tables, and friendly service. Tea is obviously *the* meal here, with all those delicious scones and cakes downstairs, but the lunch menu is good value too with the most expensive dish – fresh salmon and salad – priced about £3. Sweets include Bakewell tart and custard, fresh cream gâteau and ice creams. Coffee costs about 25p and a glass of wine around 60p. On the second floor is a grill room, the 'Drouthy Crony' with a more limited menu at similarly moderate prices.

OLDE WORLDE INN, Charlotte Street (Kirkcaldy 65431)
Open: Mon-Fri 12noon-2.30pm,

5-10.30pm
Sun 6.30-10pm

The mid 19th-century building has come a long way from its days as a schoolhouse, to a Stakis Steakhouse. The big advantage of Olde Worlde Inns is that you can be confident of knowing exactly what to expect, in terms of standard, quantity and price. A simple starter followed by gammon steak or roast half-chicken with peas and chips or baked potato will cost under £4, and the sweets and cheeseboard are each under £1. The children's menu is good value, too, a three-course meal and soft drink costing around £1.50.

THE PANCAKE PLACE, 28 Kirk Wynd (Kirkcaldy 4982)
Open: Mon-Sat 10am-5.30pm

♬ P S

Housed in a converted stone building dating from 1779, this is a comfortable restaurant specialising in pancakes-with-everything. You can start with soup, but there is a choice of twelve snack-sized pancakes with intriguing fillings such as ham and peach, each costing around 95p. For your main course, large savoury pancakes such as chicken and pineapple (about £1.80) or Rocky Mountain Burger for less than £1.60 are recommended. Alternatively you can try one of seven crisp salads, served with two thin pancakes. There are a dozen varieties of sweet pancakes available for dessert. Costing around £1.30 'Pippin', a large spicy pancake with a delicious hot apple and cinnamon filling topped with cream is a gourmet's delight.

Montrose

CORNER HOUSE HOTEL ★★
High Street (Montrose 3126)
Open: Mon-Sun 12noon-2pm, 4.30-9pm

S

This attractive hotel-restaurant is run efficiently by friendly waitresses who will serve you a three-course lunch with coffee and a glass of Hirondelle for less than £3. The daily changing menu features the old favourites such as fried haddock, lasagne, roasts and omelettes for around £1.30. Later in the day a high tea menu is available with main courses such as gammon steak and chips or cold York ham salad at around £3 including a selection of vegetables, home-made scones, cakes and tea. The à la carte menu is rather more pricey but with careful selection a meal for around £5 is possible.

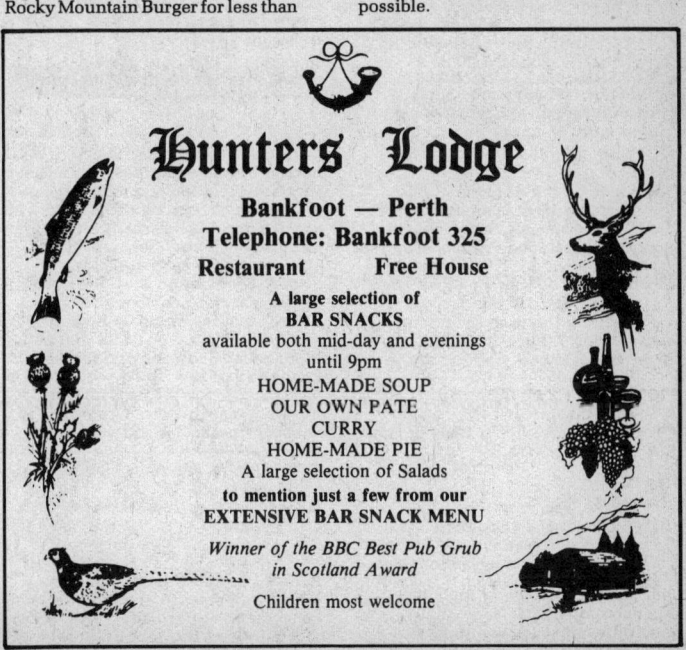

Perth

HUNTER'S LODGE, Bankfoot (Bankfoot 325) 8m north of Perth off A9 at Bankfoot services turn-off
Open: Mon-Sun 12noon-2pm, 5-9pm

[P] [♣]

This country restaurant, only eight miles north of Perth on the main road to Inverness, makes a speciality of traditional Scottish fare, both in the à la carte and bar menus. The award-winning bar food features Hunter's Lodge pâté, home-made beef steak pie and curry – all firm favourites at around £1.50. In the dining room traditional Scottish high tea is nothing short of a slap-up dinner at around £4. An extensive à la carte menu lists main courses for as little as £3.50.

KARDOMAH, St John's Square (Perth 25093)
Open: Mon-Sat 9.30am-6pm

[S] [♣]

These Trusthouse Forte restaurants are favourites with many people. This one is certainly quick and convenient if you are shopping or sightseeing. Supplementing the usual THF menu of omelettes, grills and salads is a table d'hôte lunch (two courses at around £2, three £2.30) and a high tea (including tea and toast) at about £1.90.

OLDE WORLDE INN, CITY MILL HOTEL, West Mill Street (Perth 28281)
Open: 12noon-2.30pm, 5-10.30pm

[C] [P] [♣]

Convenient, fast food of the steaks, chicken and haddock variety is served in a 19th-century mill which has been converted into a modern hotel of the Reo Stakis organisation. The mill stream and wheel can be seen through plated glass in the hotel's lounge bar and reception area. Main course prices, between £3.20 and £6 include a starter, but sweets or cheese are 75p extra.

THE PANCAKE PLACE, 10 Charlotte Street (Perth 28077)
Open: summer: Mon-Sat 10am-6pm, Sun 11.30am-5.30pm

[S] [♣]

This specialised eaterie, with its informal tea-room atmosphere, was the first to pander to pancake fans in central Scotland (other sister restaurants have since opened at Edinburgh, Kirkcaldy and St Andrews). After fruit juice or soup of the day (around 35p), you can sample a giant burger (£1.80), chicken and pineapple (£1.80) or any one of six crispy salads from £1.50-£2. And to follow? How about 'Florida' – a large pancake topped with ice-cream, peaches and fresh whipped cream – just one of a dozen exotic desserts guaranteed to ruin your diet!

THE PENNY POST ✕ 80 George Street (Perth 20867)
Open: Mon-Sat 12noon-2pm, 7-10pm

[C] [P] [S] [♣]

A cosy little restaurant which should appeal to those who find historic connections of interest, for the 18th-century building that houses The Penny Post was one of the earliest post offices, dating back to 1773. The bar downstairs is, in fact, the old Post Office counter. The à la carte menu offers such dishes as home-made Scotch broth at around 50p, and the Penny Post Special (strips of beef cooked in red wine, mushrooms and cream and served on a bed of rice) at around £4.95 and this gives a good indication of the sort of prices prevailing. The cheaper lunch menu includes beefsteak, kidney and mushroom pie or fish at about £2.

Pitlochry

GREEN PARK HOTEL ★★★ (Pitlochry 2537)
Open: Mar-Oct inclusive, Mon-Sun 8.30-9.30am, 12.30-2pm, 6.30-8pm and normal licensing hours

[P] [♣]

If you take pleasure in having your meal in beautiful surroundings, try the Green Park Hotel. This enlarged country house is set amongst lawns and fine trees, with a view across Loch Faskally. Inside, the dining room is very clean and bright. There are no à la carte meals, but the owners, Graham and Anne Brown, offer a good selection of dishes for a three-course lunch at around £4, including service and VAT. You could start with Mortadella salad, follow with beef kromeski garni and finish with sliced peaches and cream. Lunch on Sunday features a mouth-watering cold buffet, with cold meats, fish and salad galore.

THE LUGGIE, Rie-Achan Road (Pitlochry 2085)
Open: Apr-early Nov: Mon-Sun 10am-9pm

A 'luggie' is a milkmaid's bucket – appropriate since this quaint little restaurant was originally the byre of an old dairy farm. Inside, the raftered roof, white-painted rough-cast walls and stone fireplace are very welcoming. Ian and Diana Russell, the owners, ensure that home-baking and local produce are a main feature of all the fare. Lunchtime offers the choice of a self-service cold table and an excellent selection of cold meats, duck, salmon and smoked mackerel, accompanied by a variety of original salads, assorted gâteaux and fresh fruit salads, or hot dishes such as grills which are served at the table. The main course in either case will be between £3 and £4, with starters and sweets for about 60p-£2. The dinner menu offers a much wider choice of hot dishes but the price is likely to bring the full meal outside our budget.

St Andrews

THE PANCAKE PLACE, 177-179 South Street (St Andrews 75671)
Open: Mon 10am-9pm, Tue-Wed 10am-5.30pm, Thu-Sun 10am-9pm

♫ P S

The interior of this attractive speciality restaurant is surprisingly rural, with a beamed ceiling, natural stone and white-painted plaster walls. Pancakes may be sampled as a starter, main course or dessert. Soup of the day is about 35p, or you can start with a savoury pancake such as ham and peach or haddock Mornay for around 85p. For a main course you could choose a Rocky Mountain burger at about £1.80. A range of salads is also available including chicken, ham, cheese and egg, prices ranging from around £1.40-£2. There is a choice of a dozen sweet pancakes.

Stirling

BOMA RESTAURANT, KINGSGATE HOTEL ★ Kings Street (Stirling 3944)
Open: Mon-Sun 8am-9pm

S ♧

In their residential hotel, right in the town and handy for the railway station and Thistle shopping centre, Sandy and Jean Wallace have opened the 'Boma' Restaurant. Real zebra skins brought back from East Africa by the intrepid couple set the black-and-white theme of the décor. A lunch of soup or fruit juice, followed by a main course (from around £3 for chicken or ham salad, roast chicken or haddock fillet to around £4 for grilled sirloin steak garni) is available daily. Sweets, cheese and coffee are not included in the price. High tea includes a starter such as egg mayonnaise, a savoury dish with chips, scone, cake and tea at prices from about £3.60. Half portions of appropriate dishes are served for children and high chairs are available if required.

THE RIVERWAY RESTAURANT ✕
Kildean (Stirling 5734)
Open: summer: Mon-Fri 9am-7pm, Sat 9am-9pm, Sun 12noon-7pm, winter: Wed-Sun 10am-7pm

♫ P ♧

Half a mile from the town centre, on the road to the Trossachs, just off the M9 motorway and yet enjoying a panoramic view of the River Forth, the Riverway Restaurant is well-known for its excellent cuisine at reasonable prices. The three-course table d'hôte lunch costs under £3 and is good nourishing food in ample portions. High tea, the main evening meal including grills, is about the same price. The Saturday night dinner-dance, with live music, costs about £6.

STATION HOTEL ★★ 56 Murray Place (Stirling 2017)
Open: Mon-Sun 12noon-2.30pm, 5-10.30pm

C ♧

The Stakis Steakhouse at the Station Hotel offers their standard menu (as for 'The Plough' at Ayr). The wattle ceiling and dark oak settles may not be genuine antiques but the atmosphere is right for an enjoyable meal, with full waiter service, at very reasonable prices. Bar snacks run from around £1, and you might like to catch the Whistlestop Diner, also part of the Station Hotel.

Tyndrum

CLIFTON COFFEE HOUSE,
A82/A85 junction (Tyndrum 271)
Open: Apr-Oct: Mon-Sun 8.30am-5.30pm

C P S ♧

You'll be pleasantly surprised by the prices at this cheerful eaterie. It is part of a smoothly-run tourist complex that includes craft, book and whisky shops. Inside, the décor is predominantly white with strategically placed hanging baskets and hand-crafted pottery. There is an air of quality here, despite it being a self-service operation. A wide range of starters includes barley broth and cullen skink (the traditional fish-based soup). Various main courses are available throughout the day, such as beef curry (£1.95), haggis with neeps and tatties (turnip and potato) at £1.70 and venison hotpot (around £2.50).

'Farewell to the Highlands, farewell to the North,
The birthplace of valour, the country of worth,
Wherever I wander, wherever I rove,
The hills of the Highlands for ever I love.
My heart's in the Highlands, my heart is not here,
My heart's in the Highlands a-chasing the deer,
A-chasing the wild deer and following the roe,
My heart's in the Highlands wherever I go.'

ROBERT BURNS

Highland and Grampian

Regional Dishes

Aberdeen Angus roast beef
Atholl Brose (oatmeal, heather honey, whisky and cream)
Cranachan (raspberries, cream and toasted oatmeal)
Finnan Haddie (smoked haddock)
Cullen Skink (haddock, sieved potatoes and onions)

15

Aberdeen

KARDOMAH, 1 Union Bridge (Aberdeen 50459)
Open: Mon-Sat 9am-6.30pm

[C] [S]

This modern eating house provides a quick service for shoppers and holidaymakers, with a ground-floor self-service coffee shop and upstairs restaurant. The restaurant menu is reasonably priced (gammon steak around £2.50, steak and kidney pie around £2), with a waist-preserver menu for the figure-conscious and a children's menu including an exciting variety of ice creams.

THE LANTERN RESTAURANT
101 Crown Street (Aberdeen 55440)
Open: Mon-Fri 12noon-2pm, Mon-Sat 7-10.30pm

[C] [P] [S]

The Chef's Specialities menu is incredibly good value for lunch or dinner. Green bean salad is one of the delicious starters, costing around 75p. Casserole of kidney and sweetbreads (about £3) and poached salmon bonne femme (just over £3) are two of the main courses, both served with vegetables.

OLIVER'S CALEDONIAN HOTEL ★★★
Union Terrace (Aberdeen 29233)
Open: Mon-Sat 12noon-2.30pm, 6-11.30pm, Sun 6.30-11pm

[C] [P] [S]

This steak and hamburger grill is named after Oliver Hardy who, along with his buddy Stan, dominated the American screen comedy in the 1930s. The restaurant is superbly appointed, in ultra-modern design, with the all-black décor and contrasting chrome fittings giving a most striking and exciting effect. The menu is designed on a poster-style sheet and the various courses are given film-jargon titles, 'The Opening Scene' (starter), 'The Main Feature', The Supporting Role' and 'The Curtain Closer' (dessert). A 'Stars' Choice' burger costs between £2.25-£3.35. Main courses include French fries or baked potato and salad.

STAKIS STEAKHOUSE, Holburn Street (Aberdeen 56442)
Open: Mon-Sun 12noon-2.30pm, 5-11pm (10pm Sun)

[C] [P] [S]

Stakis Steakhouses have a definite appeal for inveterate meat-eaters. Main course prices, from around £3.20-£5.95 and including haddock, chicken and various steaks, cover a starter as well as vegetables and a roll and butter. Sweets are about 70p.

VICTORIA RESTAURANT
140 Union Street (Aberdeen 28639)
Open: Mon-Sat 9am-7.30pm

[S]

Enjoy a nicely-presented yet inexpensive meal right here. The à la carte menu includes a selection of starters – soup, fruit juice or grapefruit cocktail all around 50p; main dishes such as omelettes, grills, salads and fish which, with vegetables, are likely to cost between £1.75 and £3.50, and sweets at 50p or more. Very popular is a three-course lunch at around £2.70.

Aboyne

THE BOAT INN, Charleston Road (Aboyne 2137)
Open: Mon-Fri 12noon-2.30pm, Sat-Sun 9am-11pm

[P] [S]

This small inn affords good views of the River Dee, and meals at thoroughly reasonable prices. At lunchtime try macaroni cheese or shepherd's pie, either of which comes at around £2. High tea offers main dishes ranging from bacon and egg (about £2.80) to rump steak at around £4, all served with chips and vegetables and with toast, pancakes, cakes and a pot of tea included in the price. The dinner menu includes home-made pâté at about 90p.

Aviemore

CHIEFTAIN GRILL, Colyumbridge Hotel (Aviemore 810661)
Open: Mon-Sun 12.30-2pm, 5-10.15pm

[C] [P] [♧]

The Colyumbridge Hotel occupies a heather-clad site on the road to the Cairngorm ski-slopes. The spacious grill-room, being part of one of the many hotels in the Reo Stakis chain, guarantees good food at competitive prices. Among the main courses (which include the price of a starter) are fried fillet of haddock (£3.20) and gammon steak (£3.50), but the sirloin and fillet steaks are, alas, out of our league. All sweets, including peach Melba and Black Forest gâteau, are 75p. During the summer various salads augment the menu, but a special children's three-course meal is available.

Beauly

THE SKILLET, The Square (Beauly 2573)
Open: Apr-Oct, Mon-Sat 9.30am-8pm, (7pm Apr, May, Oct), Sun 11am-8pm

[P] [S] [♧]

The Skillet is an ideal place for the hungry tourist. The simple but wholesome fare is reasonably priced at around £2.50 for a three-course table d'hôte lunch and from around £4.50 for a full dinner. The à la carte menu offers a good selection of grills, fish and salads at an average price of £2.75, with bread and butter or toast plus tea included.

Buckie

THE MILL MOTEL, Tynet (Clochan 233)
Open: Mon-Sun 12.30-2pm, 7.30-9pm

[C] [♫] [P]

Only fifteen years ago this old mill was still in production, now it is a character restaurant. Evidence of milling is everywhere and the lounge bar extends into the original lofts. The dining room offers table d'hôte lunch and dinner menus. Lunch is around £3.50 and the choice is excellent but the four-course dinner is the pièce de résistance. Tynet pâté is one of eight delicious starters, with fillet sole Bercy as an entrée. Main courses include sweetbreads chasseur.

Evanton

FOULIS FERRY, 1½ miles S of Evanton on A9 (Evanton 830535)
Open: Mon-Sat 10am-11pm, Sun 12noon-6pm

[P]

Who pays the Ferryman? It's not important in this white-painted converted cottage restaurant where the Ferryman once lived and where reasonably-priced meals are now served. Salads, quiches and simple, home-baked meals are available daily. Choose with care at dinner time and an exotic à la carte meal can work out at around £5.

Forres

THE ELIZABETHAN INN ✕✕ Mondale (Forres 72526)
Open: Mon-Tue, Thu-Fri 12.30-1.30pm, 7.30-8.30pm, Wed 12.30-1.30pm

[P]

An authentic cottagey atmosphere and honest-to-goodness home-cooked fare can be found about two miles west of Forres. Built of stone and close to the River Findhorn, the interior has brick and stone walls, Victorian and antique tables and chairs and a rare air of relaxation. Meals are table d'hôte and it is advisable to book for lunch which at around £3.50 is much in demand.

Fort William

THE ANGUS RESTAURANT
66 High Street (Fort William 2654)
Open: summer: Mon-Sat 10am-10pm, winter: Mon-Sat 12noon-10pm

[S] [♧]

The Angus first-floor restaurant and ground-floor lounge bar has been strikingly created from former shop premises. Red is the colour theme of the well-appointed restaurant which offers a three-course meal from around £3. Grills predominate the à la carte lunch and dinner menus, and particularly recommended is the salmon steak, available in season for around £3.75.

McTAVISH'S KITCHEN, High Street (Fort William 2406)

Open: Restaurant: Easter and mid-May to end Sep Mon-Sun 12noon-3pm, 5-10.45pm. Self-service: Mon-Sun summer: 9am-6pm or later

[♫] [P] [S]

Excellent food, folk cabaret acts (summer evenings) and obliging staff are features here. Although prices in the main restaurant are rather near the limit, a three-course 'budget special' lunch will cost only £3.75, whereas a meal including 'A Taste of Scotland' dishes such as Tweed Kettle (a 19th-century Edinburgh dish of poached salmon fillet cooked in white wine, carrots and onion topped with a light cream sauce) can be had for around £6.50. The ground-floor Laird's Bar and self-service restaurant offer a less pricey selection of meals.

MERCURY MOTOR INN ☆☆☆
Achintore Road (Fort William 3117)
2m along the A85 to Glasgow
Open: Mon-Sun 12noon-2pm, for bar lunches, 6.30-9.30pm (9pm winter)

[C] [♫] [P] [♣]

Panoramic views from the dining room over Loch Linnhe are a bonus here. 'Bar Bites', as the Mercury calls them, include salad bowl lunches at around £3 and various hot dishes. The à la carte dinner menu boasts 'Taste of Scotland' dishes including pickled Mallaig herring, haggis wi' neeps and typically Scottish soups (at around 70p).

THE MOORINGS HOTEL, Banavie
(Corpach 550)
Open: Mon-Sun 12.30-1.30pm, 7-8pm.
Lunches served Jun to Oct only.

[P]

Take the A82 Inverness road out of Fort William turning off on to first the A830 and then the B8004 for Banavie. This family-run hotel is renowned locally for the traditional Scottish fare served in its Jacobean-style dining room. To enjoy a typical meal you might start with smoked Loch Etive mackerel, follow it with Crofter's chicken or Balmoral casserole and finish with Cranachan (a delicious concoction of raspberries, rum, oatmeal and fresh cream).

THE STAG'S HEAD HOTEL ★★
High Street (Fort William 4144)
Open: Restaurant: Mon-Sun 12.30-2.30pm, 6.30-8.30pm.
Bar Snacks: 12noon-5pm

[C] [P] [S]

A stag's head motif on the carpet and expensive dark oak furniture set the scene. The à la carte lunch and dinner menu is a little pricey for our needs but includes a good choice of reasonably-priced starters, and a selection of fish or meat dishes, all at under or around £3. But the bar lunches are the thing – chicken chasseur is around £1.20, fried scampi costs around £1.85 and a fresh salmon salad £3.50

Grantown-on-Spey

CRAGGAN MILL RESTAURANT
(Grantown-on-Spey 2288)
Open: summer: Mon-Sun 12.30-2pm, 6-10pm winter: Mon-Sun 7-10pm

[P]

A plain and rustic style is favoured by proprietors Bruno and Ann Bellini. Cuisine is a winning mixture of Italian and British, as the stylish menu reflects. A starter, such as mussels in wine or mushrooms and Stilton soup, should be followed by scampi provençale or chicken in brandy (both are under £3.75). Interesting sweets are available.

Inverness

BALMORAL RESTAURANT
19 Queensgate (Inverness 33198)
Open: Mon-Sat (also Sun Jul and Aug)
Snack Bar: 8am-5.30pm
Restaurant: 11am-7pm

[S] [♣]

The Balmoral is a popular family restaurant offering good food and friendly service both in the Snack Bar and in the Smorrebrod Restaurant. Snack bar prices range from 40p for filled rolls to about £3 top whack, for steak. The recently-opened Smorrebrod, on the first floor, offers a tempting array of open sandwiches (with salad) at around £2.

CRAWFORDS PIZZA RESTAURANT
Lombard Street (Inverness 34328)
Open: Mon-Sat 10am-11pm,
Sun 12noon-6pm (summer 8pm)

[S] [♣]

This bright, modern pizzeria is conveniently situated in a pedestrianised shopping precinct. Inside, tiled floors and stucco walls with mirrors are in pleasant contrast to the city atmosphere outside. There are sixteen varieties of pizza to choose from, as well as salads, open sandwiches and cannelloni.

OLDE WORLDE INN
Bank Street (Inverness 36577)
Open: Mon-Sat 12noon-2.30pm, 5-10.30pm,

Sun 12.30-2.30pm, 5-10.30pm

C S [symbol]

All the usual friendly, efficient service you'd expect from an establishment in the Reo Stakis chain makes this a popular Inverness eating-house. Main courses include the price of a starter and, apart from some steak options, are quite within the budget. Gammon steak with peach is an appealing choice at £3.50, and why not spoil yourself with hot apple pie and cream for 75p? Children are well catered for as well – their whole meal (that's three courses and a drink) costs only £1.45 in this charming restaurant.

Invershin

INVERSHIN HOTEL ★★
(Invershin 202)
Open: Mon-Thu 12noon-3pm, 7-9pm, Fri and Sun 12noon-3pm, 7-9.30pm, Sat 12noon-3pm, 7-10pm

C P [symbol]

You'll be encouraged to eat Scots at this traditional Highland hotel. Successful consumption of 'freshly-killed Highland haggis with tatties', roast ribs of Angus beef, and sweet little Cloutie dumplings, should leave you with a sense of achievement. And the old Scottish trait of getting good value for money holds true, too – lunch will be under £4, dinner around £5. Local fish features on all menus.

Kentallen

HOLLY TREE RESTAURANT
On A828, 3m SW of Ballachulish Bridge (Duror 292)
Open: restaurant: 10am-2.30pm, coffee shop: 10am-5.30pm

P [symbol]

This restaurant is delightfully situated at the water's edge by Kentallen pier, allowing diners to gaze across the lovely Loch Linnhe to the misty mountains beyond. The eaterie is housed in a converted extension of the old Kentallen railway station and faithfully reproduces much of the original Edwardian-style décor. There is a daily-changing set lunch menu (£2.75) and main course alternatives might be beefburger Bismarck, the 'local daily catch' or honey-baked ham with green salad. If you just fancy a snack, the coffee shop section is open throughout the day. In the evening a large à la carte menu is offered, but with prices starting at £6 it's beyond our limit.

Kingussie

WOOD'N'SPOON RESTAURANT
3-7 High Street (Kingussie 488)
Open: Mon-Sat 10am-9.30pm, Sun 12.30-2.30pm, 6.30-9.30pm

C S [symbol]

The recently renovated restaurant has exposed stonework, a log fire, natural pine partitions and a self service counter where home-made cakes, quiches and other goodies are arrayed. In the evening starters include home-made smoked fish pâté at around £1. Chef's specials include venison casserole and poached salmon, both served with baked potato and vegetables for around £3.75. Home-baked pies and venison burgers are always available. Sweets from the trolley are served with cream.

Lochton

T'MAST, Lochton House (A957, 6m SE of Banchory) (Crathes 543/585)
Open: summer: Mon-Sun 12noon-2.30pm, 4.30-10.30pm

P [symbol]

Formerly a grocer's shop, then a tearoom, this pub-cum-restaurant with its sun lounge extension now acts as a modern oasis for Grampian travellers. Lunchtime prices here are exceptionally low. For example, a simple starter, roast pork with apple sauce and peach Melba only comes to about £3. A typical high tea offering is gammon with pineapple (£3.75), including a hot drink, toast and cakes. Prices for dinner and supper are a little higher, with sirloin steak garni costing about £5.

Peterhead

COFFEE SHOP, Fraserburgh Road (Peterhead 71121)
Open: Mon-Sun 7.30am-11pm

C [symbol] P [symbol]

Inside Peterhead's newest and most modern hotel, the Waterside Inn, you will find this glowing Coffee Shop. Quick snacks include mushrooms and bacon on toast (about £1.10), pizza (around £1.50) or salads (from about £2). A three-course meal could include cream of chicken soup (about 60p), a grill such as farmhouse grill (gammon with egg, mushrooms, tomatoes and chips at around £2.75) and a knickerbocker glory (about 95p).

Stonehaven

CREEL INN, 1m E of A92, 5m S of Stonehaven (Catterline 254)
Open: Tue-Sun 12.30-2.30pm

[C] [P] [♧]

James and Avril Young's attractive white-painted inn nestles on the clifftop above the tiny harbour of Catterline. In the short period that they've owned the restaurant, the Youngs have considerably enhanced its reputation. As you'd expect from an East Grampian eaterie the accent is on sea-food. After a home-made soup you can try home-cured ham salad for £2 or a fresh prawn salad at £2.50.

Thurso

PENTLAND HOTEL ★★ Princes Street (Thurso 3202)
Open: Mon-Thu 12noon-2pm, 6.30-8.30pm, Fri-Sat 12noon-2pm, 6.30-8.30pm, Sun 12.30-2pm, 6.30-8.30pm

[S]

In the bright, cheerful dining room of the Pentland, you can be tempted by an extensive à la carte lunch, dinner, or to combine the best of two meals, a high tea (5-6pm). A three-course lunch can easily cost under £4 and may include roast Caithness ribs of beef, or for 'a few dollars more', fresh Thurso salmon. Bar lunches served during the week are again very reasonably priced.

Tomintoul

GLENMULLIACH RESTAURANT (Tomintoul 356)
2m south-east of Tomintoul
Open: Mon-Sun 10am-8pm

[P] [♧]

The Lannagan family have built their dream restaurant from scratch. Father and sons did the building work, mum took over the decorating. The result is a pleasant, modern, cottage-style building set amongst forested hills. Inside, a wood-burning stove, red-pine fittings and a cheerful atmosphere defy the occasional Scottish mist. Food-wise, the emphasis is on home-baking and Scottish fare. Day-time self-service prices can be as low as £1.75.

Ullapool

FAR ISLES, North Road (Ullapool 2385)
Open: Mon-Sun 12noon-2.15pm, 5.30-9.30pm

[P] [S] [♧]

This attractively decorated, modern restaurant and bar on the northern outskirts of this picturesque little fishing village serves reasonably-priced wholesome food. Dishes include fresh Loch Broom scallops with savoury rice and salad, or escalope of pork Cordon Bleu, French fried and croquette potatoes with vegetables for £3.50.

Wick

LAMPLIGHTER, Wellington Guest House, 41/43 High Street (Wick 3287)
Open: summer: Mon-Sat 11.30am-1.45pm, 6-8pm (closed Wed eve)
winter: Mon-Sat 11.30am-1.45pm

[P] [♧]

This well-established house has been in operation for fifty years, and now John and Rhona Houston are at the helm to provide an excellent lunch or dinner at their first-floor restaurant, or a good range of snack meals in the ground-floor cafeteria. Lunch of melon boat at 50p, followed by Caithness salmon and mixed salad at around £2.20, plus home-made sweet from the trolley for about 55p is a satisfying meal.

WALES

The Red Lion Hotel, Llangorse

Park Hill Hotel, Betws-y-Coed

La Gondola, Swansea

Plantagenant House Tenby

The Cliff Hotel, Cardigan

The Nags Head Hotel, Garthmyl

Wales

LLANDUDNO
CAERNARFON
BETWS-Y-COED
GWYNED
CRICCIETH
HARLECH
BARMOUTH
ABERYSTWYTH
DYFED
CARDIGAN
SOLVA
KEESTON
CARMARTHEN
AMMANFORD
PEMBROKE DOCK
TENBY
WEST GLA
SWANSEA
MUMBLES

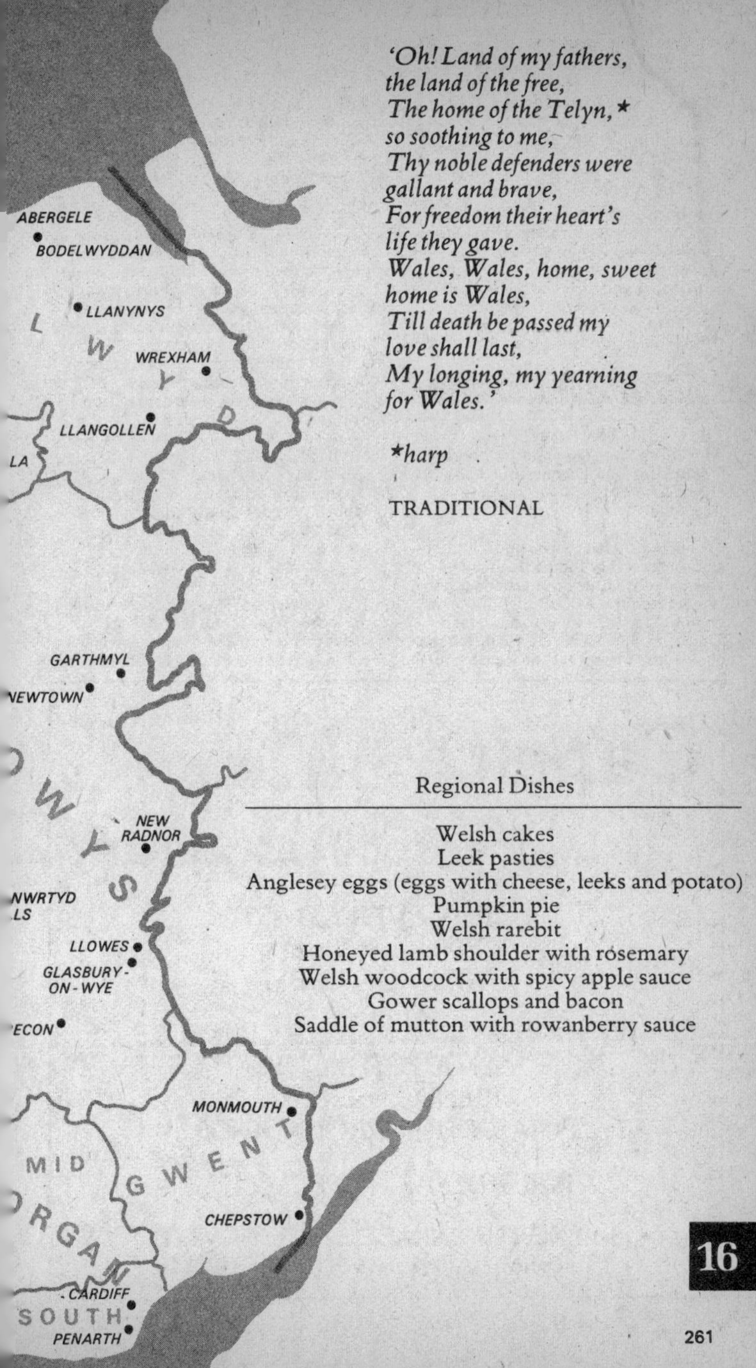

'Oh! Land of my fathers,
the land of the free,
*The home of the Telyn,**
so soothing to me,
Thy noble defenders were
gallant and brave,
For freedom their heart's
life they gave.
Wales, Wales, home, sweet
home is Wales,
Till death be passed my
love shall last,
My longing, my yearning
for Wales.'

**harp*

TRADITIONAL

Regional Dishes

Welsh cakes
Leek pasties
Anglesey eggs (eggs with cheese, leeks and potato)
Pumpkin pie
Welsh rarebit
Honeyed lamb shoulder with rosemary
Welsh woodcock with spicy apple sauce
Gower scallops and bacon
Saddle of mutton with rowanberry sauce

Abergele

BULL HOTEL, Chapel Street (Abergele 822115)
Open: Mon-Sun 12noon-2.30pm, 7-8.30pm

♫ P S

Emphasis is on good home cooking in this traditionally furnished inn with a friendly, relaxed atmosphere. The dining room menu operates for lunch and dinner and offers basic English fare, with three-courses costing from £3-£4.50. Home-made fruit pies or sherry trifle with cream are around 50p.

Aberystwyth

THE CAMBRIAN HOTEL ★★
Alexandra Road (Aberystwyth 612446)
Open: Mon-Sun 12noon-2pm, 6.30-8pm (10pm Thu-Sat, 7.30pm Sun)

P

The atmosphere is warm and friendly and the food is home-cooked, hot and well served. Three-course table d'hôte lunch is around £4.50 and includes a choice of basic English roasts or salad. The four-course table d'hôte dinner has cheese and biscuits as the fourth course. Roast dinners are around £4.50, steak dinners around £5.

CAPRICE, 8-10 North Parade (Aberystwyth 612084)
Open: Jun-Oct Mon-Sun 9am-8.30pm; the rest of the year Mon-Fri 9am-5.30pm (Closed: winter: Wed)

C ♫ S

Crabs straight from the harbour are a speciality at Jill and Alun Evans's cheerful restaurant. A three-course meal, with soup or fruit juice, a main course of roast, poultry or fish, and a sweet such as fruit tart and custard costs about £3.25. The à la carte menu is equally modestly priced, with starters from 35p for fruit juice to around £1.20 for prawn cocktail, main courses are up to about £4.

MARINE HOTEL, Marine Parade (Aberystwyth 612444)
Open: summer: Bar and dining room: Mon-Sun 12.30-2pm, 7-9.30pm, winter: 12.30-2pm, 7pm onwards, Grill room: Mon-Sat 7-9.30pm

C ♫ P S

This Welsh hotel is Welsh owned, and the lamb on the menu is Welsh too. Lunch at around £3.50 cannot be bad value, and here one has a choice of four starters, a main course followed by a pudding or lighter sweet and coffee. The table d'hôte dinner offers a wider choice than the lunch menu at around £5.50. There is also a snack menu, with sandwiches and ploughman's lunch supplemented by sausage (about £1.30) and fish or chicken (about £1.30) all served with chips. Omelettes are priced from £1 with chips. A meal from the cold table is around £2.

Y DEWIN BISTRO, Ffordd Portland Road (Aberystwyth 617738)
Open: Mon-Sat 12noon-2pm, 5-10pm

[♫] [S]

The owner has succeeded in creating a Celtic atmosphere in the heart of Wales. Murals and paintings by a local artist enhance the effect with 'Lord of the Rings' themes. Menus are in Welsh and English, though no attempt has been made to translate pizza or quiche lorraine into either language! All food is home-cooked. Specialities are cawl and syllabub.

Ammanford

EXECUTIVE RESTAURANT
46 High Street (Ammanford 4442)
Open: Tue-Sat 10.30am-2pm, 7.30-10pm

[C] [P] [♿]

Fresh from running a busy pub, owners Bobby and Ray Moring have taken a daring plunge and converted the property adjoining their home (once a vicarage) into a restaurant. A lunchtime platter of fish and chips, roast pork or roast beef with vegetables of the day costs from £1.70-£2.10, with sweet and starter prices kept very low. Bobby Moring's delicious trifle is the most popular dessert. A three-course evening meal here would be likely to take the best part of £6, but for fresh fish and generous cuts of meat, it represents good value for money.

Bala

NEUADD Y CYFNOD, High Street (Bala 520262)
Open: summer: Mon-Sun 9am-9pm, winter: Mon-Fri dinner only

[C] [P] [S] [♿]

In this imposing building, a long school hall, with its panelled walls and high ceilings, Gwyn and Ann Evans offer a taste or two of traditional Welsh cooking. Menus, with parallel text translations, include lunch at around £3 (half price for children), dinner at about £3.50 (again just over half price for children) and a particularly Welsh dinner, that includes a glass of mead, at just over £3.25. Welsh farmhouse soup, with local salmon and lamb figure among the alternatives in all three meals. A speciality of the house is an authentic Welsh tea at around £1 – unbeatable value.

Barmouth

THE ANGRY CHEESE, Church Street (Barmouth 280038)
Open: summer: Mon-Sun 12noon-2pm, 6-10.30pm, winter: Fri-Sat 6-10.30pm

C P

Inside this attractive restaurant pine tables give a cosy, rustic effect. The three-course set menu costs around £4.50. There's a choice of six items in each course, featuring main dishes such as pork schnitzel with beurre noisette or Chicken Grandmère. Vegetarians are tempted by such dishes as fruit and vegetable kebabs or peanut and parmesan pancake. If you go à la carte, potatoes and fresh vegetables of the day are included in the price of the main course dish from that menu.

Betws-y-Coed

PARK HILL HOTEL ★★ Llanrwst Road (Betws-y-Coed 540)
Open: Mon-Sun for dinner, beginning 7-7.30pm (booking essential)

C P

If 'home-made and fresh' appeals to you then you'll like this hotel restaurant. Choice is necessarily limited as proprietors John and Jenny Waite do the cooking and serving themselves. The table d'hôte dinner at around £5.50 offers a choice between soup, fruit juice and two other starters (pâté perhaps), at least three main dishes (a roast, coq au vin, plaice meunière and baked gammon in cider are examples), three sweets (raspberry tart and cream, peach lorraine, blackcurrant cheesecake for instance) and cheese and biscuits, plus tea or coffee. Just one thing – it's advisable to book well in advance.

Bodelwyddan

CROMWELL'S BISTRO, FAENOL FAWR MANOR ✕✕
(Rhuddlan 590784)
Open: Mon-Sun 12 noon-2.30pm, 7.30-11pm

C ♫ P

Faenol Fawr is a restaurant (a bit expensive for us) in a manor house built in 1597, but Cromwell's is *really* old, dating back to the early part of the 13th century. Here, you can take a pleasant yet inexpensive meal chosen from the Supper Bar menu. Starters include home-made soup at around 40p and Arbroath smokies at about £1.50. There are casseroles – duck and blackberry at around £2.20 and local pheasant in red wine (around £3) and meat platters for about £2 – with help-yourself salad and jacket potato included in the price. A home-made sweet will add 75p or so.

Brecon

RED LION INN, Llangorse
(Llangorse 238)
Open: Mon-Sun 12noon-2pm, 7-9.30pm

P ♣

A warm Welsh welcome is assured in this two hundred-year-old inn close to the famous Llangorse lake. Situated deep in the heart of the Brecon Beacons National Park, it is an ideal holiday stopping-place. Meals in the bar include snacks such as Chef's terrine, roll and butter at about 70p, cottage pie or lasagne at about £1.40. More substantial dishes such as chicken Red Lion style, veal Cordon Bleu or beef chasseur cost around £3. An à la carte meal may be had in the dining room, but this could prove beyond our means.

Caernarfon

PLAS BOWMAN, High Street
(Caernarfon 5555)
Open: Mon-Sat 12noon-1.30pm, 6-9.30pm, Sun 12noon-1.30pm, 7-8pm

S ♣

Built in 1334 for the High Sheriff, Thomas Bowman, this three-storey property now houses Posi Williams, North Wales Chef of the Year 1980, who cooks fresh meats, fish and vegetables for a brilliantly imaginative menu which changes daily. Just under £6 will get you three courses, coffee or tea and a glass of wine for lunch or dinner. The set menu offers about four choices for each course. Appetisers could include avocado vinaigrette, pâté of the house or sardine salad. Salmon with hollandaise sauces, beef Stroganoff or stuffed marrow are examples of main course dishes, and vegetarians are catered for here. It is advisable to book in advance as Plas Bowman is deservedly popular with the locals of Caernarfon.

THE STABLES RESTAURANT AND HOTEL ☆☆☆
(Llanwnda 830711/830413)
Open: Mon-Sun 12noon-1.45pm, 7-9.45pm

C ♫ P ♣

Some of the best food that Caernarfon has to offer is to be found at Mrs Jenny Howarth's Stables Restaurant, some three miles outside the town, on the A497 road to Pwllheli. Formerly the stables to Plas Fynnon, the building was very cleverly and tastefully converted for its present use in 1972. The menu is a long and impressive one but the locals, who ought to know, swear by the barbecued spare ribs starter, ham and asparagus mornay, grilled trout with almonds, local lamb chops in wine sauce and pineapple flambé, all around £3.25. A table d'hôte menu is also available for around £5.50 and about £4.50 at lunchtimes. The piped music is agreeable and discreet and live entertainment is frequently provided in the evenings.

Cardiff

THE BUNGALOW CAFE, 15 High Street (Cardiff 26932)
Open: Mon-Sat 10am-5.30pm

S ♣

The Bungalow Café has been established in Cardiff for all of seventy years. Opposite the entrance to Castle Arcade, and very handy for Cardiff Castle, The Bungalow offers a fairly comprehensive menu covering morning coffee, lunch, afternoon tea and grills in an old-fashioned tea house setting. Starters range from around 40p to £1, roasts and poultry from about £2-£3, grills from around £2.60-£3.70, fish dishes from £2-£3.50 or so and sweets from around 47p upwards. The restaurant is reached through a cake-shop via a small takeaway bar selling pasties, steak pies, cottage pies, etc. The Bungalow is unlicensed.

THE HIMALAYA RESTAURANT
24 Wellfield Road (Cardiff 491722)
Open: Mon-Sun 12noon-3pm, 6pm-2am

C ♫ S ♣

The best Indian food in Cardiff is the local verdict on Bakshi Suleman's restaurant. The Himalaya has a vaguely Oriental décor. Biriani dishes, chicken curries and meat or prawn curries cost from around £2.50 to £2.75. Be warned: the helpings are enormous.

THE PLYMOUTH ARMS RESTAURANT, St Fagans (Cardiff 569130)
Open: Tue-Sat 12noon-2.30pm, 7-9.30pm

[C] [P]

You take the A48 Swansea road out of Cardiff, following the signs for the Welsh folk museum, to reach St Fagans and The Plymouth Arms. You can get a good bar lunch for around £1.75 and a substantial three-course table d'hôte lunch for about £4.50 on Sundays, £5 on weekdays, which includes the choice of sirloin steak bordelaise. The à la carte menu is comparatively expensive, but a three-course dinner at around £6.50 is available if you go table d'hôte and keep a strong will.

SAVASTANO'S, 302 North Road (Cardiff 30270)
Open: Mon-Sat 12noon-2.30pm, 7-11.30pm (Thu-Sat 12mdnt)

Giacomo Savastano's restaurant doesn't strike one as particularly Italian, for the décor is plain and the furniture pine. But his food is very Italian, very good and – as Italian restaurants go – extremely reasonably priced, with soups around 60p, pastas at about £2.60, a number of fish, chicken or veal dishes at around £3.25 and steaks from about £3.60. Service is very efficient at this restaurant.

YE OLDE WINE SHOPPE, Wyndham Arcade, St Mary Street (Cardiff 29876)
Open: Mon-Sat 12noon-2.30pm, 7-11pm

♫ [P] [S]

Don't be put off by the name. This must be the best-stocked wine bar in Cardiff and well worth a visit, for its friendly bars and bright little bistro. The downstairs bar and bistro serve the same food at the same prices – appetisers at around 30p (fruit juices) to £3 (snails), a choice of cold table platters at about £2.50, or Chef's special pancakes with gorgeous fillings such as chicken, prawns and spices in a white wine sauce. Gâteaux and cheesecakes are about 75p a portion.

YR YSTAFELL GYMRAEG
74 Whitchurch Road (Cardiff 42317)
Open: Mon-Fri 12noon-2pm, 7-11.30pm, Sat 7-11.30pm

[C]

Yr Ystafell Gymraeg (The Welsh Room to you) is just that, with its Welsh-weave drapes, Welsh tapestry curtains, Welsh Tourist Board posters, the inevitable Welsh dresser and a Welsh menu (with English sub-titles). The owners sound Italian and, indeed, proprietor Umberto Palladino is, but his wife is just about as Welsh as it is possible to be. Starters include Penclawdd Cockles at around £1.10. Poultry dishes range in price from around £3 for chicken Snowdonia. Home-made fruit pies, gâteaux and trifle range from between 70p-£1.20.

Cardigan

THE BELL HOTEL, Pendre (Cardigan 612629)
Open: Mon-Sat 12noon-2pm, 7-9pm

[C] [P] [S]

Malcolm and Jenny Wood have a good lunchtime trade at The Bell. Hot dishes in the restaurant include steak and kidney pie at £1.95, and deep-fried scampi at around £3. The evening menu includes fresh local sea trout at around £3.75.

THE BLACK LION HOTEL
High Street (Cardigan 612532)
Open: Mon-Sat 12noon-2.30pm, 8-10pm

♫ [S]

Inglenook fireplaces, exposed beams and stone walls set the scene at the Black Lion. For about £5 you can have a satisfying three-course meal in the Linenfold Bar (rounded off by a speciality ice-cream) and perhaps even try a cocktail or two. Drivers are catered for with non-alcoholic wine and lager, and tea, coffee or hot chocolate served at the bar. Try the meals in baskets at prices from £2.55 upwards, served in the lounge.

CLIFF HOTEL ★★★ Gwbert-on-Sea (Cardigan 613241/613242/612517)
Open: Mon-Sun 12.45-2pm, 7-9pm

[C] [♫] [P] [♣]

This restaurant offers an interesting choice of menu but unfortunately, the à la carte is beyond our reach and even the table d'hote lunch and dinner at around £6 and £7 respectively strain the purse strings a bit, though they deserve a mention for special occasions. For starters hot consommé with profiteroles, main course – hot crab Gwbert style with new potatoes and tomato provençale, and a choice of sweets from the trolley. In the newly-opened buttery it is possible to dine in style on a meal of locally-caught sewin, plus starter and sweet, for under or around the £5 mark.

Carmarthen

THE OLD CURIOSITY, 20A King Street (Carmarthen 32384)
Open: Mon-Tue 10am-5pm, Wed-Fri 10am-9.30pm, Sat 10am-10pm

[♫] [P] [S] [♣]

The Old Curiosity is much, much more than a convenient place for a coffee, a snack, or a meal. The Indian salad contains brown rice, not white, and vegetarians may choose from a number of appetising dishes. The seafood salad at around £2.50 is excellent, and omelettes include mushroom, ham or chicken all at around £1.50. 'Gap fillers' at around £1 include curry butter prawns and bacon-wrapped bananas. Various quiches cost about 85p a slice.

QUEENSWAY RESTAURANT
Queen Street (Carmarthen 5631)
Open: Mon-Sat 10am-2.30pm, 6.30-11pm

[C]

This ground-floor restaurant and first-floor wine bar opens on to a sun-trap roof garden. Steaks are popular in the restaurant, where the à la carte menu includes Chef's specials priced about £3. Meals served from the wine bar include plaice and chips or roast beef and Yorkshire pudding at around £4 or steak and chips at under £4.

Chepstow

CASTLE VIEW HOTEL ★★ Bridge Street (Chepstow 70349)
Open: Mon-Sat 12.15-2pm, 6.30-9pm, Sun 12.15-1.45pm, 6.30-8.30pm and normal licensing hours

C P S

As its name suggests this charming, creeper-clad hotel is opposite Chepstow Castle. Meals in the bar include imaginative soups such as salmon and cucumber, cawl and celestial soup – potato, carrot and onion with sherry. Prawns au gratin is a popular main course choice, so is fresh Wye salmon at £3 with salad. Lemon syllabub costs around 85p. Restaurant dishes include West Country pork chop with apple, onion, cheese and cider or plaice fillet poached in white wine with mushroom and cream sauce, but these might be just out of our price range.

THE FIRST HURDLE
9 Upper Church Street
(Chepstow 2189)
Open: Mon-Sat 12noon-9pm

C P S

Just off Chepstow's town centre is this small hotel, immediately attractive because of its Edwardian furniture and pretty soft furnishings. At lunchtime, roast joints carved hot from the oven represent good value, as well as Welsh lamb chops and daily specials such as home-made steak and kidney pie or curry. In the evening diners can choose from the French menu, where a good choice would be French onion soup (70p), followed by trout with almonds and fresh vegetables (£3.60), and a sweet from the trolley, or the grill menu where prawn cocktail, gammon with pineapple, salad, peas and chips and a sweet costs about £5.

Criccieth

BRON EIFION COUNTRY HOTEL
★★★ (Criccieth 2385)
Open: Mon-Sun 8.30-9.30am, 1-2pm, 7.30-9pm

P

Bron Eifion was built in the 1870s as the summer residence of slate master John Greaves. Its main hall boasts superb wall panelling and a magnificent central galley of pitch pine. The hotel's three-course lunch is about £5 (including service) and gives a tempting choice of starters and desserts.

THE MOELWYN RESTAURANT
Mona Terrace (Criccieth 2500)
Open: Mon-Sun 12.30-2pm, 7-9.30pm (closed Mon all day and Sun pm in winter)

C P

Mr and Mrs Peter Booth worked for the previous owners for four years before purchasing the Moelwyn Restaurant, a creeper-clad Victorian house with panoramic views over Cardigan Bay and the Cambrian Range, five years ago. Readers may enjoy lunch only in this neatly furnished dining room, as the evening meal is beyond our budget. Tasty lunch offerings include a good quality home-made soup for around 65p, smoked mackerel or lasagne verdi at about £1.85, a choice of sweet or cheeseboard for 80p or so and Cona coffee at 50p. A children's menu offers three courses for about £2 and, on Sundays, a traditional roast lunch table d'hôte costs under £4.

Garthmyl

THE NAG'S HEAD HOTEL
(Berriew 287/537)
Open: Mon-Sat 10.30am-2.30pm, 6-10.30pm, Sun 12noon-2pm, 7-10.30pm

C P

Modern, colourful décor is the hallmark of the small restaurant at The Nag's Head, where Mr and Mrs Emilio Moreno attend personally to your needs. The atmosphere is cosy and intimate in the small bar where you can drink while you wait for your excellent meal. Particularly recommended is the table d'hôte – for example, you can eat Spanish omelette, roast chicken Cuban style and apple pie for under £5, or pick a 'main course special' which comes preceded by soup at £2.80.

Glasbury

LLWYNAUBACH LODGE ★★
(Glasbury 473)
Open: Mon-Sun 12noon-2.30pm, 7.30-10.30pm

C P

Llwynaubach Lodge enjoys a peaceful situation in the Wye Valley with ten acres of grounds including its own trout-filled lake and an outdoor swimming pool. At lunchtime during the week, hot and cold bar snacks and salads are available from £1-£3 – sandwiches even cheaper. Chef's carving table offers hot roast joints in the evenings and for Sunday lunch.

Harlech

CASTLE COTTAGE (Harlech 780479)
Open: summer: Mon-Sun 10.30am-2pm, 6.30-9pm (Sun eve; bookings only)
winter: Fri-Sun 10.30am-2pm, 6.30-8.30pm (closed Sun eve)

C

Castle Cottage had a variety of uses before it became a restaurant and guest house some twenty-five years ago; it was once a farm, a smithy, a butcher's shop and, originally, a gin shop. Jim and Betty Yuill cater for up to twenty-six people in their 16th-century beamed cottage which can be found adjacent to Harlech Castle. Simple lunch dishes include cottage pie, meatballs in tomato sauce and plaice and chips all at around £1 (all home-made). A special three-course table d'hôte menu is excellent value at £1.95. At dinnertime the menu is more adventurous and includes starters such as New Orleans prawn at just over £1 or eggs Florentine for around 85p. With main course of haddock in cream, and coffee granita for dessert, you have a substantial meal for less than £5.

Llandudno

COFFEE SHOP AND POOLSIDE BAR, EMPIRE HOTEL ★★★ Church Walks (Llandudno 79955)
Open: Mon-Sun 11am-3pm, 6-10pm

C P

The range of five different starters (predominantly fishy!) cost from 70p-£1.50. A variety of salads, rainbow trout and charcoal chicken are just some of the main courses that enable you to keep within the budget. Desserts are around 75p and include fresh fruit salad.

PLAS FRON DEG HOTEL
48 Church Walks (Llandudno 77267)
Open: Mon-Sun 12.30-2pm, 6.30-7.30pm

C

Lunch and dinner menus priced from around £4.50-£6 offer a real choice, with dishes such as salmon mousse, coq au vin and ratafia trifle to tempt the taste buds. 'A Taste of Wales' dishes are a feature of Plas Fron Deg, too, and well worth trying. The à la carte menu is likely to be out of our price range.

Llangollen

GALE'S WINE AND FOOD BAR
18 Bridge Street (Llangollen 860089)
Open: Mon-Sat 12noon-1.45pm, 6-10pm (also Sun Jun-Oct)

P S

There are more than a hundred wines on offer at Richard and Jill Gale's Wine and Food Bar, including one vintage port. The atmosphere is very friendly and welcoming, the menu written on a blackboard behind the bar. The food is outstandingly good for this kind of operation and very reasonable, with home-made soups at around 50p, a choice of pâtés at around 85p and a hot dish of the day from around £2.30. Very popular are pork and apple Stroganoff at around £1.90 and beef in Guinness at about £2.20.

ROYAL HOTEL ★★★ Bridge Street (Llangollen 860202)
Open: Mon-Sun 12.30-2.15pm, 7-9.30pm (10pm Sat)

C P S

There are views of the River Dee from

the restaurant of this Trusthouse Forte hotel. The à la carte menu is on the expensive side, but the three-course table d'hôte lunch at about £5.25 and dinner at around £6 are excellent value. A good, more modest bar lunch or evening meal is possible at around £2.

Llanwrtyd Wells

DOL-Y-COED HOTEL
(Llanwrtyd Wells 215)
Open: Mon-Sat 12noon-2pm, 7-8pm

[P]

Everything a simple country hotel should be, the creeper-clad Dol-y-Coed overlooks the River Irfon on the outskirts of the village. Log fires, dark, rich wood, old prints and unpretentious comfort exude a peaceful atmosphere. The three-course lunch (under £4) and dinner (around £5) present a small choice of good, fresh food. Bar meals such as home-cooked cold ham and various salads at under £2 are available.

Llanynys

THE LODGE, Llanrhaeadr, near Denbigh (Llanynys 370)
Open: Mon-Sat 9.30am-5.30pm

[C] [P] [♧]

The Lodge combines the display of fashions (from many parts of the world) and objets d'art with the provision of tasty inexpensive food. The accent is on light meals with filled baps, Welsh rarebit, hamburger, and several other items, all at under £2, but there are more substantial dishes including salads (cheese, ham, prawn or chicken) for between £1.60-£2.50 and savoury pancakes or omelettes for less than £2. Sweets and pastries are home-made. A wide variety of beverages is available – but the Lodge is not licensed.

Llowes

RADNOR ARMS (Glasbury 460)
Open: Mon-Sat 12noon-3pm, 7-10.30pm

[P] [♧]

This small, pleasant country pub is a converted house with white-painted walls. The atmosphere in the dining area with its high, beamed ceiling, is informal and relaxed. A good selection of food is chalked up on the blackboard menu with home-made soups at about 90p, quiches at around £2, lasagne or Cheshire pork and apple pie, both about £2.50 and mackerel in white wine costing a little more. There is a good selection of sweets at around £1.

Monmouth

KING'S HEAD HOTEL ★★★ Agincourt Square (Monmouth 2177)
Open: Mon-Fri 12.30-2pm, 7-9pm,
Sat 12.30-2pm, 7-10pm,
Sun 12.30-1.45pm, 7-9pm
Coach House: Mon 6.30-11pm,
Tue-Sat 12noon-3pm, 6.30-11pm,
Sun 12noon-2pm, 7-10pm

[P] [S]

Table d'hôte lunch costs around £5, but the dinner menu is £6 or more. Other informal lunches well within the budget are served in the cocktail bar – a cold buffet selection with interesting, fresh salads costs about £2, and hot dish of the day might be a casserole, pasta dish or steak and kidney pie. To the rear of the main hotel, is the Coach House. Colourful plants are arranged on the very pleasant patio area. Prices on the pub-snack menu range between 50p and £2. In the grill room, the usual selection of grills is enlivened by Barnsley chop at £2.65 or Polynesian prawn and pineapple curry at about £5.

Mumbles

LA GONDOLA, 590 Mumbles Road (Swansea 62338)
Open: Tue-Sun 12noon-2.30pm, 6.30-11pm

[C] [P]

Apart from his native Italian, Proprietor Aldo Grattarola speaks English very well, and gets by in French and German so it follows that he should keep a cosmopolitan menu. À la carte choices include veal dishes, fillet Stroganoff, Dover sole meunière and lasagne verdi al forno – a pretty cosmopolitan bag, you'll agree! More modest is the set lunch menu offering four choices of roast, plaice, trout or steak and kidney pie with vegetables and potatoes, plus a sweet and starter, around £3.

New Radnor

RED LION INN
Llanfihangel Nant Melan
(New Radnor 220)
Open: Mon-Sun 12noon-2pm, 7-11pm

[P] [♧]

A warm welcome always awaits visitors to this 300-year-old roadside inn.

Situated on the A44 between Leominster and Rhayader, the building retains its olde-worlde character and charm while also benefiting from modern comforts inside such as the cosy wood-burning stove in the lounge. Proprietors, the two man-and-wife teams of Beadle and Rowan, pride themselves in offering homely fare and for only £4.75 or so, you can sit down to a wholesome lunch of soup, and 8oz sirloin steak with trimmings followed by ice-cream or cheese and biscuits. Sunday lunch costs around £1 less – so you can afford to treat the family. Tasty bar snacks, served day or evening, include scampi or steak and kidney pie at around £1.70 and a cold buffet, served from the verandah, is a big attraction at £1.50 per head.

Newtown

BEAR HOTEL ★★★ Broad Street
(Newtown 26964)
Open: Mon-Sun 12noon-2pm, 6.30-9.30pm

C P S

Formerly a coaching inn, the Bear has all the atmosphere anyone could wish for. Food is available in the bar and in two grill rooms: the Spinning Wheel and the Severn. Bar snacks are served in the evening and are mainly substantial, including steak and kidney pie or chicken and chips. The restaurants serve an excellent three-course dinner with a large choice for each course, including fresh goujons of sole in tomato sauce or chicken Marengo at around £4.50 including coffee.

Pembroke Dock

HILL HOUSE INN, Cosheston
(Pembroke 4352/5344)
Open: Mon-Sun 12noon-2pm, 7-10pm

C P

There's a touch of Welsh patriotism at this early Georgian Inn, with Welsh gammon and lamb featuring on the table d'hôte menu amongst a good choice of international dishes. The beers are mainly Welsh brews – and the impressive Victorian-style, mahogany bar on the ground floor was made by local craftsman John Owen Hughes. There is a comfortable, welcoming atmosphere. The table d'hôte in the charming dining room is around £6 but does include a glass of house wine. Bar meals are good value, with home-made soups and pâtés at 50p and 75p respectively, and prawn Normandy (with tartare sauce, apple and tomato purée) at £1.80, or fresh local trout.

Penarth

RABAIOTTI'S, CAPRICE RESTAURANT, ××× The Esplanade (Penarth 702424)
Open: Mon-Sat 10.30am-2.30pm, 7-10.30pm, Sun 10.30am-2.30pm

[C] [♫] [P] [S] [🍷]

Situated below the Caprice Restaurant (superb cuisine but too expensive for us!) Rabaiotti's operates from the same kitchen and offers good, unpretentious food at very reasonable prices. Starters include home-made soup of the day at around 40p, potted shrimps at about £1.20 and mixed hors d'oeuvres at around £2. Dishes include lamb cutlets, peas and chips, at just over £3, and fillet steak garni with chips, at about £4.50. Sweets include a choice of gâteaux and fruit tart with cream in the 50p-80p range. The three-course Sunday lunch is very good value, the price list for the main course being inclusive of starter and sweet and costing about £4.65. Starters offer a choice of soup, fruit juice or Florida cocktail, the third course can be a fresh cream dessert or cheese and biscuits. Rabaiotti's also boasts an interesting cocktail bar open to non-diners which proves popular.

Solva

HARBOUR HOUSE, Solva (St Davids 721267)
Open: summer: Mon-Sun 8.30am-2.30pm, Mon-Sat 7-9.30pm, winter: Thu-Sat only – telephone to determine times

[P] [🍷]

The Canby-Lewis family run this small hotel with obvious enjoyment. For lunch you could do no better than to try the home-made cawl, a large bowl of steaming hot soup which comes served with a tasty cheese roll and butter at 95p. Tasty pizzas are made to order on the premises, the trout and mackerel come from local waters, and the steaks are cut from local beef. The speciality of the house is tournedos Maximillian – fillet steak wrapped in bacon, served on a croute and covered in mushroom and Madeira sauce, but it's out of our price range. However, plenty of other dishes – such as scampi with tartare sauce – are under £3. Sweets include home-made gâteau, cheesecake and chocolate mousse Basquaise. Children under twelve have their own Junior Menu with old favourites such as hamburger and chips, ice cream and lemonade.

THE OLD PHARMACY CAFE
Main Street
(Solva 232/492)
Open: Mon-Sun 9am-9pm

[P]

An old pharmacy is what this traditional, shop-fronted restaurant was before it became such a boon to this little town in the tidal-inlet valley. Daily deliveries of freshly-caught fish to the kitchen from St Brides Bay include Solva crab and sewin (Welsh salmon trout). Smoked trout from the trout farm at Llawhaden is used in the home-made pâté and is served with tomato salad and granary bread (£1.20). Steak, crab and trout are popular main course dishes, but at lunchtime the cold table prevails. Sweets such as honey snap ice with almonds and fresh cream or walnut meringue delight come at under £1.

Swansea

THE DRAGON HOTEL ☆☆☆☆
Kingsway Circle (Swansea 51074)
Open: The Birch Room: Mon-Sat 12.30-2.30pm, 7-9.30pm
The Dragon and Viking Buttery: Mon-Sun 12noon-2.45pm, 6-10.45pm

[C] [P] [S]

The Birch Room's à la carte menu is on the expensive side but a choice of table d'hôte lunches at prices from about £5, the three-course table d'hôte dinner at around £5.85 and the four-course one at the £6.50 mark are all excellent value. The Buttery prices are extremely competitive, with plaice around £3, pizza Norseman at around £1.75 and gammon steak at around £3. Prices of the lounge-bar salads run from £2 upwards.

Tenby

HOI SAN RESTAURANT
Tudor Square (Tenby 2025)
Open: Apr-Sep Mon-Sun 12noon-11.45pm, Oct-Dec, Mar Thu-Fri 6-11.45pm, Sat-Sun 12noon-11.45pm

[C] [S]

A friendly, enthusiastic Cantonese atmosphere is to be found here in the centre of Tenby. Chopsticks are laid out to test your dexterity and help is at hand should you fail the test. Special home cooking evenings are laid on when unusual family-style dishes are available. The choice of special dinners is impressive. A four-course dinner and coffee will cost about £5.15 per person, but two can share the £4.90 menu which offers three courses (a choice of four main dishes) and coffee. Particularly recommended are hot and sour soup and char siu – honey roast pork with Cantonese roast and boiled rice. Special facilities exist for mothers with young babies.

THE LION'S DEN, ROYAL LION HOTEL ★★ High Street (Tenby 2127)
Open: summer: Mon-Sun 12noon-2pm, 6.30-10pm

C

The Lion's Den restaurant and bar, with its dark oak settles and cosy alcoves, is a favourite meeting and eating place for Tenby folk and visitors alike. The cheap three-course lunch with roast chicken, plaice, steak and kidney pie and omelettes all around £3 and a special menu for children at around £1.75 are excellent value as is the à la carte menu, with main course dishes ranging from locally-caught fish to entrecôte Bordelaise. Gâteaux, fruit pies and cheesecakes come at 70p each and make an excellent sweet course.

PLANTAGENET HOUSE, Quay Hill (Tenby 2350)
Open: Etr-Oct: Mon-Sun 10am-10.30pm

C S

This 15th-century house boasts a superb example of a Flemish Chimney. As well as the more traditional meals, Barney and Tina Stone also offer an interesting selection of vegetarian and wholemeal-based dishes. Prices range from around £1 for a slice of vegetarian quiche to around £4 for local crab or salmon in season with a large mixed salad. Home-made chili con carne with brown rice or a large home-made wholemeal pizza can be enjoyed for around £2. A lighter meal of open sandwiches or burgers can be had in the downstairs Quincy Room. This historical restaurant welcomes families. Children are well-catered for.

Wrexham

THE WELSH KITCHEN
7-9 Church Street (Wrexham 263302)
Open: Mon-Sat 10am-2.30pm

C S

Ann Evans owns and runs this tranquil restaurant in a 14th-century listed building – the oldest in Wrexham. Exposed roof timbers set the scene and there is a good choice from any one of thirteen home-made main courses, all for around £2.50. Home-made desserts such as fruit pie and cream cost about 65p each.

A–Z of Towns

A

B

C

D

E

F

G

H

I

J

K

L

M

T

U

V

W

Y

Report Form 1982

You are invited to recommend your favourite restaurant for the 1983 edition of *Eat Out For Around £5.*

To: The Automobile Association
Hotel and Information Services Department
9th Floor
Fanum House
Basingstoke
Hampshire
RG21 2EA

Name of establishment ______________________

____

Address ______________________

____

____

____

Telephone number ______________________

Date of visit ______________________

Average price of a three-course meal	£	
Is the restaurant already AA-appointed?	YES	NO
If so, do you agree with the classification or recommendation?	YES	NO

Name ______________________

Address ______________________

____

____

____

Date ____________ Signature ______________________

Cut along here

Additional remarks:

Glossary

afelia Greek dish of pork fillet, red wine, cream and coriander

antipasti Italian appetisers

apfel strüdel apple in very thin pastry

Arbroath smokies haddock specially cured at Arbroath

baklava Greek sweet of flaky pastry filled with nuts and steeped in syrup

beef blanquette beef stew made with a white sauce

beef kromeski creamed mixture of meats wrapped in bacon and deep-fried in butter

beef Stroganoff strips of steak cooked with onions and mushrooms, with sour cream and sherry

beef teriyaki Japanese dish of sliced beef marinated in soy sauce, ginger, garlic and mirin

Berliner apfel kuchen German apple cake

biriani meat and rice dish flavoured with spices and saffron

bistecca pizzaiola beef steak with tomatoes, garlic and basil

blanquette de veau veal casseroled in white sauce

boeuf bourguignon beef casseroled in red wine with onions, bacon and mushrooms

bouillabaise Marseilles assorted fish and shellfish cooked in white wine, garlic, saffron and olive oil

brochette cooked on a skewer

cacciatore Italian hunter's-style sauce – with mushrooms, herbs, shallots, wine, tomatoes, ham and tongue

cannelloni tubular pasta stuffed with meat and served with sauce

carbonnade of beef beef slices, onions and herbs braised in beer

chapatis Indian unleavened bread

chasseur French hunter's-style sauce of mushrooms, tomatoes, wine, garlic and herbs

chateaubriand thick fillet or rump steak

chicken Kiev young whole chicken or chicken breast rolled and stuffed with garlic butter, rolled in fresh breadcrumbs and fried in oil

chicken à la king diced chicken with mushrooms and pimentoes in a white sauce with sherry, whisky and slivered almonds

chicken Basque style chicken cooked with onions, green peppers and tomatoes

chicken florentine chicken cooked in oil, with spices and spinach

chicken kurma mildly spiced chicken cooked with cream and nuts

chicken paesana chicken peasant-style, with bacon, potatoes, carrots, marrow and root vegetables

chicken spatchcock 'despatch cock' – small broiler, jointed and grilled at speed

chicken supreme boned chicken breast served in a thick, bland chicken stock

chicken Veronique chicken casseroled in white wine sauce with grapes

chili con carne kidney beans, minced beef, tomatoes, pimento or chili pepper and spices, with slices of raw onion

chocolate Bavarois rich, chocolate custard, set with gelatine and topped with whipped cream

chop suey stir-fried meat in gunpowder sauce, served with rice

chow chow Chinese preserve of orange peel, ginger etc

chow mein fried noodles with a topping of stir-fried meats and vegetables

clam chowder spicy clam soup

coq au vin chicken flamed with brandy and casseroled in red wine with mushrooms, bacon, onion and herbs

consommé clear soup served hot or cold

croûtons small pieces of bread toasted or fried

crudites an appetiser of raw vegetables, usually served sliced, grated or diced

Cumberland sausage a giant herb-filled sausage, containing rosemary, thyme and sage

cumquat plum-sized fruit with sweet rind and acid pulp

d'agneau grillée poivre vert lamb grilled with green peppers

devilled pôissin whole, young chicken in a hot, spicy sauce

dolci Italian pastries and cakes

dolmas vine leaves stuffed with rice and herbs

dolmades (dolmadakia) vine or cabbage leaves stuffed with rice and minced meat, braised in white sauce

dondurma makli Egyptian ice cream flavoured with mastic

egg à la Russe eggs in mayonnaise with diced vegetables

en croûte in a pastry crust

escalope of veal champignoise thin slice of veal served in mushroom sauce

escalope of veal cordon bleu breaded veal with a cheese filling

escalope of veal Holstein thin, boneless slice of veal, breaded, with fried egg and anchovies

escargots snails

fetta best-known Greek cheese, made of goat's, or ewe's milk, white and crumbly

fettuccine matriciana thin noodles served in tomato sauce, bacon or pork and sheep's milk cheese

Florida cocktail grapefruit and orange appetiser

fondue *either* melted cheese with white wine in a tureen, into which bread is dipped, *or* bite-sized pieces of beef, dipped into boiling oil in a tureen and eaten with a variety of sauces

fricasée browned pieces of meat braised with seasonings and vegetables and served in a thick sauce

gazpacho icy cold, seasoned soup with raw onions, garlic, tomato, cucumber and green peppers

gnocchi Italian dumplings

goulash beef or veal casseroled with paprika, peppers, onions and vegetables, served with sour cream

gulab jam a traditional Indian sweet

haggis boiled sheep's tripe stuffed with oatmeal, onions, chopped sheep's liver, lights and heart

horiatiko Greek rye bread

houmous Greek chick pea and sesame appetiser

jugged hare jointed hare casseroled in a mixture of herbs, onions, cloves and port or stout

kalamari squid

kateifi Greek sweet of sugared thin noodles, almonds, walnuts and syrup

kedgeree flaked fish served in a mixture of rice, eggs and butter

kleftedes spicy Greek meat balls

kleftiko Greek 'bandits meal' of lamb cooked with bay, oregano and spices

kosher pastrami lamb or beef sausage cooked in unadulterated oils

kotopoullo chicken roast with spring beans and Greek herbs

kotta kebab skewered chicken with peppers and tomatoes

kulfi Indian ice cream with nuts

lamb's kidney's turbigo kidneys chopped in batter with mushroom and sausage pieces, glazed with white wine and tomato

lamb marechella pieces of lamb fried in egg and breadcrumbs

lamb masallam whole leg of lamb or lamb pieces marinated and cooked with rare Indian herbs

lamb pasanda marinated lamb slices cooked in cream or yoghurt and mild spices

lasagne thin layers of noodle dough, baked with tomato, sausage meat, chicken liver, ham, white sauce and grated cheese

lobster bisque rich soup made from lobster, cream and brandy

lobster musalla lobster cooked with curry powder

longaniko sausage Greek sausage made with minced pork marinated in wine and smoked

marchand de vin steak poached in red wine with shallots or onions

Marsala red dessert wine from Sicily

masala Indian herbs

medaglione round fillets of beef or veal

meringue glacé Chantilly meringue served with ice cream and sweetened, whipped cream

meze (mezedes) a selection of Greek speciality dishes

mignonette small pieces of tenderloin of beef, pork or veal

milanese Milanese style: breaded, fried with Parmesan cheese and often served with saffron rice

Mortadella salad salad served with Bologna sausage

moules marinières mussels simmered in white wine and garlic

moussaka Greek dish of layers of aubergines and minced meat, topped with a white sauce and baked

mousseline a variety of Hollandaise sauce with whipped cream

moutons au haricots casserole of mutton, beans and potatoes

mozzarella soft, unripened cheese with a sweet, bland flavour, made from buffalo's milk in Southern Italy, cow's milk elsewhere

nan levened Indian bread

navarin of lamb mutton casserole with turnips

neeps Scottish turnips

noisettes choice, boneless meat usually taken from loin or rib and cut into a round shape

normande Norman style – usually cooked in white wine with gudgeon, crayfish, oysters, mussels, shrimps, mushrooms, cream or with truffles

oregano herb of the marjoram family

paella Spanish saffron rice dish with assorted seafood and/or meat

paprika huhn German paprika-cooked chicken

pâté de foie gras duck or goose liver pâté

Pavlova meringue meringue filled with ice cream and fruit such as raspberries or strawberries

peach Melba peach served in syrup with vanilla ice cream and raspberry sauce

pear Hélène pear with vanilla ice cream and chocolate sauce

Peking duck roast duck eaten wrapped in a pancake

penne carbona macaroni with ham, cream, eggs, cheese and nutmeg

pillau rice and meat cooked together in spices

pitta flat, round bread

pizza capricciosa chef's speciality pizza

pizza margherita pizza named after Italy's first Queen – tomato, mozzarella cheese and basil represent national colours

pizza marinara pizza with garlic and tomatoes

pizza napoletana classic pizza with anchovies, ham, capers, tomato, mozzarella cheese and oregano

pizza proscuitto ham pizza

pizza quattro stagioni pizza with a different topping for each quarter

pizza romana pizza with onions

pizza sardenaria pizza with sardines, anchovies, tomatoes, black olives and garlic

pizza siciliana pizza with black olives, capers and cheese

pizzaiola steak see bistecca pizzaiola

plaice meunière plaice sautèd in butter, garnished with lemon and parsley

plaice niçoise plaice served with lettuce, tomatoes, green beans, hard boiled eggs, tuna, olives, green peppers, potatoes and anchovies

polla (i) chicken (Italian)

poppadams parchment-thin discs of lentil flour, fried in very hot oil

pork tonkatsu Japanese pork in batter

potage French soup

pot-au-feu stockpot of meat and aromatic vegetables

profiteroles small choux pastry puffs filled with cream and covered with chocolate sauce

quiche shell of unsweetened pastry filled with egg custard and cheese etc

ragout stew of meat with olive oil, garlic, tomatoes, carrots and herbs

raita Indian yoghurt

rashmi kebab chicken minced with onions, chillies, fresh mint, coriander, herbs and spices

raspberry Pavlova raspberries with ice cream, baked inside a meringue casing

ratatouille Mediterranean stew of tomatoes, peppers, onions, garlic and aubergines, served hot or cold

risotto rice with butter, white wine, saffron and bouillon, served with a variety of meats (Italian)

rogan josh lamb spiced with herbs and cashew nuts

rollmop herrings pickled and rolled herrings

sangria a mixture of red wine with ice, orange, lemon and sugar

scampi alla provinciale shrimps with garlic, onion, herbs, olives and tomatoes – Italian provincial style

scampi provençale shrimps or lobster tails in Provence style with garlic, onion, herbs, olive oil and tomatoes

shabu shabu Japanese-style fondue

sheftalia (sheftalies) minced meat, onion, garlic and parsley enveloped in beef suet and cooked over charcoal

sis saslik skewered lamb with mushroom and onion slices

skirlie mixture of oatmeal, dripping, onions and seasoning in a sausage case – 'mealy pudding'

smørbrød Swedish open sandwich

smørgasbrød buffet-style meal offering wide range of appetisers, hot and cold meats, fish, cheeses, salads, relishes and desserts

sole à la bonne femme sole cooked with white wine and mushrooms

sole Bercy sole pan-boiled with a sauce of shallots in white wine

sole lasserre sole baked with asparagus, mushrooms and sauce in a pastry case

sousoukakia spicy meat balls cooked with wine and Greek mountain herbs

spaghetti bolognese spaghetti served in a sauce of tomatoes and meat, ham or cheese

steak au poivre peppered rump or entrecôte steak

steak Diane rump or entrecôte steak flamed in brandy

steak and kidney fleurons steak and kidney with small, flaky pastry toppings

stifado Greek method of braising meat with spring onions, tomatoes and wine

suvlaki spit-roast hunks of beef

syllabub light dessert of sweet wine or cider whipped with lemon, cream and sometimes eggs

tagliatelli long, narrow noodles

Tandoori Indian food cooked in clay ovens

taramasalata Greek appetiser of cod or mullet roe combined with bread, olive oil, lemon juice and seasoning such as garlic

tava Greek casserole

terrine pâté presented in its own pot

tikka selected meat pieces roasted Tandoori style

tofu soya bean curd

torte open flan or tart

tournedos Rossini round cut of prime beef, garnished with foie gras and truffles, served with Madeira wine sauce

trout almondine trout with almonds

tsatsiki Greek appetiser made of yoghurt, cucumber, garlic, olive oil and mint

veal (Wiener) schnitzel breaded veal cutlet

vindaloo highly-spiced curry with pieces of potato

vol-au-vent light puff pastry filled with meat or fish etc

waffle batter-cake, baked in a hinged iron utensil

Waldorf salad salad containing celery, walnuts, apple and sour cream

zabaglione Italian dessert of egg yolks, sugar and Marsala wine

zuppe Italian soup